If you are in need of high quality OBM content to round out coursework or enhance your applied skills, look no further than the Handbook of Organizational Performance: Foundations and Advances. Imagine hosting a dinner party where your guests are the sharpest minds in OBM and you get to listen to them discuss OBM content spanning from its history to application to future directions. Well, that is how this handbook feels! It is a well curated feast of OBM information, all in one place, that you can use to support your students or your own professional development.

Tyra Sellers, JD, PhD, BCBA-D
Owner, TP Sellers, LLC

The Handbook of Organizational Performance is an invaluable resource for students, early career practitioners, and seasoned experts in OBM alike. It strikes an impeccable balance between breadth and depth in comprehensively examining the field. This text fills critical gaps by addressing topics often overlooked in existing literature and offers a unique opportunity to learn directly from a distinguished group of subject matter experts. As a professor and practitioner, I unequivocally endorse this book as the preeminent choice for guiding early-career professionals in honing their competencies.

Shannon Biagi, MS, BCBA
CEO, Chief Motivating Officers, LLC
Academic Administrator and Professor, UWF Center for Behavior Analysis

Handbook of Organizational Performance: Foundations and Advances is an excellent resource for professors, practitioners, and students in the field of Organizational Behavior Management (OBM). I have used several of the chapters as part of my graduate level performance management class and it has greatly benefited students with their knowledge, understanding and application of both the basic and more advanced topics within the discipline. This handbook will serve as valuable text for anyone interested in learning more about the field of OBM.

Denys Brand, Ph.D.
Assistant Professor, Department of Psychology, California State University, Sacramento

I was eager to delve into this thoughtfully curated text edited by Drs. Doug Johnson and Carl Johnson. The book provides the reader with a history of OBM, including development and challenges, highlighting the importance of both systems analysis and performance management. This text is a 'must use' for instructors teaching Organizational Behavior Management (OBM) and is appropriate at the undergraduate and graduate level. The chapters are authored by faculty and experts, including new and emerging researchers, practitioners, and consultants. I'm excited to incorporate this book into a future course and to see this book support student research.

Ivy Chong, PhD, BCBA-D
Chief Clinical Officer, Little Leaves Behavioral Services
Adjunct faculty & Lead Instructor, University of Massachusetts-Lowell

Handbook of Organizational Performance, Volume I

This book covers the intersection of behavior analysis and management, including a comprehensive examination of different topics within organizational behavior management. It exemplifies how behavior science can be extended to drive business performance improvements at both the individual level and the organizational level.

Featuring some of the top researchers and consultants from across the globe, Volume I:

- covers topics from a historical foundation.
- demonstrates how the basic foundations of research, principles, and philosophy derived from behavior analysis relates to employee and organizational behavior.
- comes with a new epilogue and is supplemented by review questions.
- is an indispensable resource for instructors, practitioners, and students of organizational behavior management.

Each chapter in this volume is written as an introduction to its topic, thus making the book an ideal resource for students of business and behavior wanting to learn more about how various management tools can draw out and reward the best in employees.

The chapters in this book were originally published in the *Journal of Organizational Behavior Management.*

Douglas A. Johnson is the Global Engagement and Learning Leader for Eastman Chemical Company, USA, where he leads initiatives related to leadership development, performance improvement, employee training, instructional design, and performance management to guide learning, employee motivation, and safety outcomes. He previously spent 13 years working as a faculty member at Western Michigan University. He is certified as a Lean Six Sigma Yellow Belt and a doctoral-level Board Certified Behavior Analyst (BCBA-D). He is an expert in instructional design, training design/development, computer-based instruction, performance management, behavioral systems analysis, fluency training, incentives, feedback, and employee motivation.

C. Merle Johnson is Professor Emeritus of Psychology at Central Michigan University, USA. He serves on the editorial board for the *Journal of Organizational Behavior Management*. His research concerns organizational behaviour management, treatment of sleep disorders in children, behavioural pediatrics, and assessment and treatment of children who have low-incidence disabilities.

Handbook of Organizational Performance, Volume I

Foundations and Advances

Edited by
Douglas A. Johnson and C. Merle Johnson

Routledge
Taylor & Francis Group
LONDON AND NEW YORK

First published 2025
by Routledge
4 Park Square, Milton Park, Abingdon, Oxon OX14 4RN

and by Routledge
605 Third Avenue, New York, NY 10158

Routledge is an imprint of the Taylor & Francis Group, an informa business

British Library Cataloguing in Publication Data
A catalogue record for this book is available from the British Library

ISBN13: 978-1-032-70824-9 (hbk)
ISBN13: 978-1-032-70826-3 (pbk)
ISBN13: 978-1-032-70827-0 (ebk)

DOI: 10.4324/9781032708270

Typeset in Minion Pro
by Newgen Publishing UK

Publisher's Note
The publisher accepts responsibility for any inconsistencies that may have arisen during the conversion of this book from journal articles to book chapters, namely the inclusion of journal terminology.

Contents

Citation Information

The following chapters in this book were originally published in various volumes and issues of the *Journal of Organizational Behavior Management*. When citing this material, please use the original page numbering for each article, as follows:

Chapter 1

Revisiting the Past and Selecting for the Future: An Introduction to Handbook of Organizational Performance: Foundations and Advances
Douglas A. Johnson and C. Merle Johnson
Journal of Organizational Behavior Management, volume 42, issue 3 (2022), pp. 203–209

Chapter 2

A History of Organizational Behavior Management
Dale M. Brethower, Alyce M. Dickinson, Douglas A. Johnson and C. Merle Johnson
Journal of Organizational Behavior Management, volume 42, issue 1 (2022), pp. 3–35

Chapter 3

On Terms within Organizational Behavior Management
Douglas A. Johnson and Rachael Ferguson
Journal of Organizational Behavior Management, volume 43, issue 2 (2023), pp. 162–188

Chapter 4

Experimental Research Methodologies in Organizational Behavior Management
Tyler G. Erath, Azure J. Pellegrino, Florence D. DiGennaro Reed, Sandra A. Ruby, Abigail L. Blackman and Matthew D. Novak
Journal of Organizational Behavior Management, volume 41, issue 2 (2021), pp. 150–181

Chapter 5

Common Antecedent Strategies within Organizational Behavior Management: The Use of Goal Setting, Task Clarification, and Job Aids
Eunju Choi and Douglas A. Johnson
Journal of Organizational Behavior Management, volume 42, issue 1 (2022), pp. 75–95

Chapter 6
Pinpointing, measurement, procedural integrity, and maintenance in organizational behavior management
David Wilder and Daniel Cymbal
Journal of Organizational Behavior Management, volume 43, issue 3 (2023), pp. 221–245

Chapter 7
Performance Feedback in Organizations: Understanding the Functions, Forms, and Important Features
Douglas A. Johnson, C. Merle Johnson and Priyanka Dave
Journal of Organizational Behavior Management, volume 43, issue 1 (2023), pp. 64–89

Chapter 8
Pay-for-performance: Behavior-based recommendations from research and practice
Barbara R. Bucklin, Anita Li, Manuel Manny Rodriguez, Douglas A. Johnson and Lauren M. Eagle
Journal of Organizational Behavior Management, volume 42, issue 4 (2022), pp. 309–335

Chapter 9
Assessment of Employee Performance
Nicole Gravina, Jessica Nastasi and John Austin
Journal of Organizational Behavior Management, volume 41, issue 2 (2021), pp. 124–149

Chapter 10
Performance Assessment of Organizations
Heather M. McGee and Brian J. Crowley-Koch
Journal of Organizational Behavior Management, volume 41, issue 3 (2021), pp. 255–285

Notes on Contributors

John Austin, Reaching Results, USA.

Abigail L. Blackman, Behavior Science Technology, New London, New Hampshire, USA.

Dale M. Brethower, Western Michigan University, Department of Psychology, Kalamazoo, Michigan, USA.

Barbara R. Bucklin, The Bucklin Group Inc, Laguna Niguel, California, USA.

Eunju Choi, St. Cloud State University, St. Cloud, Minnesota, USA.

Brian J. Crowley-Koch, ALULA, Philadelphia, Pennsylvania, USA.

Daniel Cymbal, University of Central Florida, Orlando, Florida, USA.

Priyanka Dave, Western Michigan University, Department of Psychology, Kalamazoo, Michigan, USA.

Alyce M. Dickinson, Western Michigan University, Department of Psychology, Kalamazoo, Michigan, USA.

Florence D. DiGennaro Reed, Behavior Analyst Certification Board, Littleton, Colorado, USA.

Lauren M. Eagle, Ascend Wellness Holdings, Portage, Michigan, USA.

Tyler G. Erath, University of Vermont, Burlington, Vermont, USA.

Rachael Ferguson, Kalamazoo Valley Community College, Kalamazoo, Michigan, USA.

Nicole Gravina, Department of Psychology, University of Florida, Gainesville, USA.

C. Merle Johnson, Central Michigan University, Department of Psychology, Mount Pleasant, Michigan, USA.

Douglas A. Johnson, Eastman Chemical Company, Kingsport, TN, USA.

Anita Li, University of Massachusetts Lowell, Lowell, Massachusetts, USA.

Heather M. McGee, Department of Psychology, Western Michigan University, Kalamazoo, Michigan, USA.

Jessica Nastasi, Department of Psychology, University of Florida, Gainesville, Florida, USA.

Matthew D. Novak, Department of Psychiatry and Behavioral Sciences, Johns Hopkins University School of Medicine, Baltimore, Maryland, USA.

Azure J. Pellegrino, California State University, Fresno, California, USA.

Manuel Manny Rodriguez, Bueno Ventures, Doral, Florida, USA.

Sandra A. Ruby, University of Kansas, Department of Applied Behavioral Science, Lawrence, Kansas, USA.

David Wilder, Florida Institute of Technology, Florida, USA.

Acknowledgements

These two volumes (Foundations and Advances) are developed as a revision and expansion of the original *Handbook of Organizational Performance: Behavior Analysis and Management* (2001). We hope the next generation of OBM devotees enjoy learning about the roots and progress of the field during the past two decades.

We want to thank all the Associate Editors, members of the Board of Editors, and guest reviewers from the *Journal of Organizational Behavior Management* (*JOBM*) who contributed excellent reviews suggesting improvements for the 23 chapters in the two volumes. Moreover, three Editors of *JOBM* made superb suggestions and contributions that initiated and steered this project over many years. Our heartfelt appreciation to Dave Wilder, Ramona Houmanfar, and Tim Ludwig cannot express the depths of gratitude we have for their collegial support. Most of us fail to realize the amount of work expended by all the individuals who keep *JOBM* operating efficiently and brilliantly.

Finally, as editors we must express our heartfelt appreciation for the authors who deserve most of the credit for their collective efforts in completing *Handbook of Organizational Performance: Foundations and Advances*. The transition from an action plan to an accomplishment is due to their hard work and excellent contributions. Gratias tibi.

Revisiting the Past and Selecting for the Future: An Introduction to Handbook of Organizational Performance, Foundations and Advances

Douglas A. Johnson and C. Merle Johnson

ABSTRACT

Both business and behavior can be understood through the lens of variation and selection, with adaptive approaches prospering and other approaches perishing. The *Handbook of Organizational Performance: Foundations and Advances* series seeks to lay out the groundwork and direction for our field to prosper, as understood by many expert contributors in the field of organizational behavior management. Other worthwhile directions beyond the series are also noted, all guided by the notion that a science of behavior is not only possible, but also a critical missing component from the typical understanding of how to best operate a business so that it survives.

Behavior analysis, and by extension organizational behavior management (OBM), has been guided by a selectionist paradigm since the conceptual basis for B. F. Skinner's science of behavior was first developed (Palmer & Donahoe, 1992; Skinner, 1945). Behavior is a product of selection contingencies operating at three levels (Skinner, 1981, 1987, 1990): biological (natural selection of species), psychological (contingencies of reinforcement responsible for behavior of individuals), and anthropological (evolution of contingencies that maintain social environments). C. M. Johnson et al. (2001) proposed an analogous paradigm for organizational performance, suggesting three levels of variation and selection: economics (natural selection of organizations that survive competition in the marketplace), behavior analysis (contingencies of reinforcement for individual and group behavior within and between organizational settings), and social environments (organizational culture, verbal behavior, laws, workplace rules, policies and organizational practices). Two decades later there appears little reason to dismiss this evolutionary model of organizational performance. Organizations, behaviors, and social practices change over time. The adaptive ones flourish or at least maintain; those that do not evolve in changing environments undergo extinction. Although the scale of behavior is clearly vast and the units of analysis change across disciplines, variation and selection remains a constant shaping process across the levels. OBM often has needed to straddle the fence between multiple levels, looking at both individual/performer and collective/organizational levels (or contingencies and metacontingencies if one prefers).

This current series is an evolution of the *Handbook of Organizational Performance: Behavior Analysis and Management* (C. M. Johnson et al., 2001), which itself was a descendant of the two original OBM handbooks published in 1982 (Frederiksen, 1982; O'Brien et al., 1982). After 40 years of progress, OBM has grown large enough to permit tremendous variability. In fact, this was one of the greatest challenges as the editors sought to apply their own selection pressures to the contributions and topics (i.e., deciding what to include from the many possibilities, constrained by practical limitations). Despite the extensive contributions of many authors, many topics will regrettably have to be left untouched. Such a range that is incorporated in the handbook would likely be pleasing to Skinner and other pioneers in behavior analysis, who always saw our science as broad and far-reaching; not a science to be applied to just a handful of demographics or concerns (Skinner, 1953). We are honored by the contributors willing to share their hard-earned expertise and the input of the editors, associate editors, editorial review board members, and guest reviewers of the *Journal of Organizational Behavior Management* (JOBM).

To capture the aims of our many contributors and to ensure a continuity across series, we settled on the title of *Handbook of Organizational Performance: Foundations and Advances.* The subtitle is intended to emphasize the need to look both forward and backward. Foundations tell us where we originated and provide direction as we continue forward. In fact, it is traditional for OBM handbook introductions to summarize how the field came to be (Houmanfar et al., 2021; C. M. Johnson et al., 2001; Wine & Pritchard, 2018). Such an approach orients readers and honors the architects. We will not dwell on such points here for fear of stealing the thunder from contributions to the series, except to note that several will lay the groundwork with their coverage of the history of OBM pioneers, our methodology, our terminology (and thus our concepts and principles), and various motivational and diagnostic tools. Of course, our foundations include the wealth of literature built up over 40+ years, informing topics such as training, goal setting, feedback, safety, health, etc.

Advances tell us about the new territory we have recently entered and territory into which we should be venturing. Looking forward is always fraught with difficulties, as legions of past amateur futurists can surely attest. Beyond the many suggestions mentioned by our contributors, there remain a few threads that have stuck out to us as worth pulling.

One area of tremendous growth potential is providing support for other behavior analysts as they forge new organizational ventures. The most obvious candidate is behavior analysts providing professional services related to Autism Spectrum Disorder. As these services have expanded, organizations have emerged with all the employee-related needs of any other organization. Most of the behavior analysts managing such organizations lack formal training in OBM (or perhaps have attended only a workshop or two). As such, collaborations with the human service industry would be wise, or else they will surely reinvent the OBM wheel without us and our base of empirical findings.

It would help broaden the scope and mission of our field if we could find ways to contribute to the broader culture besides traditional management initiatives. How might OBM support union concerns? How can we contribute to diversity of the workforce or the development of professional skills of employees? How can we prevent layoffs or support former employees transitioning between jobs?

While on the topic of unemployment, the nature of work demands will undoubtedly change and therefore we may not be able to rely on the dependent measures of years gone by. For example, increasing automation will eliminate many jobs and types of work, but can rise to new jobs and emphases (Asimov, 1991; D. A. Johnson & Akpapuna, 2018). There will likely be a greater need for behavior analysts to understand creativity and innovation (Bradley & Johnson, in press). Quoting Jack Welch, former chief executive officer of General Electric, in his annual report, Andersen (2020) described how organizations change or die and new forms of work develop.

> "When the rate of change inside an institution becomes slower than the rate of change outside, the end is in sight. The only question is when. Learning to love change is an unnatural act in any century-old institution" (Andersen, 2020, pp. 342-343).

OBM professionals will need to continually refine their verbal skills to become more proficient in marketing and outreach. No doubt this will require us to better understand our audiences, not just our products and services, no matter how proud we may be of the processes we have developed. We need to understand and exhibit persuasive behaviors at the performer level, organizational level, and the broad cultural level.

When mapping out our plans for moving forward, it is probably wise to mark our progress by three questions: Where are we going? How shall we get there? How will we know we have arrived? (Brethower & Smalley, 1998; Mager, 1997). This introduction and the collection of articles point out several possible directions. The foundations of our field will undoubtedly provide the means for how we will get there. But how will we know we have arrived? As Dale Brethower mentioned in his contribution (who unfortunately passed away several months after the completion of the manuscript), we can "let the data be the guide!" (Brethower et al., in press). However, not just data alone, but a thoughtful and critical appraisal of the data. To illustrate how data may impact decision making differentially, let us consider the landmark study by Tversky and Kahneman (Kahneman won the Nobel Prize in 2002 for his work in economics. Tversky passed away; the Nobel Committee does not present awards posthumously).

Tversky and Kahneman (1974) were teaching flight instructors in Israel to minimize criticisms in favor of rewards supported by empirical evidence. The flight instructors disagreed and noted that when they praised trainees for good landings, trainees typically performed worse the next time. When the instructors harshly criticized poor landings, their trainees usually performed better the next opportunity. Thus, the flight instructors concluded that praise was detrimental to learning and verbal punishment was beneficial. Tversky and Kahneman suddenly realized that the statistical principle of regression to the mean was responsible for the flight instructors' erroneous conclusion. That is, events that are outliers from typical performance are more likely to return to average performance the next time (see, Figure 1). For example, poor or exceptionally great athletic performances are likely to return to a typical performance for that individual or team the next game. Similarly, exceptionally hot or cold days are likely to return to average highs or lows for that season the next day. Thus, climate change is gradual, many people fail to detect it (Easterling et al., 2000). When learning and behavior change are incremental and relatively slow, extreme outcomes are likely to return to near average performance for that individual. Regardless of whether the flight instructor yelled at the trainee or put a poor landing on extinction, the next time the

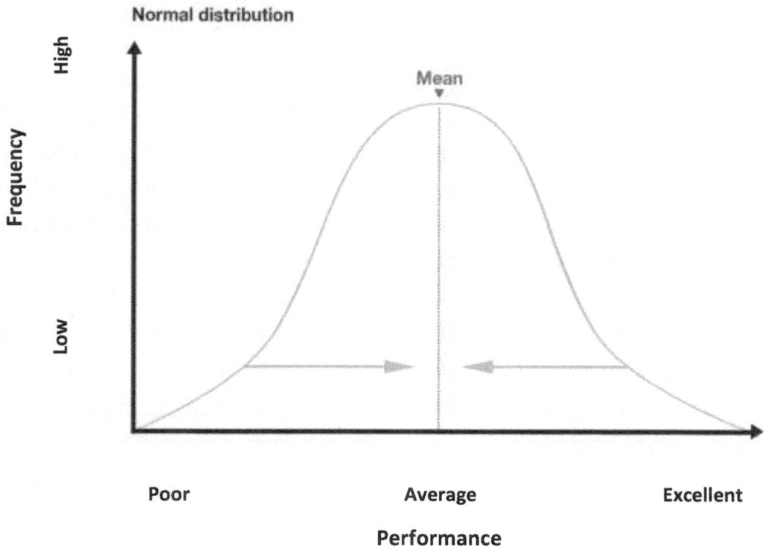

Figure 1. Regression to the mean for performance.

trainee was likely to improve. Conversely, if flight instructors praised great landings, trainees were likely to execute worse in comparison the next time and return to just above or near their average performance. Hence, criticizing flight instructors was being reinforced and the delivery of praise for outstanding performance by trainees was not reinforced by the statistical principle of regression to the mean due to the slow improvements on this complex task. Couple this regression to the mean with the immediate, yet short-term, change in employee behavior and it becomes obvious why aversive control is prevalent. Even though experts have long since warned about the perils of excessive aversive techniques (Azrin & Holz, 1966; Sidman, 1989) and the trends of data overall supported the use of praise, the data based upon the immediate and direct experiences of the instructors supported the use of criticism.

Variation and selection strike again – we are swimming upstream when we advocate the use of reinforcement over punishment to those who are not well-versed in behavior analysis research unless shaping new behavior is rapid and average performance is improving dramatically. Extinction, correcting, and differential reinforcement for alternative behaviors are more humane and effective for long-term behavior change when motivating employees to work in organizational settings (Daniels & Bailey, 2014). Reinforcement contingencies improve and sustain performance over time, but most managers and supervisors do not systematically collect data on the behavior of their subordinates. There might be well-developed outcome measures or results of staff performance, but these are frequently tied to the bottom line in a loose manner at best. We need to understand these various streams of data and plan accordingly. To advance the field, we need to push beyond the normal range of variability into new territory. The world of business is a world flooded with numerical measures. Net cash from operations, optimal size for inventory, present value of a growing perpetuity, internal rate of return, acceptable tolerance levels for machinery, and other precisely calculated quantifications are routinely developed. However, traditional business metrics are largely restricted to processes and products. Metrics involving people are rarely used outside the confines of paychecks, attendance, delivery dates, and infrequent subjective performance appraisals. When it comes to actual day-to-day workplace behavior, the level of precision approaches zero. Instead, vague theories of behavior lurk, outflowing with constructs such as emotional intelligence, drive, vision, motivation 3.0, personality, self-knowledge, level 5 leadership, and many, many more (the list is exhausting and ever-growing).

As such, products and processes are planned, with the hope that annoying human variation does not get in the way and that our exhortations and threats may somehow push the right secret internal button within our employees. As one of the first author's business professors once put, when responding to a question of how we might prevent injuries and deaths when employees hide unsafe performance, "Well, that's human behavior and there's nothing you can do about that. People will just do things wrong sometimes and you can't stop them." We respectfully disagree with such a fatalistic assumption. The science of behavior shows us how to understand human behavior with the same degree of precision as the other facets of business. This series is a solid start detailing how to achieve this objective. Of course, there remains much to do in the world of work. Join us as we traverse this expedition, varying directions and selecting many prosperous paths.

Disclosure statement

No potential conflict of interest was reported by the author(s).

ORCID

Douglas A. Johnson http://orcid.org/0000-0002-7802-3566

References

Andersen, K. (2020). *Evil geniuses*. Random House.

Asimov, I. (1991). *Robot visions*. Roc.

Azrin, N. H., & Holz, W. C. (1966). Punishment. In W. K. Honig (Ed.), *Operant behavior: Areas of research and application* (pp. 380–447). Appleton-Century-Crofts.

Bradley, J. L., & Johnson, D. A. (in press). Creating creativity: A behavior analytic approach. *The Psychological Record*. https://doi.org/10.1007/s40732-021-00480-z

Brethower, D., & Smalley, K. (1998). *Performance-based instruction: Linking training to business results*. Jossey-Bass/Pfeiffer.

Brethower, D. M., Dickinson, A. M., Johnson, D. A., & Johnson, C. M. (in press). A history of organizational behavior management. *Journal of Organizational Behavior Management*. https://doi.org/10.1080/01608061.2021.1924340

Daniels, A. C., & Bailey, J. S. (2014). *Performance management: Changing behavior that drives organizational effectiveness* (5th ed.). Performance Management Publications.

Easterling, D. R., Meehl, G. A., Parmesan, C., Changnon, S. A., Karl, T. R., & Mearns, L. O. (2000). Climate extremes: Observations, modeling, and impacts. *Science*, *289*(5487), 2068–2074. https://doi.org/10.1126/science.289.5487.2068

Frederiksen, L. W. (Ed.). (1982). *Handbook of organizational behavior management*. John Wiley & Sons.

Houmanfar, R. A., Fryling, M., & Alavosius, M. P. (Eds.). (2021). *Applied behavior science in organizations: Consilience of historical and emerging trends in organizational behavior management*. Routledge.

Johnson, C. M., Redmon, W. K., & Mawhinney, T. C. (Eds.). (2001). *Handbook of organizational performance: Behavior analysis and management*. Haworth.

Johnson, D. A., & Akpapuna, M. (2018). A pragmatic approach for building motivation to promote employee creativity and organizational innovation. In B. Wine & J. K. Pritchard (Eds.), *Essentials of Organizational Behavior Management* (pp. 242–273). Hedgehog Publishers.

Mager, R. (1997). *How to turn learners on . . . without turning them off.* Center for Effective Performance.

O'Brien, R. M., Dickinson, A. M., & Rosow, M. P. (Eds.). (1982). *Industrial behavior modification: A management handbook.* Pergamon Press, Inc.

Palmer, D. C., & Donahoe, J. W. (1992). Essentialism and selectionism in cognitive science and behavior analysis. *American Psychologist, 47*(11), 1344–1358. https://doi.org/10.1037//0003-066x.47.11.1344

Sidman, M. (1989). *Coercion and its fallout.*

Skinner, B. F. (1945). The operational analysis of psychological terms. *Psychological Review, 52* (5), 270–277. https://doi.org/10.1037/h0062535

Skinner, B. F. (1953). *Science and human behavior.* Macmillan.

Skinner, B. F. (1981). Selection by consequences. *Science, 213*(4507), 501–504. https://doi.org/10.1126/science.7244649

Skinner, B. F. (1987). *Upon further reflection.* Prentice-Hall.

Skinner, B. F. (1990). Can psychology be a science of mind? *American Psychologist, 45*(11), 1206–1210. https://doi.org/10.1037/0003-066X.45.11.1206

Tversky, A., & Kahneman, D. (1974). Judgment under uncertainty: Heuristics and biases. *Science, 185*(4157), 1124–1135. https://doi.org/10.1126/science.185.4157.1124

Wine, B., & Pritchard, J. K. (Eds.). (2018). *Organizational behavior management: The essentials.* Hedgehog Publishers.

A History of Organizational Behavior Management

Dale M. Brethower, Alyce M. Dickinson, Douglas A. Johnson, and C. Merle Johnson

ABSTRACT

Organizational behavior management (OBM) arose as early behavior analysts decided to use data in earnest to make the world a better place, first through education, then workplace training, and eventually through business and industry as a whole. The historical roots of the field are traced through the lessons learned by these pioneers and how their formative experiences created the tools and techniques that are common within the discipline today. This history also created a worldview and conceptual system that continues to distinguish OBM from alternative approaches and is reflected in recent publication trends seen today. As the levels of analysis, specializations, implementations, and problems faced continue to vary and expand within organizational behavior management, the mantra of performance-based empiricism has remained as a steady and consistent guide throughout the decades.

In order to better understand how the field of organizational behavior management (OBM) came to operate as it does today, it may be instructive to trace our historical roots to see how the legacy of several pioneers left us with certain tools, assumptions, and a general modus operandi. This cumulative history created the framework that guides our current pioneers as they seek to apply our particular brand of science to improve behavioral relations within business. It can also serve as a point of demarcation to highlight how our field evolved differently than other fields with similar interests, which could prove useful as we look to our growth going forward. OBM-like work gradually emerged during the 1950s and 1960s as individuals began to see the relevance of the experimental work being done by behavioral psychologists to the behavior of management and employees (Aldis, 1961). The OBM label was formalized when the *Journal of Organizational Behavior Management* (JOBM) was established in 1977. The publisher, Behavioral Systems Incorporated

(BSI), was a for-profit firm started in 1971 by Aubrey Daniels and Fran Tarkenton. Daniels is recognized as one of the pioneers of OBM, receiving the OBM Network's first Lifetime Achievement Award in 1988 (see Dickinson, 2000). Tarkenton is best known as a National Football League Hall of Fame quarterback for the Minnesota Vikings.

The potential for behavioral principles and derived procedures to reshape business and industry had already begun to be demonstrated in the decades that preceded the formation of OBM. For example, James Lincoln (1961) developed a system of incentives to produce lasting and economically important effects in industry. Lincoln Electric in Cleveland operated by paying production employees for only what they produced rather than paying a salary. This was different than hourly pay; the approach most American factories utilized at the time and had earned Lincoln Electric a worldwide reputation for its management practices (Handlin, 1991). The Lincoln philosophy that had guided such practices was not an inherently behavioral philosophy. The company founder believed that the key to employee motivation was to develop the workforce's sense of pride and mutual respect, which was best achieved by ensuring recognition was scaled to contribution (Lincoln, 1951). Although the philosophical core was different than the basis that guides OBM, many of the resulting practices and procedures were similar. As a businessman Lincoln believed that the fruits of business should be shared among workers, owners, and customers. He further believed that profit sharing alone was insufficient, rather there needed to be a recognition of the individual's performance (as Lincoln once put it, "an organization is composed of individuals – not charts"). There would be individual accountability for both quality and output with employees only being paid for good products and correcting any defects on their own time. Although monetary incentives were a standard part of the Lincoln approach, the company also emphasized that money is not the only form of reward. Under incentive management, wages went up and prices went down. At one point, Lincoln Electric won a lawsuit against the Internal Revenue Service; the IRS accused the company of paying workers a lot to drive up costs and thereby "hide" profits. Why else, the IRS argued, would Lincoln Electric pay workers three times as much as the industry average? The winning defense was that piecework pay yielded about three times the average compensation and three times the productivity. Also, there were special incentives for working cooperatively. The first author toured the plant in the 1970s and asked about safety. Workers got a lot done and avoided accidents, else they did not earn any money when hurt or sick.

What events drove people to look for OBM-like applications?

"Let the data be the guide!" was a rallying cry of a handful of behaviorally-oriented graduate students at Harvard, Columbia, the University of Michigan, and a few other universities during the 1960s. Rallying around the data is essential to success in the field and discovering variables that must be managed to improve performance. What excited us most was, "How can we revolutionize education?" The answer to both finding and managing the variables, we believed, was through "programmed learning," which primarily involved the careful application of fading, prompting, priming, branching, and response requests to instructional material, along with extensive testing and revisions (D. M. Brethower, 1963; Markle, 1969). Several publications inspired our emphasis on this great educational revolution, particularly those by the first author's mentor, B. F. Skinner, and his thoughts on how automated and individualized instruction might transform how students learn (Skinner, 1954, 1958). Skinner had noted how effective education requires a careful analysis and sequencing of instructional content, continual engagement by the learner, and frequent consequences closely following performance. Such an extensive management of behavioral contingencies would require behavioral science to adapt to serve large numbers of students at once, a problem of scale that would prove relevant again later on as behaviorists began trying to shape the behavior of entire workforces. Skinner's approach to educational contingencies is well-represented in a collection of his articles titled *The Technology of Teaching* (Skinner, 1968).

The preface to an updated edition of *The Technology of Teaching* was written by James G. Holland, in which he recounted how he attempted to apply Skinner's notion of teaching machines and a behavioral approach with education to Natural Science 114, an undergraduate course at Harvard University that taught about the experimental analysis of behavior. These efforts involved extensive testing and refinement of instructional material in which student responding guided every decision throughout several development cycles. Eventually the program within the teaching machine was converted into textbook form with the publication of *The Analysis of Behavior* (Holland & Skinner, 1961), which would become the most influential and well-known of the programmed learning books, of which there were many publications over the years (with the number of 'm's in programed/programmed varying across authors). Beside Holland, other key figures in the Harvard Teaching Project included Susan Meyer Markle, author of *Designs for Instructional Designers* (Markle, 1990), and Tom Gilbert, author of *Human Competence* (Gilbert, 1996). Gilbert sometimes referred to himself as "Skinner's right-hand man" as a way of acknowledging Skinner's impact on his work. The field of programmed learning developed out of enthusiasm for improving public education. The most significant early development occurred in the early 1960s when Professor Skinner went into the shop at the Psychological Laboratories in Harvard's Memorial Hall and built a teaching machine out of an old phonograph turntable. Deficiencies in public education had caught his attention when he visited his daughter's elementary school (Skinner, 1983). He set out to do something about it, wrote a paper (Skinner, 1954), got some funding, and, with the help of the members of the Harvard Teaching Machine Project, the field of programmed learning was off and running.

There was a flurry of entrepreneurship in the programmed learning business during the 1960s. Most of these businesses failed or transformed themselves into vendors in the training and human resources marketplace. Robert Mager (1997) was one who succeeded and made significant contributions to the field. When enthusiasm and hard work were not enough to support a great educational revolution, many of us began to apply behavioral principles in a variety of settings such as government agencies, institutions, private businesses, and educational organizations.

Behavioral psychologists, aware of Skinner's (1938) three-term contingency connecting relationships among antecedents, behavior, and consequences, researched reinforcement, extinction, discrimination, and other fundamental processes. Beyond that, the foundation for OBM was like loosely laid paving stones; there were solid items and many gaps. The paving stones are important in hindsight because organizational behavior management was influenced historically by a variety of sources including human learning, education research, economics, systems analysis, management, and both the experimental analysis of behavior and applied behavior analysis. For example, there was solid evidence that:

- simply practicing intellectual tasks does not have much effect on other tasks; transfer of training does not happen automatically (Woodworth & Thorndike, 1901).
- basic principles of learning can be applied to:
  - learning of emotions (Watson & Rayner, 1920)
  - treatment of emotional disorders (Ayllon & Michael, 1959; Lazarus, 1959)
  - learning by disabled humans (Fuller, 1949)
  - learning of social skills (Azrin & Lindsley, 1956)
  - learning of language skills (Skinner, 1957)
- simple tests can teach (Pressey, 1926)
- numerous variables influence how reinforcement works (Ferster & Skinner, 1957; Keller, 1954; Premack, 1959; Skinner, 1953)
- how humans process information is important; there are limitations on how much people can keep in memory at one time (G. A. Miller, 1956)
- there are serious concerns about the applications of behavioral principles to human behavior (Rogers & Skinner, 1956)
- the "systems approach" is both relevant and important (Boulding, 1956; Drucker, 1946; Skinner, 1938; Weiner, 1950)

- there are complex and important social implications related to applying the concepts and methods of science to practical human affairs (Drucker, 1973; Mayo, 1933, 1945; Roethlisberger & Dickson, 1939; Skinner, 1948)
- there exist well-developed methodologies (Flagle et al., 1960; Sidman, 1960).

The most powerful methods, described by Sidman (1960), were well-known to a few hundred people familiar with the work of B. F. Skinner at Harvard and Fred Keller at Columbia. Economists called these time-series designs. These methods were not and are not well known to psychologists, educators, social scientists, or managers outside OBM. Part of the excitement of graduate students of this period was the gaps we could fill. We did not know all the answers, but we knew how to find them. Manipulate variables related to the three-term contingency and collect data on the effects (see Sidman, 1960). From the beginning our willingness to be guided by the data was one of the most important biases of people working in OBM; science is more valuable than ideology. The data bias is one of the reasons that establishing professional journals and graduate programs is an important part of OBM history.

What lessons from Nobel Prize scientists proved important to the assumptions of OBM?

From Percy Bridgman (Nobel Prize in Physics), we can learn that one of the necessary tasks in doing an OBM project is enabling the client to see the world as we see it (Bridgman, 1959, 1961). We must integrate our knowledge into the world of the client, at least the part of the world that is within the scope of the project. One way, maybe the best way, to achieve that integration is to partner or work with the client.

Bridgman gave a presentation, *The World as I See It*, in Cambridge, MA in the early 1960s. The first author attended and saw his point was clear: the world as I see it is the world as I see it. He said he did not know if the point was trivial or profound. It was years later before the first author saw that while the point might sound trivial, nonetheless it is still profound. Getting clients and OBM professionals to see the world the same way is necessary for success; both the success of the project and success in getting repeat business and referrals (see Standard 4 of the International Society for Performance Improvement (ISPI) certification standards; ISPI, n.d.).

Different people see the world differently. Even when working with colleagues or clients who see the world in much the way we do there will be differences of opinion. What should we do first on this performance improvement/OBM project? Should we try what worked last time, even though conditions changed? There is usually no umpire to decide. Even if there is an authoritarian leader who decides, maybe collecting more data will change the Big Boss' mind. Not only are numbers important for changing minds – the data often reflect matters necessary for success. Do funding agencies consider our results good enough? Are lost time accidents decreasing? Do we have enough potential customers in the pipeline to generate enough sales to continue the business? Is the cost of production decreasing for our products? Bankers, investors, and senior executives live in a world where data rule.

OBM practitioners work in an environment in which we are not all powerful; we must work with others to achieve results. Rarely are we the ones who have the final word. "Do this because I'm the expert on behavior" rarely works. This is one reason the ISPI adopted "Partner with Clients" as #4 of the 10 Standards of Excellence. The mnemonic is RSVP: Results, System, Value-added, Partner. "Results" are decided by measures such as increases in revenues, widgets produced, profit margins, or returns on investments. A "System" is a department, company, or a division in which anything that happens can affect something else. All performance occurs in a system of some sort. "Value-added" is making things better. Getting agreement on what adds value by collecting data to discover which results might add value.

From Georg von Békésy (Nobel Prize in Physiology) we learn that what we must do is "first, make the analysis; second, make the synthesis; the synthesis tells you if your analysis is correct." The analysis identifies key variables that must be managed to get the result we seek. The synthesis includes building a system that manages the variables and gets results. von Békésy (1961) gave his talk, probably in Memorial Hall at Harvard, also in the early 1960s. The analysis/synthesis/evaluation-confirmation quote was from the beginning of the presentation. He ended by repeating it and saying, "You do the work; they give you the prize." The middle concerned how he made a model of the basilar membrane and used it to replicate many phenomena in hearing; thus, providing evidence that his analysis was correct. The first author left the talk glad he attended, but unaware he had just received a summary of how to make OBM projects successful. First do the analysis, then do the synthesis by building a system to manage variables from the analysis to yield the result. Variants of von Békésy's procedure appear under several names: the experimental analysis of behavior, applied behavior analysis, behavioral systems analysis, organizational behavior management, human performance technology, behavior engineering, and the scientific method. Whatever we name it, we are doing what von Békésy said: "First you make the analysis ... " The contemporary set of standards for certifying excellence show these remarks by two Nobel Prize recipients prophetic: ISPI 10 standards (ISPI, n.d.).

What are some of the other basic lessons learned during the history of OBM?

Analysis is always part of our work, but what is it? Analysis is nothing more nor less than finding answers to questions. An economist might analyze by asking, "How did supply and demand vary to change prices of seed corn in Iowa during the 1930s?" A performance analyst might ask, "What are the salient differences between what our best machine operators do and what our typical operators do?" "What results are we not getting that we should be getting?" Each discipline has its own tailored analysis questions. It was years into doing "subject matter analysis" for programmed learning and doing "behavior analysis" that we began to figure out differences between variables that bring about excellent performance and variables that bring about average performance. Finally, we figured out two insights that felt startling: First, analysis is always about asking questions, and second, different disciplines have tailored analysis questions. All of them. The key to performance analysis is asking the right questions. Different gurus all ask good questions. In addition, all successful gurus are good at value sharing. They have a subtext: "You and I have some of the same values; we can work together." The subtext is *not*: "I'm an expert and will show you peasants what to do."

Second, do the synthesis. Teach the average performer to do what the best performer does. For example, find out what happens when you introduce the production techniques used in the best performing manufacturing plant into an average performing plant. Crawley et al. (1982) demonstrated this approach when they recorded the top 65 sales performers' behaviors for four months (1000 hours). Then they trained these techniques to 450 sales agents across the country. This improved performance for average sales agents and the company. Gilbert's (1996) "PIP" (potential for improving performance) model of computing the ratio of top performers' accomplishments, compared to average performers, demonstrates the utility of this OBM technique. Large PIP ratios indicate opportunities to improve overall performance; small ratios suggest spending time and resources elsewhere.

Third, test the synthesis. Collect performance data, then revise and fine tune until it works. Does it always work? No. Get suggestions from performers and others, make changes, and measure the results. Call this "re-engineering," "trial-and-error," or "persistence." Discover that when the people involved get involved (the ISPI Standard 4 on Partnering) this improves overall organizational performance (ISPI, n.d.). We are biased toward science and engineering and practical matters. We tend to rely on data, often data obtained by counting such as students graduated, products sold, exam questions answered correctly, number of responses, etc.

What were the early jobs as the field tried to find opportunities?

There were and are three main markets for our sources of income: academics, consultants, and salaried personnel such as trainers, safety experts, and in more recent years, organizational development specialists and quality improvement specialists. We had to market our skills and perform useful work as best we could. We all had a common set of principles, an entrepreneurial tendency, and a reliance on data to guide our work.

Academics typically work in a publish-or-perish environment in which we earn our base pay by teaching courses, providing service to universities and organizations, and conducting research. We earn advancements and avoid perishing by publishing articles and books. Securing grants and contracts is important for major research universities. We sometimes moonlight as consultants and, occasionally, leave academia to start or work in consulting businesses. Consultants are free lancers or small business owners and employees thereof. Some are profiled in Dickinson (2000) and have informative websites. Earning a living as a trainer – now called Human Resource Developer – became the most common because of our early roots in programmed learning. The National Society for Programmed Instruction was started in 1962 and became ISPI. Several of the founding members, such as Tom Gilbert, had connections to Skinner's Harvard Teaching Machine project. The Programmed Learning Workshop at the University of Michigan contributed to the development of the field by helping businesses that sent people to the workshop develop effective self-instructional programs.

How was the OBM infrastructure built through journals and training programs?

The *Journal of the Experimental Analysis of Behavior* was established in 1958; an applied outgrowth periodical, *Journal of Applied Behavior Analysis*, was established a decade later in 1968. *Performance Improvement Journal*, started in the 60s as the Programmed Learning journal, evolved into *Performance Improvement Quarterly*. As mentioned earlier, the *Journal of Organizational Behavior Management* was established in 1977. Academic programs specializing in analysis of behavior were simply non-existent in the early 60s. Students learned by falling within the orbit of individual faculty members. That changed gradually as faculty were able to recruit colleagues. That is how all our applied behavior analysis and OBM graduate programs started. Early on, several people collected in various parts of universities such as the University of Michigan, University of Kansas, University of Nevada-Reno, West Virginia University, North Texas State University, and Western Michigan University. Some started masters and doctoral programs (Dickinson, 2000).

How did OBM move from programmed learning to workplace and organizational performance?

Influences from the Harvard Teaching Machine Project showed up at the University of Michigan in the early 1960s. Harlan Lane, a newly minted Harvard Ph.D. and author of critically acclaimed *The Wild Boy of Aveyron* (Lane, 1976), later received a MacArthur Foundation Genius Grant. He teamed with F. Rand Morton on a U.S. Office of Education project. The purpose? Build programmed learning for 5 languages. The first author went to Michigan to help. Part of the reason for joining the project was that pundits were saying the complex material could not be taught with programmed learning. Teaching languages by programmed learning was part of the proof that the pundits were wrong. Morton wrote the Spanish program. Faculty members from other universities wrote programs in French, German, and Chinese. The first author, with a couple of Thai graduate students, wrote the program in Thai. Geary Rummler, working for the University of Michigan Office of Research Administration, was assigned to monitor the project.

Lane and Morton also started the Institute for Behavioral Research and Programmed Instruction (IBRPI) with funding from a private company. IBRPI had a lofty motto, written on a medallion. Read one way the medallion said: "To Change Man to Change the World." Read another way it said: "To Change the World to Change Man." What it meant is: "to improve the performance of individuals and change the world for the better" (A very similar motto is seen throughout the works of Dick Malott, who helped pioneer the early dissemination and adoption of OBM/behavioral systems analysis and introduced these topics to generations of behavior analysts). The IBRPI mottos refer to small goals that might have a huge impact. IBRPI worked toward a small goal and initiated a workshop to train people from the private sector to write self-instructional programs. IBRPI failed as a business, but the workshop was a success. The workshop was the beginning in a series of important developments in the history of OBM. These small but impactful developments are described in detail below.

George Odiorne (primarily known for advocating "management by objectives"), Rummler's mentor in the College of Business, brought the IBRPI workshop into the University of Michigan. Odiorne opined that the new programmed learning workshop should distinguish itself from the competition by training people better, faster, and cheaper. To do that it should use programmed instruction and have workshop participants actually write programs to prove in the marketplace that the faster and cheaper (one week rather than 2 to 6 weeks) was also better. Participants in competing workshops learned a lot about programmed learning but practiced little actual writing during workshops. There was much to learn that was not put into practice. Participants went through a self-instructional program and Rummler managed them. The first author wrote the instructional material and then hid so participants would not know how very young he was. Rummler sent out a brochure advertising the workshop which would now be offered by the "Center for Programmed Learning for Business" of the College of Business at the University of Michigan. There was one problem; there was no such center. Odiorne received a phone call from the Business College Dean who chastised Odiorne and explained that such a center must go through a review process that could last years. Odiorne was properly contrite and asked "OK, but what should I do with all the checks?" "What checks?" "People have already enrolled and I have checks here from . . . " Odiorne then listed several of the largest corporations in Michigan, including Ford, General Motors, and Michigan Bell. The Center for Programmed Learning for Business became the only Center at Michigan ever established by press release. Rummler learned another lesson in entrepreneurship from his mentor; it truly is easier to get forgiveness than permission.

The program used in the workshop was later published by the first author (D. M. Brethower, 1963; there was a Japanese translation in 1965), which covers the core techniques and uses of programmed instruction. The program taught enough so that workshop participants could describe what they were trying to do; doing it was difficult because the program did not provide enough examples of material similar to what they were trying to program. The workshop staff corrected that by collecting examples from participant programs and publishing another programmed book of what we called the lean programming process and expanded the scope of the previous publication by examining how to first analyze various subject matters, then break the content down to manageable sizes, and then conduct empirical testing and revision (D. M. Brethower et al., 1965). The Center for Programmed Learning for Business workshop ran once per month for twenty years or so, long after Rummler and Brethower had earned their Ph.D.s and left the University of Michigan. Each workshop included an exercise in "subject matter analysis" in which we tried to analyze what every participant's program would teach. Not just general "business math," but "computation of the production costs of new products." The program required specific outcomes so that we knew what computations learners would master by the end of the program. We could work backwards from the computations to determine what was to be taught. Seeing 20 or so examples each month we noticed patterns in subject matter analysis. The analysis questions were quite similar regardless of the subject matter we were analyzing (e.g., "What will they do with what they learned? Examples, please!").

Our questions focused on *results*; the results added measured *value* to the organization (system) as a whole. The results required *partnering*, that is, other people in the company also must perform well. Many years later an ISPI Task Force codified essentially the same pattern as the first 4 of 10 Standards for

Excellence in performance improvement projects: Results, Systemic, Value Adding, and Partnering (see D. M. Brethower, 2008).

The programmed learning workshop spawned others at the Center: one on advanced programmed learning, a management of behavior change, and a training systems workshop. The story of how this occurred further illustrates the entrepreneurial spirit of the time and adherence to the rallying cry "Let the data guide!" We believed that workshop graduates would be successful only if they practiced applying the developmental testing process. But there was a serious problem; participants did the developmental testing on Friday. To accomplish that we used available technology; typewriters operated by paid typists who stayed up late Thursday night so that programs would be ready to test Friday. Participants had Thursday nights off, having worked until 9 or 10 PM Sunday through Wednesday. They complained and we explained that they had to work in our workshop. Participants took advantage of their free time to experience Ann Arbor's night life; some came in bleary eyed Friday morning and not ready to learn developmental testing. Rummler successfully solved the problem by scheduling a session for Thursday evening. Under the title Applied Learning Theory, the first author lectured about behavioral theory and told them stories to hold their attention. These included folklore from students at Harvard, Columbia, and Michigan in which students had changed professor behaviors. For example, Harvard students reported shaping a chemistry professor to lecture holding onto both faucets on a sink at the front of the lecture hall. Whenever the professor approached the sink they "looked alert" and took notes; when he lectured from anywhere else they sat back looking like other bored students. Within the first hour the professor touched the faucets with one hand, then both, and lectured from there. The first author told workshop participants that such antics were unethical unless students obtained the professor's permission in advance. Part of the workshop fee included follow-up telephone conversations with workshop graduates. These calls turned out to be extremely important because we learned from their successes and failures and improved the workshop. Years later a colleague published a book describing very similar techniques (Brinkerhoff, 2003).

Some graduates reported their own behavior change examples, some work related and some personal. The first author was delighted since it showed his lectures did not bore people too much; Rummler was delighted since it suggested an entrepreneurial opportunity. He sent brochures offering a 3-day workshop in "Applied Learning Theory." Participants said they had trouble convincing their bosses that 3 days of theory was worth the money. We let the data be our guide and changed to "Management of Behavior Change" so that participants could justify "management" over "theory." We ran the workshop quarterly for several years. The effort Rummler made to stay in touch with workshop graduates paid off in another offering: The Training Systems Workshop. Programmed Learning and Behavior Change graduates reported a variety of organizational problems on the job from their programs including managers with other priorities or other workers who scoffed and performed in a different way. Such problems were no surprise to us; we discovered them while doing subject matter analyses in the programmed learning workshop. We tried to show participants how to deal with such problems, but participants told us we were not successful. People wiser than we were said organizational problems were easy to discover but quite difficult to solve or even ameliorate. We offered advice, "If you can't maintain it, don't train it!" (K. S. Brethower, 1967). We set out to design a workshop to practice what we were preaching. Two tools helped participants analyze behavior change problems and create (synthesize) solutions.

The first tool guided what we called a balance of consequences analysis. The workshop experiences forced us to place a greater emphasis on the maintenance of performance after training via programmed instruction (K. S. Brethower, 1967). As we move around on the chessboard of life, every move we take has more than one consequence–some environmental outcomes will strengthen the reoccurrence of trained behavior and some outcomes will weaken the reoccurrence of trained behavior. The net effect of these daily consequences will determine whether the performers will persist in emitting that behavior beyond training. If the problem is with maintenance via consequences, then training will not be successful as an intervention, at least for the subordinate (although training for supervisors in how to provide support may be warranted). Some consequences are immediate, some are delayed. Immediate consequences, perhaps small, have more power than delayed consequences, even if the delayed consequences are larger. This had been demonstrated many times in the behavioral research literature and, for several years later on, was a mainstay of Dick Malott's teaching and public lectures at Western Michigan University. Multiple authors began to present this notion graphically as a pharmacist's set of scales balancing reinforcing and punishing consequences (see Figure 1 as an example) for desired and undesired behavior and began to classify the consequences by category (Connellan, 1978; Petrock, 1978). Consequences were classified according to their frequency-altering effect (reinforcing or punishing), magnitude (large or small), impact (personal or organizational & other), timeliness (immediate or delayed), and probability (certain or uncertain). Unhealthy organizations will typically have powerful reinforcers and weak punishers for undesired behavior and/or weak reinforcers and powerful punishers for desired behavior. The balance of consequences can be thrown off in other ways, such as with "dangerous" organizations in which both desired and undesired behaviors are excessively punished or "silly" organizations where all behaviors are met with noncontingent reinforcement (Brown, 1982). Eventually, the balance of consequences analysis was adapted into tools such as the PIC/NIC model or ABC Analysis, which focused on consequence characteristics of frequency-altering effect

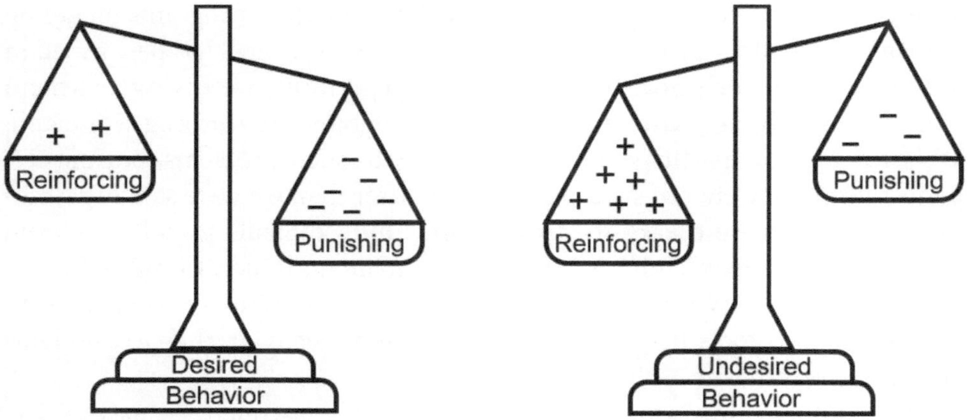

Figure 1. Balance of consequences representing an unhealthy organization.

(now labeled as positive or negative), timeliness, and probability (Braksick, 2007; Daniels & Bailey, 2014). Unfortunately, the important considerations of magnitude and whether the consequence impacts the individual, the organization, or both were lost along the way. Eventually, more prescriptive assessment tools at the performer level began to emerge over time (see Gravina et al., 2021).

One of the other products that emerged from the Training Systems Workshop was a second tool called the Total Performance System (TPS) diagram (see Figure 2). It captured the functioning of the organization at a level broader than the individual performer. General Systems Theory and Information Theory were hot topics for a few years so Center staff looked for

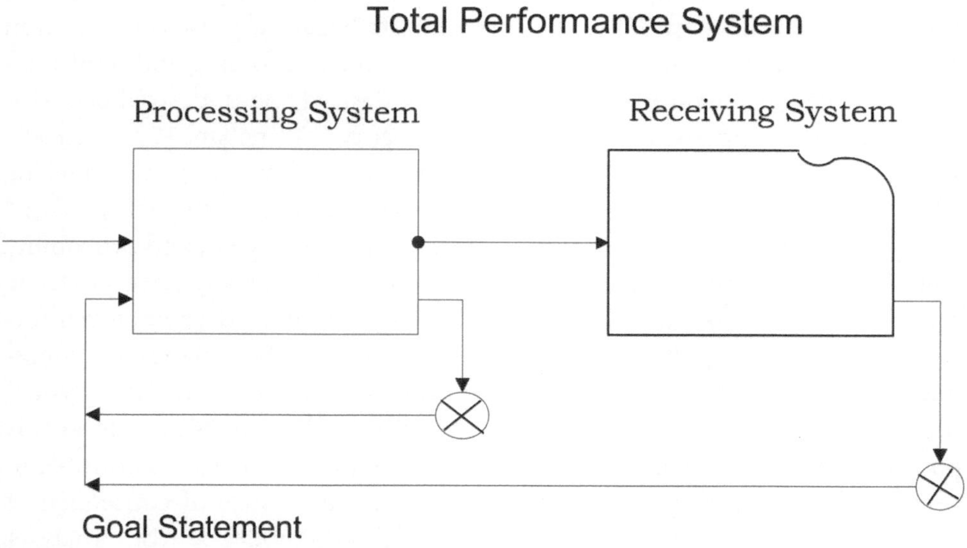

Figure 2. Total performance system map.

guidance as we designed the workshop. General Systems Theory could be applied by people with common sense, such as a Ph.D. in economics, and a penchant for thinking out of the box. The material crossed discipline lines and organizational boundaries. Our training systems workshop was designed for a broader chunk of the marketplace, so we applied programmed learning logic and tactics to the design. We had participants devise many diagrams during workshop exercises. Two turned out to be quite important: flow charts and total performance system diagrams. The idea behind flow charting is to discover how work flows better, faster, and cheaper. This became process mapping; Hammer and Champy (1993) helped that effort (see McGee & Crowley-Koch, 2021, for a discussion of various systems tools). The reason we called it the Total Performance System diagram was because clever people could use it to capture all of the most essential variables participants in the Training Systems Workshop would have to capture to manage critical business issues in their organizations. Later, Geary Rummler earned a living with process mapping and the TPS diagram expanded into the core of his Anatomy of Performance (AOP) diagram. Similarly, Maria Malott (2003) showed the world how the TPS could be applied to multiple levels of organizations. Some participants learned in the training systems workshop that Rummler should be hired as a consultant to work on strategically as well as tactically significant problems. During this time Tom Gilbert made several trips to Ann Arbor, appearing in workshops and talking with staff. Tom, Geary, and a third partner formed the Praxis Corporation headquartered in Manhattan. Geary completed his Ph.D. in adult learning and moved to New Jersey. The decade of the history of OBM in the 1960s was ending.

What are the lessons we can learn from the work at the University of Michigan?

One lesson is that innovators sometimes fail but keep on trying. Life is full of intermittent reinforcement. Jonas Salk, who discovered the polio vaccine, stated, "There is no such thing as failure, there's just giving up too soon." The IBRPI founders and staff had not found a market for programmed language learning. IBRPI failed, but Rummler and Odiorne kept programmed learning workshops. Innovators in OBM learn from both successes and failures.

Marketplace forces are more powerful than the innovators' intentions. To market a new product or service, offer it, sell it, and use the revenue to fund additional products/services. Geary knew that in advance; the first author did not. The analysis, synthesis, and test process applied to all the work at the Center for Programmed Learning for Business. We did subject matter analysis in the programmed learning workshop, followed by synthesis (writing programs) and testing (by the Friday developmental testing work). We did balance of consequence analysis in the Behavior Change Workshop and had participants devise (synthesize) practical management systems to create balances that supported improved performance. Testing occurred when they returned to their workplaces and implemented the designs. Did the designs work? It was not hard to find out; some did not work fully and needed revision. The Total Performance System diagram helps people capture complex interactions of variables in complex organizations. Some call the diagram a "model." We do not, instead preferring to call it a tool. The first author's dissertation validated the tool (D. M. Brethower, 1970).

OBM developed from practical issues in the world. The practical issues always involved improving performance in various organizations: schools, workplace, or the home. The development of the field is well chronicled (Dickinson, 2000). Participants in our workshops always focused on practical problems and these were great sources of learning for us. The performance might be reducing accidents, improving time on-task, reducing inventory shrinkage, reducing time to market for new products, or increasing prosocial behavior/reducing anti-social behavior among prison inmates. Every real-world issue had professionals eager to improve performance.

How did OBM the field start to mature as it moved from the 1960s to 1970s?

It seems the way the Center for Programmed Learning for Business grew and developed continued into the current era as new markets were discovered, new clients found, and new technology developed. For example, process mapping evolved from small flow-charting exercises to major tools in the business press. Once the idea of process mapping – drawing flow charts of the revenue producing processes – became a hot item in business there was an upsurge in demand for these services (Hammer & Champy, 1993; Rummler & Brache, 2013). Programmed learning faded as a movement over the years, but artifacts remained as "job aids." Costly training could be avoided by crafting tools such as a procedural checklist, labeled diagram, or computer-aided artificial intelligence program that show workers how to do specific tasks. The familiar "To-Do" list can be part of documentation for work completed. Some job aids are just part of the job; the airline pilot's pre-flight checklist is one example (Gawande, 2009; Rantz et al., 2009). The analysis tools – diagrams like the Total Performance System, the Behavioral Engineering Model, Rummler's Anatomy of Performance, Langdon's Language of Work, and Binder's Six Boxes are job aids for very complex tasks (Binder, 1998; D. M. Brethower, 1972; Gilbert, 1996; Langdon, 2000; Rummler, 2007). By the time the 1970s arrived, the number of business-minded individuals inspired by Skinner's general approach dramatically increased as they saw the potential for using behavioral technology to solve the concerns of business and industry. Joe

Harless (1970) textbook explicitly suggested that behavioral concepts and procedures should be applied to the management of others so that one could become a better parent, teacher, or supervisor. Corporations such as General Motors published management textbooks that were essentially behavior analysis textbooks (General Motors Institute, 1971). The relevance of operant techniques for a better understanding of classic organizational psychology events such as the Hawthorne studies began to emerge (Parsons, 1974), although myths about those studies still persist decades later in traditional textbooks as a form of academic folklore (Olson, Hogan, & Santos, 2006). Lawrence Miller published multiple books (L. M. Miller, 1974, 1978) that introduced readers to how behavioral concepts could apply to topics such as performance management, systems analysis, training, and self-management, making extensive use of case studies to illustrate his points. One of the better-publicized case studies, involving Edward J. Feeney's efforts to use feedback and reinforcement to improve sales training and save millions of dollars at Emery Air Freight, was featured in multiple textbooks, such as *Organizational Behavior Modification* (Luthans & Kreitner, 1975) and *Behavior Modification in Business, Industry, and Government* (Brown & Presbie, 1976). Before the 1970s ended, the *Journal of Organizational Behavior Management* would see its first publication.

What was happening in the field during the 1980s and 1990s?

Dickinson (2000) asserted that OBM fully matured as a field by the 1980s; there were undergraduate and graduate programs, OBM jobs in academia and in consulting firms, and jobs in both profit and nonprofit organizations. Multiple handbooks dedicated to OBM had been published in the early 1980s (Frederiksen, 1982; O'Brien et al., 1982). As in former decades, there were many publications in journals beyond the OBM-centric periodicals. ISPI grew – by the time the first author was elected President for 1999–2000 there were a dozen or so thriving chapters and about 10,000 members. The Association for Behavior Analysis International (ABAI) also prospered; Executive Director Maria Malott assured that OBM technology was applied to manage the annual conference and the entire operation. The *Journal of Organizational Behavior Management* celebrated 20 years of success by publishing a special edition of invited articles. Major books published OBM work, or Human Performance Technology as it was often called by ISPI members. One example was the edited book by Kaufman et al. (1997), *The Guidebook for Performance Improvement: Working with Individuals and Organizations*. The title indicates that the focus grew to include both individuals and organizations. One development in the 1990s foreshadowed major events that occurred at the beginning of the 21st Century. Rummler and Brache (2013; original work published 1990) released a book full of tools they used in their work,

Improving Performance: How to Manage the White Space on the Organization Chart. Rummler's fans recognized his humor; the white spaces in the org chart are the cracks that problems fall through rather than being solved.

What is the status of OBM looking backwards from the 21st Century and how do we compare to similar approaches?

The field has clearly grown; less obvious and perhaps as important is that history has performed an experiment about the folly of drifting away from evidence-based practice. ISPI has drifted and lost vitality; ABAI, including the OBM Network, remained close to the data. This can be demonstrated in a number of ways. For example, one could look at the peer-reviewed flagship journals for the two organizations: *Performance Improvement Quarterly* (PIQ) for the ISPI and *Journal of Organizational Behavior Management* (JOBM) for the OBM Network. If one excludes editorials and book reviews, the two journals published a comparable number of articles (183 for PIQ and 192 for JOBM) during the most recent decade (2011–2020; volumes 24–33 for PIQ and volumes 31–40 for JOBM). The overlap between topics covered during this decade was also comparable. For example, PIQ covered topics such as employee engagement, organizational culture, coaching, gamification, instructional design, feedback, employee incentives, performance appraisals, transfer of training, and team performance over the past decade (Ellis & Brown, 2020; Ghosh et al., 2019; Goksoy & Alayoglu, 2013; Gray et al., 2015; C. L. Miller et al., 2018; Norberg, 2016; Pousa & Mathieu, 2014; Song, 2011; Yelon et al., 2013; Zingoni, 2017). JOBM covered topics such as employee engagement, organizational culture, coaching, goal setting, rapport-building, feedback, employee incentives, performance appraisals, transfer of training, and safety over the past decade (Arnold & Van Houten, 2020; Curry et al., 2019; Gil & Carter, 2016; Gravina & Siers, 2011; Hagge et al., 2017; D. A. Johnson, 2013; Krapfl & Kruja, 2015; Ludwig & Frazier, 2012; M. V. Miller et al., 2014; Tilka & Johnson, 2018). However, the philosophical assumptions and standards for empiricism are very divergent in these two publication outlets. To illustrate this, we classified every article according to one of three categories: 1) collected data based on survey, interview, or other form of self-report (without any accompanying performance data), 2) collected data based on original performance data (summarizations of data previously published elsewhere did not qualify as original), or 3) other types of data or no data collected (e.g., literature reviews, qualitative case studies, theoretical arguments, meta-analyses, etc.). Original performance data could include actual changes in behavior or the results of behavior (e.g., sales made, units completed, etc.), including the data from customers, employees, supervisors, and/or laboratory participants. If survey data were collected in addition to performance data, this was classified as "performance data" only (i.e., no multiple category classifications).

In regard to PIQ, 56.3% of the articles were based on self-report data, 9.8% of the articles were based on performance data, and 33.8% of the articles did not fall into either prior category. The theoretical orientations, models, and framework employed are quite varied within this journal, including conceptualization such as psychological ownership (Chai et al., 2020), self-efficacy (Howard, 2019), equity theory (Kang et al., 2012), social exchange theory (De Guzman & Teng-Calleja, 2018), organizational knowledge creation theory (Kang et al., 2012), motivation-hygiene theory (Chyung & Vachon, 2013), mental models (Toker & Moseley, 2013), group-efficacy (Eatough et al., 2015), emotional intelligence (Nafukho et al., 2016), implicit mind-set (Zingoni, 2017), and cognitive load theory (Darabi & Kalyuga, 2012). In regard to JOBM, 3.6% of the articles were based on self-report data, 66.1% of the articles were based on performance data, and 30.2% of the articles did not fall into either prior category. Figure 3 shows the comparisons between the journals. The theoretical orientation, model, and framework employed within JOBM were consistently based on behavior analysis, sometimes in combination with general systems theory, economics theory, or another hybrid approach.

It is clear that PIQ (and by extension ISPI) has long since drifted from its behavioral roots. One survey (Roy & Pershing, 2012) of ISPI members found only 20% of members identified "behavior analysis" as an area that is part of

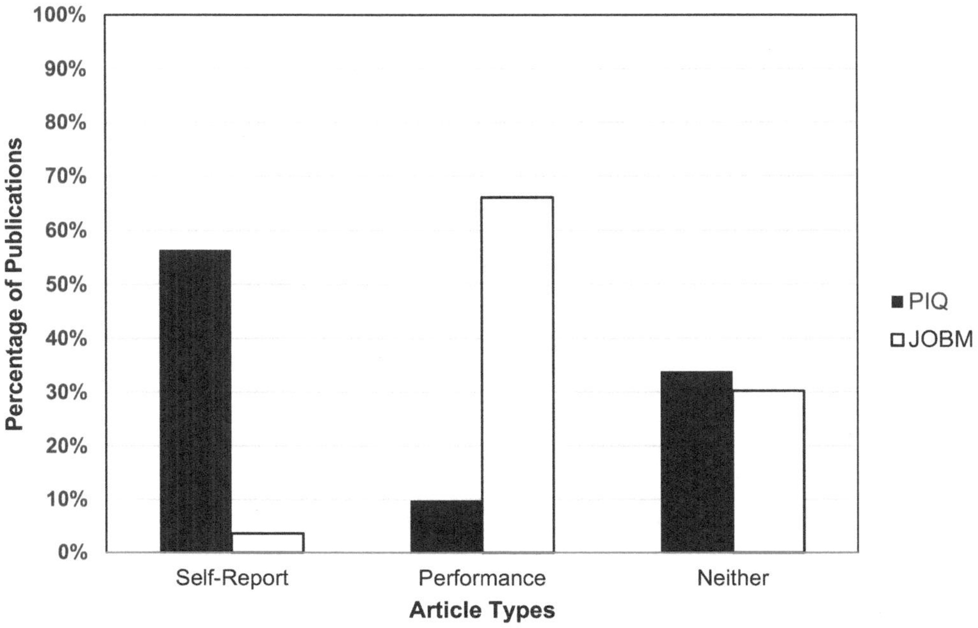

Figure 3. Comparison of PIQ and JOBM publication types.

their research or practice (note: respondents were free to identify multiple areas), outpaced by areas such as cognitive science, educational research, learning theory, and systems theory. Furthermore, respondents categorized behavior analysis as a low-tier application. This drift away from an emphasis on behavior-environmental relations may help explain why verbal reports are used as a substitute for actual performance data, such as when Frino and Desiderio (2012) asked salespeople about their performance but never measured that performance directly. One interesting observation from a reading of recent PIQ articles is how often the publications acknowledge the importance of looking at performance data and the pitfalls of relying on self-report. For example, Farrington (2011) warned that self-report data are often flawed. Duan (2011) lamented that little application of performance measurement existed, instead being eclipsed by stories, anecdotes, and single cases. Several publications (Howard, 2019; Marshall & Rossett, 2014; Williams & Nafukho, 2015) bemoan the fact that studies of training rarely go beyond Kirkpatrick's first level of evaluation (i.e., reactions of trainees) and neglect higher levels of evaluation (i.e., actual learning, changes in work performance, changes in results). While there is value in self-report research (e.g., employee burnout, customer perception of service, etc.), it should not be forgotten that what people say (derived from techniques such as questionnaires, interviews, focus groups, etc.) and what people actually do (derived from observations or demonstrations of performance) are not equivalent.

In contrast to this acknowledgment, one could not be faulted if they mistakenly thought ISPI stood for "Interviews and Surveys about Performance Improvement" given the overreliance on asking people about performance rather than measuring performance. Despite assertions that improving performance is the primary concern of the field (Kang & Molenda, 2018), the publications suggest that perceptions, constructs, and model-building may be the actual primary concern. If we only relied on self-reported perceptions in other sciences, we would still believe that the Earth is flat and that the rest of the universe moves around our stationary world. However, the empirical data told us that our perceptions were wrong, that we actually live on a rotating round planet that is flying through the universe. Data must rule, whether in deciding questions of the cosmos or how to best manage a business. It is difficult to "let the data be the guide" when there are no data available.

Although the current JOBM publications reflect a stronger interest in measuring performance rather than inferring it, the possibly of a discipline losing focus on foundations in favor of fads should serve as a cautionary tale for the OBM community. Although the creation of models and tools is a fine endeavor and can be a useful guide in practice, they are not intended to replace data. OBM successes typically have data guided analysis, data guided synthesis, and continuous data guided management of value adding performance. In addition, OBM practitioners typically maintain allegiance to science through education, networking, and research, especially the B. F. Skinner style science of human behavior. In 2000, ISPI had roughly 10,000 members. Two decades later that number dwindled by more than 80%. Several Past-Presidents, and Honorary Members for Life attribute much of the decline to ISPI's failure to remain close to evidence-based practice (D. M. Brethower, 2012; Wallace, 2012). Despite such decline, there still remains good work by many ISPI members. For example, Guy Wallace has collected dozens of interviews and publications by ISPI thought leaders (see https://hpttreasures.wordpress.com/). ABAI, including the OBM Network, has grown in membership and visibility in the world during this same period. OBM still emphasizes the performance of individuals but has expanded its reach to include product lines and total organizations.

OBM is very similar to what can be found in conventional business or management textbooks. The OBM contribution is to apply a science and engineering mind-set to real problems and opportunities in real settings. Our work helps put into practice what is easy to say in textbooks. We know why it is difficult to put good ideas into practice. Different folks have different ideas about what should be done. Getting to agreement on actions to improve performance is difficult for potential clients/customers (some say it is harder than herding cats). OBM methods can be used to gain agreement and get worthy results. However, we should remember that our clients/customers have been quite successful serving their clients and customers. They have expertise in areas we may not exhibit; we offer expertise in analyzing the behaviors to get them where they want to go. They may be the cats we are trying to herd, but we must never forget that it is their habitat we wandered into.

OBM practitioners focus sharply on performance, especially in what we measure and what variables we manage. Our focus is on what many called the ABCs of performance: Antecedents (what happens before) Behaviors (what performers do to get results) and Consequences (what good and bad things happen as a consequence of the behavior). Knowing the ABCs we can focus on training and maintenance: how can performers learn to perform? And what must the organization provide to maintain high levels of performance? For example, safety experts know that "unsafe conditions" yield accidents so part of managing antecedents (A), is reducing "unsafe conditions" as much as we can. Safety experts know that many lost time accidents result from behavior (B), especially lifting by bending the back rather than lifting with a straight back and bended knees. Safety experts and "safe lifters" also know that lifting light loads with bended back can lead to the set of consequences (C) of faster and easier lifting. That tells OBM practitioners that some serious effort will be required to maintain safe lifting.

We don't have any magic but OBM practitioners know that unless we get the ABCs right for the immediate situation (lifting this box) and the rest of the time (lifting all the boxes by the entire shift today and every day), there will be instances of improper lifting. And we know that the ABCs apply, over longer time spans, to the organization as a whole (e.g., to at least a few key managers who can keep the "safe lifting" system in place). Before, during, and after are the 3 salient time periods – that is common sense that has been fully verified in practice. We are biased toward science, engineering, and practical matters. We tend to rely on data, often data obtained by counting things such as students graduated, products sold, exam questions answered correctly, etc. There are many examples throughout OBM history (D. M. Brethower, 2016).

What major books were published in the 21st century and what "tools of the trade" from them are likely to be important in the future?

Many noteworthy and influential books focused on performance improvement have been published during the 21st century. These books contain numerous job aids that capture essential variables that enable client organizations to agree about what key players must do to achieve and maintain high levels of performance. Aubrey Daniels continued his pioneering OBM efforts into the 21st century, publishing books aimed at leaders (Daniels & Daniels, 2007), students (Daniels & Bailey, 2014), and people in general interested in understanding the business of behavior (Daniels, 2001, 2009, 2016). His books represent a continual quest to push supervisors away from an emphasis on aversive control and the latest management fads to instead find reinforcement-based approaches built upon decades of scientific understanding. Diagnostic tools such as the PIC/NIC analysis (the descendent of the earlier balance of consequences model) are used to identify why employees are only putting in the minimal effort and how to bring out discretionary effort. He is quick to operationalize commonly thrown around words like trust, vision, loyalty, and engagement so that readers are left with a blueprint of actions to take (as opposed to vague and vacuous truisms you might get from other management books that left readers inspired but directionless). As always, he uses a friendly and approachable voice that still makes readers well aware of the wealth of business consulting experiences and management stories that Aubrey has collected over the years.

Bill Abernathy published his final book, *The Liberated Workplace* (Abernathy, 2014) which was one part homage to the utopia of *Walden Two* (Skinner, 1948) and one part distillation of his years of consulting efforts to dissect typical compensation practices. Like his classic *Sin of Wages* book (Abernathy, 1996), he highlights how typical wage-and-salary system reinforce the wrong behaviors and disconnects the performer contingencies from the organization contingencies. Instead, he proposes performance scorecards and associated profits systems to motivate performers to work toward the health of the business. Of course, if a reader wants an in-depth guide to building measurement and compensation systems, he also published books to guide such endeavors (Abernathy, 2011, 2012).

Leslie Wilk Braksick published an update of her popular book *Unlock Behavior, Unleash Profits* (Braksick, 2007). This is another book exploring how antecedents and consequences drive employee performance and she walks the reader through the process of measurement, pinpointing, environmental redesign, and the maintenance of behavior change. A stronger emphasis on executive decision making and coaching than most, using the diagnostic tool of E-TIP (her particular descendant of the balance of consequences model) to guide behavior change. Roger Kaufman's work is also devoted to strategic planning; he illuminates the path toward engineering the connections. Two useful books provide tools and notions that help close the gap between "our world now" and "the way we'd like our world to be." (Kaufman, 2006; Kaufman et al., 2003). These are important examples of Kaufman's leadership in closing the gap.

Dick Grote released books on discipline systems and performance appraisal. Although not full of technical terms, both books embody the Skinnerian spirit of building a better organizational culture, especially one that tries to minimize aversive control. In his *Discipline without Punishment* book (Grote, 2006), he presents an alternative to the typical progressive discipline system to focus on how to salvage chronic problem employees through collaboration and problem-solving. Despite writing at length about disciplinary efforts, at the core of his approach is how to use analysis and recognition to build the desired performance. This theme is seen in his performance appraisal book as well (Grote, 2002), which focuses on the importance of clear expectations and feedback during the supervision process, loaded with many tips for dealing with the specific issues that may arise during implementation.

Danny Langdon published *Aligning Performance* (Langdon, 2000) to continue advancing his "language of work" model, also described in his earlier book *The New Language of Work* (Langdon, 1995). Langdon's key point across these publications is powerful and simple: organizations are created to do work. That is what any organization does. Langdon's other key point is that to be managed well, work must be described well. He offers an unabridged language of work dictionary that describes all work in an organization. The dictionary has 6 entries, which are fundamentally the same as the labels on the *Total Performance System* diagram (D. M. Brethower, 1972). Langdon considers that the simplicity and consistency of language is essential if we are to understand the complexity of organizations. Langdon and Langdon (2018) wrote three short books (*The Business Model, The Managing Model*, & *The Working Model*) that show how the new language of work model matches the roles that three levels of an organization should perform in managing work.

Rummler (2007) published a book about consulting, because he wanted to be clear that he could not speak for all consultants. The book is a fictional case study that faithfully follows actual case studies in Rummler's files. The book is intellectually honest. It shows how the work in classics such as Gilbert's (1996) *Human Competence* and Rummler and Brache (2013) *Improving Performance* (currently in its 3rd edition) books was done. Rummler's entire career was devoted to tackling worthwhile practical problems the way a good scientist/engineer/thought leader does. He learned and shared. Fortunately, in another book published posthumously, *White Space Revisited: Creating Value through Process* (Rummler et al., 2010), he shared a chockfull of diagrams and charts that are tools used to add value to clients, helping them create value for customers, employees, and investors. The tools in *Revisited* are off-putting to some who do not like technology. It may help folks by pointing out that Rummler's tools are like children's art. Anyone can make them with a little practice, yet no one knows what they mean until they talk with the artist. Geary described his art making process this way: "I'll sit down and talk with several people about the matters you've said are issues. I'll take notes and then go away and noodle a while. When I get my notes organized, I'll come back and show them to you, and you can tell me where I've gotten it wrong. We'll work together a bit and get it right." (First, make the analysis, then the synthesis, then test it.) When talking and noodling and talking again is finished there are complex-looking diagrams that transform the confused into the manageable. One other point: Geary and his colleagues at Performance Design Lab divided projects into phases so the client did not have to clarify everything in the first round. Or pay a huge fee for something they did not know would help their organization. There is a shorter book for executives without the detail (Rummler et al., 2011).

Another important book is Maria Malott's (2003), *Paradox of Organizational Change: Engineering Organizations with Behavioral Systems Analysis.* Organizations are full of complexities, contradictions, and inconsistencies. Paradoxically, organizations are formed out of simpler, coherent, consistencies. She describes the simpler parts in coherent language that demonstrates the consistencies among the parts. Find the consistencies and we can build effective and manageable organizations. "If you don't see how crazy this place is, you don't understand it." True. "If you view this place as a system you can engineer the craziness out and the productivity in." True. Mostly. We would be remiss if we did not highlight her contributions to advancing not just the knowledge of our field, but the professional organization that supports the field of behavior analysis as a whole. Maria Malott doesn't just give lip service to "practicing what we preach," she makes sure that ABAI does it. In her role as the long-serving Executive Director, she applies OBM principles, practices, and technology to the operation of ABAI. She keeps the cost of the annual conference low and affordable by academics, including students. She sponsors interns who do OBM-type projects that develop job aids for running a high-quality conference and an efficient society. Board meetings feature performance data Maria provides. ABAI is managed through evidence-based practices, guided by data, and guided by the science of behavior. She proves that the science isn't just an intellectual exercise for the books, but a better way of doing business.

Finally, the 21st century saw the publication of handbooks such as the first *Handbook of Organizational Performance* (edited by C. M. Johnson et al., 2001) and *Organizational Behavior Management: The Essentials* (edited by Wine & Pritchard, 2018). Also, the *Journal of Organizational Behavior Management* continues to publish volumes of articles every year full of performance-based empiricism and guidance for best practices. Of course, there are many other books not mentioned, especially if one starts to expand the list to sub-specializations within OBM such as safety, consumer behavior, etc. It does not matter whether readers begin with books by Daniels, Rummler, Malott, etc.; they all say fundamentally the same things – just from different perspectives. That is not obvious to most readers.

What gaps in our knowledge are important to fill in the future?

When the Michigan group began using the Total Performance System diagram in the 1960s, we always drew the Receiving System box with a missing corner. It is a visual reminder that the Receiving System is not completely known. Rummler's Anatomy of Performance diagram requires us to specify more detail, to make more of it known. The version of the AOP diagram in Figure 4 shows where the inputs to the Processing System begin (Capital Markets and Customer Markets), where the outputs go, and where the external feedbacks derive. It calls attention to the competitive environment organizations face and to the importance of both "close" and "distant" external influences. "My Enterprise," the processing system, must navigate through all those important, often unknown, and always changing influences if an enterprise is to continue and prosper. The AOP diagram visually demands strategic planning and far-sighted management. It helps managers, executives, and small business owners develop the plans and tools they need to navigate successfully. Please notice that the arrows at the top pointing down to the enterprise box from the "close" and "distant" influences boxes do not quite touch. The gap exists because Rummler never engineered the connections. The arrows signal "be aware of" and "consider as much as you can," not "Here is how to devise goals, policies, and procedures to engineer these important connections."

Two points illustrate both the scope and success of this work should become increasingly known and influential in the future. First is the work at the Technological Institute of Sonora to establish a program to "get your company a Ph.D." The faculty included Mariano Bernardez, Roger Kaufman, Ingrid

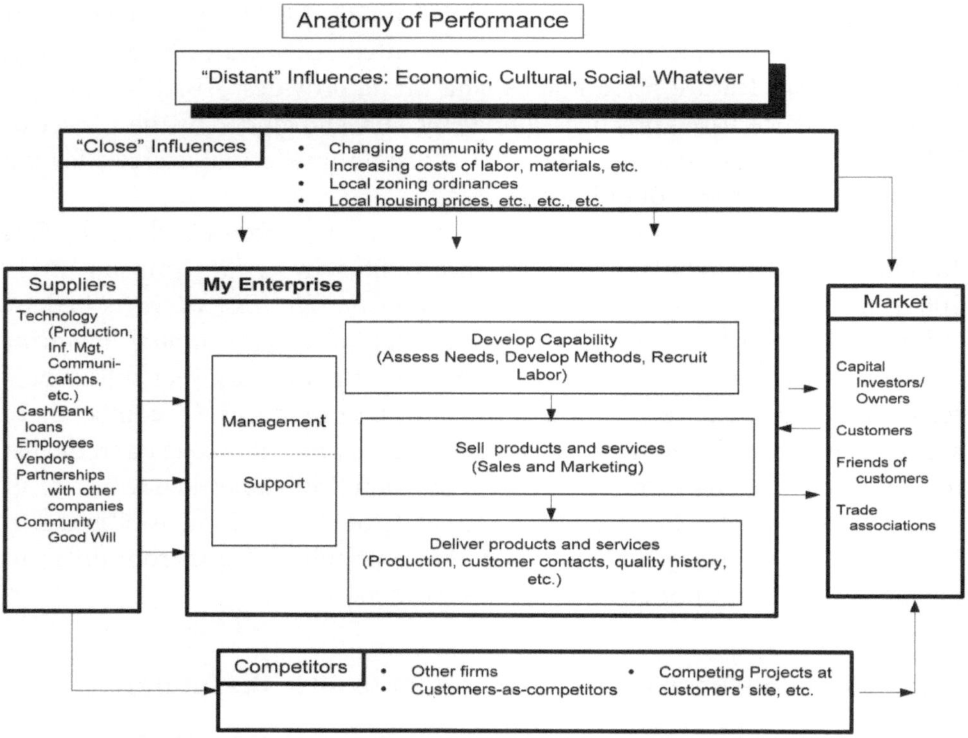

Figure 4. Anatomy of performance.

Guerra-Lopez, Geary Rummler, Dale Brethower, and a few others. The idea was that students would learn and do by starting a new business or a new product line. They did that for several years before the program foundered due to opposition from traditional academics during an economic downturn in Mexico (Guerra & Rodriguez, 2005).

Second is work primarily organized by Mariano Bernardez in the Spanish speaking world. Most of the material can be found online in both Spanish and English (http://www.piionline.org/or http://www.ispiglobal.org/) There are also links to some of this work on Kaufman's web site (https://megaplanning.com/). This work is important to OBM Network people who want to see what is being done in the Spanish speaking part of the globe and/or those who wish to know more about the increasing scope of our work. Kaufman's notion is that the people running an enterprise should start by agreeing on their ideal vision for the world they are helping create (think meaningful vision statements focused on the AOP world of distant influences). This is Mega Thinking. The Kaufman vision idea that may work best is, "We are creating a better world for tomorrow's child." Are we creating a worse world? Ignoring the plight of children? How can we operate our enterprise to create a better world for our own children? For our customers and other stakeholders' children? It is not hard to imagine that discussion, one-on-one, in every organization with which we work. It is easy to imagine Roger Kaufman, Maria Malott, or any one of a dozen or so OBM people known to us leading that discussion with a group of managers or executives. To those that know her, it is easy to imagine Maria flipping open her computer and saying, "OK, if that's our goal, what's our plan?" and hammering out a draft on the spot, using some of the OBM tools.

There is certainly a need to disseminate OBM even more broadly, including beyond its American roots, to be a more inclusive discipline. Much important work has been done by OBM researchers and practitioners working in places such as Brazil, Iceland, Ireland, Israel, Italy, Norway, South Korea, and the United Kingdom (Aljadeff-Abergel et al., 2017; Chae et al., 2020; Fagerstrøm et al. 2015; Lebbon & Sigurdsson, 2017; O'Hora & Maglieri, 2006; Porto & Foxall, 2019; Tosolin et al., 2005), but many opportunities still remain elsewhere (and more extensively in the places we have already been). Our job, after all, is to make the world a better place. Of course, there always more topics and research lines to pursue. Basically, if something matters to the world of work and the vision of tomorrow, it should matter to us as well. The topics in our books and journals will probably never exhaust the range of important ideas because the workplace is always evolving and sometimes rediscovering old lessons.

Is that your last word about the history of OBM?

Almost. One way to assess the status of OBM in the 21st century is to think about the publications within this series. The evidence-based material could not have been written 50 years ago. Another way to assess the status is to search the internet and to look into the behaviorally oriented set of academic programs in the world. In the United States, they can be found at Western Michigan University (said with a bit of bias from the authors who spent much of their careers at WMU), Florida Institute of Technology, University of Florida, University of Kansas, University of Nevada-Reno, Appalachian State University, California State University (Fresno, Northridge, and Sacramento campuses), Portland State University, and more (the OBM Network maintains a list of training programs that interested students should consult). The list of schools and programs is often in flux as faculty retire, are hired, or transition to practice or other schools and programs. But the work continues because the work is needed and will continue to be needed in the world of tomorrow. OBM grew through the work of many people who were willing to work hard to make the world a better place. They started by working in their own sandbox, then continued to work in almost every imaginable organization. They encountered a great variety of real human/organizational performance problems and attempted to improve the performance using what they already knew, a body of knowledge and common sense. If they did not already know how to do the job, they analyzed, synthesized, and tested until they got the job done. They developed tools to help. They used these tools to improve performance wherever they were. They wrote about the work, shared technology, and shared stories of successes and failures. Undoubtedly these stories will grow as OBM turns from yesterday and continues on its journey into tomorrow.

Disclosure statement

No potential conflict of interest was reported by the author(s).

ORCID

Douglas A. Johnson http://orcid.org/0000-0002-7802-3566

References

Abernathy, W. B. (1996). *The sin of wages: Where the conventional pay system has led us and how*. Performance Management Publications.

Abernathy, W. B. (2011). *Pay for profits: Designing an organization-wide performance-based compensation system*. Performance Management Publications.

Abernathy, W. B. (2012). *Human performance diagnostics: A multidisciplinary approach for analysis & improvement in organizations*. Performance Management Publications.

Abernathy, W. B. (2014). *The liberated workplace: Transitioning to Walden Three*. Performance Management Publications.

Aldis, O. (1961). Of pigeons and men. *Harvard Business Review, 39*(4), 59–63.

Aljadeff-Abergel, E., Peterson, S. M., Wiskirchen, R. R., Hagen, K. K., & Cole, M. L. (2017). Evaluating the temporal location of feedback: Providing feedback following performance vs. prior to performance. *Journal of Organizational Behavior Management, 37*(2), 171–195. doi:10.1080/01608061.2017.1309332

Arnold, M. L., & Van Houten, R. (2020). Increasing following headway in a driving simulator and transfer to real world driving. *Journal of Organizational Behavior Management, 40*(1–2), 63–81. doi:10.1080/01608061.2020.1746475

Ayllon, T., & Michael, J. (1959). The psychiatric nurse as a behavioral engineer. *Journal of the Experimental Analysis of Behavior, 2*(4), 323–334. doi:10.1901%2Fjeab.1959.2-323

Azrin, N. H., & Lindsley, O. R. (1956). The reinforcement of cooperation between children. *Journal of Abnormal and Social Psychology, 52*(1), 100–102. doi:10.1037/h0042490

Binder, C. (1998). The Six Boxes: A descendent of Gilbert's behavior engineering model. *Performance Improvement, 37*(6), 48–52. doi:10.1002/pfi.4140370612

Boulding, K. (1956). General systems theory: The skeleton of science. *Management Science, 2*(3), 197–286. doi:10.1287/mnsc.2.3.197

Braksick, L. W. (2007). *Unlock behavior, unleash profits: Developing leadership behavior that drives profitability in your organization* (2nd ed.). McGraw-Hill.

Brethower, D. M. (1963). *Programed instruction: A manual of programing techniques*. Educational Methods, Inc.

Brethower, D. M. (1970). *The classroom as a self-modifying system* (Unpublished doctoral dissertation). The University of Michigan.

Brethower, D. M. (1972). *Behavior analysis in business and industry: A total performance system*. Behaviordelia, Inc.

Brethower, D. M. (2008). Historical background for HPT certification standard 2, take a systems view, part 2. *Performance Improvement*, *47*(4), 15–24. doi:10.1002/pfi.198

Brethower, D. M. (2012). The future of HPT depends on whether practitioners focus on foundations or fads. *Performance Improvement Quarterly*, *25*(1), 47–58. doi:10.1002/piq.20139

Brethower, D. M. (2016, April 10-12). *Keeping score with scorecards* [Invited address]. ISPI Annual Conference, Philadelphia, PA.

Brethower, D. M., Markle, D. G., Rummler, G. A., Schrader, A. W., & Smith, D. E. (1965). *Programmed learning: A practicum*. Ann Arbor Publishers.

Brethower, K. S. (1967). Maintenance: The neglected half of behavior change. In G. A. Rummler, J. P. Yaney, & A. W. Schrader (Eds.), *Managing the instructional programming effort*. Bureau of Industrial Relations.

Bridgman, P. W. (1959). *The way things are*. Harvard University Press.

Bridgman, P. W. (1961). *The world as I see it. [colloquium session]*. Harvard University Department of Psychology.

Brinkerhoff, R. O. (2003). *The success case method: Find out quickly what's working and what's not*. Berrett-Koehler Publishers.

Brown, P. L. (1982). *Managing behavior on the job*. John Wiley & Sons, Inc.

Brown, P. L., & Presbie, R. J. (1976). *Behavior modification in business, industry, and government*. Behavior Improvement Associates.

Chae, S., Eagle, L. M., Johnson, D. A., Moon, K., Choi, E., & Oah, S. (2020). The impact of authority relations and feedback delivery method on performance. *Journal of Organizational Behavior Management*, *40*(1–2), 140–150. doi:10.1080/01608061.2020.1746476

Chai, D. S., Song, J. H., & You, Y. M. (2020). Psychological ownership and openness to change: The mediating effects of work engagement, and knowledge creation. *Performance Improvement Quarterly*, *33*(3), 305–326. doi:10.1002/piq.21326

Chyung, S. Y., & Vachon, M. (2013). An investigation of the profiles of satisfying and dissatisfying factors in e-learning. *Performance Improvement Quarterly*, *26*(2), 117–140. doi:10.1002/piq.21147

Connellan, T. K. (1978). *How to improve human performance: Behaviorism in business and industry*. Harper & Row.

Crawley, W. J., Adler, B. S., O'Brien, R. M., & Duffy, E. M. (1982). Making salesmen: Behavioral assessment and intervention. In R. M. O'Brien, A. M. Dickinson, & M. P. Rosow (Eds.), *Industrial behavior modification: A management handbook* (pp. 184–199). Pergamon Press.

Curry, S. M., Gravina, N. E., Sleiman, A. A., & Richard, E. (2019). The effects of engaging in rapport-building behaviors on productivity and discretionary effort. *Journal of Organizational Behavior Management*, *39*(3–4), 213–226. doi:10.1080/01608061.2019.1667940

Daniels, A. C. (2001). *Other people's habits: How to use positive reinforcement to bring out the best in people around you*. McGraw-Hill.

Daniels, A. C. (2009). *Oops! 13 management practices that waste time and money (and what to do instead)*. Performance Management Publications.

Daniels, A. C. (2016). *Bringing out the best in people: How to apply the astonishing power of positive reinforcement*. McGraw-Hill Education.

Daniels, A. C., & Bailey, J. S. (2014). *Performance management: Changing behavior that drives organizational effectiveness* (5th ed.). Performance Management Publications.

Daniels, A. C., & Daniels, J. E. (2007). *Measure of a leader: The legendary leadership formula for producing exceptional performers and outstanding results*. McGraw-Hill.

Darabi, A., & Kalyuga, S. (2012). Improvement of organizational performance and instructional design: An analogy based on general principles of natural information processing systems. *Performance Improvement Quarterly, 25*(3), 23–35. doi:10.1002/piq.21122

De Guzman, I. L. M., & Teng-Calleja, M. (2018). Development of a model for a great place to work and its perceived outcomes: An example from the Philippines. *Performance Improvement Quarterly, 31*(1), 5–34. doi:10.1002/piq.21252

Dickinson, A. M. (2000). The historical roots of organizational behavior management in the private sector: The 1950s-1980s. *Journal of Organizational Behavior Management, 20*(3–4), 9–58. doi:10.1300/J075v20n03_02

Drucker, P. F. (1946). *The concept of the corporation*. John Day.

Drucker, P. F. (1973). *Management: Tasks, responsibilities, practices*. Harper & Row.

Duan, M. (2011). Application of data collection techniques by human performance technology practitioners. *Performance Improvement Quarterly, 24*(3), 77–100. doi:10.1002/piq.20118

Eatough, E., Chang, C., & Hall, N. (2015). Getting roped in: Group cohesion, trust, and efficacy following a ropes course intervention. *Performance Improvement Quarterly, 28*(2), 65–89. doi:10.1002/piq.21183

Ellis, S., & Brown, H. Q. (2020). Can values be trained? Applying affective engagement to change organizational culture. *Performance Improvement Quarterly, 33*(3), 327–347. doi:10.1002/piq.21327

Fagerstrøm, A., Stratton, J. P., & Foxall, G. R. (2015). The impact of corporate social responsibility activities on the consumer purchasing situation. *Journal of Organizational Behavior Management, 35*(3–4), 184–205. doi:10.1080/01608061.2015.1093053

Farrington, J. (2011). Training transfer: Not the 10% solution. *Performance Improvement Quarterly, 24*(1), 117–121. doi:10.1002/piq.20105

Ferster, C. B., & Skinner, B. F. (1957). *Schedules of reinforcement*. Appleton-Century-Crofts.

Flagle, C. D., Huggins, W. H., & Roy, R. H. (1960). *Operations research and systems engineering*. The John Hopkins Press.

Frederiksen, L. W. (1982). *Handbook of organizational behavior management*. John Wiley & Sons.

Frino, M. G., & Desiderio, K. P. (2012). The role of demographics as predictors of successful performance of sales professionals in business-to-business sales organizations. *Performance Improvement Quarterly, 25*(4), 7–21. doi:10.1002/piq.21128

Fuller, P. (1949). Operant conditioning of a vegetative human organism. *American Journal of Psychology, 62*(4), 587–590. doi:10.2307/1418565

Gawande, A. (2009). *The checklist manifesto: How to get things right*. Metropolitan Books.

General Motors Institute. (1971). *Behavior . . . and what you can do about it*. General Motors Education and Training.

Ghosh, R., Shuck, B., Cumberland, D., & D'Mello, J. (2019). Building psychological capital and employee engagement: Is formal mentoring a useful strategic human resource development intervention? *Performance Improvement Quarterly, 32*(1), 37–54. doi:10.1002/piq.21285

Gil, P. J., & Carter, S. L. (2016). Graphic feedback, performance feedback, and goal setting increased staff compliance with a data collection task at a large residential facility. *Journal of Organizational Behavior Management, 36*(1), 56–70. doi:10.1080/01608061.2016.1152207

Gilbert, T. F. (1996). *Human competence: Engineering worthy performance*. International Society for Performance Improvement.

Goksoy, A., & Alayoglu, N. (2013). The impact of perception of performance appraisal and distributive justice fairness on employees' ethical decision making in paternalist organizational culture. *Performance Improvement Quarterly, 26*(1), 57–79. doi:10.1002/piq.21137

Gravina, N., Nastasi, J., & Austin, J. (2021). Assessment of employee performance. *Journal of Organizational Behavior Management*, 1–26. Advance online publication. doi:10.1080/01608061.2020.1869136

Gravina, N. E., & Siers, B. P. (2011). Square pegs and round holes: Ruminations on the relationship between performance appraisal and performance management. *Journal of Organizational Behavior Management, 31*(4), 277–287. doi:10.1080/01608061.2011.619418

Gray, C. M., Dagli, C., Demiral-Uzan, M., Ergulec, F., Tan, V., Altuwaijri, A. A., . . . Boling, E. (2015). Judgment and instructional design: How ID practitioners work in practice. *Performance Improvement Quarterly, 28*(3), 25–49. doi:10.1002/piq.21198

Grote, D. (2002). *The performance appraisal question and answer book: A survival guide for managers*. American Management Association.

Grote, D. (2006). *Discipline without punishment: The proven strategy that turns problem employees into superior performers*. American Management Association.

Guerra, I. J., & Rodriguez, G. (2005). Educational planning and social responsibility: Eleven years of mega planning at the Sonora Institute of Technology (ITSON). *Performance Improvement Quarterly, 18*(3), 56–64. doi:10.1111/j.1937-8327.2005.tb00341.x

Hagge, M., McGee, H., Matthews, G., & Aberle, S. (2017). Behavior-based safety in a coal mine: The relationship between observations, participation, and injuries over a 14-year period. *Journal of Organizational Behavior Management, 37*(1), 107–118. doi:10.1080/01608061.2016.1236058

Hammer, M., & Champy, J. (1993). *Reengineering the corporation: A manifesto for business revolution*. Harper-Collins.

Handlin, H. C. (1991). The company built upon the golden rule: Lincoln Electric. *Journal of Organizational Behavior Management, 12*(1), 151–163. doi:10.1300/J075v12n01_07

Harless, J. H. (1970). *Behavior analysis and management: A self-instructional lesson*. Stipes Publishing Company.

Holland, J. G., & Skinner, B. F. (1961). *The analysis of behavior: A program for self-instruction*. McGraw-Hill.

Howard, M. C. (2019). The effect of training self-efficacy on computer-based training outcomes: Empirical analysis of the construct and creation of two scales. *Performance Improvement Quarterly, 32*(4), 331–368. doi:10.1002/piq.21301

ISPI. (n.d.). *CPT performance standards*. Retrieved from https://ispi.org/page/CPTStandards

Johnson, C. M., Redmon, W. K., & Mawhinney, T. C. (Eds.). (2001). *Handbook of Organizational Performance: Behavior analysis and management*. Haworth.

Johnson, D. A. (2013). A component analysis of the impact of evaluative and objective feedback on performance. *Journal of Organizational Behavior Management, 33*(2), 89–103. doi:10.1080/01608061.2013.785879

Kang, I., Song, J. H., & Kim, W. (2012). The mediating effect of team-level knowledge creation on organizational procedural justice and team performance improvement. *Performance Improvement Quarterly, 25*(2), 43–64. doi:10.1002/piq.21117

Kang, S., & Molenda, M. H. (2018). How shall we define human performance technology? *Performance Improvement Quarterly, 31*(2), 189–212. doi:10.1002/piq.21276

Kaufman, R. (2006). *Change, choices, and consequences: A guide to mega thinking and planning*. HRD Press & International Society for Performance Improvement.

Kaufman, R., Oakley-Browne, H., Watkins, R., & Leigh, D. (2003). *Strategic planning for success: Aligning people, performance, and payoffs*. Jossey-Bass/Pfeiffer.

Kaufman, R., Thiagarajan, S., & MacGillis, P. (Eds.). (1997). *The guidebook for performance improvement: Working with individuals and organizations*. Jossey-Bass/Pfeiffer.

Keller, F. S. (1954). *Learning: Reinforcement theory*. Random House.

Krapfl, J. E., & Kruja, B. (2015). Leadership and culture. *Journal of Organizational Behavior Management, 35*(1–2), 28–43. doi:10.1080/01608061.2015.1031431

Lane, H. (1976). *The wild boy of Aveyron.* Harvard University Press.

Langdon, D. (1995). *The new language of work.* HRD Press.

Langdon, D. (2000). *Aligning performance: Improving people, systems, and organizations.* Jossey-Bass/Pfeiffer.

Langdon, D., & Langdon, K. S. (2018). *The language of work trilogy.* Performance International.

Lazarus, A. A. (1959). The elimination of children's phobias by deconditioning. *Medical Proceedings (South Africa), 5*, 261–265.

Lebbon, A. R., & Sigurdsson, S. O. (2017). Behavioral perspectives on variability in human behavior as part of process safety. *Journal of Organizational Behavior Management, 37*(3–4), 261–282. doi:10.1080/01608061.2017.1340922

Lincoln, J. F. (1951). *Incentive management.* The Lincoln Electric Company.

Lincoln, J. F. (1961). *A new approach to industrial economics.* Devin-Adair.

Ludwig, T. D., & Frazier, C. B. (2012). Employee engagement and organizational behavior management. *Journal of Organizational Behavior Management, 32*(1), 75–82. doi:10.1080/01608061.2011.619439

Luthans, F., & Kreitner, R. (1975). *Organizational behavior modification.* Scott, Foresman and Company.

Mager, R. F. (1997). *Preparing instructional objectives: A critical tool in the development of effective instruction* (3rded.). Center for Effective Performance.

Malott, M. E. (2003). *Paradox of organizational change: Engineering organizations with behavioral systems analysis.* Context Press.

Markle, S. M. (1969). *Good frames and bad: A grammar of frame writing.* John Wiley & Sons, Inc.

Markle, S. M. (1990). *Designs for instructional designers.* Stipes Publishing Company.

Marshall, J., & Rossett, A. (2014). Perceptions of barriers to the evaluation of workplace learning programs. *Performance Improvement Quarterly, 27*(3), 7–26. doi:10.1002/piq.21173

Mayo, E. (1933). *The human problems of industrial civilization.* Harvard University Press.

Mayo, E. (1945). *The social problems of an industrial civilization.* Harvard Business School.

McGee, H. M., & Crowley-Koch, B. J. (2021). Performance assessment of organizations. Journal of Organizational Behavior Management. Advance online publication. https://doi.org/10.1080/01608061.2021

Miller, C. L., Grooms, J. C., & King, H. (2018). To infinity and beyond—Gamifying IT service-desk training: A case study. *Performance Improvement Quarterly, 31*(3), 249–268. doi:10.1002/piq.21263

Miller, G. A. (1956). The magical number seven plus or minus two: Some limits on our capacity for processing information. *Psychological Review, 63*(2), 81–97. doi:10.1037/h0043158

Miller, L. M. (1974). *Behavior management: New skills for business and industry.* Human Behavior Institute, Inc.

Miller, L. M. (1978). *Behavior management: The new science of managing people at work.* John Wiley & Sons, Inc.

Miller, M. V., Carlson, J., & Sigurdsson, S. O. (2014). Improving treatment integrity in a human service setting using lottery-based incentives. *Journal of Organizational Behavior Management, 34*(1), 29–38. doi:10.1080/01608061.2013.873381

Nafukho, F. M., Muyia, M. H., Farnia, F., Kacirek, K., & Lynham, S. A. (2016). Developing emotional intelligence skills among practicing leaders: Reality or myth? *Performance Improvement Quarterly, 29*(1), 71–87. doi:10.1002/piq.21215

Norberg, P. A. (2016). Employee incentive programs: Recipient behaviors in points, cash, and gift card programs. *Performance Improvement Quarterly, 29*(4), 375–388. doi:10.1002/piq.21233

O'Brien, R. M., Dickinson, A. M., & Rosow, M. P. (1982). *Industrial behavior modification: A management handbook*. Pergamon Press, Inc.

O'Hora, D., & Maglieri, K. A. (2006). Goal statements and goal-directed behavior. *Journal of Organizational Behavior Management, 26*(1–2), 131–170. doi:10.1300/J075v26n01_06

Olson, R., Hogan, L., & Santos, L. (2006). Illuminating the history of psychology: Tips for teaching students about the Hawthorne studies. *Psychology Learning & Teaching, 5*(2), 110–118. doi:10.2304/plat.2005.5.2.110

Parsons, H. M. (1974). What happened at Hawthorne? *Science, 183*(4128), 922–932. doi:10.1126/science.183.4128.922

Petrock, F. (1978). Analyzing the balance of consequences for performance improvement. *Journal of Organizational Behavior Management, 1*(3), 197–205. doi:10.1300/J075v01n03_04

Porto, R. B., & Foxall, G. R. (2019). The marketing firm as a metacontingency: Revealing the mutual relationships between marking and finance. *Journal of Organizational Behavior Management, 39*(3–4), 115–114. doi:10.1080/01608061.2019.1666774

Pousa, C., & Mathieu, A. (2014). The influence of coaching on employee performance: Results from two international quantitative studies. *Performance Improvement Quarterly, 27*(3), 75–92. doi:10.1002/piq.21175

Premack, D. (1959). Toward empirical behavior laws: I. Positive reinforcement. *Psychological Review, 66*(4), 219–233. doi:10.1037/h0040891

Pressey, S. L. (1926). A simple apparatus which gives tests and scores–and teaches. *School and Society, 23*(586), 373–376.

Rantz, W. G., Dickinson, A. M., Sinclair, G. A., & Van Houten, R. (2009). The effect of feedback on the accuracy of checklist completion during instrument flight training. *Journal of Applied Behavior Analysis, 42*(3), 497–509. doi:10.1901/jaba.2009.42-497

Roethlisberger, F. J., & Dickson, W. J. (1939). *Management and the worker*. Harvard University Press.

Rogers, C. R., & Skinner, B. F. (1956). Some issues concerning the control of human behavior: A symposium. *Science, 124*(3231), 1057–1066. doi:10.1126/science.124.3231.1057

Roy, R., & Pershing, J. A. (2012). Examining the boundaries of HPT through the lens of communities of practice. *Performance Improvement Quarterly, 25*(2), 79–105. doi:10.1002/piq.21120

Rummler, G. A. (2007). *Serious performance consulting: According to Rummler*. The International Society of Performance Improvement.

Rummler, G. A., & Brache, A. P. (2013). *Improving performance: How to manage the white space on the organization chart* (3rd ed.). Jossey-Bass.

Rummler, G. A., Ramias, A. J., & Rummler, R. A. (2010). *White space revisited: Creating value through process*. Jossey-Bass.

Rummler, G. A., Ramias, A. J., & Wilkins, C. L. (2011). *Rediscovering value: Leading the 3-D enterprise to sustainable success*. Jossey-Bass.

Sidman, M. (1960). *Tactics of scientific research: Evaluating experimental data in psychology*. Basic Books.

Skinner, B. F. (1938). *The behavior of organisms: An experimental analysis*. Appleton-Century-Crofts.

Skinner, B. F. (1948). *Walden Two*. MacMillan.

Skinner, B. F. (1953). *Science and Human Behavior*. Appleton-Century-Crofts.

Skinner, B. F. (1954). The science of learning and the art of teaching. *Harvard Educational Review, 24*, 86–97.

Skinner, B. F. (1957). *Verbal behavior*. Appleton-Century-Crofts.

Skinner, B. F. (1958). Teaching machines. *Science*, *128*(3330), 969–977. doi:10.1126/science.128.3330.969

Skinner, B. F. (1968). *The technology of teaching*. Appleton-Century-Crofts.

Skinner, B. F. (1983). *A matter of consequences*. University Press.

Song, J. H. (2011). Team performance improvement: Mediating roles of employee job autonomy and quality of team leader-member relations in supportive organizations in the Korean business context. *Performance Improvement Quarterly*, *24*(3), 55–76. doi:10.1002/piq.20115

Tilka, R., & Johnson, D. A. (2018). Coaching as a packaged intervention for telemarketing personnel. *Journal of Organizational Behavior Management*, *38*(1), 49–72. doi:10.1080/01608061.2017.1325821

Toker, S., & Moseley, J. L. (2013). The mental model comparison of expert and novice performance improvement practitioners. *Performance Improvement Quarterly*, *26*(3), 7–32. doi:10.1002/piq.21152

Tosolin, F., Truzoli, R., Vigano, I., Algarotti, E., & Gatti, M. (2005). Current practice of Precision Teaching in the workplace. In G. Chiazzese, M. Allegra, A. Chifari, & S. Ottaviano (Eds.), *Methods and technologies for learning* (pp. 159–166). WIT Press.

von Békésy, G. (1961). *Untitled presentation* [colloquium session]. Harvard University Department of Psychology.

Wallace, G. W. (2012). Not every ISPI'er needs to be a researcher, but every ISPI'er needs to know how research findings apply to what they do. *Performance Improvement Quarterly*, *24* (2), 7–9. doi:10.1002/piq.20127

Watson, J. B., & Rayner, R. (1920). Conditioned emotional reactions. *Journal of Experimental Psychology*, *3*(1), 1–14. doi:10.1037/h0069608

Weiner, N. (1950). *The human use of human beings*. Houghton Mifflin.

Williams, R. C., & Nafukho, F. M. (2015). Technical training evaluation revisited: An exploratory mixed-methods study. *Performance Improvement Quarterly*, *28*(1), 69–92. doi:10.1002/piq.21187

Wine, B., & Pritchard, J. K. (Eds.). (2018). *Organizational behavior management: The essentials*. Hedgehog Publishers.

Woodworth, R. S., & Thorndike, E. L. (1901). The influence of improvement in one mental function upon the efficiency of other functions. *Psychological Review*, *8*(3), 247–261. doi:10.1037/h0074898

Yelon, S. L., Ford, J. K., & Golden, S. (2013). Transfer over time: Stories about transfer years after training. *Performance Improvement Quarterly*, *25*(4), 43–66. doi:10.1002/piq.21131

Zingoni, M. (2017). Motives in response to negative feedback: A policy-capturing study. *Performance Improvement Quarterly*, *30*(3), 179–197. doi:10.1002/piq.21249

On Terms within Organizational Behavior Management

Douglas A. Johnson and Rachael Ferguson

ABSTRACT

Understanding the distinction between organizational behavior management and similar performance improvement initiatives requires an understanding of the field's conceptual system. The components of the field's conceptual system are the individual concepts and principles that compose our terminology. To introduce novices to an understanding of the field, this paper seeks to review various basic terms and highlight how they may help us explain behavior within organizational contexts. Furthermore, the paper also features several considerations and nuances important to bear in mind when applying terminology to actual cases.

What distinguishes organizational behavior management (OBM) from other applied science fields? This question has been the subject of many student inquiries, conference panels, academic mailing lists, and social media group discussions. Members of the OBM community claim expertise on applying science to solve concerns of people, but so can a variety of disciplines such as sociology, economics, and political science. OBM professionals can narrow the scope further, arguing that OBM applies a science of behavior to solve concerns specific to workplace settings, but that will not distinguish OBM from overlapping disciplines such as industrial-organizational psychology. As such, the subject matter does not make for a clear distinction. One could use credentials as a distinguishing mark (Luke et al., 2018; Weatherly, 2021). However, an expert without credentialing remains an expert and sometimes those credentialed are of questionable quality. Disciplines exist independent of credentialing agencies; credentials should not be confused for the field itself.

One could search for differences related to specific topics, types of interventions, and methodologies typically seen within the disciplines (Bucklin et al., 2000). However, whether a discipline addresses areas such as selection and placement or performance management is likely the product of normative trends from historical origins of that discipline (Brethower et al., 2022; Dickinson, 2000), rather than inherent distinctions. For example, performance appraisals, employee attitudes, equity issues, and decision making could all be addressed by an OBM practitioner or researcher, even though these topics have more typically been concerns of traditional industrial-organizational psychology. Similarly, methodological differences (e.g., between group vs. within-subject designs; correlational vs. experimental designs) are also likely the product of history – nothing precludes an OBM researcher from utilizing designs typically seen in other disciplines (Erath et al., 2021). Regarding independent variables, it is questionable whether a *behavioral* intervention (that is, specific to OBM or behavior analysis in general) exists because procedures are atheoretical in nature. One cannot tell from a feedback intervention whether a behavior analyst, cognitive scientist, or humanistic psychologist was the one who implemented it (although one might guess based on normative trends). Empirical data and applied techniques are routinely developed by all scientific approaches to human behavior.

The difference between fields largely lies within the explanations employed by those working in those paradigms. OBM is defined by conceptual systems explaining why techniques function as they do (i.e., behavior analysis). Without a unifying theoretical framework, a field can quickly devolve into a collection of tips and tricks indistinguishable from competing approaches (Baer et al., 1968). This is probably why it can be quite contentious when professionals propose new conceptual frameworks – to tamper with a conceptual framework is to mess with the very identity of a discipline. As such, it is critical to connect procedures to the principles of behavior to ensure an integrated expansion of OBM. To fail to do so risks losing the identity of the field itself. To that end, this paper will survey concepts and principles that provide the foundation of OBM, use examples within the framework of these concepts and principles to highlight their relevance within the workplace for readers acquainted with behavior analysis (but not yet specialists in OBM), highlight terminological considerations that might be neglected by even the most experienced OBM professionals, and to encourage a continuation and expansion of conceptual analyses within the field. This paper will presume an existing familiarity with definitions of basic behavioral terminology (e.g., behavior, stimuli, respondent conditioning, operant conditioning, reinforcement), define more advanced concepts and principles, and illustrate how both basic and advanced terminology relates to the research and practice of OBM. For any readers not familiar with basic terminology, we would refer them to several excellent introductory textbooks (Chance, 2014; Cooper et al., 2020; Madden et al., 2021; Martin & Pear, 2019; Michael, 2004; Miller, 2006).

The basic units of behavioral relations being applied to OBM

The core unit of analysis within OBM (and behavior analysis in general) is the contingency (behavior itself is not our subject matter, despite the semi-misleading names of our disciplines). Of course, to fully understand a contingency, it is imperative that we understand the elements of a contingency, namely responses and stimuli, apply to workplace scenarios. Although behavior analysts often speak of targeting behavior, in practice it is more typical to target a response class. This involves a variety of responses that produce the same outcome, even if the particulars of the response may vary. For example, a consultant or researcher may target suggestive selling of appetizers to customers in a restaurant (Reetz et al., 2016). Although servers may emit a range of distinct behaviors, such as phrasing suggestions in various forms (e.g., "would you like to add fries or onion rings?," or "can I interest you in one of our appetizers?"), suggesting an appetizer early or late in customer interactions, stating suggestions quietly or loudly, speaking rapidly or slowly, or stating requests once or multiple times, these specific response variants fall into the same general response class (i.e., suggestive selling) that produces the same outcome (i.e., customers provide or withhold their assent to requests). Not only can the behaviors vary while serving the same function, the size of the behaviors that are being analyzed can vary as well. Such units of behavior vary dramatically, ranging from discrete isolated actions such as touching, grasping, or twisting (Twarek et al., 2010) to broader collections of actions such as stealing, rapport building, or marketing (Curry et al., 2019; Porto & Foxall, 2019; Rafacz et al., 2011). Over the years there has been a growing movement to analyze units of behavior that occur across individuals (by looking at series of interacting contingencies), particularly when analyzing cultural level phenomenon (Glenn et al., 2016).

Although debates have long occurred regarding whether it is best to conduct analyses using smaller moment-by-moment units (molecular) or using larger aggregated units (molar) of behavior (Baum, 2002; Shimp, 2014), it should be noted this is not necessarily a dichotomous choice. If we consider behavior along a continuum, nearly all instances can be broken down into finer grade collections or accumulated into an amalgamation of actions. The useful unit of analysis is the one that permits us to observe and manipulate predictable relations among events (Palmer & Donahoe, 1992; Skinner, 1935), regardless of a narrow or broad vantage point.

It is not uncommon for OBM professionals to focus exclusively on outcomes (thus inferring behavior from its product), such as checking to see if lights were left on or off (Clayton & Nesnidol, 2017). In fact, Gilbert (1996) argued that OBM professionals should not just target behavior, but rather the focus should be on worthy performance instead (in which value produced by outcomes exceeds the time and effort of the behavior). Indeed, it is rare for us to focus on behavior irrespective of surrounding contexts or needs of the organization. However, focusing exclusively on outcomes alone carries risks. For example, it may be tempting to focus on sales numbers alone (inferring the behaviors that produced the sales), but the risk is performers may have produced outcomes through undesirable means (e.g., false promises to customers, distorting records, neglecting long-term investments in favor of short-term payoffs). Conversely, focusing exclusively on responding may produce behavior irrelevant to organizational goals. Thus, we generally recommend measuring both behavior and outcomes. Finally, it is important to distinguish between a state and behaviors that produce a state. For example, "being asleep on the job" is a state, not a behavior (Blampied & Bootzin, 2013), therefore "being asleep on the job" is not an appropriate target for behavior change. However, the state of interest may have many related behaviors that could be targeted for change (e.g., leaning back in chair, closing office blinds, shutting eyes). The distinction between states and behaviors that produce states is relevant for a variety of workplace examples (e.g., the state of being alert, the state of being safe).

Besides behavior (whether observed or inferred), the other important component of a contingency is a stimulus. There are several important nuances worth discussing when trying to understand stimuli in organizational settings. Although we may refer to an antecedent or a consequence as a stimulus, in practice we are often talking about stimulus classes. For example, we may tell employees that when they see customers enter the restaurant, they should smile and talk with these customers (Komaki et al., 1980). In this case, "customer" is not a particular antecedent (i.e., not just a single individual), but a stimulus class containing vast numbers of widely differing people, all who belong in the category of customer. A "quality product" might also be a stimulus class, although how wide or narrow this class is depends on a company's range of acceptable tolerances for quality. Positive feedback might be a stimulus class that could be used as consequences for performance. Some suggest it is important to ensure that feedback varies by design, for a lack of variation may render the consequences ineffective (D. A. Johnson et al., 2015). For example, saying "great job!" every time as a consequent stimulus is likely to appear rote and insincere, therefore the class membership of positive feedback should contain various supportive statements.

Another important nuance of stimuli relates to sources of change – changes in the environment can be internal or external to the person. Put differently, the stimulation that occurs within our bodies also count as stimuli, even if these cannot be perceived by anyone outside of the person experiencing the sensation. These include covert events such as pain, a racing heart, contraction of stomach muscles, and other physiological events. Covert verbal events (e.g., sound of one's private dialogue, physiological sensations) also serve as stimuli and are critical to understanding many complex forms of behavior. This understanding of the private world is particularly important when interacting with verbally sophisticated individuals, which is routine within organizational settings. A willingness to include covert events is a defining feature of modern behavior analysis (Skinner, 1945), a fact often missed by critics who erroneously suggest the field excludes thoughts and feelings. However, internal events are still conceptualized as physical events; the field eschews mentalistic constructs and states (such as drives to succeed, expectancies, laziness, mental storage devices, schemas, etc.). Behavior analysis, and by extension OBM, is successful by exploring both simple and complex relationships between stimuli and responses without adding unnecessary and misleading elements.

Relations among basic units: respondent conditioning

One of the most basic types of relations between stimuli and responses are respondent relations. Respondent conditioning is sometimes overlooked in OBM and often neglected in textbooks, yet it can still play an important role in many organizational situations. Activation of the sympathetic division of the autonomic nervous system is an example; an environmental event causes multiple physiological changes including increased heart rate, directed blood flow to skeletal muscles, and other activities to increase arousal and energy generation (Poling & Braatz, 2001). This physiological syndrome can occur as an unconditioned response to life-threatening or intense stimuli or as a conditioned response due to other stimuli being regularly paired with such events. Such respondent conditioning underlies emotional reactions, anxiety, and affective behaviors of employees, which some cite as the greatest problems for managers (Scott & Podsakoff, 1985). In the realm of safety, another example of respondent conditioning is seen with habituation (in which chronic exposure to an unconditioned stimulus weakens typically elicited responses). Persistent alarms result in weakening startle responses and ultimately a failure to attend to dangerous threats (Lebbon & Sigurdsson, 2017).

The literature has long demonstrated attitudes can develop through respondent processes (Kuykendall & Keating, 1990; Staats & Staats, 1958). For example, punishment and negative evaluations often elicit negative emotional responses. If performance measurement or feedback sessions are only paired with punishment and negative evaluations, it is not surprising when employees develop negative attitudes toward any proposed measurement or feedback systems (Choi et al., 2018; Daniels & Bailey, 2014). Such attitude developments are not limited to interventions, but also impact how employees feel about certain people, tasks, items, practices, and policies (Scott & Podsakoff, 1985). Poling and Braatz (2001) give the example of an executive who chooses to only deliver good news to subordinates and delegates delivery of bad news to an underling. A probable outcome of this scenario is the executive is well-liked, whereas the underling will be discomforting to the employees. If implementation of a new technology or new set of social conduct standards threaten employees' status within an organization – if not their job entirely – then employees may show hostile attitudes and even try to sabotage new initiatives (Davidson & Walley, 1985). Even mention of an associated word or phrase (e.g., LMS system, diversity training) may elicit emotional reactions for those not well-versed in the new organizational practices. Persistent negative emotional reactions have been linked to stress, turnover, and burnout, whereas positive emotional reactions have been linked to satisfaction, job security, and productivity (Filipkowski & Johnson, 2008; Lawson & O'Brien, 1994).

The important issue is to learn how to carefully use pairing and unpairing to create more favorable respondent relations. Undesirable respondent relations can be undone via exposure techniques (Paradise, 1984), whereas desirable respondent relations can be formed through programmed pairing. For example, many attempt to influence others via a luncheon technique, in which individuals attempt to pair themselves with free food (Cialdini, 2009). Examples may include salespeople trying get buy-in with potential clients over food or executives holding meetings during lunch, so that the favorable feelings that food elicits will transfer to the people who shrewdly bought such meals. Of course, this may not be successful if preexisting negative relationships already exist. For example, N. Brown and Redmon (1990) arranged for employees to have the option of a paid lunch with their supervisors (among a variety of options for winners of a lottery incentive system), but only 3 out of 60 employees ever selected the free lunch and managerial feedback session.

There are some important considerations when analyzing respondent relations within organizational settings. One is that most relevant examples of respondent employee behaviors may be covert in nature. As such, we must rely on self-reports of internal states, typically via survey methodology. For a variety of reasons employee descriptions of themselves may not be accurate (Filipkowski & Johnson, 2008), therefore it is important to consider various overt correlates. Finally, respondent conditioning cannot create new behaviors, but only extend preexisting behavior to new sources of control (Michael, 2004; Poling & Braatz, 2001). Most behaviors of interest in OBM are quite dissimilar to our inherited relations. As such, we now turn to operant relations, in which behavior is controlled, at least in part, by consequences.

Relations among basic units: operant conditioning

The ability of a performer to operate on their environment to produce an effect makes the person an active participant in their ever-changing world, with the person changing their environment and, in turn, that environmental change altering that person. This succession of experiences leads to an accumulation of behavioral relations in new environments, including the workplace. This notion may best be captured by the concept of a repertoire – the collected and enduring tendency to behave under specific circumstances (Palmer, 2009). It is a construct we use to describe the potential behavior of an individual, which arises from a history of being exposed to contingencies. Without an organism's behavior, there is no repertoire. Without the environment, there is also no repertoire. The concept lies in the interaction between the two. We do not study responses, but rather response relations. The repertoire does not sit idly by in some other dimension within a warehouse of skills or a bag of tricks, waiting to be called forth into our world. Unfortunately, our native languages tend to lead to misinterpretation, especially with operant relations. It is important to avoid reification with the term repertoire – it is an abstraction to describe the effect of historical events, not a thing, place, or storage container. It is a strange convention to ask where a response is residing when it is not being emitted. With respondent relations, we do not ask where the blink resides when there is no irritant in the eye or where the knee jerk resides when the patellar tendon is not being tapped (Skinner, 1957). It is equally misleading to ask where the response resides when our analysis involves operant relations. Even though the repertoire is a construct, we need to not forget what type of construct it is. It is a term to summarize vast and complex environment-behavior relations that accumulate over the lifetime of the individual. It is not an internal construct that initiates action from a place separate from the physical world, a type of explanation behavior analysis has long opposed (Skinner, 1950). Instead, our discipline seeks to develop explanations that place both seen and unseen events at the same level of the natural and physical world. It is easy to forget as everyday verbal practices (e.g., grammar structures that place the initiation of action only within the individual, such as "I begin" or "we decided") seep into our more precise analyses and scientific explanations.

One outcome of viewing a repertoire in a non-mentalistic manner is we stop viewing behavior as an independent entity initiated by forces within. For example, after training it is tempting to view established knowledge, skill, or ability as a collection of things carried around with employees. However, trained behavior exists in relation to training environments and therefore is dependent on trained surroundings (or surroundings with sufficient common properties). New environments, such as daily workplace settings, will not evoke or maintain trained behavior if conditions or contingencies are too dissimilar, a finding well-known to those who have struggled with transfer of training or maintenance (Brethower & Smalley, 1998; Conard et al., 2016).

One implication of the perspective that behavior is a function of the environment is that much of our behavior is not the result of capricious free-will (Johnston, 2014). This assertion is controversial, especially with those who prefer to explain their successes and decisions in terms of self-determination, genetic makeup, or other innate factors. Thus, an OBM professional should be sensitive to how they communicate with others. Any professional who places a high degree of value on their "self-made" accomplishments may feel threatened or angered by assertions that the environmental history was the primary contributor to their success, rather than their traits or spontaneous choices (Crawley et al., 1982).

Types of consequences

Reinforcement

The supportive consequences mentioned above are considered a form of reinforcement. This principle is foundational to the field of OBM given the focus is primarily on increasing desired behavior (Austin et al., 1999). Experts have identified reinforcement as one of the most popular OBM interventions (Daniels & Bailey, 2014). This is perhaps one reason why reinforcement was determined the most common behavioral principle in a review of studies published in the *Journal of Organizational Behavior Management* (DiGennaro Reed et al., 2016). Common reinforcers include performance feedback, praise, monetary incentives, and symbolic tangibles such as plaques or trophies (Alvero et al., 2001; Daniels & Bailey, 2014). Consider the issue of compensation: workers can be paid on individual piecework and on group performance through gainsharing (Dixon et al., 2004). From a broader perspective, both systems might be reinforcing if they are performance-contingent and lead to increases in performance following their delivery. See, Bucklin et al. (2022) for details on implementing various incentive systems. With all potential reinforcers, it is critical to conduct preference assessments to increase the likelihood that consequences will function as intended (Wine et al., 2014).

Extinction

We would be remiss to discuss reinforcement without also exploring extinction within an OBM context. Extinction occurs across a variety of professions when reinforcement is infrequent. Consider workers trained to follow complex safety protocols. During training, they are presented with many different hazards. These practice sessions are further supplemented with multiple coaching opportunities, which involve a dense schedule of reinforcement. When on the job, however, hazards are rare. While the same level of complexity may be expected, the reinforcement schedule is often sparse or nonexistent. Without regular reinforcement, the safety behaviors would likely extinguish over time which could ultimately lead to an increase in injuries (Hyten & Ludwig, 2017).

Reinforcement is infrequent in other professions as well. During visual baggage screenings, transportation security administration (TSA) agents must emit frequent search behaviors over extended periods. Locating a "signal" or target item can be reinforcing. However, it is also rare. Research shows that search behavior decreases if signals are absent (Hogan et al., 2009), the tendency to search extinguishes due to lack of reinforcement.

While the previous examples demonstrate the negative effects, there are instances when extinction is beneficial for work-related behaviors. This is the case for *undesired behavior*. To revisit the prior example, imagine TSA agents being trained to detect target items. If detected items matched actual threats, managers would praise this response. However, if TSA agents flag items inappropriately and too frequently, such as when they encounter innocuous items, these incorrect responses would not be praised and would decrease or extinguish over time. Provided managers continued to reinforce correct responding, eventually stimulus control would be established such that agents would differentiate between innocuous items and potential threats. This would be particularly critical given that frequent false positives lead to unnecessary delays and decrease traveler satisfaction. Thus, extinguishing overresponding would be beneficial.

Punishment

While reinforcement is the most common technique applied in OBM, it is also critical to understand how the related term of punishment is relevant. Unlike reinforcement, punishment is uncommon in OBM (Daniels, 2016), however, it remains a popular technique among managers (Grote, 2006). Even in subfields of OBM such as behavior-based safety (which seeks to reduce accidents and injuries), the focus is on promoting safe behaviors rather than punishing unsafe behaviors or injuries (Sulzer-Azaroff et al., 1990). Some of this focus is related to the fact that OBM as a field generally attempts to improve, not worsen, the experience of people at the workplace (Abernathy, 2014; Bucklin et al., 2022). Furthermore, employees operating under aversive stimulation may very well exert various forms of undesirable countercontrol (Ludwig & Geller, 1999; Mawhinney & Fellows-Kubert, 1999). Finally, excessive use of aversive control can produce many negative side effects such as turnover, disengagement, absenteeism, and more (Camden & Ludwig, 2013; Cymbal et al., 2022; Moran et al., 2022). Still, there are instances when punishment occurs in organizational settings, especially when dealing with severe violations of workplace policies (Daniels & Bailey, 2014).

For instance, while punishers are typically not introduced by OBM specialists, there are natural punishers that can decrease desired behavior. Once again consider the TSA agents. A TSA agent who was overly cautious and had several false positives (innocuous items or people targeted as threats) would likely be verbally punished by impatient travelers. They may react negatively to being searched or complain about prospects of missing flights. The sight of a line increasing, coupled with travelers becoming anxious, may further punish searching behavior including the detection of potential targets.

Previously we mentioned that behavior is a function of the environment and trained behavior will fail to transfer or maintain within work environments if consequences fail to support it. Suppose a salesperson was trained to use high-pressure techniques to convince customers to purchase products. During training, supportive consequences such as praise were delivered by the trainer contingent on the trainee emitting high-pressure techniques when customers gave reasons for not purchasing. While the salesperson may excel during training, the tendency to emit high-pressure behaviors is a function of the environment. If the trainee progresses to the job and supportive consequences are no longer provided, or if aversive consequences begin to follow, the behavior will decrease (Daniels & Bailey, 2014; Hyten & Ludwig, 2017). Applying high-pressure techniques will likely evoke negative responses from actual customers. These act as natural punishers causing high-pressure techniques to decrease.

In addition to natural punishers, reprimands or progressive discipline are tactics that frustrated managers may use at the behest of their organization's legal department, in accordance with human resources policies, or simply in desperation when they lack expertise in other ways of changing human behavior (Grote, 2006). These tactics are not advised. Reprimands, penalties, and other punishers are forms of aversive control that can evoke a fear response. Furthermore, unless the reprimands, loss of privileges, fines, and more are consistently maintained, it is likely that a recovery from punishment will likely be seen (Daniels & Bailey, 2014).

Recovery from punishment

Behavior suppressed through punishment in the past will likely return to previous levels upon removal or termination of suppressive stimuli, which has implications for organizational settings. Consider a software engineer who must develop, input, and compile code – often a tedious task. Furthermore, the same computer on which coding is completed can become a temptation; an "entertainment vessel" that houses an abundance of competing reinforcers in the form of news, games, and social connection which may cause attention to work to stray.

Engaging in these competing activities at the office would likely lead to reprimands by supervisors, thus decreasing time off-task. However, while being punished may temporarily suppress off-task behavior, the undesired behavior would not be eliminated from the repertoire. Therefore, it would not be permanently suppressed from punishment alone and would likely return to preexisting levels once the punisher is no longer present (Daniels & Bailey, 2014).

Recovery from punishment is particularly relevant given the rising development of remote work positions and when in-person positions are temporarily shifted to remote (Howe et al., 2021; Jimenez-Gomez et al., 2021). These changes in organizational structures can impact the dynamics related to supervisor presence. For example, workers such as software engineers may have previously been confined to cubicles near their supervisors, but now find themselves working from home. This both (a) increases available off-task alternatives, and (b) eliminates presence of agents (i.e., supervisor) who historically delivered punishment. In time, off-task behavior previously punished may increase. This phenomenon can be observed across a variety of occupations, particularly those in which supervisors are unable to be present. As more individuals work remotely, the relevance of recovery from punishment increases for organizational behavior. However, recovery from punishment can be avoided. Rather than focus on decreasing undesired behavior through reprimands or using aversive techniques, managers should increase desired behavior through reinforcement. Ferguson and Rivera (2021) provide a comprehensive discussion of OBM techniques to improve behavior of independent professions and autonomous workers.

Types of antecedents

Although the last several concepts illustrate the power of consequences to impact employee behavior, antecedents are an important part of workplace contingencies (Choi & Johnson, 2022). Some powerful antecedents derive their evocative functions from their historical correlations with consequences, exemplified by discriminative stimuli. Some discriminative stimuli are based on reinforcement contingencies, such as S^D or S^Δ. The process of establishing stimulus control through discrimination training has many potential organizational applications. For example, one aspect of ensuring quality control is to make sure employees respond differentially to high- and low-quality products or services. During training, employees may be presented with a sample to evaluate. In the presence of high-quality samples (S^D), employees labeling these samples as good may be praised (Sr). In the presence of low-quality samples (S^Δ), employees labeling such samples as good would not be praised (EXT). Of course, stimulus control should also be established for the behavior of labeling these samples as poor, as shown in Figure 1.

Other applications for establishing stimulus control, besides training, include the TSA job targeting items that rarely appear (bomb attempts are very infrequent), leading to extinction of vigilance behaviors. One method of fixing this is to contrive a more regular S^D condition than what normally occurs, such as having managers periodically send prohibited items through security as a test (Hogan et al., 2009). If screeners successfully flagged these items, reinforcing consequences such as praise or being told that they stopped a dangerous item could be provided, making it more likely that vigilance would persist over time. Not only could the public be safer through planned provision of discriminative stimuli, but employee safety could improve.

Discrimination Training for Quality Control

S^D Sight of high-quality product or service	:	**R** Trainee says, "That looks good to me"	→	**Sr** Affirmation or praise from trainer
S^Δ Sight of low-quality product or service	:	**R** Trainee says, "That looks good to me"	→	**EXT** No affirmation or praise from trainer
S^D Sight of low-quality product or service	:	**R** Trainee says, "That was done wrong"	→	**Sr** Affirmation or praise from trainer
S^Δ Sight of high-quality product or service	:	**R** Trainee says, "That was done wrong"	→	**EXT** No affirmation or praise from trainer

Figure 1. Discrimination training for quality control.

Just as discriminative stimuli evoke and abate behavior due to their correlation with the availability of reinforcement, discriminative stimuli also evoke and abate due to a correlation with the availability of punishment (Hantula et al., 1991). Just as an S^D refers to the availability of reinforcement for responding, an S^{Dp} refers to the availability of punishment for responding and therefore an S^{Dp} has an abative effect on behavior (Doughty et al., 2007; O'Donnell, 2001).

For example, many organizations, concerned about potential destructive effects of rumor or gossip on organizational culture (Houmanfar & Johnson, 2004), have policies forbidding these activities and managers are likely to provide reprimands when observing such behaviors. Similarly, people who are the subject of gossip are likely to provide disapproval upon observing these behaviors due to the typical negative content. Therefore, a stimulus of someone whispering "Susan is coming" or "the boss is close" would function as an S^{Dp}, in that continued gossiping will soon be met with social punishers from Susan or the boss, respectively. Likewise, hearing a manager's voice would likely function as an S^{Dp} for opening or scrolling through social media accounts given typical organizational policies regarding off-task activities during paid hours.

Logically, this implies the need for a parallel term for stimuli correlated with non-availability of punishment. An $S^{\Delta p}$ would have an evocative effect as behavior recovers in the absence of punishment contingencies. Returning to the previous examples, someone saying "alright, Susan is gone" or "the boss left" would function as an $S^{\Delta p}$ and have a recovering effect on gossiping behavior. Likewise, the sound of the manager's voice growing distant would function as an $S^{\Delta p}$ for behaviors related to social media and an evocative effect is likely.

Motivating operations

While motivating operations (MOs) are incorporated into treatments within many specializations of applied behavior analysis, they are less common in OBM (Lotfizadeh et al., 2014). One reason could be OBM professionals experience success with consequences alone. However, including an analysis of the MO into the performance analysis could provide a comprehensive understanding of consequences and factors that influence their efficacy. This expansion of analysis could prove fruitful during planning through increasing the range of interventions considered. OBM experts rarely directly manipulate variables related to unconditioned motivating operations such as deprivation (although employees may be sleep, food, or water deprived for reasons unrelated to our manipulations; Olson et al., 2001), thus the focus of our discussion will be on conditioned motivating operations (CMOs).

There are different types of CMOs. Consider a reflexive CMO (CMO-R), in which a stimulus is correlated with some form of worsening and whose removal will function of as a form of reinforcement (Michael, 2004). This has commonly been demonstrated in the laboratory through avoidance. For example, a neutral stimulus such as a beep is first presented to an experimental organism. Over trials, this beep is reliably followed by shock. When consistently preceding the worsening situation, the beep acts as a type of "warning stimulus" that aversive event will soon follow. Therefore, that beep will be established as an CMO-R, in that it establishes its own removal as reinforcing. Subsequently, once sounded it immediately evokes behaviors that have, in the past, led to its removal.

CMO-Rs, such as this example, extend beyond the laboratory and become relevant in other settings including the workplace. For instance, observe the effects of CMOs on the behavior of doctors and nurses in hospitals. The sound of a patient's heart rate monitor is a reassuring repetitive beep signaling strong and steady heart rates. If the repetition suddenly becomes irregular and increases dramatically, then this may serve as a warning that patient is in trouble. The new signal of an abnormal pattern would be a CMO-R that precedes potential worsening states (e.g., stroke, arrhythmia). The new sound *immediately* evokes behaviors aimed at restoring a steady pulse and escaping the threatening abnormal sound (e.g., administering medication, electrical cardioversion).

While the previous example shows a beep functioning as a CMO-R, other forms of auditory stimuli exist (or more broadly, stimuli involving the other sense receptors). Feedback may function as a CMO-R. For instance, suppose one of the nurses from the previous example failed to make rounds and check patients regularly. The director of nursing provided evaluative feedback and discussed dangers of failing to check patients consistently. The current performance does not meet hospital standards and must improve to ensure patient safety. Like the tones in previous examples, evaluative feedback functions as a warning stimulus that a worsening state such as termination or lawsuits may be forthcoming. Following the meeting the nurse increases her rate of checking patients to remove the threat and avoid possible termination associated with it.

In addition to CMO-Rs, there are other types of CMOs such as transitive CMOs (CMO-T). Michael (2004) defined a CMO-T as a stimulus (S1) that helps to establish the reinforcing effectiveness of a secondary stimulus (S2). In other words, the reinforcing effectiveness of S2 depends on the presence of the first stimulus (S1). S1 then evokes behaviors that produce S2 (Michael, 2004). To consider how this concept applies to workplace behavior, imagine Jasmine, a bank teller whose primary responsibility is to deposit and withdraw customer funds. Jasmine continuously encounters customers during her busy shift as there is a constant line. Recently, the bank started a new credit card, but few customers signed up. When encountering customers prior to beginning transactions, Jasmine must ask them to open a credit card account. Getting them to express interest allows her to open an electronic form on her computer to sign them up through a series of steps. At first Jasmine is simply told to encourage customers to enroll, but there is no contingency for doing so. Lines are long and Jasmine sees this task as unreasonable additional effort. Encountering electronic forms to sign customers up (which is the S2) have little value to her. In the presence of the customers making a deposit or withdrawal, Jasmine does not open forms and ask to sign them up.

Now suppose the branch manager sends an e-mail informing the tellers that they can earn a $20 bonus for each credit card account opened and this contingency lasts until the end of the month. Jasmine reads this S1 (announcement about the incentive). As usual, she looks up and sees a line of customers. Now, both the electronic form (S2) and completed electronic form (another S2) are more valuable, so that the presence of interested customers (S^D) immediately evokes behaviors related to electronic forms. The CMO-T in this example is the S1 or e-mail announcement about the incentive. Note this is instructional control (announcement about incentives), not consequence control (the incentive itself), because incentives have not been delivered yet and therefore cannot exert control over behavior (see, Figure 2 for relevant diagrams).

A goal coupled with an incentive might also function as a CMO-T (Olson & Winchester, 2008). Imagine an adjustment in the previous example, in that Jasmine was emailed a bar graph each day showing the percentage of customers who opened new accounts. Opening the e-mail, she would see her

Diagram of Teller's Behavior

No MO No announcement	:	**S^D** Presence of customer	:	**R** Pull up electronic form and ask questions	→	**NS** Sight of complete form (stimulus not valuable)
No MO No announcement	:	**S^Δ** No customer is present	:	**R** Pull up electronic form and ask questions	→	**EXT** Sight of incomplete form (stimulus not valuable or available)
CMO-T Announcement of incentive	:	**S^D** Presence of customer	:	**R** Pull up electronic form and ask questions	→	**Sr** Sight of complete form (stimulus valuable and available)
CMO-T Announcement of incentive	:	**S^Δ** No customer is present	:	**R** Pull up electronic form and ask questions	→	**EXT** Sight of incomplete form (stimulus not available)

Figure 2. Diagram of Teller's behavior.

current percentage for the week. A performance increase on the graph (S2 in this case) may have little value in the absence of a goal or incentive. Now suppose the manager begins a bonus contingent on meeting a goal to secure credit card accounts for 40% of customers serviced that week. As before, each day he e-mails tellers their average percentage on a bar graph. However, this time he includes the goal drawn on the graph (S1). On Friday (i.e., end of the week), Jasmine reads her e-mail and learns she is currently at 37%–just shy of the 40% goal just above. The sight of this discrepancy between her current performance and the goal line (S1) will likely function as an MO (Olson & Winchester, 2008). It will immediately evoke behaviors that led to high performance in the past on the graph (S2) such as prompting customers to start credit cards and follow the process for opening accounts.

Complex verbal relations

Most of the terminology above was derived from experimental work in which events of interest are close in time to the behavior under study (e.g., a light is turned on and immediately evokes a response; food is presented less than a second later). How long delays can be before or after behavior to maintain efficacy of antecedents or consequences has never been precisely settled, although the general rule is these events lose control as temporal gaps increase (Green et al., 2004; Michael, 2004). Although time is a continuous variable, the delays in most organizational settings are so great that time might be considered dichotomous: "delayed" or "immediate" (Malott, Malott et al., 1993). That is, it is rarely a comparison of 5- versus 60-s delays, but rather delays involving days, weeks, or months between events and relevant performance. Unlike the verbal humans within the business organizations, non-verbal organisms require direct contingencies and could not be influenced by reinforcers or punishers delivered several days after performance (Michael, 2004). At first glance, the context in workplace settings does not seem to exert control through direct contingencies, but rather relies on verbal events to manage temporal gaps. Nearly all interventions in OBM involve verbally mediated contingencies with significant delays (Malott, Shimamune et al., 1993), therefore it is important to understand how verbal stimuli such as rules influence and govern behavior in workplace environments. This assertion raises a question: If much of workplace behavior is maintained through indirect acting effects, why devote so much of this paper summarizing direct acting behavioral terminology? One reason is that many instances of workplace behavior can still be explained via direct reinforcers and punishers supplied by others. Another reason is that seemingly indirect external contingencies are maintained via direct verbal contingencies, which are best understood in the conceptual framework built upon basic principles. The connection between verbal events and indirect contingencies has long been explored by OBM and behavior analysis in general.

B. F. Skinner, in one of his analyses of problem-solving, spoke about how we can construct stimuli to control our own behavior, such as marking the correct path to take on a map (Skinner, 1969). For example, imagine a truck driver wanted to learn locations for clean and safe travel plazas and truck stops (to avoid sketchy places while in search of food, fuel, and showers along their routes). He could memorize names, architecture, or locations of various buildings and cities across the country, experiencing reinforcement and extinction directly until he slowly learned which places paid off and which did not, eventually certain locales becoming S^Ds and others S^Δs for entering buildings. Alternatively, he could construct stimuli to control his behavior more efficiently, such as marking places on a map with a circled X to indicate clean and safe locations and an open circle to indicate sketchy locations. In this scenario, the trucker constructed discriminative stimuli to manage his future behavior, with the circled X functioning as a personal S^D and open circle as a personal S^Δ. Of course, such constructed stimuli need not be limited to personal use – if these discriminative stimuli are explained to others, they can then help any knowledgeable member of that community. An easier and less contrived method to construct useful discriminative stimuli for the community as a whole is to take advantage of existing verbal forms (such as word of mouth or review websites/apps), with "go there for free showers with clean towels if you buy $50 in diesel" serving as an S^D and "don't bother going there" serving as an S^Δ. These verbal rules specify the behavior (go to that location) and the consequences (presence/absence of an attractive deal) without new individuals needing to directly experience the contingency through trial and error.

This specification of the contingency (i.e., rule) takes the form of an IF-THEN connective verbal frame (Agnew & Redmon, 1992), in which the IF element specifies the behavior and the THEN element specifies the consequence for that behavior. That is, the contingency follows the pattern of IF ___, THEN ___, such as "IF you go over to that food truck now, THEN you can get tasty food" or "Because the boss has arrived, IF I start working frantically, THEN I will receive positive comments from her." These discriminative rules can be stated by others or developed by oneself. One point of clarification: stated rules do not need to formally contain the words "IF" or "THEN" to exert discriminative control through an IF-THEN frame. For example, an employee may state to themselves, "the boss said he is going to stick around and observe my performance today, so I better be on my A game." Although the sentence does not formally contain the words "IF" or "THEN," functionally it has an equivalent effect as statements such as "IF I perform well during this observation, THEN I might get some positive feedback" or "IF I take another break right now, THEN I'll get yelled at," thus immediately evoking desired and abating undesired performance. When behavior falls under the control of such rules, we call it "rule-governed behavior." One advantage of rule-governed behavior is that a seemingly endless set of potential events can be integrated into a relational frame. This changes the effects of events, if rule following is reinforced (and rule breaking punished) sufficiently in our culture, then rule following becomes a generalized skill for most members of the culture (Baum, 1993; Malott, Malott et al., 1993; Skinner, 1969). Of course, the personal learning histories of employees will remain a powerful determinant on whether rules are likely to be followed or ignored at an individual level (Skinner, 1978). Some theoretical accounts, such as relational frame theory, arose to focus exclusively on how relations among stimuli, behavior, and verbal events, including those relations that are explicitly described by others and those that are derived by the individual without explication by others (O'Hora & Maglieri, 2006). There are many areas of overlap between theoretical accounts such as relational frame theory and Skinner's attempt to delineate verbal behavior processes (such as general operant frames), but the distinctions remain controversial (Leigland, 1997; Palmer, 2008) and a full treatment of both accounts is well beyond the scope of this paper.

Rules, as verbal stimuli, are not limited to discriminative relations. Indeed, many rules involve consequences which are not immediately available after performance and many rules may not be related to availability of consequences. To illustrate, many scholars have pointed out that rules can function as motivating operations (Lipschultz et al., 2021; Squires & Wilder, 2010). Suppose an employee was told about a new measurement and incentive system, for which the rule "if you keep your desk clean and organized in a timely fashion every day, then at the end of the week you can enter a lottery for a chance to ignore the company's dress code for a day" could be derived (similar to Griffin et al., 2019). Even if this rule immediately evoked desk cleaning and organizing, the consequence of being entered into the lottery would not follow any instance of these behaviors. Rather, the rule established noncompliance with the rule as aversive (Malott, 1993). After the statement of the rule, some stimuli (previously neutral) became reinforcing, such as the sight of clean and organized desks, and other stimuli (also likely neutral prior to the rule) became punishing, such as the sight of untidy desks. Thus, the rule evokes behaviors that produce clean and organized desks and abates behaviors that produce untidy desks.

An additional nuance is that sometimes rules do not function as either discriminative stimuli or motivating operations. Both immediately evoke or abate behavior, but some rules do not have an immediate effect. In such cases, it may be better to conceptualize rules as contingency-specifying stimuli (Blakely & Schlinger, 1987; Schlinger & Blakely, 1987). Contingency-specifying stimuli operate by changing the function of other antecedents and consequences, including verbal events, because of descriptions of the relations among those events and behavior. To illustrate, assume a new employee was hired at a coal mine subject to ventilation inspections by the Mine Safety and Health Administration (Rhoton, 1980). During orientation a coworker takes him aside and says, "If you see a person wearing a beige hardhat, that's probably the MSHA inspector. It's critical that the line brattice is placed correctly and there's no loose coal dust in the area. If you see that guy, run and quickly make sure the brattice is where it is supposed to be or else we're all in trouble." Such a rule is unlikely to immediately evoke behavior (unlike the effects of S^Ds and MOs). In fact, these behaviors may not occur for several weeks or months. But the rule, as a contingency-specifying stimulus, changes the function of a beige hardhat. When it does finally appear, it will immediately evoke brattice checking. Behaviors not related to proper ventilation will likely be punished in the presence of a beige hardhat (S^{Dp}). In addition, behaviors that reduce or eliminate the forthcoming threat will also be evoked (CMO-R), so that actions that remove coal dust will be reinforced by the sight of a dust-free area (Sr). Behaviors to check and possibly move the brattice will also be evoked and reinforced by the sight of a correctly placed brattice (Sr). The rule also establishes the sight of loose coal dust as aversive (Sp) when a beige hardhat is present. In sum, the contingency-specifying stimulus established several discriminative stimuli, motivating operations, reinforcers, and punishers exhibited at a later date. All these antecedents and consequences (e. g., beige hardhat, sight of loose dust) would remain as behaviorally neutral events, if not for the rule altering their function.

It is important to look at how verbal events might prompt future behavior as well as how they may serve as effective consequences. Skinner (1957, 1969) and others noted we have a long history in which the verbal community teaches us to engage in self-descriptive behavior (e.g., "What are you doing?" "Why are you doing that?" "How are you?" "Do you see what I see?" "What are your plans for later?"). Our awareness of self probably is due to a near-constant stream of verbal self-evaluation responses, including self-evaluations of our work performance (e.g., "My desk is now clean" "That's my sixth successful sale today"). These verbal responses also produce verbal stimuli as a response product (i.e., we hear the sound of our own voice as a stimulus, whether overt or covert). When combined with rules, these evaluative self-statement stimuli may function as direct reinforcers or punishers for our own behavior.

For example, suppose an intervention included a promise for a $25 gift certificate to the employee with the best customer service evaluations at the end of two weeks (similar to M. G. Brown et al., 1980). As such, employees may form a rule such as "if I perform customer service just like they trained me, then I might get a spare 25 bucks." Although this rule may prompt good customer service, employees do not need to wait two weeks for an evaluation – they can provide their own immediately after performance. An employee may say to themselves, "Okay, I did all four service things just the way they wanted me to – now they'll be happy with me and I might even get that gift certificate in a couple of weeks." The resulting verbal stimulus from such evaluative self-statements are likely to have reinforcing properties and occur immediately at the conclusion of performance. One implication of this is even rule-governed behavior is likely maintained through direct-acting contingencies, but the direct consequences are often verbal and self-supplied (Malott, 1993; Malott, Shimamune et al., 1993).

Of course, not all evaluative self-statement stimuli will be equal in reinforcing effectiveness (or be reinforcing at all). For example, by the end of M. G. Brown et al. (1980), none of the salespeople received a $25 gift certificate because no customers completed any of the 500 evaluation forms distributed. If this study had continued past the two weeks, it should not be surprising that the discovered inaccuracy of original rules would result in revised self-statements such as "who cares if they liked my performance, those cheap liars won't stick to their word." Any stimulus resulting from such a covert description is unlikely to serve as a reinforcer for desired customer service. Self-evaluations that fit within a NOW-WILL verbal frame are likely to be powerful, such as "NOW that I've cleaned my desk, I WILL be entered into the raffle" or "NOW that I screwed up in front of the boss, I WILL get a poor performance review later this year." In comparison, a NOW-MAYBE verbal frame will probably exert weaker effects as consequences for behavior, such as "NOW that I made that sale, MAYBE I'll get a promotion eventually" or "NOW that I'm 5 minutes late, MAYBE I'll get written up." The various frames can alter the effectiveness of rules in controlling performance (R. A. R. A. Johnson et al., 2010). Approaches for classifying the effects of various derived verbal frames have been proposed and reviewed elsewhere (Maraccini et al., 2016). To briefly give some examples, it has been suggested (Ghezzi et al., 2020; O'Hora & Maglieri, 2006) that some rule-governed behavior should be classified as pliance if it is under the control of social approval (irrespective of actual contingencies), classified as tracking if it is under the control of a correspondence between instruction and actual contingencies, or classified as augmenting if the rule changes the function of other events (similar to the characteristics of contingency-specifying stimuli or motivating operations). Much of OBM involves developing rules to prompt desired behavior and ensure verbal events continue to support that desired behavior.

With any terminology, including those involved in complex verbal events, it is important to avoid nominal fallacies and not treat terms such as "rule-governed behavior" as magical phrases to preclude analysis. Invoking this phrase means potential functional relations must still be specified as part of the explanation to exceed nontechnical lay understanding of rules (Blakely & Schlinger, 1987; Schlinger & Blakely, 1987). Simply naming terms is not an analysis; we risk only being left with labeling a behavior and no more. A critical attribute of behavior *analysis* requires more investigation. Although it can be tempting to neglect terminological precision, Michael (2004) pointed out that clearly understanding the underlying mechanisms that drive our interventions is likely to have both theoretical and practical implications.

Conclusion

We hope this overview of terminology serves as an entry point for neophytes looking to connect behavioral concepts and principles to workplace practices as well as remind seasoned professionals about points sometimes forgotten. In conclusion, we return to the question that opened this paper: In short, what makes OBM different? At the core of this question is an attempt to define and differentiate the field from its competitors and complementary professions. By describing the terminology of the field, several themes are noted and worth making explicit. OBM professionals investigate and intervene upon workplace phenomena using a paradigm founded upon a natural science and selectionist account. This account emphasizes empirical data based upon actual performance and eschews hypothetical constructs or explanatory variables that take place at levels or dimensions different than our observations (e.g., training outcomes explained by schemas, success of incentives explained by expectancies or drives, leadership decisions explained by neurotransmitters or brain structures). We reject mentalistic approaches rooted in non-behavioral phenomena, but that should not be taken as a rejection of biological, cognitive, or internal events (as illustrated by our consideration of physiological stimulation, feelings, perceptions, and private verbal behaviors). This framework lies at the heart of a radical behaviorism position (Skinner, 1945, 1950), from which behavioral technologies developed.

Our terms and assumptions define us more than our procedures. Practices have evolved over the decades (Brethower et al., 2022) and will continue to advance. The field of OBM originated with individual performers, but early on recognized a need to grow toward organization-wide improvements (Hall, 1980). The challenges encountered along the way have varied, but our explanatory framework consistently guided us. This is what distinguishes OBM from other approaches and may be best exemplified by our terminology. By marking the boundaries of the field, we believe a definition is finally warranted: Organizational behavior management is a scientific discipline that uses explanations derived from radical behaviorism to develop, coordinate, and implement performance improvement applications that range from individual performers in organizations to large-scale programs of change. This conceptualization can be witnessed across many contributions and analyses shown in this handbook series (D. A. Johnson & Johnson, 2022) and proven to be productive and pragmatic in understanding human behavior in the workplace.

Disclosure statement

No potential conflict of interest was reported by the author(s).

ORCID

Douglas A. Johnson http://orcid.org/0000-0002-7802-3566

References

Abernathy, W. B. (2014). *The liberated workplace: Transitioning to Walden three*. Performance Management Publications.

Agnew, J. L., & Redmon, W. K. (1992). Contingency specifying stimuli: The role of "rules" in organizational behavior management. *Journal of Organizational Behavior Management, 12* (2), 67–76. https://doi.org/10.1300/J075v12n02_04

Alvero, A. M., Bucklin, B. R., & Austin, J. (2001). An objective review of the effectiveness and essential characteristics of performance feedback in organizational settings (1985-1998). *Journal of Organizational Behavior Management, 21*(1), 3–29. https://doi.org/10.1300/J075v21n01_02

Austin, J., Carr, J. E., & Agnew, J. L. (1999). The need for assessment of maintaining variables in OBM. *Journal of Organizational Behavior Management, 19*(2), 59–87. https://doi.org/10.1300/J075v19n02_05

Baer, D. M., Wolf, M. M., & Risley, T. R. (1968). Some current dimensions of applied behavior analysis. *Journal of Applied Behavior Analysis, 1*(1), 91–97. https://doi.org/10.1901/jaba.1968.1-91

Baum, W. M. (1993). For parsimony's sake. *Journal of Organizational Behavior Management, 12*(2), 81–84. https://doi.org/10.1300/J075v12n02_06

Baum, W. M. (2002). From molecular to molar: A paradigm shift in behavior analysis. *Journal of Experimental Analysis of Behavior, 78*(1), 95–116. https://doi.org/10.1901/jeab.2002.78-95

Blakely, E., & Schlinger, H. (1987). Rules: Function-altering contingency-specifying stimuli. *The Behavior Analyst, 10*(2), 183–187. https://doi.org/10.1007/BF03392428

Blampied, N. M., & Bootzin, R. R. (2013). Sleep: A behavioral account. In G. J. Madden (Ed.), *APA handbook of behavior analysis: Vol. 2 translating principles into practice* (pp. 425–453). American Psychological Association. https://doi.org/10.1037/13938-017

Brethower, D., & Smalley, K. (1998). *Performance-based instruction: Linking training to business results.* Jossey-Bass/Pfeiffer.

Brethower, D. M., Dickinson, A. M., Johnson, D. A., & Johnson, C. M. (2022). A history of organizational behavior management. *Journal of Organizational Behavior Management, 42* (1), 3–35. https://doi.org/10.1080/01608061.2021.1924340

Brown, M. G., Malott, R. W., Dillon, M. J., & Keeps, E. J. (1980). Improving customer service in a large department store through the use of training and feedback. *Journal of Organizational Behavior Management, 2*(4), 251–265. https://doi.org/10.1300/J075v02n04_02

Brown, N., & Redmon, W. K. (1990). The effects of a group reinforcement contingency on staff use of unscheduled sick leave. *Journal of Organizational Behavior Management, 10*(2), 3–17. https://doi.org/10.1300/J075v10n02_02

Bucklin, B. R., Alvero, A. M., Dickinson, A. M., Austin, J., & Jackson, A. K. (2000). Industrial-organizational psychology and organizational behavior management: An objective comparison. *Journal of Organizational Behavior Management, 20*(2), 27–75. https://doi.org/10.1300/J075v20n02_03

Bucklin, B. R., Li, A., Rodriguez, M., Johnson, D. A., & Eagle, L. M. (2022). Pay-for-performance: Behavior-based recommendations from research and practice. *Journal of Organizational Behavior Management*, Advance online publication. . https://doi.org/10.1080/01608061.2022.2047868

Camden, M. C., & Ludwig, T. D. (2013). Absenteeism in health care: Using interlocking behavioral contingency feedback to increase attendance with certified nursing assistants. *Journal of Organizational Behavior Management, 33*(3), 165–184. https://doi.org/10.1080/01608061.2013.814521

Chance, P. (2014). *Learning and behavior* (7th ed.). Cengage Learning.

Choi, E., Johnson, D. A., Moon, K., & Oah, S. (2018). Effects of positive and negative feedback sequence on work performance and emotional responses. *Journal of Organizational Behavior Management, 38*(2–3), 97–115. https://doi.org/10.1080/01608061.2017.1423151

Choi, E., & Johnson, D. A. (2022). Common antecedent strategies within organizational behavior management: The use of goal setting, task clarification, and job aids. *Journal of Organizational Behavior Management, 42*(1), 75–95. https://doi.org/10.1080/01608061.2021.1967834

Cialdini, R. B. (2009). *Influence: Science and practice* (5th ed.). Pearson.

Clayton, M., & Nesnidol, S. (2017). Reducing electricity use on campus: The use of prompts, feedback, and goal setting to decrease excessive classroom lighting. *Journal of Organizational Behavior Management, 37*(2), 196–206. https://doi.org/10.1080/01608061.2017.1325823

Conard, A. L., Johnson, D. A., Morrison, J. D., & Ditzian, K. (2016). Tactics to ensure durability of behavior change following the removal of an intervention specialist: A review of temporal generality within organizational behavior management. *Journal of Organizational Behavior Management, 36*(2–3), 210–253. https://doi.org/10.1080/01608061.2016.1201036

Cooper, J. O., Heron, T. E., & Heward, W. L. (2020). *Applied behavior analysis* (3rd ed.). Pearson.

Crawley, W. J., Adler, B. S., O'Brien, R. M., & Duffy, E. M. (1982). Making salesmen: Behavioral assessment and intervention. In R. M. O'Brien, A. M. Dickinson, & M. P. Rosow (Eds.), *Industrial behavior modification: A management handbook* (pp. 184–199). Pergamon Press.

Curry, S. M., Gravina, N. E., Sleiman, A. A., & Richard, E. (2019). The effects of engaging in rapport-building behaviors on productivity and discretionary effort. *Journal of Organizational Behavior Management, 39*(3–4), 213–226. https://doi.org/10.1080/01608061.2019.1667940

Cymbal, D. J., Litvak, S., Wilder, D. A., & Burns, G. N. (2022). An examination of variables that predict turnover, staff, and caregiver satisfaction in behavior-analytic organizations. *Journal of Organizational Behavior Management, 42*(1), 36–55. https://doi.org/10.1080/01608061.2021.1910099

Daniels, A. C., & Bailey, J. S. (2014). *Performance management: Changing behavior that drives organizational effectiveness*. Aubrey Daniels International, Inc.

Daniels, A. C. (2016). *Bringing out the best in people: How to apply the astonishing power of positive reinforcement*. McGraw-Hill Education.

Davidson, R. S., & Walley, P. B. (1985). Computer fear and addiction: Analysis, prevention, and possible modification. *Journal of Organizational Behavior Management, 6*(3), 37–52. https://doi.org/10.1300/J075v06n03_03

Dickinson, A. M. (2000). The historical roots of organizational behavior management in the private sector. *Journal of Organizational Behavior Management, 20*(3), 9–58. https://doi.org/10.1300/J075v20n03_02

DiGennaro Reed, F. D., Henley, A. J., Rueb, S., Crabbs, B., & Giacalone, L. (2016). Discussion of behavioral principles in journal of organizational behavior management: An update. *Journal of Organizational Behavior Management, 36*(2–3), 202–209. https://doi.org/10.1080/01608061.2016.1200938

Dixon, M. R., Hayes, L. J., & Stack, J. (2004). Changing conceptions of employee compensation. *Journal of Organizational Behavior Management, 23*(2–3), 95–116. https://doi.org/10.1300/J075v23n02_06

Doughty, A. H., Doughty, S. S., O'Donnell, J., Saunders, K. J., & Williams, D. C. (2007). Stimulus control of punishment effects: Determining the controlling variables. *Revista Mexicana de Análisis de la Conducta [Mexican Journal of Behavior Analysis], 33*(1), 57–66.

Erath, T. G., Pellegrino, A. J., DiGennaro Reed, F. D., Ruby, S. A., Blackman, A. L., & Novak, M. D. (2021). Experimental research methodologies in organizational behavior management. *Journal of Organizational Behavior Management, 41*(2), 150–181. https://doi.org/10.1080/01608061.2020.1869137

Ferguson, R., & Rivera, L. (2021). Self-management in organizational behavior management. *Journal of Organizational Behavior Management*. 1–20. Advance online publication. https://doi.org/10.1080/01608061.2021.1996502

Filipkowski, M., & Johnson, C. M. (2008). Comparisons of performance and job insecurity in union and nonunion sites of a manufacturing company. *Journal of Organizational Behavior Management, 28*(4), 218–237. https://doi.org/10.1080/01608060802454437

Ghezzi, E. L., Houmanfar, R. A., & Crosswell, L. (2020). The motivative augmental effects of verbal stimuli on cooperative and conformity responding under a financially competing contingency in an analog work task. *The Psychological Record, 70*(3), 411–431. https://doi.org/10.1007/s40732-020-00400-7

Gilbert, T. F. (1996). *Human competence: Engineering worthy performance*. International Society for Performance Improvement.

Glenn, S. S., Malott, M. E., Andery, M. A. P. A., Benvenuti, M., Houmanfar, R. A., Sandaker, I., Todorov, J. C., Tourinho, E. Z., & Vasconcelos, L. A. (2016). Toward consistent terminology in a behaviorist approach to cultural analysis. *Behavior and Social Issues, 25*(1), 11–27. https://doi.org/10.5210/bsi.v25i0.6634

Green, L., Myerson, J., Holt, D. D., Slevin, J. R., & Estle, S. J. (2004). Discounting of delayed food rewards in pigeons and rats: Is there a magnitude effect? *Journal of the Experimental Analysis of Behavior, 81*(1), 39–50. https://doi.org/10.1901/jeab.2004.81-39

Griffin, M., Gravina, N. E., Matey, N., Pritchard, J., & Wine, B. (2019). Using scorecards and a lottery to improve the performance of behavior technicians in two autism treatment clinics. *Journal of Organizational Behavior Management, 39*(3–4), 280–292. https://doi.org/10.1080/01608061.2019.1632241

Grote, D. (2006). *Discipline without punishment: The proven strategy that turns problem employees into superior performers*. American Management Association.

Hall, B. L. (1980). Editorial. *Journal of Organizational Behavior Management, 2*(3), 145–150. https://doi.org/10.1300/J075v02n03_01

Hantula, D. A., Stillman, F. A., & Waranch, H. R. (1991). A comparison of strategies for facilitating smoking survey return in low-SES employees. *Journal of Organizational Behavior Management, 11*(2), 47–59. https://doi.org/10.1300/J075v11n02_04

Hogan, L. C., Bell, M., & Olson, R. (2009). A preliminary investigation of the reinforcement function of signal detections in simulated baggage screening: Further support for the vigilance reinforcement hypothesis. *Journal of Organizational Behavior Management, 29*(1), 6–18. https://doi.org/10.1080/01608060802660116

Houmanfar, R., & Johnson, R. (2004). Organizational implications of gossip and rumor. *Journal of Organizational Behavior Management, 23*(2), 117–138. https://doi.org/10.1300/J075v23n02_07

Howe, D. C., Chauhan, R. S., Soderberg, A. T., & Buckley, R. M. (2021). Paradigm shifts caused by the COVID-19 pandemic. *Organizational Dynamics, 50*(4), 1–9. https://doi.org/10.1016/j.orgdyn.2020.10080

Hyten, C., & Ludwig, T. D. (2017). Complacency in process safety: A behavior analysis toward prevention strategies. *Journal of Organizational Behavior Management, 37*(3–4), 240–260. https://doi.org/10.1080/01608061.2017.1341860

Jimenez-Gomez, C., Sawhney, G., & Albert, K. M. (2021). Impact of COVID-19 on the applied behavior analysis workforce: Comparison across remote and nonremote workers. *Behavior Analysis in Practice, 14*(4), 873–882.https://doi.org/10.1007/s40617-021-00625-0

Johnson, R. A., Houmanfar, R., & Smith, G. S. (2010). The effect of implicit and explicit rules on customer greeting and productivity in a retail organization. *Journal of Organizational Behavior Management, 30*(1), 38–48. https://doi.org/10.1080/01608060903529731

Johnson, D. A., Rocheleau, J. M., & Tilka, R. E. (2015). Considerations in feedback delivery: The role of accuracy and type of evaluation. *Journal of Organizational Behavior Management, 35*(3–4), 240–258. https://doi.org/10.1080/01608061.2015.1093055

Johnson, D. A., & Johnson, C. M. (2022). Foundations and advances: Revisiting the past and selecting for the future. *Journal of Organizational Behavior Management*, Advance online publication. 1–7. https://doi.org/10.1080/01608061.2022.2029797

Johnston, J. M. (2014). *Radical behaviorism for ABA practitioners*. Sloan Publishing, LLC.

Komaki, J., Blood, M. R., & Holder, D. (1980). Fostering friendliness in a fast food franchise. *Journal of Organizational Behavior Management, 2*(3), 151–164. https://doi.org/10.1300/J075v02n03_02

Kuykendall, D., & Keating, J. P. (1990). Altering thoughts and judgements through repeated association. *British Journal of Social Psychology, 29*(1), 79–86. https://doi.org/10.1111/j.2044-8309.1990.tb00888.x

Lawson, D. A., & O'Brien, R. (1994). Behavioral and self-report measures of staff burnout in developmental disabilities. *Journal of Organizational Behavior Management, 14*(2), 37–54. https://doi.org/10.1300/J075v14n02_04

Lebbon, A. R., & Sigurdsson, S. O. (2017). Behavioral perspectives on variability in human behavior as part of process safety. *Journal of Organizational Behavior Management, 37*(3–4), 261–282. https://doi.org/10.1080/01608061.2017.1340922

Leigland, S. (1997). Is a new definition of verbal behavior necessary in light of derived relational responding? *The Behavior Analyst, 20*(1), 3–9. https://doi.org/10.1007/BF03392757

Lipschultz, J. L., Wilder, D. A., Sleiman, A., Cruz, N., Curry, S., & Gravina, N. E. (2021). The effects of feedback accuracy and trainer rules on performance during an analogue task. *Journal of Organizational Behavior Management, 41*(3), 215–235. https://doi.org/10.1080/01608061.2021.1903646

Lotfizadeh, A. D., Edwards, T. L., & Poling, A. (2014). Motivating operations in the journal of organizational behavior management: Review and discussion of relevant articles. *Journal of Organizational Behavior Management, 34*(2), 69–103. https://doi.org/10.1080/01608061.2014.914010

Ludwig, T. D., & Geller, E. S. (1999). Undesirable side-effects reflect countercontrol. *Journal of Organizational Behavior Management, 19*(2), 25–34. https://doi.org/10.1300/J075v19n02_03

Luke, M. M., Carr, J. E., & Wilder, D. A. (2018). On the compatibility of organizational behavior management and BACB certification. *Journal of Organizational Behavior Management, 38*(4), 288–305. https://doi.org/10.1080/01608061.2018.1514347

Madden, G. J., Reed, D. W., & DiGennaro Reed, F. D. (2021). *An Introduction to Behavior Analysis*. Wiley.

Malott, R. W., Malott, M. E., & Shimamune, S. (1993). Comments on rule-governed behavior. *Journal of Organizational Behavior Management, 12*(2), 91–101. https://doi.org/10.1300/J075v12n02_08

Malott, R. W., Shimamune, S., & Malott, M. E. (1993). Rule-governed behavior and organizational behavior management. *Journal of Organizational Behavior Management, 12*(2), 103–116. https://doi.org/10.1300/J075v12n02_09

Malott, R. W. (1993). A theory of rule-governed behavior and organizational behavior management. *Journal of Organizational Behavior Management, 12*(2), 45–65. https://doi.org/10.1300/J075v12n02_03

Maraccini, A. M., Houmanfar, R. A., & Szarko, A. J. (2016). Motivation and complex verbal phenomena: Implications for organizational research and practice. *Journal of Organizational Behavior Management, 36*(4), 282–300. https://doi.org/10.1080/01608061.2016.1211062

Martin, G. L., & Pear, J. J. (2019). *Behavior modification: What is it and how to do it* (11th ed.). Routledge.

Mawhinney, T. C., & Fellows-Kubert, C. (1999). Positive contingencies versus quotas: Telemarketers exert countercontrol. *Journal of Organizational Behavior Management, 19* (2), 35–57. https://doi.org/10.1300/J075v19n02_04

Michael, J. L. (2004). *Concepts and principles of behavior analysis*. Association for Behavior Analysis International.

Miller, L. K. (2006). *Principles of everyday behavior analysis* (4th ed.).

Moran, D. J., Batten, S., Gamble, M. A., & Atkins, P. (2022). Acceptance and commitment training: Improving performance in organizations with applied contextual behavioral science. In R. Houmanfar, M. Fryling, & M. Alavosius (Eds.), *Applied behavior science in organizations: Consilience of historical and emerging trends in organizational behavior management* (pp. 177–196). Taylor & Francis.

O'Donnell, J. (2001). The discriminative stimulus for punishment or S^{Dp}. *The Behavior Analyst, 24*(2), 261–262. https://doi.org/10.1007/BF03392036

O'Hora, D., & Maglieri, K. A. (2006). Goal statements and goal-directed behavior. *Journal of Organizational Behavior Management, 26*(1), 131–170. https://doi.org/10.1300/J075v26n01_06

Olson, R., Laraway, S., & Austin, J. (2001). Unconditioned and conditioned establishing operations in organizational behavior management. *Journal of Organizational Behavior Management, 21*(2), 7–35. https://doi.org/10.1300/J075v21n02_03

Olson, R., & Winchester, J. (2008). Behavioral self-monitoring of safety and productivity in the workplace: A methodological primer and quantitative literature review. *Journal of Organizational Behavior Management, 28*(1), 9–75. https://doi.org/10.1080/01608060802006823

Palmer, D. C., & Donahoe, J. W. (1992). Essentialism and selectionism in cognitive science and behavior analysis. *American Psychologist, 47*(11), 1344–1358. https://doi.org/10.1037//0003-066x.47.11.1344

Palmer, D. C. (2008). On Skinner's definition of verbal behavior. *International Journal of Psychology and Psychological Therapy, 8*(3), 295–307.

Palmer, D. C. (2009). Response strength and the concept of the repertoire. *European Journal of Behavior Analysis, 10*(1), 49–60. https://doi.org/10.1080/15021149.2009.11434308

Paradise, R. C. (1984). Introducing a phobia program into a community mental health center. *Journal of Organizational Behavior Management, 6*(2), 15–21. https://doi.org/10.1300/J075v06n02_04

Poling, A., & Braatz, D. (2001). Principles of learning: Respondent and operant conditioning and human behavior. In C. M. Johnson, W. K. Redmon, & T. C. Mawhinney (Eds.), *Handbook of organizational performance: Behavior analysis and management* (pp. 23–49). Routledge.

Porto, R. B., & Foxall, G. R. (2019). The marketing firm as a metacontingency: Revealing the mutual relationships between marketing and finance. *Journal of Organizational Behavior Management, 39*(3–4), 115–144. https://doi.org/10.1080/01608061.2019.1666774

Rafacz, S. D., Boyce, T. E., & Williams, W. L. (2011). Examining the effects of a low-cost prompt to reduce retail theft. *Journal of Organizational Behavior Management, 31*(2), 150–160. https://doi.org/10.1080/01608061.2011.570087

Reetz, N. K., Whiting, S. W., & Dixon, M. R. (2016). The impact of a task clarification and feedback intervention on restaurant service quality. *Journal of Organizational Behavior Management, 36*(4), 322–331. https://doi.org/10.1080/01608061.2016.1201035

Rhoton, W. W. (1980). A procedure to improve compliance with coal mine safety regulations. *Journal of Organizational Behavior Management, 2*(4), 243–249. https://doi.org/10.1300/J075v02n04_01

Schlinger, H., & Blakely, E. (1987). Function-altering effects of contingency-specifying stimuli. *The Behavior Analyst, 10*(1), 41–45. https://doi.org/10.1007/BF03392405

Scott, W. E., & Podsakoff, P. M. (1985). *Behavioral Principles in the Practice of Management*. Wiley.

Shimp, C. P. (2014). How molecular, molar, and unified analyses change the meaning of behavioral variability. *International Journal of Comparative Psychology*, *27*(2), 82–105.

Skinner, B. F. (1935). The generic nature of the concepts of stimulus and response. *The Journal of General Psychology*, *12*(1), 40–65. https://doi.org/10.1080/00221309.1935.9920087

Skinner, B. F. (1945). The operational analysis of psychological terms. *Psychological Review*, *52* (5), 270–277. https://doi.org/10.1037/h0062535

Skinner, B. F. (1950). Are theories of learning necessary? *Psychological Review*, *57*(4), 193–216. https://doi.org/10.1037/h0054367

Skinner, B. F. (1957). *Verbal behavior*. Prentice-Hall.

Skinner, B. F. (1969). *Contingencies of reinforcement: A theoretical analysis*. Prentice-Hall.

Skinner, B. F. (1978). *Reflections on behaviorism and society*. Prentice-Hall.

Squires, J., & Wilder, D. A. (2010). A preliminary investigation of the effect of rules on employee performance. *Journal of Organizational Behavior Management*, *30*(1), 57–69. https://doi.org/10.1037/h0042782

Staats, A. W., & Staats, C. K. (1958). Attitudes established by classical conditioning. *Journal of Abnormal and Social Psychology*, *57*(1), 37–40.

Sulzer-Azaroff, B., Loafman, B., Merante, R. J., & Hlavacek, A. C. (1990). Improving occupational safety in a large industrial plant: A systematic replication. *Journal of Organizational Behavior Management*, *11*(1), 99–120. https://doi.org/10.1300/J075v11n01_07

Twarek, M., Cihon, T., & Eshleman, J. (2010). The effects of fluent levels of big 6 + 6 skill elements on functional motor skills with children with autism. *Behavioral Interventions*, *25* (4), 275–293. https://doi.org/10.1002/bin.317

Weatherly, N. L. (2021). The ethics of organizational behavior management. *Journal of Organizational Behavior Management*, *41*(3), 197–214. https://doi.org/10.1080/01608061.2021.1890664

Wine, B., Reis, M., & Hantula, D. A. (2014). An evaluation of stimulus preference assessment methodology in organizational behavior management. *Journal of Organizational Behavior Management*, *34*(1), 7–15. https://doi.org/10.1080/01608061.2013.873379

Experimental Research Methodologies in Organizational Behavior Management

Tyler G. Erath, Azure J. Pellegrino, Florence D. DiGennaro Reed, Sandra A. Ruby, Abigail L. Blackman, and Matthew D. Novak

ABSTRACT

Organizational behavior management (OBM) is a scientific approach to understanding behavior and its relation to the workplace. As a natural science it relies on the use of sound experimental research methodology. This methodology has been critical to the field's success in demonstrating the application of behavioral principles across the basic–translational–applied continuum, from laboratory to natural workplace settings. The purpose of this paper is to present an overview of experimental methods commonly used within the field. We attempt to highlight the range and diversity of OBM research by providing examples of different approaches to research and design methodologies. In doing so, we review strengths, limitations, and examples of various single-case and group research designs.

> Experimental observations must be brought into some kind of order before they can be said to contribute to a science of behavior. (Sidman, 1960, p. 12)

Organizational behavior management (OBM), with its roots in behavior analysis, is a natural-science approach to understanding behavior and its relation to the workplace (Wilder, Austin, & Casella, 2009). Like many other branches of behavior analysis, OBM has experienced growth – both in its publications and its applications – since its inception as a subdiscipline (DiGennaro Reed, Henley, Rueb, Crabbs, & Giacalone, 2016; Gravina et al., 2018; Wilder, Lipschultz, King, Driscoll, & Sigurdsson, 2018). As a science whose focus is on changing behavior in organizational contexts, findings from this literature have demonstrated robust effects from the application of behavioral principles to workplace settings. Moreover, these findings have demonstrated the adeptness of OBMers to use and modify experimental designs to meet the environmental conditions of the setting, all while maintaining a high degree of experimental rigor.

The purpose of this manuscript is to present an overview of experimental methods found within the field of OBM. We will attempt to highlight the range and diversity of OBM research by providing examples of different approaches to research and design methodologies. In doing so, we describe various experimental designs – including both single-case and group designs – and relevant examples of their application within the literature. We begin by providing a brief synopsis of critical components to science in general and the behavior of the scientist in particular.

The goals of science and approaches to research

The goal of science is to understand phenomena and their underlying causes – that is, to discover nature's truths (Cooper, Heron, & Heward, 2020). The role of the scientist, then, is to discover truths through observation and controlled investigation. Scientific knowledge is obtained through experimentation, which broadly involves identifying relations between two or more events (Kazdin, 2011; Skinner, 1965). A researcher demonstrates a functional relation when one event (i.e., *independent variable*) reliably and consistently produces an effect on another event (i.e., *dependent variable*). Through controlled experimentation, a researcher rules out variables other than the independent variable (i.e., *extraneous variables or confounding variables*) as potential explanations for the observed relation, thereby increasing the researcher's confidence in the findings (Johnston & Pennypacker, 2009).

Experimental design is critical to making accurate inferences about the relation between events, as scientific knowledge is only as valid as its procedures. *Internal validity* refers to the extent to which the independent variable is responsible for the change in the dependent variable (Campbell & Stanley, 1963; Kazdin, 2011). As a continuum, internal validity is related to the degree to which an experimental design controls for extraneous variables or threats, such as history, maturation, selection biases, and others. The type of experimental design employed is a critical feature in determining the degree to which different threats are controlled (for a more detailed review regarding between-subject designs, see Campbell & Stanley, 1963; Shadish, Cook, & Campbell, 2002; for a more detailed review regarding single-case designs, see Kazdin, 2011). *External validity* refers to the extent to which findings are generalizable to different populations, times, and environmental settings (Baron & Perone, 1998; Zedeck, 2014). Internal validity is necessary (though not sufficient) for external validity; thus, to make inferences about the generality of the findings, there must first be a causal relation between events (Perone & Hursh, 2013).

Scientific research can vary along a continuum ranging from basic research conducted in the laboratory to applied research conducted in real-world settings (e.g., Hake, 1982). The approach adopted by a researcher and the methods used in an experiment will vary depending on the research aims.

Considerations include the gains in fundamental understanding of the principles under investigation and the intended ecological validity, or practical use of the findings (Stokes, 1997). These two aims may appear to be at odds with one another. An experiment conducted in a natural setting may have strong ecological validity, but potential confounds in the natural environment may limit a researcher's understanding of the effects of the independent variable. With the hopes of maintaining experimental control, a researcher may conduct an experiment in a tightly controlled laboratory setting. This heightened experimental control allows for increased understanding of the variables under study, but with less utility for natural settings. As noted by Skinner (1959), "Laboratory experimentation is designed to make a process as obvious as possible, to separate processes one from the other, and to obtain quantitative measures. These are indeed the very heart of an experimental science. The history of science shows that the results can be effectively extended to the world at large" (p. 106). Although there may appear to be a tradeoff between internal and ecological validity, a third approach combines the pure basic and pure applied ends of the research continuum. *Use-inspired basic research*, or *translational research*, seeks fundamental understanding of basic principles while also investigating areas of practical importance (Critchfield, 2011).

The publication practices of OBM's flagship journal reflect that OBM research spans the basic–translational–applied continuum. In a review of articles published in the *Journal of Organizational Behavior Management* between 1992 and 1997, Normand, Bucklin, and Austin (1999) reported that both field (i.e., applied; $n = 22$) and laboratory (i.e., basic/translational; $n = 5$) research were published during this period. DiGennaro Reed et al. (2016) replicated this finding for articles published between 2006 and 2015 and found similar results for the publication rates of field and laboratory research – with approximately four times as many field-research publications ($n = 102$) as laboratory-research publications ($n = 25$).

Basic OBM research seeks to discover fundamental understanding of behavior by simulating workplace settings within the laboratory. This approach maximizes experimental control by isolating relevant variables. Basic OBM experiments often involve measuring discrete responses during a computer simulation with a highly controlled independent variable. To be most useful, the experimental tasks and methodological arrangements should ensure that (a) behavior occurs at a high rate, so participants are unable to easily self-monitor their behavior; (b) the task is not too fun, to prevent ceiling effects; and (c) the task is not too aversive, to avoid floor effects (D. Johnson, personal communication, August 19, 2020).

To simulate a busy workplace environment, Bucklin, McGee, and Dickinson (2003) measured the number of points undergraduate participants earned on a computer program that concurrently presented memory, arithmetic, visual monitoring, and auditory monitoring tasks. The researchers observed participant performance under three conditions: an incentive pay system for earning a certain number of points, an incentive pay system for earning a certain number of points plus feedback on the number of points earned after each session, and an hourly pay system plus feedback on number of points earned after each session. Although the dependent and independent variables did not necessarily match behaviors and interventions typically encountered in the workplace, this experimental arrangement allowed the researchers to examine independent and combined effects of the two intervention components – performance feedback and contingent incentives. Specifically, they observed the greatest point totals when the two components were presented together, in the incentive system plus feedback condition, and the lowest point totals when only feedback was presented, in the hourly pay system plus feedback condition. These findings, like others conducted in controlled settings, could set the stage for future research studying similar variables in more naturalistic approximations of workplace settings (e.g., Johnson, Dickinson, & Huitema, 2008), eventually leading to effective translation into a workplace setting.

Translational OBM research seeks to balance internal and ecological validity. It uses information gleaned from basic OBM research to potentially observe the same phenomena in increasingly naturalistic workplace settings. Although the research may not be conducted with employees or in actual workplace settings,[1] scenarios are created within the experimental context to evoke behavior that may be observed within an organization. For example, Henley and DiGennaro Reed (2015) evaluated the efficacy of the feedback sandwich – a corrective feedback statement "sandwiched" between two positive feedback statements – using a translational approach. Undergraduate student participants completed four office tasks, such as filing time sheets, in a simulated workplace. Three of the tasks were each associated with one of three different feedback sequences (positive–corrective–positive, positive–positive–corrective, corrective–positive–positive); the fourth task was assigned to a control condition wherein the researchers did not provide feedback. This arrangement permitted the researchers to evaluate the efficacy of the feedback sandwich in relation to other sequences while controlling for feedback content. Henley and DiGennaro Reed showed that the feedback sandwich was neither the least nor most efficacious feedback sequence. The selection of the work task – as an approximation of a real-world workplace behavior – likely strengthens the ecological validity of the arrangement, despite the simulated nature of the experiment.

The focus of applied research is to improve behaviors of social importance, whereas the focus of basic research is to enhance the understanding of underlying behavioral principles (i.e., to gather additional knowledge for knowledge sake; Baer, Wolf, & Risley, 1968; Mace & Critchfield, 2010). Despite these differences, basic and applied sectors often rely on each other to inform future research questions. Therefore, applied research is typically derived from the principles observed in basic research and extended to a variety of populations and behaviors to produce socially important outcomes (Lerman, Iwata, & Hanley, 2013).

Additional differences between basic and applied areas of research include where the research is conducted, the populations that serve as participants, the behaviors addressed, and the interventions assessed. Applied research is conducted within the natural environment with participants who can directly benefit from participation in the experiment. A quick glance of recent publications in the *Journal of Organizational Behavior Management* revealed variability in the settings where such research took place, including restaurants (e.g., Downing, Capriola, & Geller, 2018), retail stores (e.g., Smith & Wilder, 2018), and human service settings (e.g., Griffin, Gravina, Matey, Pritchard, & Wine, 2019). The types of participants involved in research also varied and included direct support professionals (Griffin et al., 2019), cashiers (Downing et al., 2018), and employees with disabilities (e.g., Smith & Wilder, 2018), among others. Applied research has addressed numerous performance issues, with the most prevalent involving productivity and quality, safety and health, and customer-service tasks (VanStelle et al., 2012). Applied interventions often comprise multiple intervention components (e.g., antecedents, training, feedback; Gravina et al., 2018) to observe performance improvements in real time.

Research methodologies

Using an appropriate experimental design is a critical component of research. The experimental design determines the degree to which accurate inferences can be made about observed relations. Ideally, our experiments would involve *the same person* experiencing condition A (but not condition B) while at *the same time* experiencing condition B (but not condition A) to control for both time and person variables. This experimental arrangement is obviously impossible; thus, all experiments have limitations because they deviate from this ideal arrangement. Experimental designs can, broadly, be categorized into two types – single-case and group designs – with uses for each spanning the basic-to-applied continuum. Single-case designs better control for person variables because the behavior of the same participants is repeatedly measured across different conditions. Group designs assign groups of participants to different conditions at the same time; thus, they better control for time variables. Next, we expound on both types of designs and their variations, including a discussion of methodological strengths, weaknesses, and relevant examples of their implementation found within the OBM literature.

Single-case design

Like other specialties within behavior analysis, single-case design is prevalent in OBM research (Balcazar, Shupert, Daniels, Mawhinney, & Hopkins, 1989; Nolan, Jarema, & Austin, 1999; VanStelle et al., 2012). Single-case design allows for the measurement of a dependent variable before, throughout, and after the implementation of an independent variable (Perone & Hursh, 2013). The primary advantage of single-case design is that the level of analysis allows for each participant to serve as their own control (Sidman, 1960); that is, the researcher can directly compare the dependent variable before and after the independent variable is introduced for each participant. Relatedly, single-case design allows for repeated measurement of a dependent variable across each participant (Johnston & Pennypacker, 2009). This repeated measurement – particularly during the baseline phase – helps control for several potential threats to internal validity, including maturation, instrumentation, and testing. Another advantage of single-case design is its flexibility. Repeated measures allow for session-by-session analysis and decision-making regarding the introduction, withdrawal, and adjustment of the independent variable. In addition, the participants studied in single-case design can range from single individuals (e.g., employees) to large groups of individuals (e.g., branches of an organization), depending on the research question.

OBM researchers who employ single-case design observe the effects of an independent variable on a dependent variable using visual inspection, which is the systematic interpretation of graphically displayed data, typically presented within time-series line graphs (Cooper et al., 2020). Although OBM researchers analyze data both within and across experimental phases, the change that occurs to the dependent variable upon the introduction of the independent variable is of primary interest. A methodological strength of single-case design is that researchers can observe exactly when changes in the dependent variable occur due to the design's repeated measurement within participants. If changes in the dependent variable reliably and predictably follow changes in the independent variable, the researcher has demonstrated a functional relation (Sidman, 1960; Skinner, 1965). Another strength is that single-case design permits researchers to analyze data and make necessary changes in real time, which is appealing for applied settings.

With single-case experimental designs, a critical step toward ensuring strong internal validity is to visually analyze repeated measures within each experimental phase or condition (Bourret & Pietras, 2013; Cooper et al., 2020; Johnston & Pennypacker, 2009; Komaki & Goltz, 2001; Sidman, 1960). Repeated measures data should be depicted in a graphical display to visually assess the level, trend (i. e., ascending, descending, stable), and variability, which is critical in determining when to introduce the independent variable. Although there is no specific rule regarding the introduction of an independent variable (Barlow, Nock, & Hersen,

2009), most researchers agree that to attribute the effects of the independent variable accurately, the introduction should take place when the baseline data are within a steady state (Sidman, 1960). There are differing interpretations of a steady state; however, a commonly agreed-upon definition involves a data path that is stable with negligible session-to-session changes.

A steady state is also necessary to meet the criteria of baseline logic (Cooper et al., 2020). Baseline logic involves three components to analyze graphical data: prediction, verification, and replication. Prediction involves forecasting future baseline data based on existing baseline data. That is, the researchers would predict that the baseline data (level, trend, and variability) would remain unchanged in the absence of the independent variable. Verification requires incorporating design features that allow the researchers to substantiate the accuracy of their prediction (we describe these design features below). Prediction and verification increase the likelihood of a functional relation; that is, that the independent variable, rather than other confounds or extraneous variables, is responsible for changes in the dependent variable. Replication, or the application of the independent variable more than once (within or across participants) and obtaining the same results, further increases the likelihood of a functional relation.

Finally, repeated measurement within single-case design permits researchers to examine trends that are not possible to observe when data are averaged or collected at a single point in time. For example, suppose we averaged the hypothetical data in Figure 1 (McGee & Johnson, 2015) or only considered the first data point within each phase, which would be a plausible approach with other experimental designs. A logical conclusion would be that performance is higher in the first phase compared to the third phase, whereas visual inspection of repeated measurement suggests that performance in the first and third phases is similar.

Although single-case design is the most prevalent experimental approach within OBM research, it is not without limitations. First, the repeated measures during baseline that strengthen the methodological rigor of single-case design can also present disadvantages. There are situations in which extended exposure to baseline may not be ideal for participants, such as when safety or ethical concerns exist. Data collection resources and organizational logistics may also make repeated measures improbable. However, different types of single-case designs (described below) may be better suited for situations such as these. Second, threats to external validity – namely, sample, stimulus, and setting characteristics (Kazdin, 2002) – may decrease the extent to which the findings generalize outside of the experimental arrangement. Depending on the type of design employed, an experiment employing single-case design may be susceptible to other threats, such as contrast and sequence effects (Komaki & Goltz, 2001), which could limit the degree to which comparative research can be conducted.

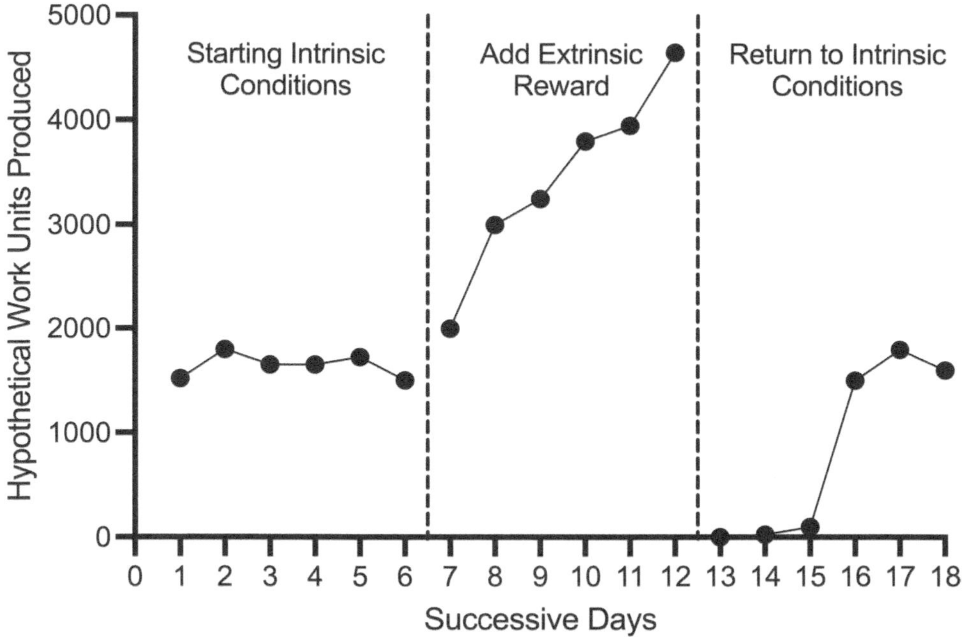

Figure 1. Hypothetical data of repeated-measures design modeled after McGee and Johnson (2015). See published data for actual data and full context.

Another concern of single-case design is the typically limited number of participants in experiments compared to group design, which could cause a reader to question the generality of an experiment's results. This concern, however, is addressed through replication, both direct and systematic,[2] which can further validate the effects of the independent variable(s) (Sidman, 1960).

Finally, researchers using single-case design do not generally analyze data statistically and thus do not often report statistical power and effect size measures. Visual inspection often is both sufficient and most appropriate for analysis, thereby limiting the need to include such measures. Various methods have emerged to calculate effect sizes for single-case design (e.g., nonoverlap of all pairs; Parker & Vannest, 2009), and recent advances make these calculations a promising option for researchers. It should be noted, though, that statistical significance reported with single-case design should be used as a supplement to and not in lieu of visual analysis.

Depending on the research question, dependent and independent variables, and the resources available, OBM researchers may choose from and combine aspects of several single-case designs. A summary of the most common single-case designs, including methodological strengths and weaknesses and examples in published OBM research, is presented next.

AB design

The simplest single-case design is the AB design (Johnston & Pennypacker, 2009). Within this design, a dependent variable is measured repeatedly during a baseline phase (A) and an intervention phase (B), or when an independent variable is introduced. A methodological strength of the AB design is that researchers can potentially observe changes in the dependent variable immediately after introducing the independent variable. Figure 2 (panel A) contains a hypothetical example of an AB design; notice that the target behavior (i.e., dependent variable) increases upon the introduction of the independent variable. However, a researcher cannot draw strong conclusions from the results of this design because there is only one instance in which a researcher can analyze changes in the dependent variable (Petursdottir & Carr, 2018). It is possible that one or more confounding variables caused the change in the dependent variable, which cannot be detected without replication. Replication of the independent variable's effects within or across participants increases the methodological strength of a single-case design.

Despite its limitations, the AB design has its place in OBM research. An OBM researcher or practitioner may observe the need for an intervention but lack the resources to implement more complex research designs. Similarly, an OBM consultant may have time constraints that prevent replication of the effects of an intervention, or an organization may prohibit use of other single-case designs. Using an AB design could be a practical alternative to more complex research designs under these methodological and environmental constraints.

Parsons, Schepis, Reid, McCarn, and Green (1987) employed a series of AB designs to evaluate a staff management program on increasing student involvement in functional activities within a classroom setting (see Figure 3). The staff management program consisted of (a) an in-service training to discuss the importance of teaching functional skills (e.g., teaching a student to put on a coat), (b) supervisor prompting (i.e., unannounced visits to ask staff about the functional activities being implemented), and (c) supervisor feedback. The percentage of on-task intervals with functional activities was low during baseline. Upon introduction of the staff management intervention, an immediate and sustained increased in performance was observed across a period of approximately 24 months. Although this AB design does not allow for a determination of causality, the cumulative number of replications suggests an effect that may be sufficient for OBM researchers, consultants, and practitioners seeking to improve an organization's practices.

ABAB design

An ABAB (also referred to as a withdrawal or reversal[3]) design is an extension of the AB design. In the ABAB design, baseline (A) precedes an intervention (B), in which the independent variable is implemented. Upon meeting level,

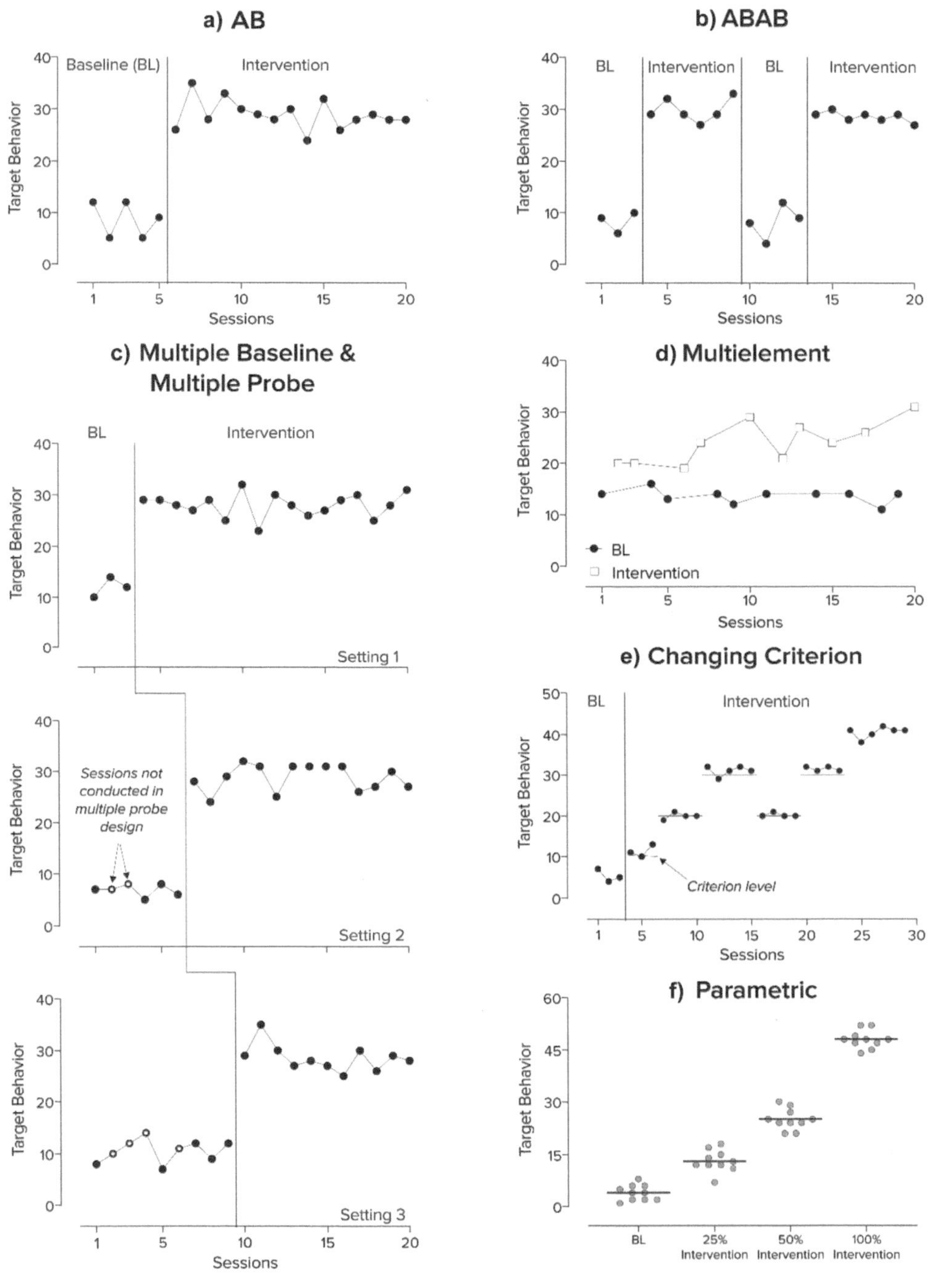

Figure 2. Generic examples of common single case designs.

trend, and stability criteria, the intervention is withdrawn, creating conditions similar to baseline (A). Finally, the intervention is reinstated (B) (Gast & Baekey, 2014). In other words, the ABAB design replicates the AB design within the same participant. If the target behavior changes with the

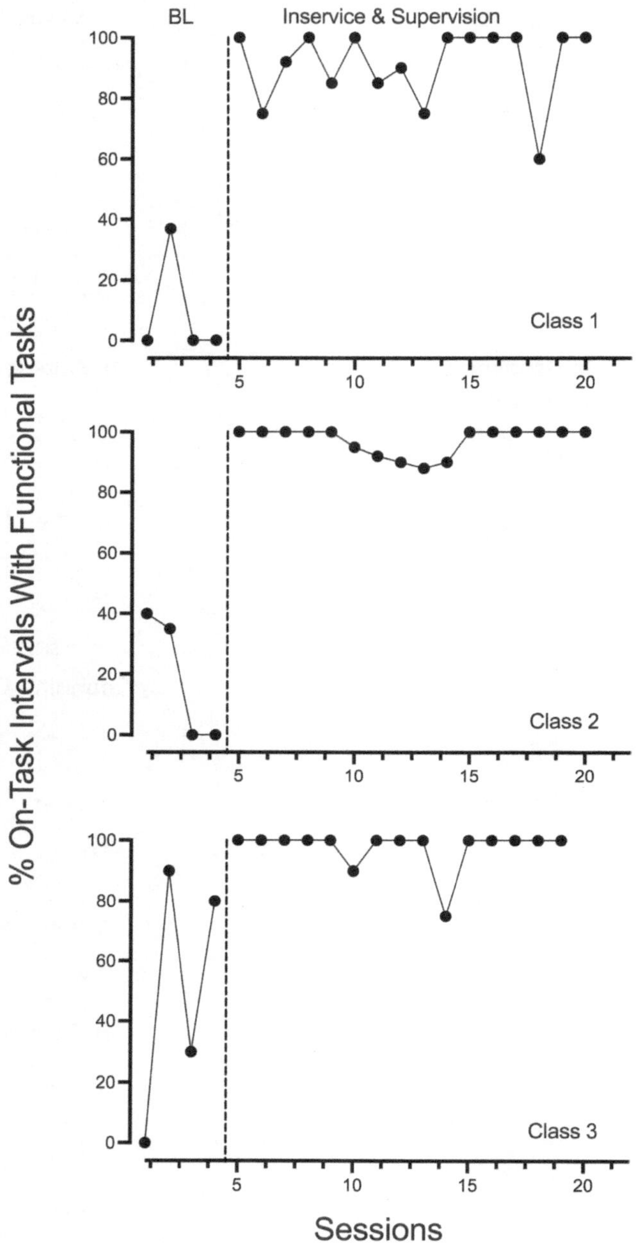

Figure 3. Hypothetical data of AB design modeled after Parsons et al (1987). See published data for actual data and full context.

introduction of the intervention, reverts to the previous baseline level when the intervention is withdrawn, and returns to the previous intervention level when it is reinstated (see Figure 2, panel B), one can say with greater certainty that a functional relation exists between the independent and dependent variables. It is this replication of the independent variable's effect on the dependent variable within the same participant that makes the ABAB design one of the most robust single-case designs.

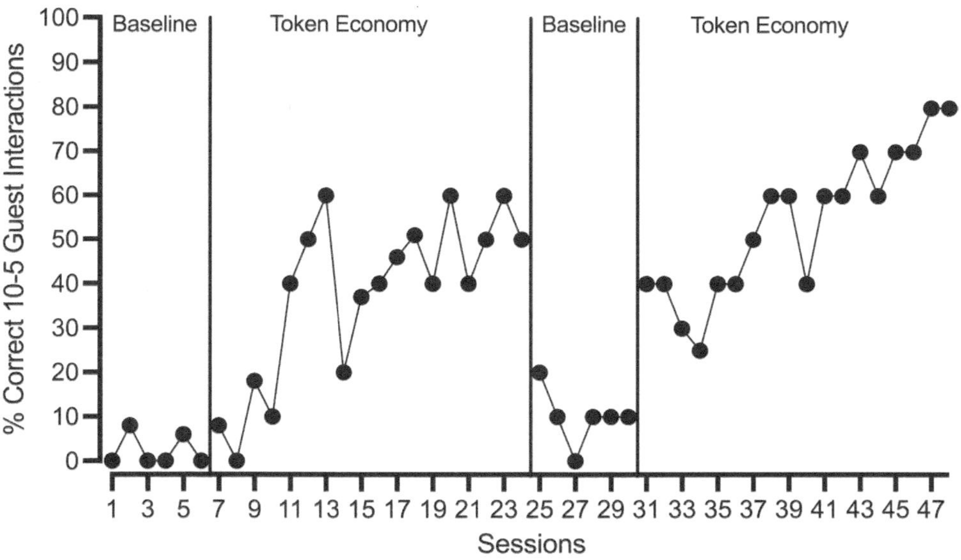

Figure 4. Hypothetical data of ABAB design modeled after Vergason and Gravina (2020). See published data for actual data and full context.

Vergason and Gravina (2020) used an ABAB design to evaluate the effects of a token economy on employee interactions with guests (see Figure 4). In the first baseline (A) phase, employees demonstrated low interactions with guests. In the first intervention (B) phase, employee interactions increased throughout the implementation of the token economy. When the token economy was withdrawn and conditions returned to those similar to baseline (A), employee–guest interactions decreased and remained low. Upon reinstatement of the token economy (B), interactions increased. The replication of effects in the second baseline and intervention phases strengthens the claim that the token economy, and only the token economy, was the variable responsible for increased employee–guest interactions.

Sometimes OBM researchers are interested in the individual effects of more than one independent variable on a dependent variable. It is possible to study the separate effects of multiple independent variables in a variation of an ABAB design. For example, an OBM researcher could measure the effects of one independent variable on a dependent variable in one phase, followed by measuring the effects of a second independent variable on the dependent variable in the following phase (ABC). Implementation of these independent variables could be repeated (ABCBC), separated by baseline phases (ABACABAC), or studied separately and combined (ABACAB+C) depending on the research question. A variety of other sequences can be used, but they are all based on the ABAB design.

The experimental control of the ABAB design is a strength, but the design also has limitations. An ABAB design takes more time to complete than an AB design due to its replication of phases. Taking the time to withdraw and reinstate an intervention may not be feasible within an organization, especially if intervention planning and implementation is a systems-level change within an organization. Additionally, withdrawing and reinstating an intervention may be unethical if withdrawing an effective intervention could cause harm to participants. For example, it may not be ethical to withdraw a safety intervention that prevents potentially fatal injuries within an industrial workplace setting. There are also workplace behaviors that are not reversible; that is, there are behaviors that, once learned, are unlikely to be performed again at baseline levels (Johnston & Pennypacker, 2009). Some examples of irreversible behaviors include workplace behaviors learned through training and practice as well as behaviors that, once learned, contact natural reinforcers. If baseline is reinstated for participants who have learned how to complete a particular behavior, the participants' performances will likely remain unchanged because the researchers cannot undo the participants' previous learning. Fortunately, there are other single-case designs that can demonstrate experimental control while also controlling for variables like time, safety, and previous learning.

Multiple baseline and multiple probe design

A multiple baseline design individually introduces an independent variable across multiple (a) participants' or groups' behavior, (b) behaviors of the same participant or group, or (c) conditions (e.g., settings; Gast, Lloyd, & Ledford, 2018). Multiple baseline designs may possess both within-participant (i.e., replication across multiple behaviors for the same participant) and between-participant (i.e., replication across multiple participants) methodological features. A within-participant comparison is also possible via an AB design implemented with each participant. For example, Figure 2 (panel C) depicts a multiple baseline design across three settings. Notice the separate, stacked panels (or tiers) that graphically display the target behavior for each setting. The participant experienced a baseline phase (A) followed by the introduction of the independent variable in an intervention phase (B) in each setting that effectively increased the target behavior. Notice how the introduction of the independent variable occurs after a different number of baseline sessions for each setting. This staggered introduction of the independent variable across differing baseline sessions contributes additional control to the design. The fact that the participant showed low levels of the target behavior during baseline in settings 2 and 3 and an increase in the target behavior with the introduction of the independent variable in setting 1 makes researchers more confident that the independent variable, not an extraneous variable, caused the increase. The strength of the design increases with each staggered replication across panels, as the replication of effects increases the likelihood that the change in the dependent variable is due only to the independent variable. That is, when and only when the independent variable is introduced is a change observed in the dependent variable. Each replication of an effect across panels further strengthens the likelihood of a functional relation within multiple baseline designs.

The multiple baseline design is the most common design published in behavior-analytic research (Coon & Rapp, 2017) and is used frequently in OBM research. As an example of how these designs are used in organizational settings, Fox, Hopkins, and Anger (1987) demonstrated the effectiveness of a token economy on employee safety performance – measured across groups – in two open-pit mines (see Figure 5). During baseline, groups of employees were subject to adhering to Mining Safety and Health Administration regulations and procedures (e.g., new employee training, ongoing refresher training, frequent mine inspections). During the token economy, trading stamps were used as tokens to reward safety-related behaviors, both at the individual and group levels. At the individual level, employees could earn trading stamps for no lost-time injury or compensation injuries requiring medical care. At the group level, trading stamps could be earned for workgroups not being in a safety-related or equipment-damaging incident, making suggestions to enhance worksite safety, and engaging in unusual behaviors to prevent an accident or injury. The researchers found significant reductions in the number of missed workdays due to injury, the total number of worksite injuries, and the yearly costs resulting from accidents and injuries. In addition, these results were shown to maintain across multiple years for all dependent measures, thereby furthering the effectiveness of the intervention.

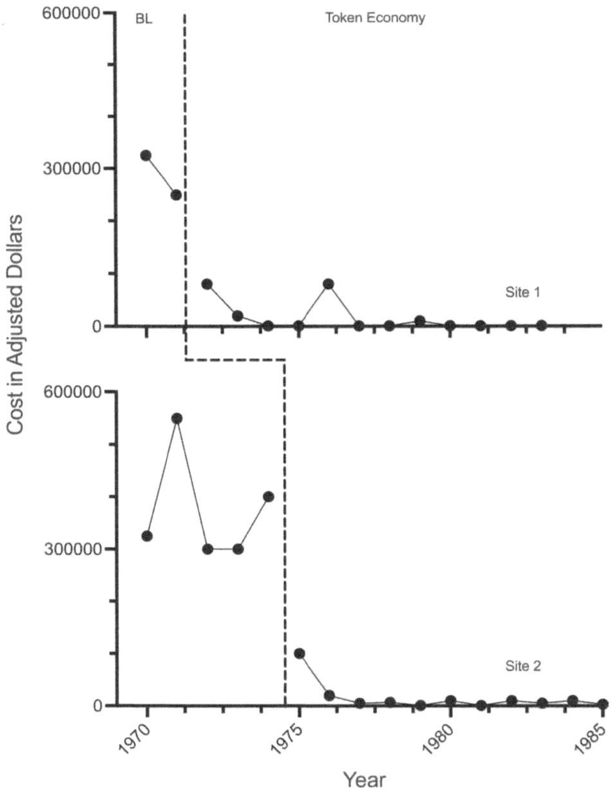

Figure 5. Hypothetical data of multiple baseline design modeled after Fox et al. (1987). See published data for actual data and full context.

Practicality issues may present difficulties for an OBM researcher to conduct sessions across multiple participants, behaviors, or conditions within the same time frame (Carr, 2005). A variant of the multiple baseline design – a nonconcurrent multiple baseline design – provides the researcher flexibility in session timing. Within a nonconcurrent multiple baseline design, the panels do not temporally align session-by-session, which may make its use more practical. However, a nonconcurrent multiple baseline design may not allow a researcher to observe extraneous variables that could affect responding within and across panels at points within an experiment. Using a concurrent multiple baseline design mitigates this risk, although its implementation may be temporally difficult.

Another variation of the multiple baseline design is a multiple probe design (Horner & Baer, 1978). This design is identical to a multiple baseline design except for systematic intermittent measurement rather than continuous measurement during baseline (See Figure 2, panel C; the white data points denote sessions that would not be conducted in a multiple probe design). The primary advantage of the multiple probe design is that it can minimize the number of baseline sessions while still demonstrating experimental control. Typically, researchers conduct baseline sessions for the remaining panels (e.g., settings, participants, behaviors) when the independent variable is introduced for one setting. Arranging baseline sessions in this way demonstrates that upon introduction of the independent variable in the first setting, performance does not change (i.e., remains similar) to other baseline performances in the remaining settings.

Alavosius and Sulzer-Azaroff (1986) evaluated the effects of individual written and verbal performance feedback on safe behavior of employees (i.e., safely performing transfers of clients with physical disabilities). The authors describe their design as a multiple baseline across settings and subjects design; however, one could conceptualize their design as a multiple probe design due to the intermittent measurement of the dependent variable (see Figure 6). Notice how sessions are not always conducted consecutively but are timed in a way that researchers could observe that the percentage of safe behavior in Wards C and D remained low when the percentage of safe behavior increased following feedback in Ward A and B Cottage. Also note that the percentage of safe behaviors in Wards C and D similarly increased only after the employees received feedback. These researchers' use of a multiple probe design allowed for fewer baseline sessions while still demonstrating experimental control.

Multielement

Multielement designs (sometimes described as alternating treatment designs) allow for the semi-randomized, rapid presentation of multiple conditions to participants, limiting the likelihood of maturation, history, testing, and instrumentation effects – or at least equating them across conditions (Perone & Hursh, 2013). The multiple conditions might include baseline and a single

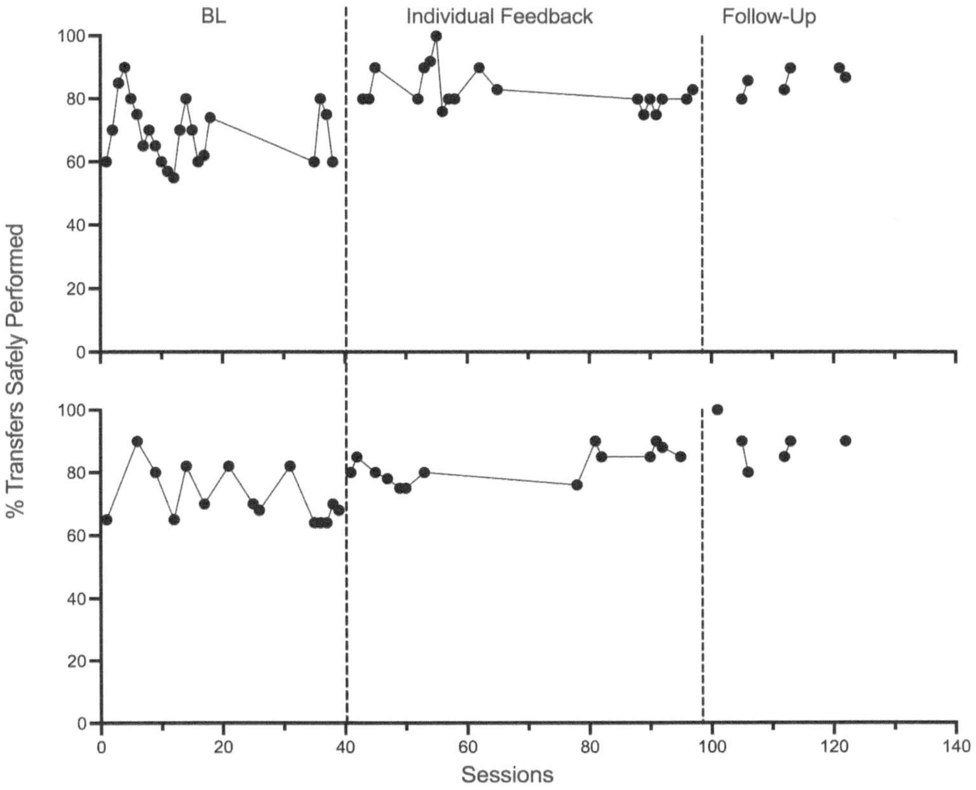

Figure 6. Hypothetical data of multiple probe design modeled after Alavosius and Sulzer-Azaroff (1986). See published data for actual data and full context.

intervention, baseline and more than one intervention, or more than one intervention without a baseline comparison. Notice how the hypothetical participant in Figure 2 (panel D) is exposed to an intervention during sessions 2, 3, 6, 7, 10, 12, 13, 15, 17, and 20. This participant experienced baseline during all other sessions. Experiencing these conditions in this semi-randomized order increases the likelihood the participant's increased performance in each intervention session is due to the independent variable alone. A risk, however, with multielement designs is that the rapid fashion in which the conditions are presented could cause them to interact in a way that they would not have if the participants experienced each condition in a separate phase (e.g., ABACAD). This confound is known as multiple treatment interference wherein the influence of one intervention impacts the influence of another intervention on the dependent variable (Campbell & Stanley, 1963). To reduce the likelihood of this interaction occurring, signals have been used to aid discrimination between the conditions. Because neurotypical adults are usually the participants in OBM research, rules describing the contingencies within the conditions could be all that is required for participants' behavior to differentiate across conditions.

Therrien, Wilder, Rodriguez, and Wine (2005) used a multielement design to evaluate timely customer greetings of sandwich shop employees. The multielement component was a preintervention analysis where performance was assessed under five antecedent conditions: manager presence, a door chime, having the radio on, uncontrolled (i.e., no programmed manipulations), and a control (i.e., no manager, door chime, or radio). The researchers presented the conditions in a rapidly alternated fashion (see Figure 7). This rapid alternation of antecedent conditions increased the likelihood that employee performance was in response to the current contingencies of each session rather than the history of, for example, an entire phase of sessions with a manager present. Using this multielement design, Therrien et al. found that the door-chime condition produced the highest percentage of timely customer greetings, followed by a manager's presence. The data collected from this preintervention analysis were then used to inform the components implemented in the intervention package, which included both the door chime and a manager's presence.

Changing criterion

A changing criterion design is used to produce systematic changes in a single dependent variable in a stepwise fashion (Hartmann & Hall, 1976; Ledford & Gast, 2014; Perone & Hursh, 2013). Within this design, stable responding during an intervention phase can simultaneously act as a baseline for the next phase (Sidman, 1960). Experimental control is demonstrated each phase when

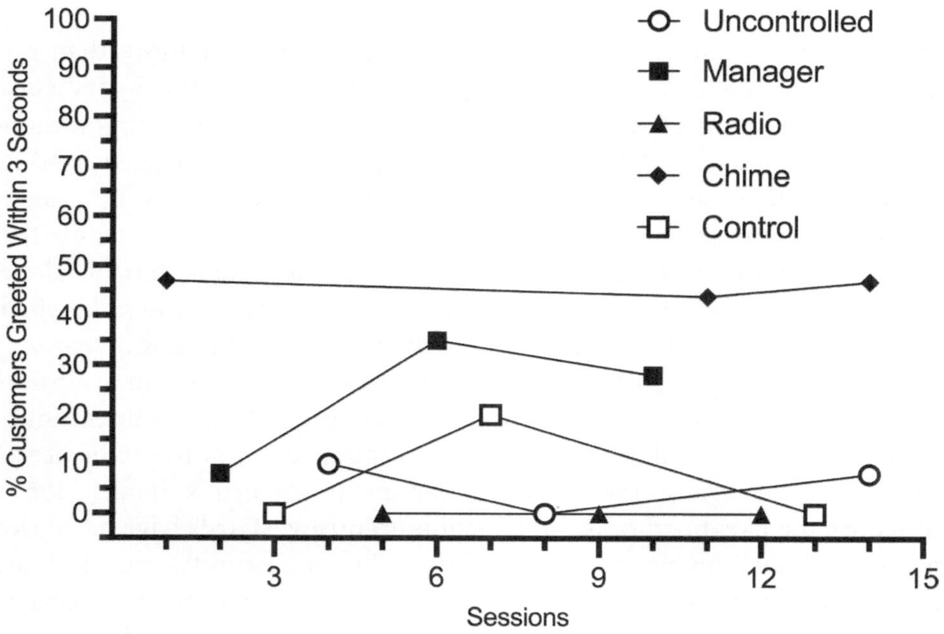

Figure 7. Hypothetical data of multielement design modeled after Therrien et al. (2005). See published data for actual data and full context.

(a) the participant has the opportunity to respond freely (i.e., responding is unconstrained) and (b) the dependent variable (i.e., the participant's behavior) reliably matches the phase's corresponding criterion. Using Figure 2 (panel E) as an example, following a stable baseline, a participant experienced an intervention until there was stable responding at the prescribed criterion, followed by additional phases in which the target behavior increased to its corresponding criterion. To further demonstrate experimental control, the researcher incorporated a reversal to a previous criterion at session 16. This demonstration increases confidence that the intervention is responsible for the behavior change. An advantage of a changing criterion design is that it targets gradual change in behavior to achieve the overall outcome. This gradual change can be desirable in situations where immediate large behavior change is not feasible, while still demonstrating experimental control. A disadvantage is that the changing criteria may slow or delay change in the dependent variable due to the within-phase demonstrations of stability. In addition, a changing criterion design may not be appropriate for measuring certain behaviors (e.g., unlearned skills); thus, this design is most appropriately used for behaviors that a participant can perform prior to or during baseline.

Malott, Glasgow, O'Neill, and Klesges (1984) used a changing criterion design to test the efficacy of two worksite smoking programs. During baseline, participants smoked between 20 and 24 cigarettes per day (see Figure 8). During intervention, which included coworker support, researchers initially implemented a 25% smoking reduction goal phase, during which participants reduced their cigarette consumption accordingly. Following the 25% smoking reduction goal phase, researchers implemented a 50% smoking reduction goal phase, during which participants again reduced their cigarette consumption accordingly. Notice the stepwise decrease that occurs with the introduction of each criterion. The reduction of cigarette consumption in accordance with the specified goal is the demonstration of experimental control.

Parametric analysis

Similar to how a changing criterion design systematically manipulates the dependent variable criteria, a parametric analysis systematically manipulates a parameter of the independent variable to determine the parameter range that is most effective (Perone & Hursh, 2013). That is, a parametric analysis determines the precise number, quality, magnitude, or immediacy of an independent variable needed to produce desired results. For example, Figure 2 (panel F) depicts the target behavior of a participant who experienced differing magnitudes (25%, 50%, and 100%) of an intervention in addition to baseline. Notice how increases in the intervention magnitude causes increases in the target behavior. An advantage of a parametric analysis is its ability to identify the point at which the resources allocated outweigh their benefits.

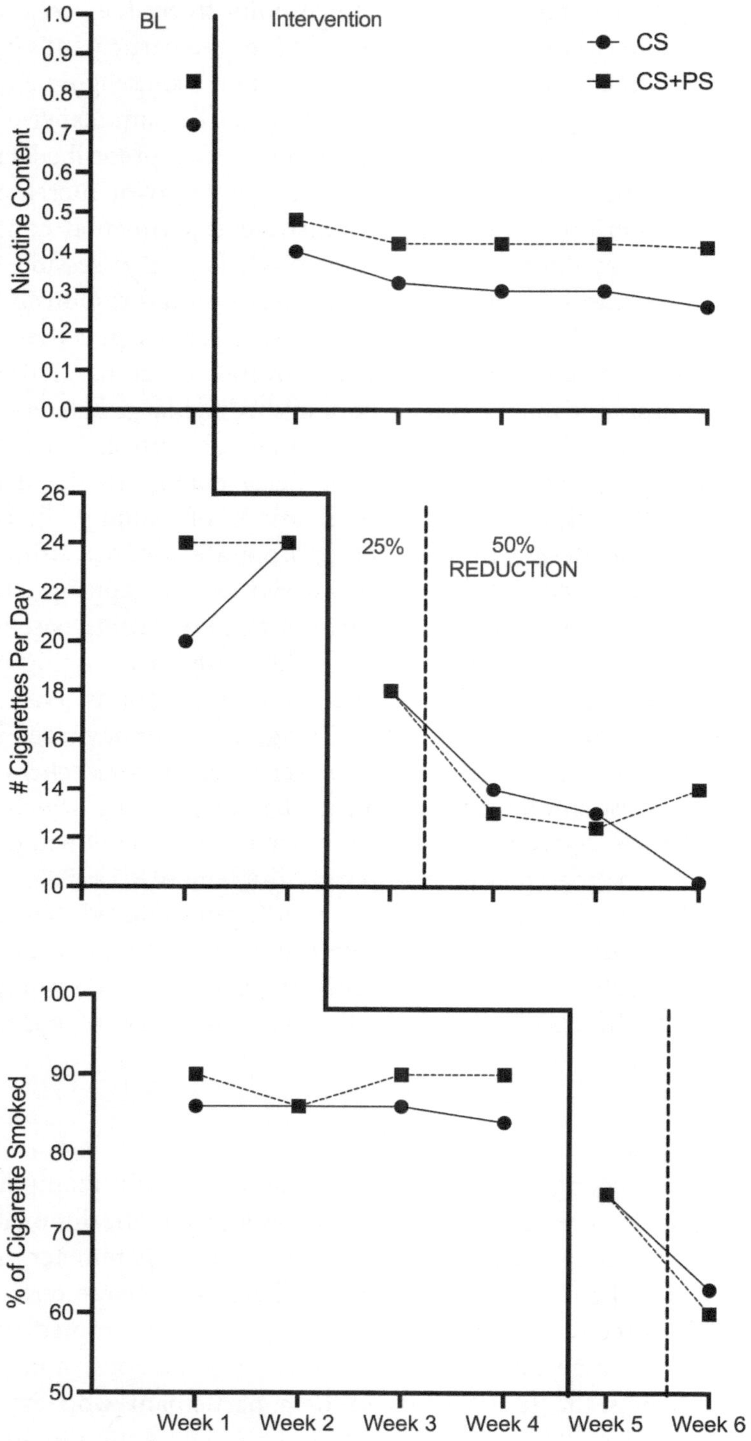

Figure 8. Hypothetical data of changing criterion design modeled after Malott et al. (1984). See published data for actual data and full context.

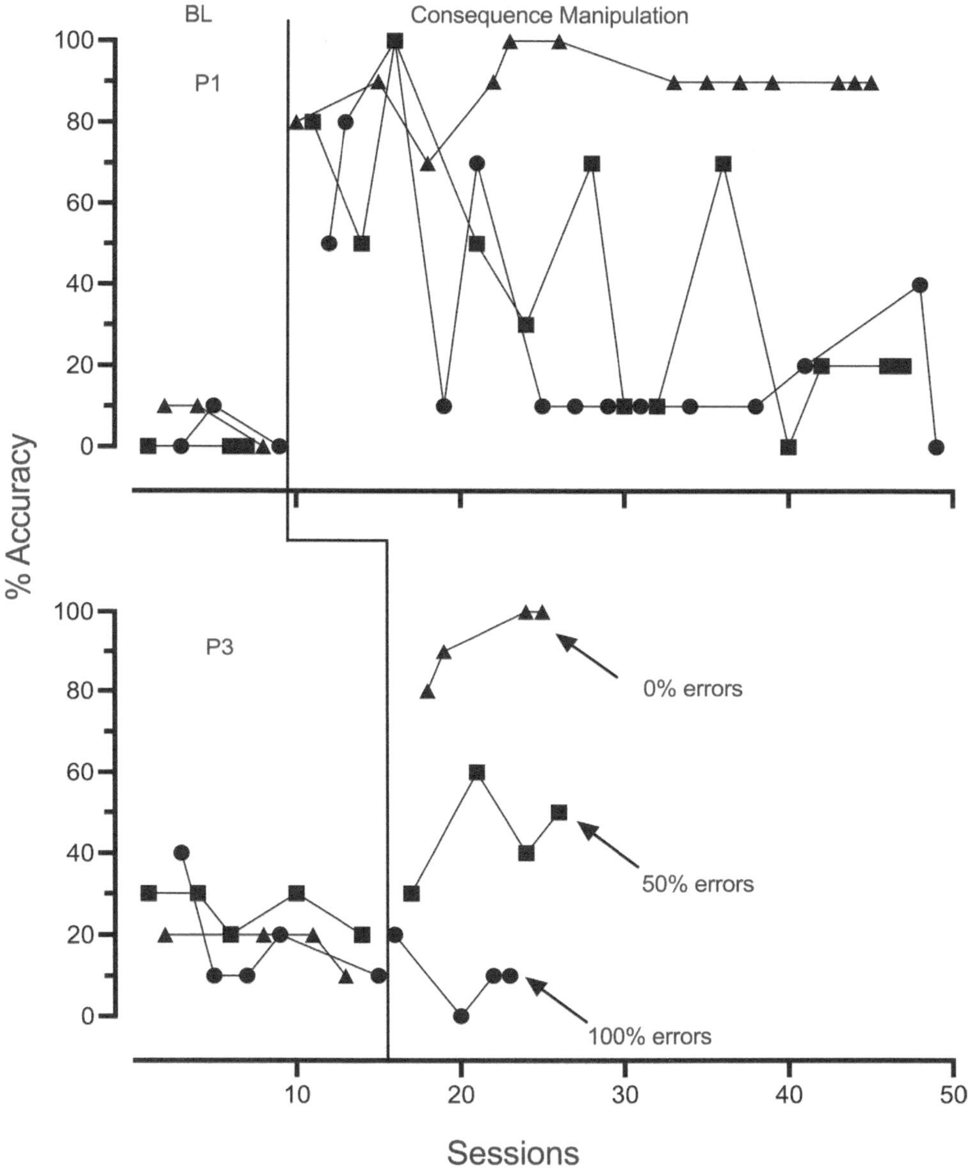

Figure 9. Hypothetical data of parametric analysis modeled after DiGennaro Reed et al. (2011). See published data for actual data and full context.

From an organizational standpoint, determining the ideal parameters of an independent variable could save an organization resources while producing effective results.

DiGennaro Reed, Reed, Catania, and Maguire (2011) used a parametric analysis to determine the effects of teaching errors on participant responding during discrete trial instruction of a match-to-sample task. Figure 9 shows this analysis, which was conducted using a multielement comparison within a multiple baseline design. During baseline, the researchers demonstrated that participating children with autism had not acquired the target skill (i.e., matching number cards). During consequence manipulation, the researcher introduced errors into the teaching procedure by manipulating the proportion of trials featuring consequence errors (0%, 50%, or 100% errors of commission). The participating children with autism performed best under teaching conditions that did not contain errors. This knowledge could impact how organizations train behavior technicians or provide ongoing coaching to decrease the likelihood of teaching errors. By manipulating the proportion of trials with errors, the researchers could systematically observe that perfect teaching integrity produced better learning outcomes compared to teaching that featured errors. The results from this experiment and other parametric analyses in OBM could have implications for efficient and effective training practices.

Component analysis

A component analysis (also known as a dismantling study) systematically evaluates components of an intervention to determine each component's effect on the dependent variable (Wolery, Gast, & Ledford, 2014). Intervention packages containing several independent variables are common in OBM research; thus, it can be valuable to determine the most efficacious components of the intervention package. It is possible that a component analysis could indicate that all the components are unnecessary to demonstrate an effect on the dependent variable. From an OBM perspective, including only the most efficacious components within a packaged intervention could result in reductions in the time needed for participants to be trained or for the intervention to be implemented, thereby saving organizations both time and resources.

Researchers can adopt a variety of single-case designs to complete a component analysis. Ward-Horner and Sturmey (2012) used a multielement design to assess which components of behavior skills training (BST) were critical for training the accuracy of conducting an assessment. The researchers individually assessed modeling, rehearsal, and feedback on separate portions of the assessment using a multielement design within an ABC design with one participant (Sandy; see Figure 10) and within an ABCD design

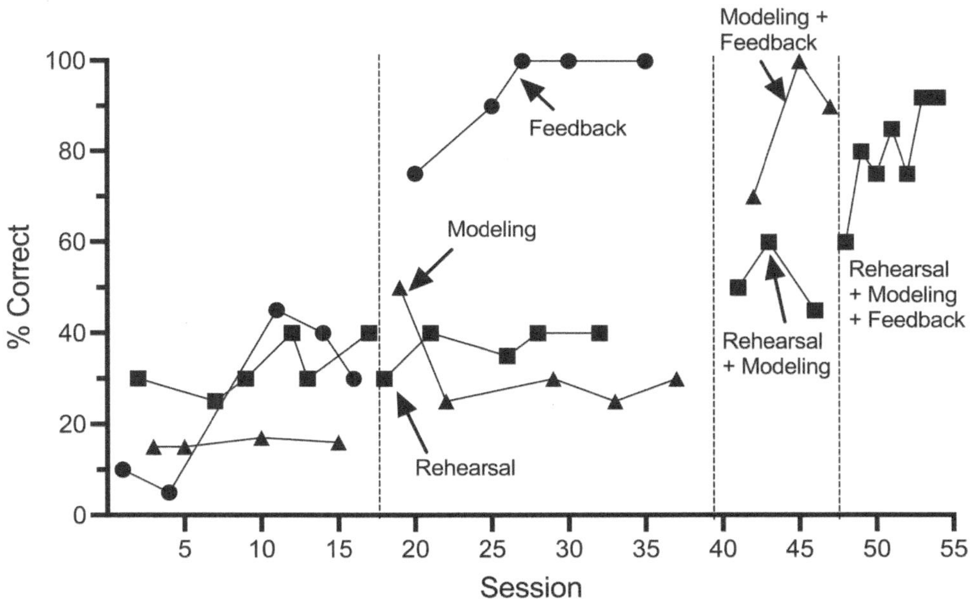

Figure 10. Hypothetical data of component analysis modeled after Ward-Horner and Sturmey (2012). See published data for actual data and full context.

with the remaining two participants (Carol and Debby). Notice in Figure 10 that accuracy did not substantially increase with the introduction of rehearsal compared to baseline containing written instructions. Accuracy substantially increased, however, when modeling was introduced for Carol and Sandy and when feedback was introduced with all three participants. The arrangement of this component analysis allowed the researchers to observe that modeling and feedback were the most effective components of BST, whereas written instructions and rehearsal were ineffective.

The above section describes the most common single-case designs. Although each design is described on its own, an OBM researcher may find it beneficial – based on the research question or other relevant variables – to combine elements of multiple single-case designs to best answer their research question. One example of such an approach is the embedding of a withdrawal or multielement design within a multiple baseline design, and it is not uncommon for researchers to adopt this strategy. As noted by Sidman, there are no set rules for scientific practice, but there are certain ways productive scientists act (1960, 2002). We encourage OBM researchers to adopt such an approach and to view experimental design from the perspective of a productive scientist rather than as a concrete set of rules.

Group designs

OBM researchers may find themselves in a situation where their question of investigation may be particularly well-suited or more appropriately answered – given methodological or environmental constraints – using a group-based design. From a procedural perspective, group designs provide behavior-analytic researchers with an additional set of methodological techniques to evaluate questions of interest regarding the impact of an independent variable on a dependent variable. Like single-case designs, group designs can vary in their level of experimental rigor, from quasi-experimental (e.g., one-group posttest only) to more controlled experimental (e.g., pretest–posttest control group, factorial) designs (Christensen, Johnson, & Turner, 2011; Shadish et al., 2002).

Several premises and assumptions must be met for an experiment to demonstrate a high degree of experimental control when using a group design. At a minimum, these methodological premises include experimental manipulation of one or more independent variables on a dependent variable (e.g., the use of a treatment and control group) and random assignment of participants between or across conditions (Shadish et al., 2002). Many of the considerations regarding recommended practices and ways to control for threats to validity (i.e., extraneous variables and experimental confounds) discussed in the section on single-case design also apply here. For a more detailed discussion on topic of validity in group design methodology, we encourage readers to review Shadish et al. (2002).

Experimentation using group design methodology can be broadly categorized into two types: between-subjects and within-subjects designs. Whereas a between-subjects design evaluates aggregated behavior between two or more groups with varying experimental conditions, a within-subjects design evaluates behavior in multiple conditions using the same group of participants. Thus, the notable methodological difference is how and to whom the researcher applies the independent variable and under what conditions. More information regarding design variations, including a brief overview, with methodological strengths, weaknesses, and a published example in the OBM literature, is provided below.

Between-subjects design

A between-subjects design is a type of design with two or more experimental conditions, with each condition consisting of a different group of participants (i.e., independent samples). This type of methodological design, at a minimum, involves the comparison of two levels of an independent variable (e.g., a treatment and a control condition) on a dependent variable. Methodological strengths of a between-subjects design include procedural controls that help to limit various potential experimental confounds and extraneous variables including history, maturation, and order effects.

However, there are also several limitations of a between-subjects design, including threats to the internal and external validity of the findings. Some threats to internal validity include sample variations (e.g., individual differences) between conditions and the potential for a limited number of testing observations – an artifact of the experimental design. With regard to the use of such a design in OBM research, a between-subjects design may be used when there are limited opportunities to collect data, limited resources to observe behavior over extended periods of time, or environmental restrictions inhibiting the ability to observe behavior at the individual level.

A between-subjects design may also be appropriate when the purpose of a research question is to evaluate the effects of a one-time intervention. For example, LeBlanc, Sump, Leaf, and Cihon (2020) employed a group design to compare standard and enhanced data sheets on the procedural integrity with which behavior therapists correctly implemented recommended practices when ordering and counterbalancing learning opportunities (i.e., trials) using a teaching procedure known as discrete trial instruction. The researchers randomly assigned participants to one of the two experimental conditions, matching each group to control for variability regarding length of experience. Using this design, LeBlanc et al. were able to assess the efficacy of each type of data sheet across participants, thus providing the researchers with data that could be used to inform training practices.

Matched pairs. A matched pairs design is a type of between-subjects design where groups are arranged based on important characteristics or variables (e.g., age, level of experience) presumed to impact performance on the dependent measure. Methodological strengths of a matched pairs design include procedural controls for threats to internal validity such as history, maturation, and putative individual differences,[4] as potential extraneous variables affecting the results. Methodological weaknesses include threats to internal validity such as non-controlled individual differences and limited testing observations and threats to external validity such as interaction effects due to selection biases.

Moon, Lee, Lee, and Oah (2017) embedded a matched pairs component into their methodological procedures when evaluating the effects of feedback content type (social comparison vs. objective feedback) of high vs. low performers on a simulated bank-money-transfer task. The matched pairs component involved participant completion of a 20-min pre-session exposure to the work task followed by assignment of the upper 40% and lower 40% of performers to each of their respective groups. The incorporation of the matched pairs component permitted the researchers to evaluate potential variations in the effects of feedback content type across the two performance levels.

Factorial design. A factorial design is a type of between-subjects design that consists of a manipulation or observation of two or more variables to study their joint and separate influence on a dependent variable (Zedeck, 2014). Depending on the number of manipulations and experimental conditions, factorial designs can vary greatly in their level of complexity and, subsequently, the amount of data they provide. Factorial designs produce two types of effects: a main effect, which refers to the effect of one independent variable on the dependent variable, and an interaction effect, which refers to the effect of a combination (i.e., two or more) of independent variables on a dependent variable. Advantages for using a factorial design include the opportunity for researchers to test two or more hypotheses at the same time as well as the ability to assess any potential combinatorial effects. Methodological strengths also include many of those described previously for between-subjects designs. Methodological weaknesses – and ones that may be of particular relevance to the OBM researcher – include limitations to the generalizability of the findings and ability to use such a design in non-laboratory-based (i.e., field) studies due to the highly controlled nature of the procedures (Shadish et al., 2002).

Park, Johnson, Moon, and Lee (2019) used a factorial design to evaluate the effects of feedback frequency (frequent vs. infrequent) and specificity (specific vs. global) on a computerized order-fulfilling task. Using college undergraduates as participants, the researchers assessed both main and interaction effects on order-fulfilling error rates, their primary dependent variable. This methodological arrangement provided the researchers with the opportunity to observe potential main effects for feedback frequency and feedback specificity as well as interaction effects between the two independent variables. As a result, the researchers found little effect of specificity on performance when controlling for frequent feedback delivery. However, when feedback delivery was infrequent, feedback specificity impacted participant performance. Thus, the use of a factorial design provided the researchers with the ability to preliminarily indicate that the specificity of feedback may not be as important if feedback is delivered on a frequent schedule.

Within-subjects design

A within-subjects design (also referred to as a repeated-measure design) is a type of experimental design wherein each participant experiences two or more experimental conditions. When compared to a between-subjects design, methodological advantages include fewer participants needed to conduct the experiment and better experimental control over individual differences as a potential extraneous variable, thereby enhancing sensitivity and the ability to detect an effect (Christensen, 2012). Disadvantages to using a within-subjects design include potential threats to internal validity (e.g., order effects, carryover effects, maturation, multiple-treatment interference, and attrition) as well as threats to the external (e.g., ecological and population) validity as it relates to the generalizability of the results to other participants and settings.

An example of a within-subjects design in the OBM literature can be found in Experiment 2 of Palmer, Johnson, and Johnson (2015). In this experiment, the researchers embedded a repeated measures component into a factorial design to evaluate the effects of numerical accuracy on a computer check processing data entry task. The repeated measures component allowed the researchers to assess the effects of the different types of feedback at both the session level and cumulatively (i.e., over multiple sessions) as well as the opportunity to collect baseline levels of performance prior to the feedback manipulation.

Mixed methods design

Under the right experimental conditions or given various environmental parameters, an OBM researcher may also be interested in using a mixed methods design. Several definitions for a mixed methods design have emerged in the literature and, although there are similarities between the definitions, two types may be of interest to the OBM researcher, with a noteworthy point of deviation between the two. For example, a mixed methods design has been defined as a "type of research in which a researcher or team of researchers combines elements of qualitative and quantitative research approaches [e.g., use of qualitative and quantitative viewpoints, data collection, analysis, inference techniques] for the broad purposes of breadth and depth of understanding and corroboration" (Johnson, Onwuegbuzie, & Turner, 2007, p. 123). Based on these criteria, experiments combining a group methodology (i.e., *quantitative*) and open-ended social validity questions (i.e., *qualitative*; Wolf, 1978) to inform the results and interpretation of an intervention would be just one example of its use in OBM research. Alternatively, quantitative research methodology has also referred to a mixed methods design as a type of experimental design that combines methodological components from both between-subject and within-subject procedures (Christensen, 2012).

Using a mixed methods framework, Johnson and Dickinson (2012) evaluated the effects of three variations of computer-based instruction (CBI) – standard instruction, instruction plus incentives and disincentives, and instruction plus postfeedback delays – on participant learning of instructional content and satisfaction with the intervention. Initially, the researchers employed a between-subject component using a pre–post design to assess differences in performance between the variations of CBI. Subsequently, upon completion of the posttest, the researchers used an alternating treatments (i.e., within-subject) design to assess participant satisfaction with the variations of CBI. Overall, the researchers found higher posttest scores, yet lower satisfaction, for the postfeedback delays condition when compared to the other two conditions.

Power analysis

When using a group design and making inferences via statistics, a critical variable to take into consideration is statistical power, which refers to the ability of a statistical test to detect a difference (i.e., an effect) if in fact such a difference exists (Cohen, 1962, 1988; Kyonka, 2019). As a statistical measure, power – which can be conceptualized as a type of test sensitivity – is dependent on four parameters including (a) sample size, (b) hypothesized effect size, (c) variability, and (d) significance level (Motulsky, 2018).

Researchers can conduct an a priori power analysis to obtain quantitative information about the most appropriate parameters and criteria to use for a proposed experiment – including sample size and the minimum number of participants to assign to each condition. A power analysis can be completed using one of several software programs (e.g., G*Power [Erdfelder, Faul, & Buchner, 1996]; powerandsamplesize.com) that are freely available to users across computer platforms and operating systems. Recommended practice is for a power analysis to be conducted *a priori* as opposed to *retrospectively*, especially when researchers plan to use inferential statistics when interpreting results (Faul, Erdfelder, Lang, & Buchner, 2007[5]; Hoenig & Heisey, 2001). "To consult the statistician after an experiment is finished is often merely to ask him to conduct a postmortem examination. He can perhaps say what the experiment died of" (Fisher, 1938).

Conclusion

This article provides a summary of experimental designs and approaches to research found within the field of OBM. We have attempted to review designs spanning the basic-to-applied continuum using both single-case and group designs; we also discuss potential tradeoffs, threats to reliability and validity, and other notable variables of consideration. This summary is not an exhaustive account of all relevant scientific activities regarding methodology. For example, we did not describe quality indicators in research, such as independent and dependent variable reliability (i.e., procedural integrity and interobserver agreement, respectively), human subject research considerations (e.g., consent, protections), or researcher behavior regarding the interpretation of findings, to name a few. Omission of these and other related areas does not relegate these activities as unimportant; in fact, it is the contrary – such activities are vital to, and a requisite for, conducting high-quality experimental research.

With its rich literature, OBM now has decades of research demonstrating the implementation of various experimental methods and their use to answer questions across both laboratory and field settings – an outcome we have attempted to highlight through noting the range and diversity of designs and approaches. This literature provides researchers with exemplar methods that demonstrate strong experimental rigor as well as a foundation from which to use and extend these methodological practices to address new questions, variables, and workplace topics of societal importance.

> Regard no practice as immutable. Change and be ready to change again. Accept no eternal verity. Experiment. (Skinner, 1979, p. 346)

Notes

1. Translational OBM studies do not always recruit undergraduate participants. Some experiments have been conducted with employees while at work, but may involve a simulated task (e.g., Wilder, Therrien, & Wine, 2006).
2. Direct replication refers to repeated demonstrations of an experimental effect under similar conditions, wherein the primary purpose is to establish the reliability of findings (i.e., the phenomenon under observation; Sidman, 1960, pp. 73–109). Systematic replication is an extension of direct replication, wherein the generality of the findings is extended by repeated demonstrations of an effect under varying experimental conditions (Sidman, 1960, pp. 110–139).
3. A reversal design is noted when the independent variable is presented contingently and noncontingently on the target behavior and another behavior in the functional class. This design feature differs slightly from a withdrawal design in which the independent variable is presented and removed.
4. The control of individual differences refers to greater experimental control of variability related to the variable(s) upon which groups are arranged.
5. We encourage readers to review Faul et al. (2007) for an excellent tutorial on G*Power.

Disclosure statement

No potential conflict of interest was reported by the authors.

References

Alavosius, M. P., & Sulzer-Azaroff, M. (1986). The effects of performance feedback on the safety of client lifting and transfer. *Journal of Applied Behavior Analysis, 19*(3), 261–267. doi:10.1901/jaba.1986.19-261

Baer, D. M., Wolf, M. M., & Risley, T. R. (1968). Some current dimensions of applied behavior analysis. *Journal of Applied Behavior Analysis, 1*(1), 91–97. doi:10.1901/jaba.1968.1-91

Balcazar, F., Shupert, M., Daniels, A. C., Mawhinney, T. C., & Hopkins, B. L. (1989). An objective review and analysis of ten years of publication in the *Journal of Organizational Behavior Management*. *Journal of Organizational Behavior Management, 10*(1), 7–37. doi:10.1300/J075v10n01_02

Barlow, D. H., Nock, M. K., & Hersen, M. (2009). *Single case experimental designs: Strategies for studying behavior change* (3rd ed.). Boston, MA: Pearson.

Baron, A., & Perone, M. (1998). Experimental design and analysis in the laboratory study of human operant behavior. In K. A. Lattal & M. Perone (Eds.), *Handbook of research methods in human operant behavior* (pp. 45–91). Plenum. doi:10.1007/978-1-4899-1947-2_3

Bourret, J. C., & Pietras, C. J. (2013). Visual analysis in single-case research. In G. J. Madden, W. V. Dube, T. D. Hackenberg, G. P. Hanley, & K. A. Lattal (Eds.), *APA handbook of behavior analysis: Vol. 1. Methods and principles* (pp. 199–217). American Psychological Association. doi:10.1037/13937-009

Bucklin, B. R., McGee, H. M., & Dicksinson, A. M. (2003). The effects of individual monetary incentives with and without feedback. *Journal of Organizational Behavior Management, 23* (2), 65–94. doi:10.1300/J075v23n02_05

Campbell, D., & Stanley, J. (1963). *Experimental and quasi-experimental designs for research.* Chicago, IL: Rand-McNally.

Carr, J. E. (2005). Recommendations for reporting multiple-baseline designs across participants. *Behavioral Interventions, 20*(3), 219–224. doi:10.1002/bin.191

Christensen, L. B. (2012). Types of designs using random assignment. In H. E. Cooper, P. M. Camic, D. L. Long, A. T. Panter, D. E. Rindskopf, & K. J. Sher (Eds.), *APA handbook of research methods in psychology: Vol 2. Research designs: Quantitative, qualitative, neuropsychological, and biological.* American Psychological Association. doi:10.1037/13620-000

Christensen, L. B., Johnson, R. B., & Turner, L. A. (2011). *Research methods, design, and analysis* (11th ed.). Boston, MA: Pearson.

Cohen, J. (1962). The statistical power of abnormal-social psychological research: A review. *Journal of Abnormal & Social Psychology, 65*(3), 145–153. doi:10.1037/h0045186

Cohen, J. (1988). *Statistical power analysis for the behavioral sciences* (2nd ed.). Mahwah, NJ: Lawrence Erlbaum.

Coon, J. C., & Rapp, J. T. (2017). Application of multiple baseline designs in behavior analytic research: Evidence for the influence of new guidelines. *Behavioral Interventions, 33*(2), 160–172. doi:10.1002/bin.1510

Cooper, J. O., Heron, T. E., & Heward, W. L. (2020). *Applied behavior analysis* (3rd ed.). Hoboken, NJ: Pearson.

Critchfield, T. S. (2011). Translational contributions of the experimental analysis of behavior. *The Behavior Analyst, 34*(1), 3–17. doi:10.1007/BF03392227

DiGennaro Reed, F. D., Henley, A. J., Rueb, S., Crabbs, B., & Giacalone, L. (2016). Discussion of behavioral principles in *Journal of Organizational Behavior Management*: An update. *Journal of Organizational Behavior Management, 36*(2–3), 202–209. doi:10.1080/01608061.2016.1200938

DiGennaro Reed, F. D., Reed, D. D., Catania, C., & Maguire, H. (2011). A parametric analysis of errors of commission during discrete trial training. *Journal of Applied Behavior Analysis, 44*, 611–615. doi:10.1901/jaba.2011.44-611

Downing, C. O., Jr., Capriola, N., & Geller, E. S. (2018). Preventing credit-card fraud: A goal-setting and prompting intervention to increase cashiers' ID-checking behavior. *Journal of Organizational Behavior Management, 38*(4), 335–344. doi:10.1080/01608061.2018.1514349

Erdfelder, E., Faul, F., & Buchner, A. (1996). GPOWER: A general power analysis program. *Behavior Research Methods, Instruments, & Computers, 28*(1), 1–11. doi:10.3758/BF03203630

Faul, F., Erdfelder, E., Lang, A. G., & Buchner, A. (2007). G* Power 3: A flexible statistical power analysis program for the social, behavioral, and biomedical sciences. *Behavior Research Methods, 39*(2), 175–191. doi:10.3758/BF03193146

Fisher, R. A. (1938). Presidential address to the First Indian Statistical Congress. *Sankhya: The Indian Journal of Statistics, 4*, 14–17.

Fox, D. K., Hopkins, B. L., & Anger, W. K. (1987). The long-term effects of a token economy on safety performance in open-pit mining. *Journal of Applied Behavior Analysis, 20*(3), 215–224. doi:10.1901/jaba.1987.20-215

Gast, D. L., & Baekey, D. H. (2014). Withdrawal and reversal designs. In D. L. Gast & J. R. Ledford (Eds.), *Single case research methodology: Applications in special education and behavioral sciences* (pp. 211–250). New York, NY: Routledge. doi:10.4324/9780203521892-10

Gast, D. L., Lloyd, B. P., & Ledford, J. R. (2018). Multiple baseline and multiple probe designs. In J. R. Ledford & D. L. Gast (Eds.), *Single case research methodology*. New York, NY: Routledge/Taylor & Francis Group. doi:10.4324/9781315150666

Gravina, N., Villacorta, J., Albert, K., Clark, R., Curry, S., & Wilder, D. (2018). A literature review of organizational behavior management interventions in human service settings from 1990 to 2016. *Journal of Organizational Behavior Management, 38*(2–3), 191–224. doi:10.1080/01608061.2018.1454872

Griffin, M., Gravina, N. E., Matey, N., Pritchard, J., & Wine, B. (2019). Using scorecards and a lottery to improve the performance of behavior technicians in two autism treatment clinics. *Journal of Organizational Behavior Management, 39*(3–4), 280–292. doi:10.1080/01608061.2019.1632241

Hake, D. F. (1982). The basic-applied continuum and the possible evolution of human operant social and verbal research. *The Behavior Analyst, 5*(1), 21–28. doi:10.1007/BF03393137

Hartmann, D. P., & Hall, R. V. (1976). The changing criterion design. *Journal of Applied Behavior Analysis, 9*(4), 527–532. doi:10.1901/jaba.1976.9-527

Henley, A. J., & DiGennaro Reed, F. D. (2015). Should you order the feedback sandwich? Efficacy of feedback sequence and timing. *Journal of Organizational Behavior Management, 35*(3–4), 321–335. doi:10.1080/01608061.2015.1093057

Hoenig, J. M., & Heisey, D. M. (2001). The abuse of power: The pervasive fallacy of power calculations for data analysis. *The American Statistician, 55*(1), 19–24. doi:10.1198/000313001300339897

Horner, R. D., & Baer, D. M. (1978). Multiple-probe technique: A variation on the multiple baseline. *Journal of Applied Behavior Analysis, 11*(1), 189–196. doi:10.1901/jaba.1987.11-189

Johnson, D. A., & Dickinson, A. M. (2012). Using postfeedback delays to improve retention of computer-based instruction. *The Psychological Record, 62*(3), 485–496. doi:10.1007/BF03395815

Johnson, D. A., Dickinson, A. M., & Huitema, B. E. (2008). The effects of objective feedback on performance when individuals receive fixed and individual incentive pay. *Performance Improvement Quarterly, 20*(3–4), 53–74. doi:10.1002/piq.20003

Johnson, R. B., Onwuegbuzie, A. J., & Turner, L. A. (2007). Toward a definition of mixed methods research. *Journal of Mixed Methods Research, 1*(2), 112–133. doi:10.1177/1558689806298224

Johnston, J. M., & Pennypacker, H. S. (2009). *Strategies and tactics of behavioral research* (3rd ed.). New York, NY: Routledge.

Kazdin, A. E. (2002). *Research design in clinical psychology* (4th ed.). Boston, MA: Pearson.

Kazdin, A. E. (2011). *Single-case research designs: Methods for clinical and applied settings* (2nd ed.). New York, NY: Oxford University Press.

Komaki, J. L., & Goltz, S. M. (2001). Within-group research designs: Going beyond program evaluation questions. In C. M. Johnson, W. K. Redmon, & T. C. Mawhinney (Eds.), *Handbook of organizational performance: Behavior analysis and management* (pp. 81–137). Binghamton, NY: Haworth Press.

Kyonka, E. G. E. (2019). Tutorial: Small-N power analysis. *Perspectives on Behavior Science, 42*(1), 133–152. doi:10.1007/s40614-018-0167-4

LeBlanc, L. A., Sump, L. A., Leaf, J. B., & Cihon, J. (2020). The effects of standard and enhanced data sheets and brief video training on implementation of conditional discrimination training. *Behavior Analysis in Practice, 13*(1), 53–62. doi:10.1007/s40617-019-00338-5

Ledford, J. R., & Gast, D. L. (Eds.). (2014). *Single case research methodology: Applications in special education and behavioral sciences.* New York, NY: Routledge.

Lerman, D. C., Iwata, B. A., & Hanley, G. P. (2013). Applied behavior analysis. In G. J. Madden, W. V. Dube, T. D. Hackenberg, G. P. Hanley, & K. A. Lattal (Eds.), *APA handbook of behavior analysis: Vol. 1. Methods and principles* (pp. 81–104). American Psychological Association. doi:10.1037/13937-004

Mace, F. C., & Critchfield, T. S. (2010). Translational research in behavior analysis: Historical traditions and imperative for the future. *Journal of the Experimental Analysis of Behavior, 93* (3), 293–312. doi:10.1901/jeab.2010.93-293

Malott, J. M., Glasgow, R. E., O'Neill, H. K., & Klesges, R. C. (1984). Co-worker social support in a worksite smoking control program. *Journal of Applied Behavior Analysis, 17*(4), 485–495. doi:10.1901/jaba.1984.17-485

McGee, H. M., & Johnson, D. A. (2015). Performance motivation as the behaviorist views it. *Performance Improvement, 54*(4), 15–21. doi:10.1002/pfi.21472

Moon, K., Lee, K., Lee, K., & Oah, S. (2017). The effects of social comparison and objective feedback on work performance across different performance levels. *Journal of Organizational Behavior Management, 37*(1), 63–74. doi:10.1080/01608061.2016.1236059

Motulsky, H. (2018). *Intuitive biostatistics: A nonmathematical guide to statistical thinking* (4th ed.). New York, NY: Oxford University Press.

Nolan, T. V., Jarema, K. A., & Austin, J. (1999). An objective review of the *Journal of Organizational Behavior Management. Journal of Organizational Behavior Management, 19*(3), 83–114. doi:10.1300/J075v19n03_09

Normand, M., Bucklin, B., & Austin, J. (1999). The discussion of behavioral principles in *JOBM. Journal of Organizational Behavior Management, 19*(3), 45–56. doi:10.1300/J075v19n03_04

Palmer, M. G., Johnson, C. M., & Johnson, D. A. (2015). Objective performance feedback: Is numerical accuracy necessary? *Journal of Organizational Behavior Management, 35*(3–4), 206–239. doi:10.1080/01608061.2015.1093059

Park, J., Johnson, D. A., Moon, K., & Lee, J. (2019). The interaction effects of frequency and specificity of feedback on work performance. *Journal of Organizational Behavior Management, 39*(3–4), 164–178. doi:10.1080/01608061.2019.1632242

Parker, R. I., & Vannest, K. (2009). An improved effect size for single-case research: Nonoverlap of all pairs. *Behavior Therapy, 40*(4), 357–367. doi:10.1016/j.beth.2008.10.006

Parsons, M. B., Schepis, M. M., Reid, D. R., McCarn, J. E., & Green, C. W. (1987). Expanding the impact of behavioral staff management: A large-scale, long-term application in schools serving severely handicapped students. *Journal of Applied Behavior Analysis, 20*(2), 139–150. doi:10.1901/jaba.1987.20-139

Perone, M., & Hursh, D. E. (2013). Single-case experimental designs. In G. J. Madden, W. V. Dube, T. D. Hackenberg, G. P. Hanley, & K. A. Lattal (Eds.), *APA handbook of behavior analysis: Vol. 1. Methods and principles* (pp. 107–126). American Psychological Association. doi:10.1037/13937-005

Petursdottir, A. I., & Carr, J. E. (2018). Applying the taxonomy of validity threats from mainstream research design to single-case experiments in applied behavior analysis. *Behavior Analysis in Practice, 11*(3), 228–240. doi:10.1007/s40617-018-00294-6

Shadish, W. R., Cook, T. D., & Campbell, D. T. (2002). *Experimental and quasi-experimental designs for generalized causal inference.* Boston, MA: Houghton Mifflin.

Sidman, M. (1960). *Tactics of scientific research: Evaluating experimental data in psychology*. Boston, MA: Basic Books.

Sidman, M. (2002). Notes from the beginning of time. *The Behavior Analyst, 25*(1), 3–13. doi:10.1007/BF03392040

Skinner, B. F. (1959). *Cumulative record*. New York, NY: Appleton-Century Crofts.

Skinner, B. F. (1965). *Science and human behavior*. New York, NY: Free Press.

Skinner, B. F. (1979). *The shaping of a behaviorist*. New York, NY: Knopf.

Smith, M., & Wilder, D. A. (2018). The use of the performance diagnostic checklist-human services to assess and improve the job performance of individuals with intellectual disabilities. *Behavior Analysis in Practice, 11*(2), 148–153. doi:10.1007/s40617-018-0213-4

Stokes, D. E. (1997). *Pasteur's quadrant: Basic science and technological innovation*. Washington, DC: Brookings Institution Press.

Therrien, K., Wilder, D. A., Rodriguez, M., & Wine, B. (2005). Preintervention analysis and improvement of customer greeting in a restaurant. *Journal of Applied Behavior Analysis, 38* (3), 411.415. doi:10.1901/jaba.2005.89-04

VanStelle, S. E., Vicars, S. M., Harr, V., Miguel, C. F., Koerber, J. L., Kazbour, R., & Austin, J. (2012). The publication history of the *Journal of Organizational Behavior Management*: An objective review and analysis: 1998–2009. *Journal of Organizational Behavior Management, 32*(2), 93–123. doi:10.1080/01608061.2012.675864

Vergason, C. M., & Gravina, N. E. (2020). Using a guest- and confederate-delivered token economy to increase employee–guest interactions at a zoo. *Journal of Applied Behavior Analysis, 53*(1), 422–430. doi:10.1002/jaba.599

Ward-Horner, J., & Sturmey, P. (2012). Component analysis of behavior skills training in functional analysis. *Behavioral Interventions, 27*(2), 75–92. doi:10.1002/bin.1339

Wilder, D. A., Austin, J., & Casella, S. (2009). Applying behavior analysis in organizations: Organizational behavior management. *Psychological Services, 6*, 202–211. doi:10.1037/a0015393

Wilder, D. A., Lipschultz, J. L., King, A., Driscoll, S., & Sigurdsson, S. (2018). An analysis of the commonality and type of preintervention assessment procedures in the *Journal of Organizational Behavior Management* (2000–2015). *Journal of Organizational Behavior Management, 38*(1), 5–17. doi:10.1080/01608061.2017.1325822

Wilder, D. A., Therrien, K., & Wine, B. (2006). A comparison between survey and verbal choice methods of identifying potential reinforcers among employees. *Journal of Organizational Behavior Management, 25*(4), 1–13. doi:10.1300/J075v25n04_01

Wolery, M., Gast, D. L., & Ledford, J. R. (2014). Comparison designs. In D. L. Gast & J. R. Ledford (Eds.), *Single case research methodology* (pp. 297–345). New York, NY: Routledge.

Wolf, M. M. (1978). Social validity: The case for subjective measurement or how applied behavior analysis is finding its heart. *Journal of Applied Behavior Analysis, 11*(2), 203–214. doi:10.1901/jaba.1978.11-203

Zedeck, S. (Ed.). (2014). *APA dictionary of statistics and research methods*. American Psychological Association. doi:10.1037/14336-000

Common Antecedent Strategies within Organizational Behavior Management: The Use of Goal Setting, Task Clarification, and Job Aids

Eunju Choi and Douglas A. Johnson

ABSTRACT

Despite organizational behavior management placing a great deal of emphasis on interventions that alter consequences for performance, antecedent interventions play an important role in the practice of our field. Antecedent interventions utilizing variables such as goal setting, task clarification, and job aids are common. Each of these variables are examined in terms of research findings and potential behavioral functions. Being well-versed in such outcomes should inform both researchers and practitioners in their efforts to identify efficient and cost-effective solutions for workplace performance.

Our world is flooded with events competing to induce our behavior. A brief tour of a typical office setting quickly identifies a rich tapestry of stimuli fighting for our attention: the notification from the computer as a new e-mail arrives, signs and post-it notes reminders, a display stating the company's mission, the sight of your coworker about to ask a favor, and the sight of the supervisor approaching with a forthcoming demand. Such objects and events are considered various forms of antecedents, stimuli which occur before and exert control over behavior (Martin & Pear, 2019). Antecedents are often stated as *triggering* or *stimulating* behavior (Daniels & Bailey, 2014). This contrasts with consequences, which are stimuli that temporally follow the behavior of interest. It is often implied, if not outright stated, that antecedents only exercise a small impact on behavior. Some authors suggest antecedents exert only 20% influence on behavior, whereas consequences exert 80% (Biteler, 2008; Braksick, 2007). Such non-empirical derivations of the Pareto principle attempt to quantify the relative impact of the components that constitute targeted behavioral relations, but these statements are potentially misleading. Misleads may be understandable considering organizational consultants routinely deal with clients whose standard solutions are to implement trainings, distribute memos and edicts, and to threaten, cajole, and/or harass subordinates (Daniels, 2016). Such techniques can be subsumed under the general category of antecedent control and consultants likely want to redirect the focus of their clients to oft-neglected variables of consequent control. However, such simple categorization may create artificial boundaries that are permeable in practice.

When behavior occurs in the natural environment, there is rarely a clear-cut method for attributing a percentage of that performance to antecedent or consequent control (with occasional exceptions such as respondent behaviors which are completely controlled by antecedent stimuli), especially considering operant behavior is multiply determined. Adding to the complexity of identifying controlling variables is that the delivery of a consequence may generate lasting antecedent effects. For example, suppose an employee is paid a monetary incentive for increased productivity immediately following a work shift. Although the incentive is clearly a consequence for performance during the prior shift, it may induce the employee to describe the contingency of reinforcement as "If I produce more, then I may get paid more." Such contingency-specifying verbal stimuli may be repeatedly self-stated by the performer covertly, including immediately before their next shift and during several later shifts right before they are to engage in performance. This response-produced verbal antecedent may evoke rule-governed behavior resulting in higher performance (Agnew & Redmon, 1992; Malott, 1993). Although the monetary consequence was the variable that was explicitly delivered, antecedent control likely played a role that was equally important to the production of behavior, especially for verbally sophisticated organisms such as employees. A sustained improvement in performance over the duration of an entire subsequent work shift (perhaps even several workdays) could not persist under the control of a single consequence delivery many hours or days prior, at least not without continued verbally mediated aid from events such as antecedent rules.

It is also important to note that interventions that only target antecedents can be very successful even when explicit attention is not paid to consequences, such as a training procedure (the antecedent of interest) that brings performers into contact with existing natural sources of reinforcement. According to VanStelle et al. (2012), antecedent manipulations were the second most popular intervention utilized in the organizational behavior management (OBM) literature. Many other interventions classified by VanStelle et al. could potentially also function as antecedents, such as feedback or incentives that are delivered right before a session (Bechtel et al., 2015; Wine et al., 2019).

One advantage of antecedent interventions is that these can be both cost-effective and time efficient for companies when implemented properly. Suppose an organization wants to increase employee hand washing. To implement a consequence intervention, such as feedback, supervisors would have to observe the current status of employee hand washing to provide timely feedback. This may be both awkward and unfeasible in certain situations (e.g., male supervisor in female restroom) so providing reminder signs or sending out a memo to employees may be more practical. To better understand some strategies, this paper will review the literature on goals, task clarification, job aids, and checklists, since these are common examples of successful antecedent interventions in the literature.

Goal setting

Goal setting remains a simple yet effective antecedent intervention successfully implemented across many organizations. At its most basic level, goal setting involves specifying a criterion (i.e., goal) for performance (Daniels & Bailey, 2014). Beyond this initial requirement, implementation takes many forms. Goals can be self-set or determined by supervisors, easy or difficult to achieve, set for an individual or collectively set for a group of employees, broken into several sub-goals or just a single specified level, etc. The logic behind goal setting is similar to the logic for a changing criterion experimental design in that each phase entails specific goals to achieve (Erath et al., 2020), except in this context goal setting is the intervention itself rather than a methodology to evaluate another intervention. Wilk and Redmon (1998) provide an example of goal setting in which they investigated the effectiveness of goal setting and feedback on the productivity and satisfaction of clerical employees in a university admissions department. In consultation with the researchers, the supervisor provided a specific goal that included a precise number of tasks that employees needed to attain (e.g., enter application information on 55 students and update the records for 15 files) and was adjusted daily based upon previous performance and current workplace needs. A multiple baseline design across job roles was applied. During the intervention, individualized daily goal setting and verbal feedback were applied (praise if goal met and prompting if goal unmet). During phase two graphic feedback was added to the first intervention. The results showed both interventions significantly increased productivity and satisfaction among clerical employees. Furthermore, the effects successfully maintained at follow up.

Another representative goal setting study was conducted at a multinational manufacturing plant. Jessup and Stahelski (1999) investigated effects of an intervention package comprised of goal setting, feedback, and performance contingent rewards at a large aluminum smelter. During intervention in a reversal design, progressively more difficult goals were implemented for reductions of defective products with various rewards available for meeting established criteria. This intervention showed consistent reductions in defects, meeting both production and organizational goals that realized a significant cost savings (which was critical since competition and excessive supply had forced the business to reduce half of its operations). During the return to baseline, there was a clear increase in defective products, demonstrating the intervention package was responsible for prior improvements. The authors mentioned that feedback alone did not appear sufficient to improve performance because quality did not improve until a difficult-to-attain goal was set. Furthermore, goal setting in the absence of rewards and feedback (the reversal phase) also appeared ineffective, demonstrating the need for the packaged components.

Amigo et al. (2008) studied the effects of task clarification, goal setting, and feedback on employee busing time at a high-volume pizza restaurant. Busing behavior was defined and measured as the amount of time it took waitstaff to correctly clear dirty dishes and reset the table. Baseline data were collected for 2 weeks and the average busing time was over 300 seconds. During the first phase of intervention, employees were given a memo with task clarification and a goal set by managers to reduce table busing time to 180 seconds or less. During this initial phase busing time decreased to 284 seconds. In the second intervention phase, a mixture of individual verbal and graphic feedback as well as group feedback were delivered by managers weekly. Weekly group feedback was posted on a large graph in the back of the restaurant. Upon completion of this phase the average busing time was reduced to 152 seconds. Note that initial goals were only successfully met when feedback supplemented the initial intervention package. When feedback was removed during follow-up, busing times reversed to near baseline.

As illustrated with the above examples, goal setting is simply information about the standard by which performance is considered successful. Such goal setting has been shown to positively impact employee behavior across a variety of settings, job types, and research designs. Properly set goals can drive improved performance whereas improperly set performance goals run the risk of being ignored or even demotivating performers. Therefore, understanding potential variables for successful implementation of goal setting is important. The aforementioned studies already hinted at how goal setting can be enhanced or attenuated by the presence of other experimental variables. The variables that impact goal setting have been extensively investigated by both behavior analysts and traditional organizational psychologists. One widely investigated variable is degree of goal difficulty. For example, Roose and Williams (2018) examined different levels of goals (i.e., set at 150% and 175% of baseline performance) and two types of feedback on performance. A group design was used with participants receiving one of two goal levels and two different types of feedback. The authors found the types of feedback did not impact performance. However, as goal difficulty increased, the performance improved until goals became so difficult that performance could not improve. Similarly, Tammemagi et al. (2013), exposed 26 participants to a computer-based data entry task. Performance was measured during the first phase with no goal, then either a low attainable goal (i.e., 20 correct data entry in 12 minutes) followed by a high unattainable goal (i.e., 40 correct data entry in 12 minutes) counterbalanced with a group which got a high unattainable goal followed by a low attainable goal. Introducing the higher goal demand first showed a greater benefit for performance than leading with the lower goal demand, although performance deteriorated over time under unattainable conditions for both sequences. Ultimately, even though high goals stimulate performance, these short-term gains come with a risk of eventual loss in performance if employees do not contact reinforcement due to goals persistently beyond current skill levels. This summary was corroborated by Locke and Latham (1990), who reviewed 400 empirical research articles and found goal difficulty and performance have a linear relationship. The more difficult the goal the better the performance. Therefore, it is best to set goals high, however, with the caveat that such goals should not be out of reach.

One consideration that helps mediate especially difficult goals are subgoals. Subgoals are small and obtainable steps that lead to the ultimate goal. If assigned a single ultimate goal, employees only have a single opportunity for success. However, subgoals enable employees to receive frequent reinforcement for goal attainment (Daniels & Bailey, 2014). For example, Sulzer-Azaroff et al. (1990) set successively higher goals to improve safety behaviors in a large industrial plant. Approximately 200–250 employees in three different departments where injuries showed the highest rates were involved. Safety behaviors were determined by reviewing accident and injury records, interviewing job incumbents, and conducting direct observations. Based on information gathered by this selection of safety behavior procedures, the dependent variable was determined as a percent of safety achievements, the aggregated percentages of correctly performed behaviors. Intervention consisted of feedback, reinforcement, and goal setting with subgoals for 4–5 weeks. Subgoal levels were determined by the highest percent scored from previous weeks. Employees received weekly graphic feedback with social recognition and low-cost rewards for the first goal achievement. Additionally, monthly special rewards (e.g., refreshments) were distributed. Employees' safety performance improved and eventually exceeded the targeted goal. Although successful in this case, deciding on the specific criteria for goals and subgoals can be challenging as one works across different settings and industries. As a general rule, Daniels and Bailey (2014) suggested that the initial goal be determined by the level of failure the organization can accept. Then, as time passes and success is met, more challenging yet attainable goals can be determined.

Another variable that will affect goal setting is specificity. According to Locke and Latham (1990), a specific and difficult goal is better in improving performance than a vague goal such as "do your best." One reason is that "do your best" goals do not provide clear criteria from the organization and therefore individual employees may infer different expected performance standards from their supervisors (Locke & Latham, 2002). In this situation, employees give themselves the benefit of the doubt concerning adequacy of their performance and maximum effort will not be exerted (Kernan & Lord, 1988). When such self-directed goals fall short of management's expectations, the corresponding consequences (e.g., recognition, rewards, incentives, etc.) are withheld following employee performance, despite the fact the employee may have labeled their performance as fulfilling "do your best." This mismatch between employee's verbal self-appraisals and managerial evaluations may unintentionally create an extinction procedure which culminates in deterioration of performance and may also add conflict between subordinates and supervisors. A specific goal eliminates ambiguity as to what constitutes successful performance and precludes any arguments about the criteria. Furthermore, specific goals elucidate behavioral constitutions that lead to successful performance and these facilitate feedback on goal attainment since that feedback will be interpreted in relation to the goals (Latham, 2005).

Several studies have demonstrated the abovementioned argument. For example, Locke and Bryan (1967) conducted a series of experiments to identify a relationship between goal level and degree of interest in the task. Participants completed simple addition, perceptual speed, and psychomotor coordination tasks. In the first experiment participants were assigned either a specific and difficult goal or "do your best" goal. The specific and difficult goal group scored 9% higher than the "do your best" group. Latham and Baldes (1975) applied specific and difficult goals with truck drivers to increase net weight of log transporting trucks. A 94% truck net weight was determined as a difficult but attainable goal. Before implementing the specific and difficult goal, a nonspecific goal to simply "do their best" was presented. In this phase, the 36 logging trucks were reported between 55% and 65% of net weight. After the onset of a specific and difficult goal, substantial increase to approximately 90% net weight was shown and this maintained across time.

One long running debate during the 1970s and 1980s concerned whether goals should be assigned or set participatively (Latham & Arshoff, 2013). Fellner and Sulzer-Azaroff (1984) reviewed a series of articles on this topic and concluded that goals selected by employees were as effective in influencing performance as goals assigned by others. Similarly, Locke and Latham (1990) confirmed that if goal difficulty is held constant, an assigned goal is as effective as one set participatively. Even though assigned goals are as effective, many authors favored participative goals for reasons beyond direct performance (Fellner & Sulzer-Azaroff, 1984; Ludwig & Geller, 1997). Most research on goal setting only examines one or two goal-directed behaviors. However, in the real world, employee behaviors are intertwined such that success of one task will impact success of other tasks. Therefore, it is practical to assume employees' behaviors may share functional similarities to each other. In other words, non-target behaviors that share behavioral functions increase when the behavior targeted by goal-setting intervention increases (Ludwig, 2002). Therefore, employees articulate their implicit goals when participating in goal setting to provide opinions about the performance that shares behavioral functions (Locke & Latham, 1990). Success of implicit goals within an intervention can be considered by the association of functionally related behaviors. That is, by utilizing targeted behaviors which maintain a previous functional relationship with nontargeted behaviors, the likeliness of generalization is further augmented. Though, a central consideration is whether the implicit goal behavior is maintained externally. If so, it is unlikely that response generalization will occur for related but nontargeted behavior (Ludwig & Geller, 1997).

For instance, Ludwig and Geller (1997) investigated the relative effects of participative and assigned goals on target and non-target behaviors. Pizza deliverers from three different restaurants were observed departing for and arriving from deliveries. Intersection stopping was selected for a target behavior. Signal use and safety belt use were also observed, but not targeted for intervention. After baseline, employees at restaurant 1 participated in goal setting that targeted complete stops. Employees at restaurant 2 were assigned a goal while the third served as control. Over 4 weeks, the intervention groups' percentages of complete intersection stopping were posted as feedback. Results showed both intervention groups significantly increased complete intersection stops during intervention. The participative goal setting group also showed significant increases in turn signal and safety belt use (non-targeted behaviors) concurrent with their increases in intersection stopping (targeted behaviors). Assigned goal drivers decreased their turn signal and safety belt use concurrent with targeting complete stops. The authors explained that participative goal setting facilitated implicit rules, which, in turn, influenced behavior beyond the external consequence of the intervention.

Organizations have shifted their structures from hierarchical individualized performance to group-based structures over the last few decades (Kramer et al., 2013). Due to this reason there is increasing demand for research on group-based goal setting. However, little research has compared the relative effects of individual-based and group-based goals. In a representative study by Gowen (1985), the relative effects of an individual-based goal, team-based goal, and a combination of individual and team-based goals were investigated. Gowen (1985) defined an individual-based goal as "an overt statement about the desired level of future personal performance" and a group-based goal as "an overt statement about the desired level of future group performance." The experimental task was a sentence construction exercise to stimulate group behavior for an interdependent task. Three participants in a group performed the experimental task independently from other groups. The participants were divided into two groups: experimental and control. Participants in the experimental group were exposed to three intervention phases which were no goal, individual-based goal, and group-based goal consecutively. The participants in the control group had no goal conditions during these phases. Results found that individual-based goal increased 19% in group performance compared to no goals; group-based goal increased 12% compared to no goals; the combination of individual and group-based goals increased 31% compared to no goals. In an individual goal setting situation, the responsibility for correctly completed tasks rested solely with the individual. Therefore, differential efforts reliably resulted in differential task completion, which in turn led to differential consequences. Contrasted with group-based goals, a high performer's behavior may be unrewarded when other performers show a deficit on tasks. Since aggregated performance determines results, consequences may or may not match the group members' behaviors. If individual goals were not added to group goals, performers' effort would decline and collectively decrease organizational performance.

Jeffrey et al. (2012) revealed an important implication regarding individual and group goals. The authors pointed out previous studies exclusively implemented "one goal for all" in which group members had the same goal. Alternatively, they suggested ability-based goals where individuals of similar ability level receive the same goal. One hundred thirty-eight undergraduate students decoded numbers to the alphabet test for the experiment, half in one-goal-for-all condition. The other half in ability-based goal were divided into three levels (i.e., lower, medium, and higher ability). Repeated measures analysis revealed lower-ability individuals in the ability-based group increased their performance the most. Moreover, lower and moderate ability participants in the one goal for all condition showed larger decreases in performance.

Since goal setting depends upon other variables with which it is packaged, it may be useful to understand and isolate potential functions goal setting may serve. Goal setting can supply information regarding the desired behavior and be correlated with the availability of a consequence subsequent to behavior. In this case, goal setting functions as a discriminative stimulus for reinforcement (e.g., Daniels & Bailey, 2014). A discriminative stimulus is a condition that has frequency-altering effects because of a historical relation between behavior and the availability of an effective consequence (Michael, 2004). Suppose a supervisor is present at the workstation of an employee and states a goal that they would like that employee to meet. The authority figure making such a statement is, in essence, stating that "I will now pay attention to what you are doing." For many, verbal stimuli with properties that suggest management is currently attending to performance of subordinates have historically been paired with sudden availability of approval, bonuses, monetary incentives, or other reinforcing stimuli for superior or improved performance (S^D), whereas such consequences were unavailable when management does not provide such monitoring notifications (S^Δ). Not only are reinforcement-based discriminative relations possible, but punishment-based discriminative relations would also likely be relevant. Such a monitoring notification could also function as a threat or warning. Criticism, reprimands, or other punishing stimuli will suddenly be available for substandard performance or off-task behaviors (S^{Dp}), whereas such aversive consequences were historically absent of goal setting initiatives from management ($S^{\Delta p}$). Due to prior learning while under direct supervision, the presence of a stated goal may immediately evoke improved performance and abate other behavior.

Not only may goals be correlated with the availability of consequences, but goals could potentially make normally available consequences more effective as reinforcement (Agnew, 1998). This functional relation is best captured by the concept of a conditioned motivating operation (CMO), which is an environmental variable that evokes behavior because that variable also alters the value of some stimulus, object, or event due to prior learning history (Michael, 2004). This can be accomplished through a variety of means. For example, suppose a goal is set as part of a disciplinary measure following a manager and employee discussing a performance improvement plan. Following this meeting, the transitory but pervasive status of the employee's performance being below the goal serves to threaten their job security under such circumstances. This possibility of job termination while the goal remains unmet (the CMO) is a condition that will evoke behaviors to fulfill that goal and the removal of the threat will function as a source of reinforcement. To put it differently, job security did not become more available, but more valuable after the performance improvement plan. Another example could involve a goal being set for collecting and turning in completed customer satisfaction cards at a restaurant. Previously, satisfaction cards were typically ignored at customer tables and often thrown in the trash by waitstaff. However, due to the newly established goal (the CMO), behaviors such as seeking, collecting, and turning in satisfaction cards will be evoked. Although the availability of these satisfaction cards remained constant, their reinforcing effectiveness is now increased due to this goal setting intervention. Naturally, stimuli such as goals could serve multiple functions at once, such as a stated goal that functions as a CMO to evoke behaviors relevant to job security (e.g., collecting satisfaction cards) and an S^{Dp} that abates behavior that is not relevant to job security (e.g., talking to the line cooks despite being warned to attend to customer tables) due to the correlation between the set goal and the availability of punishment for nonproductive performance.

Besides the immediate evocative and abative properties seen with possible discriminative and motivational aspects of goal setting, goals may also function as or produce stimuli that can successfully control delayed behavior. Most employees possess adequate verbal skills of how relevant verbal contingencies operate, even for the simplest of interventions. Employees, like all verbally sophisticated individuals, routinely describe themselves, their world, and the possible relationships among events they observe. Such descriptive repertoires impact goal setting, including descriptions of relations between behavior and environmental outcomes explicitly echoed from the goal statements or inferred by the employee due to informal goals or unspoken elements of vague goals. Either way, the contingency is specified and the resulting verbal stimulus functions as a rule which can govern future behavior as performers restate the rule to themselves. Therefore, organizations can use goal statements to prompt employees to efficiently engage in desirable performance without shaping direct contingencies (Agnew & Redmon, 1992; Baum, 1995; Fellner & Sulzer-Azaroff, 1984).

A typical rule statement includes the relationship among a goal, goal-directed behavior, and corresponding consequences (Catania et al., 1989; Malott, 1993). For example, suppose that a brewery had a high rate of accident and injuries among employees. The safety manager gathers employees together at the end of one of their shifts and announces, "If we see safety improve by at least 20% over the next six months, then everyone can expect a nice bonus at the end of the year." Performers may state the contingency to themselves as "If I wear my helmet, gloves, goggles, and safety vest for the next six months, then I will probably get $500 or something like that." Note that this vague goal (i.e., improve safety) resulted in performers inferring unspoken elements (i.e., wear helmet, gloves, goggles, and safety vest; outcome of $500) in their description of the contingency. In practice, it would be better for the safety manager to explicitly state-specific behaviors, results desired, as well as consequences to be delivered, to prevent undesirable misinterpretations or disconnects (e.g., "We should hide accidents and injuries" or employees discovering the bonus was less than assumed). However, contingency-specifying stimuli can still be produced by performers in the absence of best practices. The end-of-shift goal announcement does not immediately evoke behaviors related to safety gear, but the newly created verbal stimulus (i.e., rule) can evoke rule-governed behavior for the next six months even before the incentive is delivered. This behavior is maintained by self-delivered covert verbal stimuli to mediate temporal gaps (e.g., "I'm another day closer to getting that payout"). Again, the more explicit the rule is, the better results likely achieved. Furthermore, rule-governed behavior cannot persist in perpetuity and eventual consequences should match verbal descriptions by performers to maintain productive behaviors, or else alternative verbal descriptions may produce undesirable behavior (e.g., "I can't trust the promises of management, so I might as well just do my own thing and ignore their lies about goals").

As seen in these examples, consequences that follow goal achievement are key to successful implementation of goal setting. Feedback, monetary incentives, and social reinforcement (e.g., praise, acknowledgment) are the most representative consequences. Goal setting is effective when consequences follow. In goal setting alone, performance may not be adequately reinforced in the presence of the goal (Fellner & Sulzer-Azaroff, 1984). However, when a goal is combined with consequences, goal attainment may not only increase reinforcement opportunity, but also eventually function as a conditioned reinforcer for specific employees due to their unique reinforcement history (Kang et al., 2005). Thus, organizations use packaged interventions with goal setting and consequences. For example, Gil and Carter (2016) investigated the effectiveness of a single intervention (i.e., graphic feedback) and a packaged intervention (i.e., goal setting and graphic feedback) in a human service organization. Using a multiple baseline design, these two independent variables were compared which showed that goal setting with graphic feedback yielded better performance than graphic feedback alone, but interventions were not counterbalanced to control for order effects. Numerous articles demonstrate this result (e.g., Bateman & Ludwig, 2004; Calpin et al., 1988; Downing & Geller, 2012; Eikenhout & Austin, 2005; Goomas et al., 2011; Huberman & O'Brien, 1999; Loewy & Bailey, 2007; Nicol & Hantula, 2002; Stephens & Ludwig, 2005; Wilk & Redmon, 1990).

Task clarification

Task clarification is another effective antecedent intervention. Crowell et al. (1988) defined task clarification as the precise behavioral descriptions of a performance. Such descriptions clarify and prompt behavioral components that lead to successful performance (Amigo et al., 2008). Unlike goal setting, which involves the evaluative standards for exemplary or improved performance, task clarification involves evaluative standards for minimal performance. Evaluative standards of task clarification will detail the expectations, responsibilities, and criteria used to consider performance acceptable. Task clarification not only reminds employees of existing contingencies but also introduces a new set of contingencies (Palmer & Johnson, 2013). For example, Anderson et al. (1988) evaluated the effects of task clarification and feedback on eleven low-probability cleaning behaviors (e.g., putting up bar stools, emptying trash cans) at a university bar. The dependent variable was mean percent of completed checklist for each cleaning behavior. Task clarification was achieved by providing checklists along with explicit description of each cleaning activity to bar staff. Task descriptions involved necessary behaviors for each cleaning activity and corresponding outcomes. Public individual feedback was provided after completion of the task clarification phase. Results showed introduction of task clarification increased overall completion of the checklist by 13%. Subsequent feedback posting increased 23% of completed checkmarks.

A similar result was obtained by Crowell et al. (1988) who investigated task clarification, performance feedback, and praise in improving customer service for bank tellers. Eleven target verbal behaviors of teller-customer interactions had assigned points based on tellers' performance. For example, the first was time to service. When customers approached the teller window within a yard, tellers needed to make vocal acknowledgments within 5 seconds. If the latency of acknowledgment was 0 to 5 seconds, 12 points were given. If from 6 to 11 seconds, 7 points were given. When the latency was over 11 seconds, no points were provided. The dependent variable was mean of quality points assigned for target behaviors. After baseline, task clarification was introduced to tellers by providing a memo of clear definitions of target behaviors. Then public graphic feedback was delivered on individual tellers' performance, coded to maintain anonymity. Managers also provided verbal feedback for individual tellers in weekly meetings. Next, in a praise phase, if individual teller's quality points were over 85 or their current score was higher than the previous day, managers complimented them individually. Task clarification abruptly increased teller performance an average 12% over baseline. Feedback and praise gradually increased teller performance more by 6% and 7%, respectively. As in the previous research, task clarification alone effectively increased performance.

Most task clarification investigations are part of intervention packages. Austin et al. (2005) evaluated task clarification and feedback to improve closing task completion at a restaurant. The dependent variable was the percent of completed checklist per shift. Task clarification (i.e., posted checklist), verbal feedback, and graphic feedback were provided to servers and dishwashers. Results demonstrated task completion increased by 15% among servers and 38% among dishwashers. Another task clarification study (Amigo et al., 2008) reduced busing time among servers at a restaurant. Task clarification with goal setting and manager feedback were applied. Task clarification in a memo included detailed steps and goal time of busing tables. Mean busing time slightly reduced from 315 seconds in baseline to 284 seconds after the memo. When the manager's verbal feedback was provided, busing time decreased to 152 seconds.

Durgin et al. (2014) employed task clarification and supervisor training to improve the performance of animal (i.e., pouched rats) trainers at a nongovernmental organization located in East Africa. As a part of supervisor training, job aids were created for total of 11 tasks. The job aids included a brief explanation of ways to monitor animal trainers' performance as well as provide appropriate prompts and feedback. Job aids served as data collection, task clarification, and appropriate feedback delivery to animal trainers. For example, when determining "the trainers never pull the rope/rat," trainers were only allowed to tug when the rat stopped to groom for more than 15 seconds. Having this task clarification list on hand, supervisors marked yes or no based on trainer observations. If supervisors marked no, they provided corrective feedback to trainers. The dependent variable was a percent of correct score calculated by number of correctly completed items divided by total items. Scores were collected from both supervisors and animal trainers. During the baseline, a mean percent score for supervisor A, B, and C were 68.6%, 53.7%, and 49.7%, respectively. A mean percent score for trainers A, B, and C were 66.8%, 45.5%, and 49%, respectively. Supervisor training and a job aid increased mean scores by 86.4%, 100%, and 91.7% for each supervisor and 79.6%. 81%, and 86.3% for animal trainers. Finally, during the independent supervision session, while a mean score for supervisor A, B, and C showed 98.4%, 98.5% and 95.9% respectively, a mean score for trainers A, B, and C indicated 96%, 87.3%, and 90.7%, respectively.

Task clarification can be conceptualized as low-level training. Typical behavioral training components are as follows: 1) instruction of job responsibilities, 2) task demonstration, 3) employee practice with feedback delivery until meeting the predetermined criteria, and 4) evaluation. Task clarification can be categorized as the first part of training in that it specifies job duties. In other words, operational definitions for job duties essentially become task clarification itself. This most likely functions as a contingency-specifying stimulus, it precisely specifies behaviors to be performed with an implied or explicit statement related to outcomes. Since task clarification details minimal performances, there remains a possibility it also functions as a CMO if it implies a social warning that current performance is not meeting minimal levels required to maintain employment. For example, an employee designated to unload food products from a delivery truck to refrigerator may simply group new and old items with minimal organization (e.g., lettuce goes with lettuce, sauce with sauce). This practice may irritate coworkers and the supervisor, but the employee may remain oblivious to such negative appraisals. The behavior may be under control of a faulty rule, such as "unload the truck as fast as possible and just match product types when placing them in the fridge." Task clarification specifies the importance of ensuring older stock is placed in front of newer and imply or outright state that criticisms and possible disciplinary measures follow failure to adhere to this policy. This specification of performance standards will likely result in the employee revising their verbal description of the contingency related to product deliveries. Further, the implied threat may evoke performance such as going and immediately rearranging stock from the previous delivery.

Job aids and checklists

Checklists and other forms of job aids have also been frequently utilized by both OBM researchers and practitioners (Gawande, 2009; Gravina & Cunningham, 2010; McSween, 2010; Smith, 2010). Unlike goal setting and task clarification, which may be verbally described once or as part of periodic sessions, job aids provide ongoing support that can be consulted by performers during their performance, typically as signage, documents, schedules, and other forms of readily available descriptions for expected actions. As such, job aids may prompt job-relevant behaviors and outcomes. A prompt is a stimulus that arranges the environment to evoke a particular behavior (Mcconville et al., 1998). An inexpensive but moderately effective intervention, prompts have a successful history in organizations. For example, Clayton and Blaskewicz (2012) evaluated visual aids to decrease urinal splatter on men's restrooms at a college campus. Three men's restrooms in the same building were selected, one was a control to evaluate follow-up. In both settings the visual prompt was located between two urinals with the text of "For Pete's sake, Gentleman. Please Stand Closer. Thank you." Additionally for setting 2, bull's-eye with the heat-activated message was located inside of urinals. When users hit the bull's-eye for several seconds, the message "Help the Cleaners. Please Aim Straight" appeared. The dependent variable was the number of floor tiles (1.3 cm × 1.3 cm) with urinal splatter. Introduction of text signs decreased urinal splatter by 37.5% in setting 1 and 40.2% in setting 2. In setting 2, when a heat-activated target was introduced, the splatter further decreased by 24%. Follow-up data indicated a continued reduction for both restrooms.

Warman et al. (2019) evaluated static and variable prompt effectiveness on employee performance at a private day school for students diagnosed with developmental disabilities. In experiment 1, the static prompt included the message "Please sign your student out using the form." Variable prompts consisted of the same message with random changes in font size, font type, color, and position of the sign. Humorous versions of these job aids were also employed, such as the cartoon character Popeye stating a variation of his catchphrase: "I am what I am, but at least I signed out before exiting to the playground." Signing in and out rates did not increase with static signs, but both variable and humorous signs changed behaviors. In experiment 2 static and humorous signs located in a café where staff members were likely to see the prompt were compared. The static sign was: "Please ensure the students are clocked-in and clocked-out." The humorous prompt was similar to experiment 1. During baseline, no clock-ins and outs were observed. As the static prompt was introduced, adherence increased by 3 times but returned to zero after 6 days. Humorous signs increased responses immediately and its effect maintained over time. Static signs showed transitory effect while humorous signs showed continuous and high level adherence. As such, simple ongoing prompts proved to be effective, although innovative variation was necessary to maintain the effects over time.

A checklist is distinguished from other types of job aids by the fact that a checklist involves a list of specified activities, rather than just a single activity, to be prompted. For example, Bacon et al. (1983) developed a checklist system for employees in a large midwestern university. The checklist included 17 items of specified tasks with reference to outcome measures. Employees were given handouts including performance criteria for each item. Employees completed checklists daily and the experimenter examined checklists weekly, while task completion was covertly observed on major permanent measures. Results showed task completion among employees increased by 28.8% under the checklist intervention.

In another example, Doll et al. (2007) implemented a public checklist to increase cleaning behavior at a ski shop. Using Austin's Performance Diagnostic Checklist (2000) and Daniels and Daniels' PIC/NIC Analysis (2004), seven target behaviors were identified. A packaged intervention including task clarification, a checklist, and feedback was applied. During a task clarification meeting, a store manager specified how to correctly complete behaviors of interest and a checklist of cleaning behaviors was posted next to the cash register. Weekly graphic feedback was given to employees in a public place. In a second phase, task-specific daily feedback was provided. Cleaning behavior improved by 52% in the packaged intervention and task-specific daily feedback increased cleaning by 12%.

Job aids and checklists are particularly advantageous for safety situations in which trial-and-error learning via direct consequences would be hazardous and potentially life-threatening, such as operating an aircraft (Gawande, 2009; Rantz et al., 2009). Job aids and checklists seem better alternatives to reliably prompt appropriate behaviors. For example, Clayton et al. (2006) evaluated prompts to reduce cell phone and improve seat belt use while exiting a parking lot. Individuals presented a sign (i.e., "Please Hang Up, I Care" or "Please Buckle Up, I Care") to drivers and flipped the prompt to provide a consequence (i.e., "Thank You") when drivers adhered. Results indicated seat belt use averaged 44% in the baseline and increased to 56% in intervention. The proportion of drivers hanging up their cell phones was similar to seat belt use, although this unsafe behavior was lower initially.

Job aids and checklists function as an indirect contingency shaping under control of overt or covert rules that provide the information of consequences (Mueller et al., 2001). When the existing contingencies are not in effect, job aids and checklists can be added to employees' environment as an alternative (Weatherly & Malott, 2008). When used in public, job aids and checklists can function as a CMO because they create social warning when the current behavior is not meeting what is described in job aids or checklists. Suppose that a manager posted visual signage that described putting on safety helmets before entering workstations. If employees entered workstations without safety helmets, coworkers might stare at them. This situation would create an aversive situation and alter the probability of employees putting on safety helmets.

Conclusion

Antecedents, when appropriately used, can be powerful, which should be compelling considering their relative ease and lack of expense. Naturally, consequences will probably dominate OBM, given its origin from operant conditioning. Indeed, the notion that antecedent control alone will not maintain performance has long been accepted throughout the history of the field (Brethower et al., 2021). However, the potential of simply using antecedent control, or carefully aligning antecedent with consequent control, should not be neglected. Goal setting, task clarification, job aids, and checklists all show substantial effectiveness in improving performance. Our purpose was to illustrate the general utility of popular antecedent interventions within OBM. To achieve this objective, representative research examples, variables for successful implementation, and behavioral functions for each antecedent were articulated. However, not all variables that might impact performance were examined. There remain many variants of antecedent control, both in isolation and in combination with consequences, that merit exploration and represent fruitful potential research lines. For example, the effects of multiple or tiered goals on performance lacks research (Locke & Latham, 2013), including how such goals might interact with monetary incentives.

Despite positive signs from the literature, the effectiveness of task clarification, job aids, and checklists still warrants caution with interpretation. Most research has been implemented as parts of a packaged intervention. Concerning the purpose of OBM research, this situation might be expected. Most OBM studies apply consequence-based interventions such as feedback, monetary incentives, or social reinforcers due to their powerful results. The increasing effectiveness of interventions is important since most research investigated performance in businesses and industries. Due to this reason, investigating the effects of antecedent interventions might have been neglected. However, component analyses or dismantling studies for task clarification, job aids, and checklists are necessary to identify the independent effects of these interventions. Perhaps antecedent interventions might be overused or underused in packaged interventions due to a lack of understanding of their independent efficacy. Identification of their own success will eventually demonstrate time- and cost-efficiency.

Finally, researchers and practitioners must be cautious not to rely excessively on goal setting, task clarification, job aids, and checklists. Since these antecedents seem undemanding to implement, corporate initiatives tend to overuse them to increase desired performance (Braksick, 2007). Without scrutinizing environmental components, introduction of antecedents will not change behavior in the long term. If corresponding consequences do not follow behavior evoked by the antecedent, the behavior will be eventually extinguished. We hope this paper serves as an antecedent, prompting further study and evaluation, so that the consequences of applied best practices maintain investigative efforts over the long term.

Disclosure statement

No potential conflict of interest was reported by the author(s).

ORCID

Douglas A. Johnson http://orcid.org/0000-0002-7802-3566

References

Agnew, J. L. (1998). The establishing operation in organizational behavior management. *Journal of Organizational Behavior Management*, *18*(1), 7–19. https://doi.org/10.1300/J075v18n01_02

Agnew, J. L., & Redmon, W. K. (1992). Contingency specifying stimuli: The role of "rules" in organizational behavior management. *Journal of Organizational Behavior Management*, *12*(2), 67–76. https://doi.org/10.1300/J075v12n02_04

Amigo, S., Smith, A., & Ludwig, T. (2008). Using task clarification, goal setting, and feedback to decrease table busing times in a franchise pizza restaurant. *Journal of Organizational Behavior Management*, *28*(3), 176–187. https://doi.org/10.1080/01608060802251106

Anderson, D. C., Crowell, C. R., Hantula, D. A., & Siroky, L. M. (1988). Task clarification and individual performance posting for improving cleaning in a student-managed university bar. *Journal of Organizational Behavior Management*, *9*(2), 73–90. https://doi.org/10.1300/J075v09n02_06

Austin, J. (2000). Performance analysis and performance diagnostics. In J. Austin & J. Carr (Eds.), *Handbook of applied behavior analysis* (pp. 304–327). Context Press.

Austin, J., Weatherly, N. L., & Gravina, N. E. (2005). Using task clarification, graphic feedback, and verbal feedback to increase closing-task completion in a privately owned restaurant. *Journal of Applied Behavior Analysis*, *38*(1), 117–120. https://doi.org/10.1901/jaba.2005.159-03

Bacon, D. L., Fulton, B. J., & Malott, R. W. (1983). Improving staff performance through the use of task checklists. *Journal of Organizational Behavior Management*, *4*(3–4), 17–25. https://doi.org/10.1300/J075v04n03_03

Bateman, M. J., & Ludwig, T. D. (2004). Managing distribution quality through an adapted incentive program with tiered goals and feedback. *Journal of Organizational Behavior Management*, *23*(1), 33–55. https://doi.org/10.1300/J075v23n01_03

Baum, W. M. (1995). Rules, culture, and fitness. *The Behavior Analyst*, *18*(1), 1–21. https://doi.org/10.1007/BF03392688

Bechtel, N. T., McGee, H. M., Huitema, B. E., & Dickinson, A. M. (2015). The effects of the temporal placement of feedback on performance. *The Psychological Record*, *65*(3), 425–434. https://doi.org/10.1007/s40732-015-0117-4

Biteler, M. C. (2008). When the client won't move: Understanding the causes of resistance by leveraging the laws of human behavior. *Journal of Practical Consulting*, *2*(2), 28–34. https://www.regent.edu/acad/global/publications/jpc/vol2iss2/home.htm

Braksick, L. W. (2007). *Unlock behavior, unleash profits: Developing leadership behavior that drives profitability in your organization* (2nd ed.). McGraw-Hill.

Brethower, D. M., Dickinson, A. M., Johnson, D. A., & Johnson, C. M. (2021). A history of organizational behavior management. *Journal of Organizational Behavior Management.* Advance publication. https://doi.org/10.1080/01608061.2021.1924340

Calpin, J. P., Edelstein, B., & Redmon, W. K. (1988). Performance feedback and goal setting to improve mental health center staff productivity. *Journal of Organizational Behavior Management, 9*(2), 35–58. https://doi.org/10.1300/J075v09n02_04

Catania, A. C., Shimoff, E., & Matthews, B. A. (1989). An experimental analysis of rule-governed behavior. In S. C. Hayes (Ed.), *Rule-governed behavior.* Springer.pp 119-150. https://doi.org/10.1007/978-1-4757-0447-1_4

Clayton, M., Helms, B., & Simpson, C. (2006). Active prompting to decrease cell phone use and increase seat belt use while driving. *Journal of Applied Behavior Analysis, 39*(3), 341–349. https://doi.org/10.1901/jaba.2006.153-04

Clayton, M. C., & Blaskewicz, J. (2012). The use of visual prompts to increase the cleanliness of restrooms on a college campus. *Journal of Organizational Behavior Management, 32*(4), 329–337. https://doi.org/10.1080/01608061.2012.729393

Crowell, C. R., Anderson, D. C., Abel, D. M., & Sergio, J. P. (1988). Task clarification, performance feedback, and social praise: Procedures for improving the customer service of bank tellers. *Journal of Applied Behavior Analysis, 21*(1), 65–71. https://doi.org/10.1901/jaba.1988.21-65

Daniels, A. C. (2016). *Bringing out the best in people: How to apply the astonishing power of positive reinforcement* (3rd ed.). McGraw-Hill Inc.

Daniels, A. C., & Bailey, J. S. (2014). *Performance management: Changing behavior that drives organizational effectiveness* (5th ed.). Performance Management Publications.

Daniels, A. C., & Daniels, J. E. (2004). *Performance management: Changing behavior that drives organizational effectiveness* (4th ed.). Performance Management Publications.

Doll, J., Livesey, J., McHaffie, E., & Ludwig, T. D. (2007). Keeping an uphill edge: Managing cleaning behaviors at a ski shop. *Journal of Organizational Behavior Management, 27*(3), 41–60. https://doi.org/10.1300/J075v27n03_04

Downing, C. O., Jr., & Geller, E. S. (2012). A goal-setting and feedback intervention to increase ID-checking behavior: An assessment of social validity and behavioral impact. *Journal of Organizational Behavior Management, 32*(4), 297–306. https://doi.org/10.1080/01608061.2012.729383

Durgin, A., Mahoney, A., Cox, C., Weetjens, B. J., & Poling, A. (2014). Using task clarification and feedback training to improve staff performance in an East African nongovernmental organization. *Journal of Organizational Behavior Management, 34*(2), 122–143. https://doi.org/10.1080/01608061.2014.914007

Eikenhout, N., & Austin, J. (2005). Using goals, feedback, reinforcement, and a performance matrix to improve customer service in a large department store. *Journal of Organizational Behavior Management, 24*(3), 27–62. https://doi.org/10.1300/J075v24n03_02

Erath, T. G., DiGennaro Reed, F. D., Sundermeyer, H. W., Brand, D., Novak, M. D., Harbison, M. J., & Shears, R. (2020). Enhancing the training integrity of human service staff using pyramidal behavioral skills training. *Journal of Applied Behavior Analysis, 53*(1), 449–464. https://doi.org/10.1002/jaba.608

Fellner, D. J., & Sulzer-Azaroff, B. (1984). A behavioral analysis of goal setting. *Journal of Organizational Behavior Management, 6*(1), 33–51. https://doi.org/10.1300/J075v06n01_03

Gawande, A. (2009). *The checklist manifesto: How to get things right.* Metropolitan Books.

Gil, P. J., & Carter, S. L. (2016). Graphic feedback, performance feedback, and goal setting increased staff compliance with a data collection task at a large residential facility. *Journal of Organizational Behavior Management, 36*(1), 56–70. https://doi.org/10.1080/01608061.2016.1152207

Goomas, D. T., Smith, S. M., & Ludwig, T. D. (2011). Business activity monitoring: Real-time group goals and feedback using an overhead scoreboard in a distribution center. *Journal of Organizational Behavior Management, 31*(3), 196–209. https://doi.org/10.1080/01608061.2011.589715

Gowen, C. R. (1985). Managing work group performance by individual goals and group goals for an interdependent group task. *Journal of Organizational Behavior Management, 7*(3–4), 5–27. https://doi.org/10.1300/J075v07n03_02

Gravina, N. E., & Cunningham, T. R. (2010). "Check" this out: A review of Gawande's *The checklist manifesto. Journal of Organizational Behavior Management, 30*(3), 271–277. https://doi.org/10.1080/01608061.2010.499035

Huberman, W. L., & O'Brien, R. M. (1999). Improving therapist and patient performance in chronic psychiatric group homes through goal-setting, feedback, and positive reinforcement. *Journal of Organizational Behavior Management, 19*(1), 13–36. https://doi.org/10.1300/J075v19n01_04

Jeffrey, S. A., Schulz, A., & Webb, A. (2012). The performance effects of an ability-based approach to goal assignment. *Journal of Organizational Behavior Management, 32*(3), 221–241. https://doi.org/10.1080/01608061.2012.698116

Jessup, P. A., & Stahelski, A. J. (1999). The effects of a combined goal setting, feedback and incentive intervention on job performance in a manufacturing environment. *Journal of Organizational Behavior Management, 19*(3), 5–26. https://doi.org/10.1300/J075v19n03_02

Kang, K., Oah, S., & Dickinson, A. M. (2005). The relative effects of different frequencies of feedback on work performance: A simulation. *Journal of Organizational Behavior Management, 23*(4), 21–53. https://doi.org/10.1300/J075v23n04_02

Kernan, M. C., & Lord, R. G. (1988). Effects of participative vs assigned goals and feedback in a multitrial task. *Motivation and Emotion, 12*(1), 75–86. https://doi.org/10.1007/BF00992473

Kramer, W. S., Thayer, A. L., & Salas, E. (2013). Goal setting in teams. In E. A. Locke & G. P. Latham (Eds.), *New developments in goal setting and task performance* (pp. 287–310). Routledge/Taylor & Francis Group.

Latham, G. P. (2005). Performance appraisal/performance management. In S.Catwright (Ed.), Human Resource Management, V, The Blackwell Encyclopedia of Management, 2nd ed. Malden, MA: Blackwell Publishing

Latham, G. P., & Arshoff, A. S. (2013). The relevance of goal setting theory for human resource management. In E. A. Locke & G. P. Latham (Eds.), *New developments in goal setting and task performance* (pp. 331–342). Routledge/Taylor & Francis Group.

Latham, G. P., & Baldes, J. J. (1975). The "practical significance" of Locke's theory of goal setting. *Journal of Applied Psychology, 60*(1), 122–124. https://doi.org/10.1037/h0076354

Locke, E. A., & Latham, G. P. (2013). Goal setting theory: The current state. In E. A. Locke & G. P. Latham (Eds.), *New developments in goal setting and task performance* (pp. 623–630). Routledge/Taylor & Francis Group.

Locke, E. A., & Bryan, J. F. (1967). Performance goals as determinants of level of performance and boredom. *Journal of Applied Psychology, 51*(2), 120–130. https://doi.org/10.1037/h0024471

Locke, E. A., & Latham, G. P. (1990). *A theory of goal setting & task performance.* Prentice-Hall, Inc.

Locke, E. A., & Latham, G. P. (2002). Building a practically useful theory of goal setting and task motivation: A 35-year odyssey. *American Psychologist, 57*(9), 705–717. https://doi.org/10.1037/0003-066X.57.9.705

Loewy, S., & Bailey, J. (2007). The effects of graphic feedback, goal setting, and manager praise on customer service behaviors. *Journal of Organizational Behavior Management, 27*(3), 15–26. https://doi.org/10.1300/J075v27n03_02

Ludwig, T. D. (2002). On the necessity of structure in an arbitrary world: Using concurrent schedules of reinforcement to describe response generalization. *Journal of Organizational Behavior Management, 21*(4), 13–38. https://doi.org/10.1300/J075v21n04_03

Ludwig, T. D., & Geller, E. S. (1997). Assigned versus participative goal setting and response generalization: Managing injury control among professional pizza deliverers. *Journal of Applied Psychology, 82*(2), 253–261. https://doi.org/10.1037/0021-9010.82.2.253

Malott, R. W. (1993). A theory of rule-governed behavior and organizational behavior management. *Journal of Organizational Behavior Management, 12*(2), 45–65. https://doi.org/10.1300/J075v12n02_03

Martin, G., & Pear, J. J. (2019). *Behavior modification: What it is and how to do it*. Routledge.

Mcconville, M. L., Hantula, D. A., & Axelrod, S. (1998). Matching training procedures to outcomes: A behavioral and quantitative analysis. *Behavior Modification, 22*(3), 391–414. https://doi.org/10.1177/01454455980223011

McSween, T. (2010). The checklist manifesto: A practitioner's perspective. *Journal of Organizational Behavior Management, 30*(3), 278–279. https://doi.org/10.1080/01608061.2010.499036

Michael, J. L. (2004). *Concepts and principles of behavior analysis*. Association for Behavior Analysis International.

Mueller, M. M., Moore, J. W., Tingstrom, D. H., & Doggett, R. A. (2001). Increasing seating opportunities using a behavioral prompt. *Journal of Organizational Behavior Management, 21*(2), 99–109. https://doi.org/10.1300/J075v21n02_10

Nicol, N., & Hantula, D. A. (2002). Decreasing delivery drivers' departure times. *Journal of Organizational Behavior Management, 21*(4), 105–116. https://doi.org/10.1300/J075v21n04_07

Palmer, M. G., & Johnson, C. M. (2013). The effects of task clarification and group graphic feedback on early punch-in times. *Journal of Organizational Behavior Management, 33*(4), 265–275. https://doi.org/10.1080/01608061.2013.843492

Rantz, W. G., Dickinson, A. M., Sinclair, G. A., & Van Houten, R. (2009). The effect of feedback on the accuracy of checklist completion during instrument flight training. *Journal of Applied Behavior Analysis, 42*(3), 497–509. https://doi.org/10.1901/jaba.2009.42-497

Roose, K. M., & Williams, W. L. (2018). An evaluation of the effects of very difficult goals. *Journal of Organizational Behavior Management, 38*(1), 18–48. https://doi.org/10.1080/01608061.2017.1325820

Smith, A. J. (2010). The checklist manifesto: Examples from the hotel industry. *Journal of Organizational Behavior Management, 30*(3), 280–282. https://doi.org/10.1080/01608061.2010.499252

Stephens, S. D., & Ludwig, T. D. (2005). Improving anesthesia nurse compliance with universal precautions using group goals and public feedback. *Journal of Organizational Behavior Management, 25*(2), 37–71. https://doi.org/10.1300/J075v25n02_02

Sulzer-Azaroff, B., Loafman, B., Merante, R. J., & Hlavacek, A. C. (1990). Improving occupational safety in a large industrial plant: A systematic replication. *Journal of Organizational Behavior Management, 11*(1), 99–120. https://doi.org/10.1300/J075v11n01_07

Tammemagi, T., O'Hora, D., & Maglieri, K. A. (2013). The effects of a goal setting intervention on productivity and persistence in an analogue work task. *Journal of Organizational Behavior Management, 33*(1), 31–54. https://doi.org/10.1080/01608061.2013.758001

VanStelle, S. E., Vicars, S. M., Harr, V., Miguel, C. F., Koerber, J. L., Kazbour, R., & Austin, J. (2012). The publication history of the Journal of Organizational Behavior Management: An objective review and analysis: 1998–2009. *Journal of Organizational Behavior Management, 32*(2), 93–123. https://doi.org/10.1080/01608061.2012.675864

Warman, A. S., Wine, B., Newcomb, E. T., Chen, T., & Morgan, C. A. (2019). An evaluation of static versus variable antecedents on employee performance. *Journal of Organizational Behavior Management, 39*(3–4), 257–265. https://doi.org/10.1080/01608061.2019.1666775

Weatherly, N. L., & Malott, R. W. (2008). An analysis of organizational behavior management research in terms of the three-contingency model of performance management. *Journal of Organizational Behavior Management, 28*(4), 260–285. https://doi.org/10.1080/01608060802454643

Wilk, L. A., & Redmon, W. K. (1990). A daily-adjusted goal-setting and feedback procedure for improving productivity in a university admissions department. *Journal of Organizational Behavior Management, 11*(1), 55–75. https://doi.org/10.1300/J075v11n01_05

Wilk, L. A., & Redmon, W. K. (1998). The effects of feedback and goal setting on the productivity and satisfaction of university admissions staff. *Journal of Organizational Behavior Management, 18*(1), 45–68. https://doi.org/10.1300/J075v18n01_04

Wine, B., Lewis, K., Newcomb, E. T., Camblin, J. G., Chen, T., Liesfeld, J. E., Matthews, K. M., Morgan, C. A., & Newcomb, B. B. (2019). The effects of temporal placement of feedback on performance with and without goals. *Journal of Organizational Behavior Management, 39*(3–4), 308–316. https://doi.org/10.1080/01608061.2019.1632244

Pinpointing, Measurement, Procedural Integrity, and Maintenance in Organizational Behavior Management

David Wilder and Daniel Cymbal

ABSTRACT

Organizational behavior management (OBM) is the application of behavioral principles to individuals and groups working in business, industry, government, and human service settings. In this paper, we describe OBM methodology in research and practice, highlighting pinpointing, measurement of performance, procedural integrity, and maintenance. We conclude by noting some limitations of contemporary OBM methodology and by suggesting some topics for future research.

Organizational behavior management (OBM) can be generally described as the application of behavioral principles to individuals and groups in business, industry, government, and human service settings (Daniels & Bailey, 2014; Wilder et al., 2009). Behavioral principles are natural laws that govern behavior and apply to all living organisms. OBM is sometimes referred to as a subdiscipline of applied behavior analysis (ABA), which is the application of behavioral principles to problems of social significance (Baer et al., 1968). However, OBM can historically claim influence from a variety of disciplines outside of behavior analysis as well, such as systems theory and other business-related fields (Brethower et al., 2021; Dickinson, 2001). Hyten (2017) also notes that social significance in OBM cannot be simply asserted as the behavior's importance to the behaver, as in other ABA practices, but rather in the broader context of the functioning and survival of the constituent organization. Therefore, the scope of OBM methodology and practice may be wider than other behavior analytic disciplines (Hyten, 2022), with corresponding differences in approaches to ethics, regulatory practices (e.g., credentialing and certification), and consumer protection (Hantula, 2022; McSween, 2022; Wine, 2021). In this sense, OBM is distinct from ABA and other practice areas.

Regardless, many OBM procedures have roots in radical behaviorism and retain common methodological features from other behavior analytic disciplines (Erath et al., 2021). Moreover, OBM and practices within its common constituent sub-disciplines (e.g., Performance Management, Behavioral Systems

Analysis and Behavior-Based Safety) frequently intervene in health and human services organizations where ABA practitioners are most common (Gravina et al., 2018). The commonality of this relationship is only likely to deepen as OBM instruction is slated to become a larger component of the Board Certified Behavior Analyst certification process (Behavior Analyst Certification Board, 2022). Thus, given present debate and projected future interest, it may be valuable to elucidate the parameters of the field and critical features of OBM approaches to measurement. The purpose of this chapter is to delineate some contemporary methodological features of OBM research and practice, highlighting pinpointing, measurement of performance, procedural integrity, and maintenance. We conclude by noting some limitations of contemporary OBM methodology and by suggesting some topics for future research.

Overview of research methodology

OBM eschews hypothetical constructs (e.g., self-esteem) and focuses instead on behavior, defined as anything an organism does. The goals of behavior analysis, and by extension OBM, are prediction and control, with an emphasis on control (Hayes & Brownstein, 1986). As guided by these goals, much of OBM research and application involves identifying situations under which a given behavior is most likely to occur and arranging environmental conditions to increase or decrease that behavior. Although behavior analysts recognize that biological variables affect behavior, the focus of behavior analysis is on environmental variables. In OBM, the behavior of interest is typically contextualized in relation to the production of important work results (i.e., performance; Daniels & Bailey, 2014; Hyten, 2009). Example measures could include productivity (e.g., rate of products produced) or safety (e.g., percentage of opportunities in which protective equipment is worn). Behavior that occurs privately, such as thinking and problem solving, is also considered behavior and subject to the same laws that govern overt actions. While examination of variables surrounding cognition, language, and their subsequent impact on performance remains relatively limited compared to similar fields such as industrial-organizational (I-O) psychology et, some applied work has successfully blended contemporary behavior analytic frameworks of language with common OBM intervention components (e.g., Pingo et al., 2020).

Limited measurement and intervention on private behavior is unsurprising, as direct observation of behavior is, historically, the preferred method of measurement in OBM and other behavior-analytic disciplines (Brethower et al., 2021). That is, instead of using subjective instruments in which the behavior of interest is subjectively reported or described, OBM typically strives for objective measurement of the frequency, duration, or some other dimension of behavior as it occurs in the natural environment, although initial assessments often comprise indirect or reported measures for practical reasons (e.g., Wilder et al., 2018). This focus on direct observation and measurement represents a key feature distinguishing OBM from I-O psychology (Johnson & Beehr, 2013).

Another methodological difference between OBM and other behavior science disciplines (e.g., psychology, political science) is that OBM researchers commonly use single subject experimental designs (e.g., VanStelle et al., 2012) while other behavior science disciplines typically rely almost solely on between subject (group) experimental designs (Erath et al., 2021). This is largely because behavior analysis tends to favor examination of behavior at the individual level, which is difficult with most group experimental designs. Some advantages of single subject designs (in addition to enabling examination of individual participant data) are that fewer participants are needed, and they fit well with real-world responsibilities like conducting assessments and evaluating intervention effects. Of course, single subject designs have some potential disadvantages as well. For example, generality of the data produced by these designs is established through repeated direct and systematic replications to ascertain parameters of intervention effects rather than through sampling procedures within individual studies (Walker & Carr, 2021).

Historically, OBM has used visual analysis of single case data to identify intervention effects. Researchers examine the level, trend, and variability in one condition (e.g., baseline) relative to another condition (i.e., the intervention). Often, visual analysis is sufficient to identify effects, in part because many of the interventions employed in OBM are robust. However, statistical analysis can be used to supplement the evaluation of data from single case designs. Statistical analysis is particularly useful when the differences between conditions are small, and when a large amount of variability exists in the data (Johnston et al., 2020).

While single subject designs are often utilized in behavior analytic research, it is the research question that guides the research design (i.e., the goals of the individual study; Walker & Carr, 2021). So, although OBM research frequently relies upon single subject designs, group designs and correlational designs are also used as aggregate employee or organizational performance is often relevant. Some OBM investigators begin a line of research with single-subject methods, which are ideal for identifying specific intervention components that may be effective and later progress to large-scale group evaluations, which are particularly useful to establish external validity. Of course, OBM research or applied use of techniques cannot occur without specifying the performance of interest and determining which features to measure. Thus, the remainder of this manuscript will describe some relevant, specific aspects of OBM practice and research: pinpointing, measurement, procedural integrity, and maintenance.

Pinpointing

In OBM, the word "pinpointing" is used to describe the process of operationally defining the target performance (i.e., the behavior and its results; Gilbert, 2007; Hyten, 2009), or dependent variable. Pinpointing is a crucial first step in OBM research and application. Without an operational definition of the pinpoint, measurement of performance is difficult. Good pinpoints are precise, reliable, measurable, and observable (Daniels & Bailey, 2014).

Precision

However, the reasons managers provide explaining poor employee performance may often not be measurable, observable, precise or reliable. Alternatively, organizational leaders may be interested in improving more nonspecific, global features of their organization (e.g., culture, engagement, satisfaction; McGee & Crowley-Koch, 2021). In these instances, it is the job of the OBM practitioner (e.g., managers, supervisors, researchers, and/or consultants) to interpret these reasons and/or constructs and produce precise definitions of performance(s). Therefore, pinpointing is an important skill to master. For example, imagine a manager or supervisor citing "laziness" as the variable explaining poor employee performance. However, the term "lazy" is imprecise and could refer to a number of behaviors such as not staying late at work or providing low quality customer care. Moreover, merely specifying behavior does not comprise a good pinpoint. In the former example, "not staying late" is neither behavior (i.e., it is the absence of staying) nor does it seem to specify that anything meaningful to the organization is occurring (i.e., the employee may only be occupying the office and browsing social media). At least "low quality customer care," while not a perfect pinpoint, describes some aspect of what the employee should actively be doing (i.e., addressing consumer needs) which can be subsequently linked to an important organizational accomplishment (e.g., sales and repeat business). A good pinpoint will precisely describe what aspects of an employee's performance to measure (Daniels & Bailey, 2014), contextualized within important organizational outcomes.

Reliability

As described above, another characteristic of a good pinpoint is that it is reliable. Reliability refers to consistency of measurement (Johnston et al., 2020). In other words, if repeated observation of the same events produces the same values, reliability can be asserted. Reliability is commonly determined by having two independent observers measure a pinpoint and then compare outcomes (i.e., interobserver agreement; IOA). If their outcomes produce at least 80% agreement, the pinpoint is generally, though not always, assumed to be reliable. In this sense, managers should be guided away from mentalistic pinpoints, pinpoints that reference hypothetical constructs such as self-esteem, or internal subjective states such as motivation, personality, or rapport (Daniels & Bailey, 2014). While formal, validated constructs may have utility in measurement (e.g., Mawhinney, 2011), in practice, these words often mean different things to different people, and therefore make unreliable pinpoints.

What to observe and measure

When deciding what aspects of performance to pinpoint, it is often best to consider the results of the behavior or accomplishment first since results (e.g., number of products sold, hours of services provided) are often indices of revenue. Revenue is often what is most important to organizations and it is logical to, at least initially, create a pinpoint around related results. Moreover, if there is limited potential to improve results, there may be little need to invest in behavioral change. In other words, "there can be no purpose in identifying deficiencies in rifle handling until we have established that there are deficiencies in hitting the target" (Gilbert, 2007, p. 23).

However, since a focus on results provides no information about which behaviors produced the results, managers should also measure ongoing behavior or performance (Daniels & Bailey, 2014). One area in which behavioral measures are critical is behavior-based safety. In other words, situations when outcomes occur infrequently but could have large negative impacts (Chase & Smith, 1994). While lagging indicators (e.g., incident rate) are important measures of outcome and necessary reporting variables for regulatory agencies, they do little to specify the day-to-day behaviors that influence the likelihood of incidents and may obscure ongoing unsafe practices (Agnew & Daniels, 2011). For example, if results are only measured, this may hide a pattern of unsafe behavior producing potentially severe consequences. Thus, effective behavior-based safety programs typically will pinpoint measures of specific overt behavior as well as results. Myers et al. (2010) provide an example of an effective safety improvement program at an oil refinery. As part of this program, the researchers measured specific safety practices by employees, in addition to the organization's overall safety record.

In fact, there are multiple situations in which a manager should default to pinpointing ongoing behavior instead of accomplishments or results. One situation in which is better to pinpoint and measure ongoing behavior is when employees begin learning tasks. When an employee is new and learning job duties, managers need to be sure they perform each specific duty or task. Focusing on measuring specific tasks, instead of results, may pay off under these circumstances (Daniels & Bailey, 2014). In a recent study,

Guadalupe and Alvero (2021) pinpointed data entry skills. Although a less effortful pinpoint might have been the product of data entry (e.g., a completed spreadsheet), the participants in this study had little experience with data entry, and therefore the most appropriate pinpoint was the act of entering the data.

Another situation is when there is a large discrepancy between exemplary and poor performance. If an employee is performing well below average, they are doing more or less of something than their coworkers or peers. By focusing only on results, a manager will not know what aspect of their performance is preventing them from improving. Under these circumstances, a focus on ongoing behavior (i.e., those aspects of their performance that are preventing them from achieving results consistent with their peers) is justified (Daniels & Bailey, 2014). Gilbert (2007) advocated calculation of employees' potential for improving performance (PIP), which is a ratio of exemplary performance to typical performance. A performer or group of performers with a large PIP suggests a significant discrepancy between their performance and the best performer(s), which in turn may hint at specific aspects of deficient performance to target.

A third situation is when there is concern that the employee may be falsifying information or behaving unethically in some way. Perhaps sales have increased because they are misinforming customers about sales terms of the product. To identify whether unethical behavior is occurring while an employee is producing a product or delivering a service, supervisors must measure ongoing behavior (Daniels & Bailey, 2014). Downing et al. (2018) provide an example of pinpointing identity checking behavior by cashiers in a restaurant. Although the restaurant manager could have more simply measured a result such as the amount customers spent or the number of food items purchased, they chose to measure identity checking to prevent fraud.

A fourth situation is when results are far removed in time from the ongoing performance. Many job duties involve complex sequences of steps that take a long time to complete. If managers pinpoint and measure only the outcome of those steps, an employee will learn only infrequently and if performance is sub-par, it may be too late to improve. Measuring each aspect of performance as it occurs enables managers to provide timely feedback before results are in. Kelley and Gravina (2018) provide an example of pinpointing ongoing behaviors instead of task completion by examining door-to-discharge duties in a hospital. Rather than focus on time to discharge, these researchers measured the steps involved in serving and discharging a patient. Researchers have also examined other large-scale tasks such as completing a thesis (Dillon et al., 1980).

Last, a critically important aspect of identifying pinpoints is that they should be under the control of the performer. Pinpoints not under the performer's control will be of little benefit because when managers attempt to improve the pinpoint, any intervention will have to be applied to many people. An intervention applied only to the performer will not likely be of benefit because the performer cannot directly improve the pinpoint. For example, pinpointing the number of billable hours per month will not be very useful if the number of patients an employee can serve is restricted by the organization's primary external funders. Of course, in addition to contingencies at the individual performer level, group contingencies are also common in OBM. Teams are common in many organizations, and pinpoints and interventions are directed at this level as well. Ideally, group or team pinpoints are under the control of the team.

To summarize, pinpointing is a fundamental skill in OBM and is a critical feature of organizational improvements in areas ranging from safety (e.g., Geller, 2005) to leadership (e.g., Laipple, 2012). Identifying critical observable behaviors and results, as well as insuring that they can be measured precisely and with fidelity takes practice and some knowledge of the conditions under which pinpointing behavior or results is most important. However, the payoff is well worth the investment of time and energy. The next section describes another important aspect of OBM practice and research, which is measurement.

Measurement in OBM

Once an appropriate performance is pinpointed, the next step for a manager, consultant, or researcher is to select an appropriate method to quantify and chronicle relevant variables. The direct, repeated measurement of variables of interest is a hallmark of behavior analysis (Johnston et al., 2020). OBM and its constituent subfields are no exception. Objective and ongoing measurement as the lens through which performance is influenced remains a key philosophical distinction between OBM and common popular psychological constructs of motivation (cf., Kohn, 1993), traditional approaches to management (Daniels & Bailey, 2014), as well as subjective approaches in analogous disciplines such as Industrial and Organizational Psychology (I-O Psychology; Gravina & Siers, 2011).

For example, I-O psychologists have customarily used performance appraisals as a method to sample employee ability, guide organizational decisions, and affect performance management initiatives at the group level. In contrast, performance appraisal in OBM is better characterized as output of performance management (i.e., the result of ongoing measurement and development of pinpoints), suggesting an approach more focused on individual employee growth and development (Gravina & Siers, 2011). Thus, rather than relying solely upon estimation, aggregation, or measurement of presumed correlates (e.g., tests; Gilbert, 2007), common measurement practices in OBM also represent a unique competitive advantage, producing a more continuous record of the performance of interest. This is not to say that OBM practitioners and researchers never utilize aggregate data, subjective assessments or group designs (see Erath et al., 2021), but that measurement rarely eschews the objective and measurable variables that comprise performance, studying them in ways that, often, may be more palatable to organizational constituents (e.g., Crowell, 2005).

Choosing appropriate measurement procedures is critical for a number of reasons. One principal concern is evaluating intervention efficacy. Any given OBM intervention can be conceptualized as an experiment (Poling et al., 1993). Though levels of methodological rigor vary in applied settings, OBM practitioners verify the intervention (i.e., independent variable) has a demonstrable impact on the specific performance of the constituent members through measurement. Moreover, the verifiable changes in performance should impact group, department, and, hopefully, organization-wide results. Absent an accurate and reliable measurement system, ongoing iteration and support of the intervention is hampered. Moreover, measurement is also intrinsic to many common OBM interventions. For example, the most evaluated independent variable in the *JOBM* is performance feedback (VanStelle et al., 2012). Feedback, commonly defined as information about performance to direct behavioral change (e.g., Sleiman et al., 2020) can only be conveyed to a performer if that information is measured. Moreover, poor measurement will likely reduce the efficacy of feedback. For example, inaccurate feedback can dampen its impact (e.g., Johnson et al., 2015) or diminish its value in promoting acquisition of new skills (e.g., Brand et al., 2020) and may influence the timing of delivery, deliverer(s) of feedback, and modality, all of which will likely modulate its effectiveness (Sleiman et al., 2020).

OBM practitioners are not always concerned with individual performance either. Precise measurement is fundamentally important at all levels of organizations. Systems approaches, such as BSA, customarily measure organizational, process, and performer level variables (e.g., Brethower, 1982; Diener et al., 2009; Rummler & Brache, 2013). An organization that measures performance can set appropriate goals, define important roles, distribute resources efficiently, and monitor ongoing performances (Rummler & Brache, 2013). In other words, measurement enhances the ability of managers to manage. Measurement permits establishment of critical management skills, including performance expectations, identification of deficits, and critical decision making. Conversely, if managers are measuring inaccurately or not measuring at all, then they risk making important decisions through subjective evaluation and managing by perception alone (Abernathy, 2014). Use of data derived from measurement supports unbiased, credible management that can accurately assess progress and is responsive to change (Daniels & Bailey, 2014). These benefits are apparent to the employee, who can receive clear communication and information about which job duties to perform and how to perform them. More broadly, the emphasis on objective measurement in OBM empowers the employee to monitor and improve their own performance by focusing on the observable behavior and results they control (Crowell, 2005).

Measuring the dependent variable in OBM

As mentioned above, some systems-based approaches in OBM can encompass multiple layers of the organizational function, most often at three levels (e.g., organization, process, performer; McGee & Crowley-Koch, 2021). For example, BSA approaches often begin with identifying the organization's goals, internal structure, and management systems (e.g., Rummler & Brache, 2013), with assessment and measurement often examining organizational outputs, external threats, and current management systems. Measurement at this level is primarily concerned with using these data to uncover deficiencies in organizational processes, internal measurement, and monitoring systems in relation to broad organizational outcomes and its survival. When examining at the process level, measurement is typically concerned with defining the impact of deficient processes as well as identifying problematic steps, roles, and redundancies (i.e., "disconnects") for improvement (Diener et al., 2009). However, in most published OBM literature, measurement is conducted at the performer level (i.e., related to specific work tasks) and is typically evaluated through within-subject designs (VanStelle et al., 2012).

Specific, observable behavior is of critical interest in OBM. However, in contrast to other applications of behavior analysis, such as therapeutic ABA services, there are key differences. For instance, OBM is more likely to favor measurement of behavioral products over behaviors (VanStelle et al., 2012). As discussed above, there are some situations in which measurement of ongoing behavior is preferred, but these are exceptions. This is unsurprising, however, because OBM measurement is concerned with *performance* as opposed to *behavior*. While Hyten (2009) notes the terms may be used synonymously, performance is commonly defined as a summation of behavior and results (e.g., Daniels & Bailey, 2014), or as a cost/benefit ratio of the two (e.g., Gilbert, 2007). Thus, measurement of performance can comprise many different variables (e.g., counting responses, measuring response products).

As such, performance can be conceptualized in multiple ways (see Table 1). Gilbert (2007) suggested three dimensions by which performance should be measured: quality, quantity/productivity, and cost. Quality performances can be further delineated by three distinct categories, including accuracy (i.e., the proportion of errors to the accomplishments), class (i.e., features ancillary to accuracy that distinguish quality), and novelty (i.e., the uniqueness or creativity of the performance). Quantity refers to the rate (e.g., per hour production), timeliness (i.e., products delivered on time), and/or volume (i.e., production

Table 1. Measurement of the dependent variable in OBM, adapted from Gilbert (2007).

Dimension*	Subtype	Definition	Example Performance and Pertinent Measures
Quality	Accuracy	Proportion of errors to accomplishments, typically in comparison to a model or exemplar	Manufacturing (e.g., products made to specification without defects) Medical billing (e.g., claims filed correctly)
	Class	Comparative quality distinguished by other factors besides accuracy	Filmmaking (e.g., opinion ratings, critical reviews) Commercial fishing (e.g., condition/freshness of the catch)
	Novelty	Uniqueness or creativity of a performance	Clothing design (e.g., aesthetically distinct) Food science (e.g., novel meat-substitutes)
Quantity (or Productivity)	Rate	Performance or product per unit of time	Housekeeping (e.g., rooms cleaned per day) Teaching a class (e.g., learning units delivered per class hour)
	Timeliness	Performance dependent on time criterion/criteria	News writing (e.g., story completed in time for evening news) Food delivery (e.g., pizza delivered in fewer than 30 minutes)
	Volume	Production absent time criterion	Car sales (e.g., number of new cars sold) Farming (e.g., pounds of produce harvested)
Cost	Labor	Amount spent to procure or purchase labor	Legal defense (e.g., cost of paralegals) Building a new road (e.g., liability insurance for contractors)
	Materials	Material costs to produce performance	Video game design (e.g., server costs) Breeding livestock (e.g., housing and stable costs)
	Management	Internal and external administrative costs associated with performance	Importing/exporting (e.g., port charges, tariffs) Therapy provision (e.g., supervision and credentialing costs)

without a time criterion). Daniels and Bailey (2014) note that quantity is the most frequently utilized dimension because, at its most basic, it merely involves counting. Cost refers to the net resources consumed in the performance or invested in the results, typically reported as a monetary amount. Labor (e.g., wages, insurance costs), materials (e.g., real estate, raw materials, tools), and management (e.g., administrative and managerial needs) are common expressions of cost. Additionally, measurement may also include specification of a standard for the performance, either through industry benchmarks or past performance, to inform expectations. While measurement of a performance can and, ideally should be quantified in each dimension, each category may not be practically useful to evaluate pinpoints. The manager, consultant, or researcher must exercise discretion to choose the relevant dimensions (Daniels & Bailey, 2014) and, subsequently, select precise units of measurement (e.g., count, frequency, duration). Such decisions may be based on aspects of the specific performance (e.g., is the performance discrete?), feasibility (e.g., can the performance be observed and/or quantified in this way?), and custom (e.g., has the performance been historically measured this way, successfully?)

Choosing a measurement system

The dimension of performance measured influences the assumptions a researcher, consultant, or manager must make about their data. Direct measurement typically refers to measuring the same events under analysis (i.e., counting specific occurrences of the dependent variable; Johnston et al., 2020). Indirect measurement refers to measuring a variable different than the event under analysis (e.g., a questionnaire written about the dependent variable). Some dimensions of performance (e.g., quantity, accuracy) are much more amenable to direct measurement, while some (e.g., novelty) almost necessitate indirect measures (i.e., creativity will likely be subjectively ranked). Indirect measures are not inherently problematic, so long as there is strong evidence that the variable measure correlates well to the dependent variable under analysis (Johnston et al., 2020). There is also a question of the observation procedures to capture the most complete record of the performance, leveraged against other practical concerns. Continuous measurement procedures permit detection of all responses during the observation period, while discontinuous measures approximate the number of responses that can be detected. The former is likely more accurate, but requires an attentive and, potentially intrusive, observer. The latter will likely be easier but risks missing critical occurrences of the performance. In general, continuous, direct measurement of the behavior of interest is often held as the preferred standard in behavior analytic disciplines, including OBM (Daniels & Bailey, 2014).

In OBM applications, Daniels and Bailey (2014) distill this into two primary methods of measuring dependent variables (i.e., performance): counting and judgment. Counting generally refers to all numerically based forms of quantifying performance. This could include continuously tallying frequency of permanent products or responses or merely sampling their occurrence. Most, if not all, industries feature performances that could be measured with counting. For example, human services organizations might count the hours billed or services rendered. In manufacturing, supervisors might sample the number of products made to specification in an hour (or, alternatively, the number of defects). Judgment refers to a subjective evaluation of performance, typically comprising rating and ranking scales. This method is typically reserved for performances that are difficult to distill into discrete, countable categories. Such methods are commonly observed in the service and hospitality sector, where customers are often asked to rate multiple dimensions of their experience on various numerical scales. Daniels and Bailey suggest counting is arguably the more reliable and, thus, preferred method.

That is not to say that more subjective measures have no place in OBM, however. Use of judgment as a method might also permit a consultant or researcher to consider a performance in such a manner that leads to a novel way count. Judgment methods are also useful when quantifying and analyzing complex performances. If ranking or rating scales are deemed necessary to use, repeated measurement and increased specificity of rating criteria can help improve their reliability. Some methods use objective performance pinpoints to reduce subjectivity. For example, Behaviorally Anchored Rating Scales (BARS) use numerical rating scales, with each value associated (i.e., "anchored") with an objective description of performance. This allows for rating of performance at multiple levels from exemplary to subpar, through a more reliable delineation of differences between them. A more complex version of a judgment method that incorporates features of BARS and other judgment-based measurements (e.g., checklists and rankings) is the performance matrix or scorecard. Performance matrices incorporate a variety of pinpoints and anchor them to a weighted score (Abernathy, 2014). When computed, the overall score provides a normalized index of job performance, allowing for comparison across different jobs and alignment with organizational goals. Performance scorecard outcomes can be linked to employee compensation (e.g., Abernathy, 2014) as well as to general incentive systems (e.g., lotteries; Griffin et al., 2019). In addition, subjective measurement is frequently utilized in assessment of social validity concern such as procedural acceptability (e.g., Nastasi et al., 2021).

What to measure in OBM

As OBM has grown over the decades, some debate has ensued regarding the aspects of performance most important to measure. Hyten (2009) links the historical development of the PM and BSA sub-fields of OBM to a clear divide in the dependent variables measured. Most of what is described today as PM follows what Hyten calls a "behavior-focused" approach, which developed as a direct derivative of ABA and Skinnerian tradition. In behavior-focused traditions, contingency management to influence individual performer behavior is the primary goal; the engineering of positive reinforcement strategies is emblematic of the behavioral tradition (e.g., Daniels & Bailey, 2014). Much of the publication history of *JOBM* is arguably steeped in a behavior-focused approach. Concurrently with the development of PM, what is now commonly referred to as BSA, was established. A blending of systems theory and behavior analysis resulted in what Hyten (2009) deems the "results-focused" approach (e.g., Brethower, 1982; Diener et al., 2009; Malott, 2003). In the results-focused approach, an emphasis is placed on analyzing behavior as a single variable in the larger context of an organization. This divide in approach was elaborated first by Gilbert (2007, pp. 102–105), in emphasizing that influence and control of human behavior is not the sole focus on engineering performance, but one part of the construction of work cultures. Behavior, in this conceptualization, is not the dependent measure, but another independent variable that produces the results (Hyten, 2009).

Research on measurement in OBM

However, the efficacy of one approach over the other remains largely speculative and clearly delineating the two is difficult. Behavior-focused studies have often accounted for results and other contextual variables in the literature. BSA, too, does not shun a behavior-focused approach, but instead subsumes it (Hyten, 2009). The record of published OBM literature hints at a mixture of approaches, suggestive more of a gradient than a dichotomy. For example, in *JOBM*, the focus on behavioral measures is currently decreasing in favor of product (i.e., results) measures. Yet, published research studying individual performance remains more common than evaluation of systems approaches (VanStelle et al., 2012). Therefore, it may be more beneficial to view behavior- and results-focused approaches as complementary, with pragmatic benefit to utilizing both when possible, similar to choosing appropriate performances to pinpoint (see above).

Despite some disagreement over *what* to measure and emphasize in terms of primary dependent variables, there does seem to be consensus that more frequent measurement of secondary variables is necessary in OBM. In addition to robust outcomes, a successful OBM intervention must be both worthwhile to the organization's bottom line and its constituents. These impacts are scarcely evaluated in research. Data on money are reported in less than half of OBM studies (Poling et al., 1993; Wells et al., 2013). Moreover, a formal cost-benefit calculation, the positive fiscal impacts of interventions compared to the costs incurred, remains even rarer (VanStelle et al., 2012). Measurement of consumer ratings of the intervention or the performances targeted to gauge social validity is also inconsistent. VanStelle et al. note that measurement of social validity has varied greatly across *JOBM*'s publication history. Certain forms of assessment (e.g., procedural acceptability) appear to be increasing over time, but measurement standards appear to be inconsistent and vary by industry (Nastasi et al., 2021). Moreover, measurement of social validity continues to rely predominantly on subjective measures and, therefore, data must be interpreted cautiously (Poling et al., 1993). Last, OBM research has historically demonstrated robust impact on increasing valuable performances, but the extent to which these interventions influence the overall quality of the work experience for employees remains under measured. Hantula (2015) notes that job satisfaction, despite its inconsistent ability to predict other organizational outcomes (e.g., attrition), should be a key consideration of OBM practitioners in structuring work environments.

In addition to answering *what* should be measured, the research literature has also examined *how* and *when* measurement should be conducted. As mentioned previously, continuous and direct measurement is ideal, but this is often not feasible for implementers especially for managers and supervisors with other duties. Moreover, observation may influence the behavior of observed (i.e., reactivity) as well as the observer (i.e., King et al., 2018; Sasson & Austin, 2004). Practitioners might choose to allow subjects to monitor and manage their own behavior (see Ferguson et al., 2021 for a review) to leverage these impacts to produce unique effects (i.e., the observer effect; Sasson & Austin, 2004). However, changes in the behavior of the observed may risk obfuscation of the "real" performance by introducing an unwanted extraneous variable. Thus, researchers might choose to utilize discontinuous procedures. For example, time-sampling procedures allow implementers to estimate the occurrence of the behavior by conducting and recording observations at regular time intervals. Alvero et al. (2008) compared three common time sampling procedures: whole-interval (WIR), partial-interval (PIR), and momentary time sampling (MTS) and their ability to accurately estimate levels of safe performance. In WIR, the performance must occur for the entire sampling interval to be marked as an occurrence, while in PIR, the performance only needs to occur (or partially occur) to be recorded as an occurrence. MTS requires a response to occur at the end of an interval to be recorded as an occurrence (Johnston et al., 2020). Similar to findings in ABA, Alvero et al. noted that PIR consistently overestimated behavior, WIR underestimated behavior, and MTS varied but was generally the most accurate procedure. Subsequent studies support that MTS is the preferred measurement procedure over WIR (Taylor et al., 2012) and that MTS could be accurate across longer time spans (Alvero et al., 2011).

In short, choosing the key performance variables to measure is likely dependent on the experimental question, consult focus, and/or relative costs and benefits. Measurement approaches from a systems viewpoint remain popular in discussion but relatively infrequent in practice. This is likely, in part, due to a methodological constraint. Systems analyses typically account for myriad variables at multiple organizational levels (Diener et al., 2009). Control and manipulation of variables solely at the job level is likely more amenable to demonstrating experimental control. Another reason that various approaches to measurement have not been rigorously compared is due to lack of reporting. Conard et al. (2016) suggest that consultants might be reluctant to publish proprietary data and materials that could represent a larger variety of approaches to organizational issues (e.g., techniques promoting the generality of interventions). In addition, measurement of other variables to inform context should also be explored (e.g., social validity, cost/benefit data) as they remain generally underreported in OBM research. Moreover, the way measurement is conducted can influence its accuracy (e.g., sampling procedures). Thus, ensuring reliability of measurement and fidelity of intervention is critical.

Reliability and procedural integrity measurement

Daniels and Bailey (2014) note that counting is generally more preferred to ranking or rating due to its objective nature. However, such a dichotomy belies the issue that certain forms of counting (i.e., direct observation), though superior to measurement of hypothetical constructs, are often still reliant on the judgments of the observer. In this regard, some form of subjectivity is always present in measurement (Gravina & Siers, 2011). Therefore, the assurance of the measurement system's reliability and the integrity of independent variable implementation is likely as important as the choice of measurement. This is even more important when considering that, as an applied science, a great deal of OBM research is conducted in the field (VanStelle et al., 2012). In addition to less control over extraneous variables, field studies may also incorporate a variety of implementers ranging from researchers to front-line employees. Thus, confidence in the outcomes of an intervention should always be considered in relation to the validity and accuracy of its measurement system.

Reliability generally refers to the consistency of the observers. Formal measurement of reliability occurs when two or more observers record data on the same performance and these data are evaluated for agreement (Kazdin, 2020). In behavior analytic research, this is typically calculated as some proportion of agreements to disagreements (i.e., IOA), though there are alternative correlational (e.g., Pearson Product-Moment) and statistical (e.g., computing Cohen's *k*) methods to quantify reliability available as well. Consistency of observers enhances the believability of the data collected (VanStelle et al., 2012). In behavior-analytic research, a calculated IOA of 80% or higher observed across approximately 30% of experimental sessions is generally deemed acceptable, though measurement should be adjusted based on a variety of factors, such as the skill of the observers and the rate of the targeted behavior (Hausman et al., 2022). Ultimately, the "right" amount of agreement is what is deemed acceptable by the researcher to assert reliability and minimize errors in context of the experimental conditions and question (Kazdin, 2020).

Procedural integrity measurement in OBM

Inaccuracies in recording the dependent variable are not the only potential sources of error when evaluating a procedure or conducting an experiment. Procedural integrity or fidelity measures typically describe the degree to which the independent variable was implemented as designed (Cymbal et al., 2021). Procedural integrity can be measured informally (e.g., descriptively) or formally (e.g., numerical estimation; Poling et al., 1993). When formally reported, integrity data can be calculated as a percentage of correct implementations of the procedure or the percentage of correct components (Vollmer et al., 2008). Integrity data are most frequently reported numerically in OBM studies (Cymbal et al., 2021), typically by sampling delivery of the intervention, calculating the number of steps or opportunities implemented correctly, and converting that number to a percentage. A fraction of studies also report monitoring to procedural integrity without calculating a score. This could include narrative reporting of integrity data (e.g., reporting that a checklist was used to ensure that the procedure was implemented correctly) or simply noting that the level of integrity was monitored throughout. However, these anecdotal methods should likely not serve as a standard as it reduces the replicability of the findings and may diminish confidence in the results. Of course, procedural integrity is not always a necessary feature of studies in OBM, such as when interventions are automated or mechanically introduced. All other studies, and even OBM consults, should include at least some measure of procedural integrity because some measurement is superior to none. Even simple checks integrity can yield valuable insight into intervention refinement by allowing the researcher, manager, or consultant to quickly identify problematic steps within the procedure and adapt their methods accordingly (Poling et al., 1993).

Research and procedural integrity in OBM

In general, behavior analytic research tends to underreport procedural integrity, especially compared to measurement of IOA (Falakfarsa et al., 2021; Peterson et al., 1982). Studies in *JOBM* show a similar pattern. Cymbal et al. (2021) found that, from 2000–2020, IOA was measured in over half of studies, while integrity was measured in less than half. This remains alarming when considering the risk of implementation errors remains high in most OBM studies due to the number of implementers and complexity of the interventions.

One area of procedural integrity that remains under studied in OBM research, relative to ABA, is the degree to which fidelity errors impact treatment. Multiple studies noted the detrimental impact of procedural integrity errors in therapeutic ABA applications (Carroll et al., 2013; Pipkin et al., 2010). It is likely that reduced procedural integrity in OBM also affects intervention efficacy. However, typical participants in OBM studies (i.e., typically developing adults) likely possess markedly different repertoires (e.g., advanced language, rule-governed behavior) than typical participants in ABA settings (e.g., children and individuals with intellectual disabilities) and the results of integrity failures could be different due to these variations.

Maintenance and related concepts

Generality of behavior change procedures was identified by Baer et al. (1968) as one of the critical features of ABA. As an applied science, OBM shares many of the same tenets as ABA. In common areas of OBM intervention (e.g., safety and health; VanStelle et al., 2012), it is easy to envision how a weak or brief intervention might lead to disastrous results (i.e., injury or death). Failure of interventions then could undermine confidence in applications of OBM. Thus, one critical area is ensuring the selected interventions and, thereby, subsequent behavior and organizational changes persist over time. The durability of the observed changes in behavior is commonly referred to as response maintenance (Foxx, 2013). Maintenance, topographically defined as a sustained or increased performance across time, is a seemingly simple concept. However, there are a variety of functional variables that are presumed to account for maintenance and other long term intervention effects in applied settings, leading to diverse strategies to promote long-term outcomes.

Response maintenance

The term "maintenance" has been utilized in the context of operant learning for some time (e.g., Skinner, 1953, p. 98), but most modern usages of the term are in relation to applied intervention contexts. In OBM, for example, maintenance commonly refers to some persistence of the dependent variable(s) following cessation of the formal intervention (Conard et al., 2016; Sigurdsson & Austin, 2006). This has led to multiple disparate characterizations of maintenance effects, including generalization of the behavior change and resistance to extinction. However, invoking the term generalization with regard to maintenance is likely a misrepresentation of the specific phenomena. Relatedly, resistance to extinction is likely not the best explanation for organizational instances of maintenance, as extinction oversimplifies the variety of variables involved and ignores the more likely explanation (i.e., other variables come to control performance; McSween & Matthews, 2001). In addition, assuming that an intervention is designed to be removed is flatly incorrect, especially in cases of behavior-based safety (Fleming, 2001). Some authors have suggested that determinants of maintenance are fundamentally different than the variables that promote acquisition (e.g., Boyce & Geller, 2001) or the key feature of maintenance in OBM settings is adoption of the intervention by the organization (i.e., institutionalization; Kessler, 2001).

Institutionalization

The term institutionalization refers to the transfer of intervention management and/or implementation from the consultant, trainer, or researcher to managers or other organizational stakeholders. While some authors suggested that because the outcome (i.e., sustained behavior change) is the same, there is no need to distinguish between the terms maintenance and institutionalization (Kessler, 2001). However, there are clear instances where maintenance can occur without institutionalization (e.g., when the intervention is training-based; Conard et al., 2016). Thus, the two are distinct but often interrelated concepts. Maintenance is likely best conceptualized as sustained change in the performance of interest following formal evaluation of the intervention, while institutionalization, by definition requires the involvement of other performers and performances to sustain the change. Thus, maintenance best suggests a single contingency while institutionalization specifies, at a minimum, an interlocking behavior contingency.

Research on maintenance and related concepts

Research on maintenance remains relatively sparse in OBM, especially as the main phenomena of interest. Most studies examining determinants of maintenance come from behavior-based safety interventions. Long-term evaluation of safety interventions has identified a variety of variables that likely promoted maintenance, including social mediation, contact with natural contingencies, pre-intervention systems analysis, and institutionalization of intervention contingencies (e.g., Alavosius & Sulzer-Azaroff, 1990; Boyce & Geller, 2001; Grindle et al., 2000). In short, interventions that sustain are those that continue to contact contingencies, even when formal involvement is discontinued. This can be effectively accomplished when pinpointed performance leads to relevant natural consequences (e.g., health and well-being), when new social contingencies are established, either formally or as a byproduct of intervention, and/or when these contingencies become culturally-normalized practices of the organizational setting.

Because determinants of maintenance are unique to the specific intervention setting, some research sought to identify general strategies that increase the likelihood of maintenance and institutionalization. Sigurdsson and Austin (2006) created a taxonomy of dimensions along which institutionalization can be promoted, including employee involvement in design, internal staff training, as well as formal data collection and consequence systems. In thirty-one studies, they found that addition of these variables predicted reported institutionalization of intervention. Conard et al. (2016) furthered this research by curating a larger taxonomy of "temporal generality" tactics, distilled from tactics to promote generalization (i.e., Stokes & Baer, 1977), the institutionalization taxonomy (Sigurdsson & Austin, 2006) and literature in BSA and social validity. They found most studies in OBM infrequently utilized generality strategies.

Overall, research on maintenance and institutionalization in OBM is predominantly based on reviews of prior literature and focuses on two specific areas. The first area is reviews of studies wherein interventions continued past the formal involvement of researchers. Second is reviews of studies to extract general tactics and strategies to promote these variables. To date, few tactics have been empirically validated (Conard et al., 2016). Arguably, some of the tactics outlined are also based on conceptually inconsistent technology (e.g., generalization) and broad assumptions about the nature of the performance problems (see, McSween & Matthews, 2001). Broadly, more direct manipulation of these variables is needed.

Recommendations and conclusions

The field of OBM is young and holds much promise. In this section, we offer some directions for future work on each topic described in this chapter. For pinpointing, researchers and practitioners should continue to work on identifying the conditions under which pinpointing specific behaviors takes precedent over pinpointing results. Our decision-making process regarding pinpointing behaviors versus results will undoubtedly improve as additional research becomes available.

For measurement, researchers and practitioners should continue identifying the most appropriate measure of behavior given the topography of performance and the context in which it occurs. For example, we know that MTS is superior to WIR, at least under some conditions (Taylor et al., 2012). However, there is a dearth of research on other methods of measurement in OBM and very little research on comparative efficacy of measurement procedures. Additional research might result in guidelines that are more specific for researchers and practitioners when developing measurement systems. Furthermore, "judgment" methods (e.g., ranking, rating, and survey) are an area that requires more study in OBM. Indices of employee experience such as procedural acceptability (Nastasi et al., 2021) and job satisfaction (Hantula, 2015) are under-measured in the literature. Some methods of rating traditionally held as more objective, such as BARS and performance scorecards have conflicting literature on efficacy (Martin-Raugh et al., 2016; Tziner et al., 2000) or few empirical studies (e.g., Griffin et al., 2019), respectively.

More research is also needed on the commonality of procedural integrity measurement in practice. Currently, research on the need for and use of procedural integrity in practice is nonexistent. In addition, research on the effect of integrity failures is needed. Some ABA interventions (e.g., differential reinforcement) have been shown to be effective even when implemented with only 50%-75% integrity (St. Peter-Pipkin et al., 2010). Some OBM interventions (e.g., feedback) might be similarly impacted by reduced procedural integrity, but this has not been evaluated formally in research.

For maintenance, researchers and practitioners should collect formal data, as well as evaluate the necessary variables or techniques to promote lasting change. Both monitoring of intervention effects and research on maintenance remain a weaker aspect of the OBM literature. Specifically, researchers and practitioners should examine how long OBM intervention effects persist after the intervention or when some of its components are removed. Researchers should also examine if intervention effects can be sustained with simple environmental manipulations such as signals. Finally, future research distinguishing maintenance from institutionalization is needed.

In conclusion, OBM researchers and practitioners developed a robust, natural science-based approach to understanding, predicting, and improving performance in organizations. The field has accomplished much, and yet also has much to systematically study and learn about its subject matter and methodology. Hopefully, the next 50 years will be even more productive than the last 50 years!

Disclosure statement

No potential conflict of interest was reported by the author(s).

ORCID

David Wilder http://orcid.org/0000-0002-6586-4841

References

Abernathy, W. B. (2014). *The liberated workplace: Transitioning to walden three.* Performance Management Publications.

Agnew, J. L., & Daniels, A. C. (2011). *Safe by accident? Take the luck out of safety leadership practices that build a sustainable culture.* Performance ManagementPublications.

Alavosius, M. P., & Sulzer-Azaroff, B. (1990). Acquisition and maintenance of health-care routines as a function of feedback density. *Journal of Applied Behavior Analysis, 23*(2), 151–162. http://doi.org/10.1901/jaba.1990.23-151

Alvero, A. M., Struss, K., & Rappaport, E. (2008). Measuring safety performance: A comparison of whole, partial, and momentary time-sampling recording methods. *Journal of Organizational Behavior Management, 27*(4), 1–28. http://doi.org/10.1300/J075v27n04_01

Alvero, A. M., Rappaport, E., & Taylor, M. A. (2011). A further assessment of momentary time-sampling across extended interval lengths. *Journal of Organizational Behavior Management, 31*(2), 117–129. http://doi.org/10.1080/01608061.2011.569203

Baer, D. M., Wolf, M. M., & Risley, T. R. (1968). Some current dimensions of applied behavior analysis. *Journal of Applied Behavior Analysis, 1*(1), 91–97. https://doi.org/10.1901/jaba.1968.1-91

Behavior Analyst Certification Board (2022, March, 30). March 2022 newsletter. *BACB Newsletter,* https://www.bacb.com/wp-content/uploads/2022/01/BACB_March2022_Newsletter-220330-4.pdf

Boyce, T. E., & Geller, E. S. (2001). Applied behavior analysis and occupational safety: The challenge of response maintenance. *Journal of Organizational Behavior Management, 21*(1), 31–56. http://doi.org/10.1300/J075v21n01_03

Brand, D., Novak, M. D., DiGennaro Reed, F. D., & Tortolero, S. A. (2020). Examining the effects of feedback accuracy and timing on skill acquisition. *Journal of Organizational Behavior Management, 40*(1–2), 3–18. http://doi.org/10.1080/01608061.2020.1715319

Brethower, D. M. (1982). The total performance system. In R. O'Brien, A. Dickinson, & M. Rosow (Eds.), *Industrial behavior modification: A management handbook* (pp. 350–369). Pergamon.

Brethower, D. M., Dickinson, A. M., Johnson, D. A., Johnson, C. M., Brodkin, E. S., & Connell, J. E. (2021). A history of organizational behavior management. *Journal of Organizational Behavior Management, 41*(1), 2–15. https://doi.org/10.1080/01608061.2021.1924340

Carroll, R. A., Kodak, T., & Fisher, W. W. (2013). An evaluation of programmed treatment-integrity errors during discrete-trial instruction. *Journal of Applied Behavior Analysis, 46*(2), 379–394. http://doi.org/10.1002/jaba.49

Chase, P. N., & Smith, J. M. (1994). *Performance analysis: Understanding behavior in organizations.* Envision Development Group, Inc., Publishers.

Conard, A. L., Johnson, D. A., Morrison, J. D., & Ditzian, K. (2016). Tactics to ensure durability of behavior change following the removal of an intervention specialist: A review of temporal generality within organizational behavior management. *Journal of Organizational Behavior Management, 36*(2–3), 210–253. http://doi.org/10.1080/01608061.2016.1201036

Crowell, C. R. (2005). Beyond positive reinforcement: OBM as a humanizing approach to management practices. *Journal of Organizational Behavior Management, 24*(1–2), 195–202. http://doi.org/10.1300/J075v24n01_13

Cymbal, D., Wilder, D., Cruz, N., Ingraham, G., Llinas, M., Clark, R., & Kamlowsky, M. (2021). Procedural integrity reporting in the *journal of organizational behavior management* (2000–2020). *Journal of Organizational Behavior Management, 41*(1), 2–15. https://doi.org/10.1080/01608061.2021.2014380

Daniels, A. C., & Bailey, J. S. (2014). *Performance management: Changing behavior that drives organizational effectiveness* (5th ed.). Performance Management Publications.

Dickinson, A. M. (2001). The historical roots of organizational behavior management in the private sector. *Journal of Organizational Behavior Management, 20*(3–4), 9–58. https://doi.org/10.1300/j075v20n03_02

Diener, L. H., McGee, H. M., & Miguel, C. (2009). An integrated approach for conducting a behavioral systems analysis. *Journal of Organizational Behavior Management, 29*(2), 108–135. https://doi.org/10.1080/01608060902874534

Dillon, M., Kent, H., & Malott, R. W. (1980). A supervisory system for accomplishing long-range projects. *Journal of Organizational Behavior Management, 2*(3), 213–227. https://doi.org/10.1300/J075v02n03_07

Downing, C. O., Capriola, N., & Geller, E. S. (2018). Preventing credit-card fraud: A goal-setting and prompting intervention to increase cashiers' ID-checking behavior. *Journal of Organizational Behavior Management, 38*(4), 335–344. https://doi.org/10.1080/01608061.2018.1514349

Erath, T. G., Pellegrino, A. J., DiGennaro Reed, F. D., Ruby, S. A., Blackman, A. L., & Novak, M. D. (2021). Experimental research methodologies in organizational behavior management. *Journal of Organizational Behavior Management, 41*(2), 150–181. https://doi.org/10.1080/01608061.2020.1869137

Falakfarsa, G., Brand, D., Jones, L., Godinez, E. S., Richardson, D. C., Hanson, R. J., Velazquez, S. D., & Wills, C. (2021). Treatment integrity reporting in behavior analysis in practice 2008–2019. *Behavior Analysis in Practice, 15*(2), 443–453. https://doi.org/10.1007/s40617-021-00573-9

Ferguson, R., Rivera, L., Pallathra, A. A., Eckerman, D. A., Brodkin, E. S., & Connell, J. E. (2021). Self-management in organizational behavior management. *Journal of Organizational Behavior Management, 41*(1), 2–15. https://doi.org/10.1080/01608061.2021.1996502

Fleming, R. (2001). Diverse problems call for diverse analyses and interventions in behavioral safety. *Journal of Organizational Behavior Management, 21*(1), 65–69. https://doi.org/10.1300/J075v21n01_05

Foxx, R. M. (2013). The maintenance of behavioral change: The case for long-term follow-ups. *American Psychologist, 68*(8), 728–736. https://doi.org/10.1037/a0033713

Geller, E. S. (2005). Behavior-based safety and occupational risk management. *Behavior Modification, 29*(3), 539–561. https://doi.org/10.1177/0145445504273287

Gilbert, T. F. (2007). *Human competence: Engineering worthy performance* (3rd ed.). Pfeiffer/John Wiley & Sons.

Gravina, N. E., & Siers, B. P. (2011). Square pegs and round holes: Ruminations on the relationship between performance appraisal and performance management. *Journal of Organizational Behavior Management, 31*(4), 277–287. http://doi.org/10.1080/01608061.2011.619418

Gravina, N., Villacorta, J., Albert, K., Clark, R., Curry, S., & Wilder, D. (2018). A literature review of organizational behavior management interventions in human service settings from 1990 to 2016. *Journal of Organizational Behavior Management, 38*(2–3), 191–224. https://doi.org/10.1080/01608061.2018.1454872

Griffin, M., Gravina, N. E., Matey, N., Pritchard, J., & Wine, B. (2019). Using scorecards and a lottery to improve the performance of behavior technicians in two autism treatment clinics. *Journal of Organizational Behavior Management, 39*(3–4), 280–292. https://doi.org/10.1080/01608061.2019.1632241

Grindle, A. C., Dickinson, A. M., & Boettcher, W. (2000). Behavioral safety research in manufacturing settings: A review of the literature. *Journal of Organizational Behavior Management, 20*(1), 29–68. http://doi.org/10.1300/J075v20n01_03

Guadalupe, J. K., & Alvero, A. M. (2021). A comparison of the effects of various performance feedback presentations on typing accuracy and speed. *Journal of Organizational Behavior Management, 41*(4), 289–304. http://doi.org/10.1080/01608061.2021.1919590

Hantula, D. A. (2015). Job satisfaction: The management tool and leadership responsibility. *Journal of Organizational Behavior Management, 35*(1–2), 81–94. https://doi.org/10.1080/01608061.2015.1031430

Hantula, D. A. (2022). The code is irrelevant: Organizational behavior management is not applied behavior analysis. *Journal of Organizational Behavior Management*, 1–8. https://doi.org/10.1080/01608061.2022.2029796

Hausman, N. L., Javed, N., Bednar, M. K., Guell, M., Schaller, E., Nevill, R. E., & Kahng, S. (2022). Interobserver agreement: A preliminary investigation into how much is enough? *Journal of Applied Behavior Analysis, 55*(2), 357–368. https://doi.org/10.1002/jaba.811

Hayes, S. C., & Brownstein, A. J. (1986). Mentalism, behavior-behavior relations, and a behavior-analytic view of the purposes of science. *The Behavior Analyst, 9*(2), 175–190. https://doi.org/10.1007/BF03391944

Hyten, C. (2009). Strengthening the focus on business results: The need for systems approaches in organizational behavior management. *Journal of Organizational Behavior Management, 29*(2), 87–107. http://doi.org/10.1080/01608060902874526

Hyten, C. (2017). OBM is already using the "fuzzy concept" criteria for applied behavioral research: Commentary on Critchfield and reed. *The Behavior Analyst, 40*(1), 179–182. https://doi.org/10.1007/s40614-017-0096-7

Hyten, C. (2022). On ethics codes, licensure and OBM. *Journal of Organizational Behavior Management*, 1–4. https://doi.org/10.1080/01608061.2022.2027320

Johnson, C. M., & Beehr, T. A. (Eds.). (2013). *Integrating organizational behavior management with industrial and organizational psychology*. Routledge.

Johnson, D. A., Rocheleau, J. M., & Tilka, R. E. (2015). Considerations in feedback delivery: The role of accuracy and type of evaluation. *Journal of Organizational Behavior Management, 35*(3–4), 240–258. http://doi.org/10.1080/01608061.2015.1093055

Johnston, J. M., Pennypacker, H. S., & Green, G. (2020). *Strategies and tactics of behavioral research (4th ed.)*. Routledge.

Kazdin, A. E. (2020). *Single-case research designs: Methods for clinical and applied settings* (3rd ed.). Oxford University Press.

Kelley, D. P., & Gravina, N. (2018). Every minute counts: Using process improvement and performance feedback to improve patient flow in an emergency department. *Journal of Organizational Behavior Management, 38*(2–3), 234–243. http://doi.org/10.1080/01608061.2017.1423150

Kessler, M. L. (2001). Transitioning from maintenance to institutionalization: Critical additions to the Boyce and Geller analysis. *Journal of Organizational Behavior Management, 21* (1), 71–73. http://doi.org/10.1300/J075v21n01_06

King, A., Gravina, N., & Sleiman, A. (2018). Observing the observer. *Journal of Organizational Behavior Management, 38*(4), 306–323. https://doi.org/10.1080/01608061.2018.1514346

Kohn, A. (1993). *Punished by rewards: The trouble with gold stars, incentive plans, A's, praise, and other bribes*. Houghton Mifflin and Company.

Laipple, J. (2012). *Rapid change: Immediate action for the impatient leader*. Performance Management Publications.

Malott, M. E. (2003). *Paradox of organizational change: Engineering organizations with behavioral systems analysis*. Context Press.

Martin-Raugh, M., Tannenbaum, R. J., Tocci, C. M., & Reese, C. (2016). Behaviorally anchored rating scales: An application for evaluating teaching practice. *Teaching and Teacher Education, 59*, 414–419. https://doi.org/10.1016/j.tate.2016.07.026

Mawhinney, T. C. (2011). Job satisfaction: I/O psychology and organizational behavior management perspectives. *Journal of Organizational Behavior Management, 31*(4), 288–315. https://doi.org/10.1080/01608061.2011.619419

McGee, H. M., & Crowley-Koch, B. (2021). Performance assessment of organizations. *Journal of Organizational Behavior Management, 41*(3), 255–285. https://doi.org/10.1080/01608061.2021.1909687

McSween, T., & Matthews, G. A. (2001). Maintenance in safety behavior management. *Journal of Organizational Behavior Management, 21*(1), 75–83. http://doi.org/10.1300/J075v21n01_07

McSween, T. (2022). Reflections on ethics and licensure in OBM. *Journal of Organizational Behavior Management*, 1–6. https://doi.org/10.1080/01608061.2022.2032532

Myers, W., McSween, T. M., Medina, R. E., Rost, K., & Alvero, A. M. (2010). The implementation and maintenance of a behavioral safety process in a petroleum refinery. *Journal of Organizational Behavior Management, 30*(4), 285–307. http://doi.org/10.1080/01608061.2010.499027

Nastasi, J., Simmons, D., & Gravina, N. (2021). Has OBM found its heart? An assessment of procedural acceptability trends in the *journal of organizational behavior management*. *Journal of Organizational Behavior Management, 41*(1), 64–82. http://doi.org/10.1080/01608061.2020.1853000

Peterson, L., Homer, A. L., & Wonderlich, S. A. (1982). The integrity of independent variables in behavior analysis. *Journal of Applied Behavior Analysis, 1*(4), 477–492. https://doi.org/10.1901/jaba.1982.15-477

Pingo, J. C., Dixon, M. R., & Paliliunas, D. (2020). Intervention enhancing effects of acceptance and commitment training on performance feedback for direct support professional work performance, stress, and job satisfaction. *Behavior Analysis in Practice, 13*(1), 1–10. https://doi.org/10.1007/s40617-019-00333-w

Pipkin, C. S. P., Vollmer, T. R., & Sloman, K. N. (2010). Effects of treatment integrity failures during differential reinforcement of alternative behavior: A translational model. *Journal of Applied Behavior Analysis, 43*(1), 47–70. http://doi.org/10.1901/jaba.2010.43–47

Poling, A., Smith, J. F., & Braatz, D. (1993). Data sets in organizational behavior management: Do we measure enough? *Journal of Organizational Behavior Management, 14*(1), 99–116. http://doi.org/10.1300/J075v14n01_04

Rummler, G. A., & Brache, A. P. (2013). *Improving performance: How to manage the white space on the organization chart.* Jossey-Bass.

Sasson, J. R., & Austin, J. (2004). The effects of training, feedback, and participant involvement in behavioral safety observations on office ergonomic behavior. *Journal of Organizational Behavior Management, 24*(4), 1–30. https://doi.org/10.1300/J075v24n04_01

Sigurdsson, S. O., & Austin, J. (2006). Institutionalization and response maintenance in organizational behavior management. *Journal of Organizational Behavior Management, 26* (4), 41–77. http://doi.org/10.1300/J075v26n04_03

Skinner, B. F. (1953). *Science & human behavior.* Free Press.

Sleiman, A. A., Sigurjonsdottir, S., Elnes, A., Gage, N. A., & Gravina, N. E. (2020). A quantitative review of performance feedback in organizational settings (1998-2018). *Journal of Organizational Behavior Management, 40*(3–4), 303–332. https://doi.org/10.1080/01608061.2020.1823300

Stokes, T. F., & Baer, D. M. (1977). An implicit technology of generalization. *Journal of Applied Behavior Analysis, 10*(2), 349–367. http://doi.org/10.1901/jaba.1977.10-349

Taylor, M. A., Skourides, A., & Alvero, A. M. (2012). Observer error when measuring safety-related behavior: Momentary time sampling versus whole-interval recording. *Journal of Organizational Behavior Management, 32*(4), 307–319. http://doi.org/10.1080/01608061.2012.729389

Tziner, A., Joanis, C., & Murphy, K. R. (2000). A comparison of three methods of performance appraisal with regard to goal properties, goal perception, and ratee satisfaction. *Group & Organization Management, 25*(2), 175–190. https://doi.org/10.1177/1059601100252005

VanStelle, S. E., Vicars, S. M., Harr, V., Miguel, C. F., Koerber, J. L., Kazbour, R., & Austin, J. (2012). The publication history of the *journal of organizational behavior management*: An objective review and analysis: 1998–2009. *Journal of Organizational Behavior Management, 32*(2), 93–123. http://doi.org/10.1080/01608061.2012.675864

Vollmer, T. R., Sloman, K. N., & Pipkin, C. S. P. (2008). Practical implications of data reliability and treatment integrity monitoring. *Behavior Analysis in Practice, 1*(2), 4–11. https://doi.org/10.1007/BF03391722

Walker, S. G., & Carr, J. E. (2021). Generality of findings from single-case designs: It's not all about the "N." *Behavior Analysis in Practice, 14*(4), 991–995. https://doi.org/10.1007/s40617-020-00547-3

Wells, J., Reimer, D., & Houmanfar, R. (2013). Money and *journal of organizational behavior management* interventions: A Review. *Journal of Organizational Behavior Management, 33* (4), 276–298. https://doi.org/10.1080/01608061.2013.843491

Wilder, D. A., Casella, S., & Austin, J. (2009). Applying behavior analysis in organizations: Organizational behavior management. *Psychological Services*, *6*(3), 202–211. https://doi.org/10.1037/a0015393

Wilder, D. A., Lipschultz, J. L., King, A., Driscoll, S., & Sigurdsson, S. (2018). An analysis of the commonality and type of preintervention assessment procedures in the journal of organizational behavior management (2000–2015). *Journal of Organizational Behavior Management*, *38*(1), 5–17. https://doi.org/10.1080/01608061.2017.1325822

Wine, B. (2021). More musings on ethics: A response to weatherly (2021). *Journal of Organizational Behavior Management*, 1–5. https://doi.org/10.1080/01608061.2021.1957744

Performance Feedback in Organizations: Understanding the Functions, Forms, and Important Features

Douglas A. Johnson, C. Merle Johnson, and Priyanka Dave

ABSTRACT
Feedback surrounds our personal and professional worlds, informing us about what worked and what did not. Within workplace settings, it is important to understand how feedback operates in order to deliberately and carefully craft performance information that, when delivered, generates desirable organizational outcomes. The current paper examines the many potential functions of feedback, including details on how such functions might be established. Behavioral investigations into how to best structure and deliver feedback are detailed, along with considerations of factors that may impact the reception of feedback. Finally, using the current literature as a blueprint, several possible research directions are suggested that would fit well within a behavior analytic perspective.

Feedback for performance has long been important, if not foundational, for improvements and adaptations, as noted by scholars in general, including the founders of our field. Consider the following quote by B. F. Skinner:

> Reflexes, conditioned or otherwise, are mainly concerned with the internal physiology of the organism. We are most often interested, however, in behavior which has some effect upon the surrounding world. Such behavior raises most of the practical problems in human affairs and is also of particular theoretical interest because of its special characteristics. The consequences of behavior may "feed back" into the organism. When they do so, they may change the probability that the behavior which produced them will occur again. The English language contains many words, such as "reward" or "punishment," which refer to this effect, but we can get a clear picture of it only through experimental analysis. (Skinner, 1953, p. 59)

Skinner introduces readers to the concept of operant conditioning, in which organisms are more than poor creatures at the mercy of the surrounding environment. Instead, our behavior operates to change the environment, just as much as we are changed by that same environment, in a reciprocal dance of control. Feedback is intrinsic to the successful adaptation of our repertoire to the world around us. Performance feedback is built-in during the delivery of immediate consequences. This is evidenced across many aspects of our lives, including social behaviors (e.g., does our audience laugh or scowl at our attempt at humor?), cooking (e.g., do our seasonings repulse or please taste buds?), gaming (e.g., avatars perish or triumph following our button press combinations), sporting (e.g., free throw made or missed; golf shot hits the green or goes out-of-bounds), document editing (e.g., software indicates misspelling of our typing behaviors or accepts words without judgment), and a seemingly endless list of examples. Feedback used in organizational settings would be included in this list and can be expanded to include non-immediate consequences, although formal attempts to implement feedback are often lacking due to issues related to immediacy, frequency, objectivity, and efficacy (Daniels, 2016; Duncan & Bruwelheide, 1985). Unlike many natural sources of feedback, performance feedback in organizations is defined as the provision of information specifically given to change or maintain performance.

This paper is intended to serve several purposes centered on a behavioral understanding of the effects of feedback within organizational settings. First, this paper will cover the potential functions of feedback, adding to and elaborating upon earlier conceptual analyses (Duncan & Bruwelheide, 1985). Fully understanding such potential functions is important to ensure our field is conceptually coherent rather than a simple roster of procedural recipes (Baer et al., 1968) indistinguishable from other performance change disciplines. A comprehensive understanding of multiple functions can suggest potential evocative effects and stimulus transformations to be attentive toward. Furthermore, there may be important implications for prediction and control by understanding how different histories with feedback may result in different functional relations (Michael, 2004). As such, this paper will tend to focus on the usage of feedback within the conceptual framework of organizational behavior management (OBM), although it will not be exclusively restricted. Beyond functional and theoretical considerations, practitioners and researchers need guidance on how to best utilize feedback to maximize performance. Furthermore, this paper will outline feedback strategies in terms of how to craft feedback, how to deliver feedback, and how to receive feedback through an informal review of the OBM literature. As always, more research needs to be conducted, and this paper will highlight some of the paths forward. Lastly, this paper is meant to complement the other contributions in this series of articles (Johnson & Johnson, 2022) by highlighting one of the most commonly used and studied independent variables within OBM.

The history of feedback

Performance feedback has a long and diverse history in both OBM and beyond and was one of the earliest variables investigated by experimental psychologists (Ammons, 1956). For example, Thorndike's (1927) classic study helping to establish the law of effect was a feedback study. Participants estimated lengths of lines and within 2 seconds were told "right," "wrong," or given no announcement at all. Practice with feedback improved greater than practice alone. That is, practice does not make perfect, *practice with feedback makes perfect.* A systematic replication (Trowbridge & Cason, 1932) found blindfolded subjects given specific objective feedback after drawing lines improved more than when told "right" or "wrong." Both groups performed better than no feedback or nonsense-syllables control groups. Such "knowledge of results" research (Travers, 1977) in early experimental psychology evolved into the present terminology of "feedback."

Probably the first comprehensive feedback system informed by behavioral principles in a corporate environment was guided by Edward J. Feeney and implemented at Emery Air Freight (Emery Air Freight Corporation, 1971; Feeney, 1982) during the 1970s. The extensive use of feedback and reinforcement saved Emery millions of dollars over just a few years (At Emery Air Freight: Positive reinforcement boosts performance, 1973). As Feeney liked to describe it, *problem finding* was much more important to performance improvement than *problem solving* (Feeney, 1972). Often, managers and employees were unaware of gaps between assumed and actual performance. Once discrepancies were brought to light by feedback, dozens of solutions could easily be proposed. The approach was successful enough that Emery was featured in a film titled *Business, Behaviorism, and the Bottom Line*, along with B. F. Skinner and Edward Feeney (Jordan, 1972).

Since early demonstrations, such as Feeney's work at Emery, feedback became one of the most extensively used and studied variables within OBM (Van Stelle et al., 2012). Numerous articles examined the usage of feedback in applied settings, some of which used visual inspection and some of which quantified changes through effect sizes (Alvero et al., 2001; Balcazar et al., 1985; Sleiman, Sigurjonsdottir et al., 2020). Overall, feedback was shown to be effective, although these effects were inconsistent, which suggests the need for careful control of potential confounds during implementation or identification of which variables are most effective in specific contexts. Publication trends of research within the *Journal of Organizational Behavior Management* show that feedback is the most frequently used independent variable across studies (Van Stelle et al., 2012).

There are several reasons to better understand performance feedback beyond the mere commonality of its usage. All things being equal, behavior naturally varies and tends toward the response of least effort (Timberlake, 1977). To put this in organizationally relevant terms, in the absence of either natural or programmed consequences, employee performance might gravitate toward off-task, sloppy, and substandard levels. Feedback is one type of consequence that can maintain behavior when natural outcomes are insufficient, which should be important for daily on-the-job tasks (Johnson &

Akpapuna, 2018). Feedback helps develop new behaviors when individuals cannot self-evaluate so that employees are not "flying blind" while waiting for a formal performance appraisal (Grote, 2002). Improvements in supervisor-subordinate communication made possible by feedback benefit performance by directing employee focus and effort but also show positive effects on job satisfaction and organizational commitment (Aguinis et al., 2012; Ashford & Cummings, 1983; Jawahar, 2006; Kuchinke, 2000; O'Reilly & Anderson, 1980; Pearce & Porter, 1986)

Understanding the function of feedback

Despite the many reasons to better understand the function of feedback, this is not a simple proposal. Part of the complexity and confusion lies in the fact that feedback can be classified as an antecedent, consequence, or both (Mangiapanello & Hemmes, 2015; Peterson, 1982). It may be useful not to lose track of what is probably the only consistent behavioral classification for feedback: it is a stimulus. As every teaching textbook on behavior analysis demonstrates, stimuli can take on any number of functions, some of which may be occurring simultaneously. This suggests that efforts to discover any single function of feedback would be pointless, as it can serve several functions and there is no reason to expect its function to be ubiquitous. This possibility of diverse functions in application means it may be of value to review the potential functions feedback likely acquires, including functions related to pairing history, discriminative functions, evocative effects as a motivating operation, and potential status as a contingency specifying stimulus.

Simple functions based on pairing

One possible function feedback can serve as a respondent conditioned stimulus. When supervisors deliver feedback, it is likely they utilize emotionally laden words (e.g., impressive, great, excellent, failure, disappointed, substandard). Although humans do not have a genetic predisposition to have a positive or negative reaction to such words, common cultural contingencies mean such words are likely to be paired with other stimuli that elicit emotional reactions from most members of a social community (Choi et al., 2018; Kuykendall & Keating, 1990; Staats & Staats, 1958). In other words, most verbally sophisticated individuals will have positive or negative reactions to such words (Critchfield & Doepke, 2018; Critchfield et al., 2017). Depending on the context, the resulting physiological reactions are tacted (i.e, labeled) differentially with terms such as nervous, pride, shame, satisfaction, anger, and more. As such, the emotional learning underlying feedback should not be neglected and has potential to impact other behaviors. For example, the stimuli resulting from physiological changes (e.g., anxiety) could generate tacts (accurate or otherwise) about self, world, and future ("I'm a walking disaster," "everyone is against me," "I'll never succeed") that then interfere with other behaviors (e.g., employees become inattentive to training because they are upset or they miss an important customer interaction because they are ruminating about a harsh evaluation).

Feedback also has the possibility to function as a conditioned reinforcer or conditioned punisher (Bucklin et al., 2003; Duncan & Bruwelheide, 1985; Johnson et al., 2008). For example, supervisors may provide on-the-job immediate feedback, including evaluative statements such as praise or criticisms, which will likely have behavior-altering effects on performance. The consequences do not necessarily have to be spoken by the supervisors; stimuli such as gestures or mannerisms indicating approval or disappointment during feedback could function as reinforcers or punishers for behavior preceding feedback sessions. Even feedback devoid of explicit evaluative indicators from supervisors can function as a conditioned reinforcer or punisher if the information from feedback is reliably paired with other reinforcers or punishers within the organization. Furthermore, objective statements about performance improvements or deterioration are culturally typical reinforcers and punishers, even prior to any pairing procedures within the organization. One advantage of such on-the-spot feedback sessions is the potential to be delivered more frequently and at lower costs than other organizational rewards and disciplinary stimuli.

Discriminative functions

Feedback also has the potential to serve different discriminative functions, depending on how it is implemented (Balcazar et al., 1985). Feedback can function as an S^D if the presence of feedback is positively correlated with the availability of reinforcement for performance. For example, feedback from a supervisor may not only provide details regarding the employee's previous performance, but it may also provide notification that the supervisor is monitoring subsequent performance, which could have a powerful impact (Komaki, 1986). As a result, the employee's efforts to engage in valued performance are more likely to be rewarded following such notification and will therefore evoke improvements. Notifications can also have an abative effect on performance if feedback is positively correlated with the availability of punishment. Notifications of monitoring may simultaneously indicate that undesired behaviors will now likely be punished, such as taking extended breaks, completing work in a manner against regulations, excessive socialization. Under these conditions feedback will begin functioning as an S^{Dp} for unacceptable performances.

Feedback can also be negatively correlated with the availability of consequences. In regard to reinforcing consequences, vague or inaccurate feedback indicating little or no monitoring may extinguish performance improvements (i.e., "no one is paying attention, so why bother trying?"). Such feedback is functioning as an S^{Δ} and may hinder organizational improvements. The organization could also be hindered by an $S^{\Delta p}$ in which previously punished behavior begins to recover. The same vague or inaccurate feedback could also evoke harmful behaviors (i.e., "no one is paying attention, so now I'll do whatever I want"). The preceding examples involve discriminative functions related only to performance monitoring, which does not exhaust all possible discriminative functions related to feedback.

Functions as motivating operation

Discriminative stimuli are not the only type of operant antecedent; feedback can also play a role as a conditioned motivating operation (CMO) if it establishes other events as reinforcing (Agnew, 1998; Johnson et al., 2015; Michael, 2004; Palmer et al., 2015). Any feedback correlated with the onset of some form of worsening has the potential to serve as a reflexive CMO (CMO-R) if the removal of the conditions generated by the feedback function as reinforcement. For example, feedback may consist of some warning about a forthcoming social worsening or loss of privilege and income (e.g., "I better not have to come back and have this conversation again," "if you don't resolve this problem by next week, you'll be suspended," "if your performance stays in this range, we might have to talk about your future in our company."). Threatening conditions generated by such feedback may now function as a CMO-R and evoke behaviors to remove implied or explicit threats. From the organization's perspective, the evoked behavior would ideally be improvements in performance relevant to the organization's goals. Such aversive control may not go as planned, especially if targeted performance is unclear, if demands are beyond the skills or control of the performer, or if alternative behaviors require less response effort to be successful. For example, the employee may attempt to remove threats established from performance feedback by directing the manager's attention to another employee's poor performance (or falsely describing that employee's performance), hiding evidence of insufficient performance, flattering that manager or superiors higher in the hierarchy, pleading excessively until the situation becomes aversive for the manager, or by making appeals for pity.

Feedback could also potentially function as a transitive CMO (CMO-T) if it alters the value of some other stimulus and evokes responding that will produce that other stimulus. For example, the provision of objective feedback regarding performance may establish evaluations as suddenly more reinforcing (such as an employee starts asking others, "hey, do my numbers look good to you or not?"). The objective feedback was a CMO-T that established evaluation as more reinforcing and evoked evaluation-seeking behaviors. Evaluative feedback from a supervisor could establish multiple consequences as reinforcing and evoke a variety of behaviors if the evaluation was multi-faceted. For example, suppose a manager completed a feedback session with an employee stating that they lost a promotion because a) they lacked some skills the manager was looking for, b) that their numbers had been looking bad lately, c) that their colleague had been making a better impression, and that d) their equipment usage had not been up-to-standards recently. This feedback session may establish a) training workshops ("I need this certification to rise in the company"), b) information related to self ("what are my numbers lately?"), c) information to others ("what is the person who ranked above me doing different?"), and tools ("where's that screwdriver that my supervisor keeps criticizing me for not having?") as more valuable and evoke behaviors to produce such stimuli. Evaluative feedback could even come from outside the organization, such as when customer praise as a CMO-T makes the sight of an observing manager more reinforcing (or more aversive in the case of customer complaints).

Role as rules: function-altering contingency specifying stimulus

Beyond potential direct evocative effects of feedback, there lies the possibility of feedback having several indirect effects by changing the function of other events. Feedback can operate as a contingency specifying stimulus (Agnew & Redmon, 1992; Blakely & Schlinger, 1987). The feedback might describe the relation between workplace antecedents, employee performance, and consequences for performance. Such descriptions of the organizational contingencies could alter the function of other stimuli – both verbal and non-verbal – without immediately evoking behavior and may aid in the development of rule-governed behavior (Malott, 1992; Weatherly & Malott, 2008). For example, a manager may give subordinates feedback such as, "when you are dealing with a hostile call from a customer, I want to see you follow the new corporate script rather than just ending the call or transferring to another department." Such feedback may not have any immediate evocative effect (especially if a hostile call is not encountered for some time) but will still likely alter the function of certain antecedents and consequences. Previously, an angry phone call would have evoked behaviors to end or transfer it, but now evokes a recitation of the corporate script. The sight of one's finger on the transfer call button may now, for the first time, have aversive properties. The sound of one's own voice saying the script may, for the first time have reinforcing properties. The employee may emit covert verbal behavior ("I'm following protocol") and resulting response products (i.e., covert verbal stimuli) may have reinforcing aspects. The ultimate outcome is that several environmental products may now have reinforcing and punishing aspects due to the feedback. Even if the manager does not explicate the contingencies during feedback, employees may still describe the contingencies based on feedback. For example, if an employee receives critical feedback every time their performance is within a certain range, they may derive expected performance standards even without the supervisor stating the expectations explicitly. Such feedback may lead to self-generated rules that then alter future instances of behavior ("if I keep my closing percentages above this number, then the boss will leave me alone").

The effects of feedback can be subtle and the function(s) it serves may depend on the particular learning history of the individual. This may be part of why presenting feedback alone does not consistently improve performance (Johnson, 2013). To be clear, feedback alone does have the potential to improve performance, but it likely requires that feedback brings the performer into contact with naturally occurring sources of reinforcement or requires idiosyncratic learning histories. Absent such preexisting provisions, feedback will likely need to be combined with some other maintaining variable. Pairing feedback with goal setting, consequences (praise, reprimands, tangible rewards & reinforcers), or both increases efficacy (Alvero et al., 2001; Balcazar et al., 1985; Duncan & Bruwelheide, 1985; Sleiman, Sigurjonsdottir et al., 2020). Coupling feedback with goal setting and consequences, however, makes performance feedback multifaceted. Moreover, the type, schedule, mode, source, and content are just some parameters that potentially confound the efficacy of performance feedback (Prue & Fairbank, 1981). Clearly performance feedback is multiply-controlled and usually has multiple effects on the behavior of individuals and groups; thus, managers and supervisors need to develop efficacious feedback systems to create maximal organizational impact. We believe most managers and practitioners are not aware of this and do not comprehend these concerns. They believe they provide feedback to employees and cannot understand why performance is not improving. We hope the contents of this article provide useful information to improve performance feedback systems for readers.

How to craft feedback: components and elements

Despite many aforementioned successes, feedback has not been uniformly successful, likely because it is not uniformly implemented in either research or practice (Alvero et al., 2001). Just as there are many potential functions of feedback, the components and formal elements that constitute feedback also vary widely and can pose a challenge for understanding from both a research and practice perspective (Duncan & Bruwelheide, 1985; Ford, 1980; Johnson, 2013). In fact, given the robust literature demonstrating feedback can improve performance, there is probably little need for more of this type of general research. Instead, research is needed on specific components and elements that modulate success of feedback interventions.

Type of feedback appraisal

Daniels and Bailey (2014) point out that feedback should provide objective information about past performance. Objective feedback is essential as it directs people toward factors that contribute to performance and provides clear measures for improvement. However, simply providing such information by itself may not have performance enhancing effects (Johnson et al., 2008; Kluger & DeNisi, 1996). Instead, several considerations must be taken into account. One consideration is whether the feedback contains any evaluative components. Supervisors rarely just state the performance data of their subordinates – they also incorporate appreciative or critical statements into their delivery. Research by Johnson (2013) recommended that evaluation of performance and objective details are essential components for performance feedback. In this study, participants completed an experiment modeled after a check processor job in a bank. Participants received objective feedback alone, evaluative feedback alone, combined, or no feedback. Results demonstrated that all three feedback groups performed considerably better than the no-feedback group. The author noted that, though it takes a few more minutes to administer, a combination of evaluative and objective feedback produced significant improvements in performance than general and objective evaluation alone.

Specificity of feedback

Another important consideration involves specificity. An early demonstration (Frederiksen et al., 1982) involved recordkeeping in a university psychology clinic and the experiment was conducted in two phases. Chart maintenance by therapists was the object of intervention; four types of charting errors (status error, error of completeness, format error, and signature error) were tracked and experimenters controlled the delivery of feedback. In the first part of the study, two charting errors (status and completeness) were specifically targeted using an ABA design, while the other two (format and signature) were only measured. The second part was an AB replication of the first using a second group of employees, this time targeting two different charting errors (format and signature) while the other two (status and completeness) were tracked but untargeted. In both phases during staff meetings, supervisors described individuals' specific information about the number and type of errors, along with praise when appropriate. Overall, only the behaviors receiving specific feedback during intervention phases improved (and reverted to baseline levels during withdrawal), while performance for untargeted behavior remained largely unchanged throughout the study. This showed that simply delivering feedback alone was insufficient, rather feedback needed to be tailored to the performance of interest.

Similarly, Goodman and Wood (2004) investigated specificity using a work simulation called Furniture Factory, in which participants served as department managers. The simulation required managers to complete four trials involving a sequence of decisions related to job allocation, goals set, feedback given, and the distribution of rewards. Based upon relevant literature for those areas, participants received feedback on each trial on their decision according to three levels of specificity. Low specificity simply provided participants details on how their employees performed after decisions, with no information on whether their decision was correct or not (thus requiring inference of their performance). Moderate specificity added details in which participants were told whether their decisions were correct for each worker. High specificity added more detail, informing participants on how their decisions with each worker were correct or incorrect, thus requiring almost no inference by participants.

How specificity influenced performance depended upon the type of performance. When correct, highly specific feedback was superior. When participants made errors, low feedback specificity was best for learning. Thus, when participants needed to learn from their mistakes, it was best to require them to figure out what went wrong. The opposite was true for learning from one's successes. Thus, the simple rule of "more specific feedback is always best" may not hold true across all contexts and demands (i.e., learning versus maintenance, positive versus corrective).

K. Lee et al. (2014) looked at the relative and generalization effects of global and specific feedback on safety performance and safety items at a road construction site in South Korea. Findings indicated that specific feedback is not always effective as global feedback. Global feedback could compel recipients to analyze their own behavior afterward. For feedback interventions in applied settings, cost and time are important variables and they argued that global feedback could be easy, quick, and cost-effective compared to specific feedback. The researchers found that both global and specific feedback produced comparable performance and furthermore global feedback demonstrated a greater degree of generalization for non-targeted items.

Finally, Park et al. (2019) explored the effects between feedback specificity (specific vs. global) and frequency of feedback (frequent vs. infrequent) on the quality of work performance. Participants were randomly assigned to one of four feedback groups (specific and frequent, global and frequent, global and infrequent, and specific and infrequent) and asked to complete a simulation of stocking at a distribution center. One variable examined was how global (e.g., average overall rate of errors) or specific (e.g., error rates in the following performance areas) feedback influence the average rate of errors. Specific feedback was more effective than global when feedback was infrequent. However, no differences were found in terms of specificity when feedback was provided frequently. Thus, the theme of research on specificity seems to be that more specific feedback is generally more effective, but this relationship is not so consistent that one can blindly follow a simple heuristic.

Comparative feedback

The basis for comparisons is another important element for feedback – whether the evaluation involves a comparison to standards or goals, the performance of others, or one's individual prior performance. Hartwell and Campion (2016) examined a way to reduce rating errors that increased the reliability and validity of structured interview ratings using normative performance feedback. The experimenters provided feedback reports to over 100 experienced full-time interviewers which anonymously listed each interviewer rating and the average rating across all interviewers (individuals could identify their specific scores using an identification code). Such normative feedback reduced deviations from the average ratings (beyond what could be expected from regression to the mean), with lenient interviewers being more impacted than severe interviewers. Therefore, normative interviewer feedback shared by organizations made interview ratings more reliable and normative feedback was found to be effective (at least for predicting ratings, although it may be important to note that these measures were not tied to any objective measures).

In a related line of research, Goltz et al. (1989) examined the effects of adding individualized feedback after performers were already receiving feedback based on average group performance. This study was carried out with employees at a Midwestern microelectronics plant and assessed performance using an ABCB design (A = baseline, B = group feedback, C = group and individual feedback). The addition of individual feedback exerted a clear improvement upon performance, although the reversal to group only feedback showed a more ambiguous loss of performance (mean was lower but not to a significant degree). This outcome strongly suggests that group feedback will not maximize performance; other means of feedback should be added or used in place of group feedback. This aligned well with the findings of Newby and Robinson (1983), who found individual feedback (with and without reinforcement) positively impacted multiple measures of cashier performance, but group feedback was ineffective.

Moon et al. (2017) directly compared normative feedback (i.e., social comparison) to objective feedback using high and low performers. Undergraduate students at a large university were in three computer laboratories simulating an online bank money transfer. Social comparison feedback was more effective for high performers than objective feedback, while objective feedback was more effective than social comparison feedback for low performers. In this scenario, it can be presumed that social feedback could work as a powerful reinforcer to increase performance in organizational settings. However, for those whose performance is low, social comparison feedback might function as a punisher. In these cases, the effects of feedback might depend on performance levels and the basis of comparison.

A similar lesson of how performance levels might matter with normative feedback was found by Mesch et al. (1994), but with different outcomes in regard to positive versus negative normative feedback. In their study, 59 three-person groups were randomly assigned to positive or negative feedback following performance on a word recognition task. Participants were given a sheet with feedback indicating the number of correct words, the number of total words attempted, and the mean score of other groups (mean scores were contrived to indicate team performance was either above or below average group performance, depending on random assignment). Unlike Moon et al. (2017), "low" performers did better during a subsequent session than "high" performers. It is difficult to account for the experimental differences that might be responsible for the differences between studies (e.g., cultural differences, individual versus group data, tasks, genuine versus fake normative comparisons). Mesch et al. pointed out that teams in their study were able to communicate and set self-goals between performance sessions and performers would reliably set higher goals for themselves after getting negative feedback. In essence, negative normative feedback implies higher performance standards are necessitated, thus blurring the lines between feedback and goal setting interventions. Mesch et al. also cautioned against regular use of negative feedback, as negative feedback performers showed higher levels of dissatisfaction and extensive exposure to signs of failure could result in learned helplessness.

In general, there appear to be many important qualifiers for feedback based on group performance. A general rule of thumb is to provide feedback to recipients with all the essential information to precisely identify instances of appropriate and inappropriate goal-directed behavior (Prue & Fairbank, 1981). If aggregated feedback is sufficient to enable performers to identify how to improve their individual performance, then group or normative feedback is likely to be effective (how effective may depend on the extent to which performers can accurately pinpoint strengths and deficits).

As mentioned above, negative feedback could potentially harm performance. However, there are times when such appraisal may be warranted, if not necessary. Unfortunately, feedback procedures describing substandard performance often involve multiple terms, such as constructive, negative, or corrective feedback, that often conflate subtle but important distinctions among these labels (Simonian & Brand, 2022). Many of the differences depend upon whether the feedback procedures contain objective or subjective elements (Johnson, 2013). For the sake of clarity, this paper will use "corrective feedback" to refer to objective descriptions of substandard or erroneous performance (e.g., "you achieved 85% of the expected performance" or "you did not include the third step of the protocol") and "negative feedback" to refer to subjective descriptions of substandard or erroneous performance (e.g., "you performed poorly during your last shift") or a mixture of objective and subjective (e.g., "you keep forgetting the closing statement and I expect to see you do better next time").

Feedback combinations

To avoid or minimize any harmful effects of subpar evaluations, some advocate that corrective or negative feedback be couched in the context of positive feedback. For example, delivering one positive comment, followed by the negative comment, and concluding with a second positive comment (sometimes labeled as a "feedback sandwich"). There are multiple sequences possible, such as one negative followed by one positive (or vice-versa), multiple negatives followed by multiple positives (or vice-versa), or a variety of interspersed combinations. Supporters of these various feedback sandwiches claim the method is more effective and preferred because it makes corrective feedback more acceptable to the receiver and reduces discomfort between recipient and deliverer (Berger, 2013). Whereas critics claim it obscures the message and devalues the corrective feedback because employees receive more positive statements overall than negative statements (Daniels, 2009).

Several studies investigated these various feedback sequences (Bottini & Gillis, 2021; Choi et al., 2018; Henley & DiGennaro Reed, 2015) across numerous settings and skills. Overall, the consensus seems to be there is no beneficial effect of mixing negative with positive appraisals, at least for performance (although this consensus may not hold for nonperformance measures such as emotional reactions). Interestingly, one study (Choi et al., 2018) that compared congruent feedback (all positive or all negative comments) to blended feedback (mixture of positive and negative) showed congruent feedback was superior. In other words, if an employee needs a critique or disciplinary action, it may be best to simply deliver negative feedback by itself and not confuse the evaluation with positive feedback before or after the negative message.

Accuracy of feedback

Accuracy of feedback is another important consideration. There may be many reasons feedback is inaccurate, such as inconsistent data collection, imprecise or indirect measurement of performance, inattention by supervisors to collected data, avoidance by supervisors when delivering potentially uncomfortable evaluations, or even intentional distortion to boost performance (such as a manager making normative standards look higher than they are in reality). However, it has been suggested that trust in feedback is critical to both employer-employee relations and the effect feedback will have on performance (O'Reilly & Anderson, 1980). In general, the empirical relationship seems clear, feedback that is accurate is more effective than inaccurate across numerous settings and tasks (Brand et al., 2020; Hirst & DiGennaro Reed, 2015; Johnson et al., 2015). Although some research suggested that inaccuracy may not be a problem if performers are unaware of the inaccuracy (Palmer et al., 2015), the inaccuracy can become problematic and harm performance once performers become aware that feedback cannot be trusted (Brett & Atwater, 2001; J. Lee et al., 2020).

How to give feedback: important practices and procedures

Private versus public delivery

Just as it is important to understand components and elements that constitute effective feedback, it is also important to understand the important practices and procedures for delivery of feedback. When specific performer information needs to be shared with a recipient, it is generally recommended feedback be provided privately and confidentially (Daniels, 2016). This is despite some research that suggested public feedback may have a greater effect than private (Welsch et al., 1973). However, whether performance information should be provided publicly or privately is determined by variety of factors in addition to just performance. For example, when individuals are performing low, public display of performance data may adversely affect employees as a form of punishment.

Frequency of feedback delivery

The frequency of feedback delivery is another crucial component. Authors such as DeNisi and Pritchard (2006) suggested performance feedback be a regular part of any appraisal system. This assertion has been borne out by both laboratory and field research; more frequent feedback improves performance than infrequent (Kang et al., 2005; Pampino et al., 2004; So et al., 2013). Although practical constraints will probably impose limits on how frequently managers can personally deliver feedback, the general rule appears to be the more frequent, the better, especially for workers learning new jobs compared to seasoned employees.

Timing of feedback

Another temporal consideration involves timing feedback. According to Lechermeier and Fassnacht (2018), feedback varies across two broad categories: immediate and delayed. However, the conceptualization of immediate versus delayed may be problematic for the typical workplace. In most settings, it is probably quite rare that a task would occur only once (at least rare for any performance for which we would bother to provide feedback). Instead, it is typical that behavior will be repeated by employees and such repetition means that as feedback becomes more distal from previous performance, it also becomes more proximal to subsequent performance. Therefore, it may be more important to look at the categories of after-session and before-session feedback. The importance of this distinction becomes clearer when examining research on feedback timing.

For example, Mason & Redmon, 1993) reported a comparison of immediate and delayed feedback upon performance. Participants completed a quality control task and received feedback either less than a second after a response or at the end of each session, about 10–15 minutes long. Although one of the experimental conditions was labeled as immediate, it is probably better conceptualized as frequent and ongoing, since feedback was not delivered immediately after finishing a complete session but instead delivered after each response throughout the session. Since participants engaged in continuous performance, feedback both followed and preceded responding. Furthermore, the delayed feedback was based on a summary of several responses and was not specific to particular responses. Finally, the experimental arrangements meant several instances of behavior were each followed by feedback in the immediate condition, whereas a single instance of feedback followed several behaviors in delayed conditions. Although the authors correctly concluded that immediate was more effective than delayed feedback, the study compared ongoing, specific, and repeated feedback against delayed, global, and singular feedback. Qualitative and quantitative confounds make it difficult to separate controlling variables and confuse underlying conceptual issues.

Later researchers pinpointed feedback timing characteristics more precisely. For example, Bechtel et al. (2015) compared feedback placed immediately after or immediately before sessions when completing a medical data entry task. No performance differences were found between the different feedback timings. This in contrast to Aljadeff-Abergel et al. (2017), who found feedback immediately preceding was superior to feedback following sessions for the performance of implementing a teaching protocol. Wine et al. (2019) reached a different conclusion than Aljadeff-Abergel et al., finding no performance differences between feedback following or preceding performance for staff operating a locking mechanism at a private school. These authors suggested simple tasks (such as data entry or lock operation) may not depend on a particular timing of feedback, whereas complex performance (such as implementing a teaching protocol) may benefit from antecedent feedback as a form of task clarification. Brand et al. (2020) used a fairly simple task (matching-to-sample with names of shapes) and also found no differences between after-session and before-session feedback.

A conceptual analysis may explain some of the inconsistency across studies. The aforementioned results suggest feedback for complex behaviors may rely quite heavily on rule control since feedback was not superior as an immediate consequence but was effective as an antecedent, even before it could be correlated with differential outcomes (thus precluding simple discriminative functions). Verbal mediation generated by feedback right before performance may be similar to verbal mediation generated right after performance. The critical question is whether repetition of the verbal rules persist over time. If not, then feedback right before performance may be necessary. If so, then no differences may be seen with before- or after-session feedback. It may be telling that studies with typical durations of a day or less between sessions found no performance differences (Bechtel et al., 2015; Brand et al., 2020; Wine et al., 2019), whereas the study in which a duration of multiple days between sessions (Aljadeff-Abergel et al., 2017) found improved performance with before-session feedback. That is, if one performs a task again in 10 min, it probably does not matter if you receive feedback 1 min after previous performance or 1 min before subsequent performance (any verbal self-statements are likely to persist during the duration and thus maintain any behavior strengthening aspects). However, if one performs the task again in 10 weeks, it is possible verbal self-statements may dissipate over time and therefore placing feedback right before performance may be beneficial. To our knowledge, this consideration has yet to be examined in the research (e.g., explicit control of differing durations between sessions for various behaviors with differing feedback timings). Meanwhile, there appears to be no drawbacks to providing feedback right before performance, at least for well-learned skills (skills being acquired may still benefit from ongoing corrections during performance; Bacotti et al., 2021). Further, there is some evidence that people may prefer feedback placed right before their next performance (Bacotti et al., 2021; Bechtel et al., 2015).

Feedback source

Another importance feature of performance feedback is the source. For example, does the impact of praise for performance improvement alter if delivered by a high-ranking authority figure, low-ranking authority figure, peer, friend, enemy, family member, stranger, automated computer program, or self? Differences in social histories and relationship dynamics could plausibly make similar forms of feedback effective, neutral, or even counterproductive.

In one of the few studies explicitly examining these possibilities, Chae et al. (2020) compared how college students completing an assembly task responded to feedback from an established authority figure (an experimenter who previously or currently was the professor for one of their classes) or a non-authority figure (an experimenter that the participants had not previously met). The results showed that feedback from an authority figure was more consistently effective than feedback from a non-authority figure. When provided by an authority figure, their feedback was effective when delivered either face-to-face or via e-mail. However, Chae et al. (2020) found non-authority figures could also be effective, but only when delivering feedback face-to-face.

Feedback modality

Thus, feedback modality appears important, especially as advancing technology opens up a plethora of options for feedback delivery (in-person, virtual, printed, e-mail, etc.). As Warrilow et al. (2020) point out, remote supervision is on the rise and the health concerns related to COVID-19 will likely accelerate this preexisting trend. Therefore, it is important to identify benefits and issues when supervision is provided remotely, especially when employees are juggling office work, household chores, parenting responsibilities, and more. Like Chae et al., Warrilow et al. examined the impact of different feedback modalities on performance, specifically feedback delivered via computer message, text message, and face-to-face. In alignment with Chae et al., these researchers found face-to-face feedback the most effective medium, although they noted the potential of unexplored modalities to approximate such control (e.g., one-on-one video conferencing). It is important to discover the controlling features that make certain modalities effective and, if possible, replicate those features across alternative situations.

The reception of feedback

These aforementioned studies largely focused on the elements of feedback and how people (typically managers and other authority figures) should best deliver feedback. Naturally, it would be of interest to also examine critical practices for the reception of feedback (typically by employees and other subordinates) and how the reactions of recipients might influence the delivery of feedback. For example, Matey et al. (2019) investigated the latter issue when participants were asked to deliver feedback classifying posture as "safe" or "at-risk" to confederates who would periodically act safe or unsafe. The researchers noted that participants felt uncomfortable delivering corrective feedback in particular and often classified "at-risk" behaviors as "safe." In a follow-up study, Matey et al. (2021) systematically evaluated the effect of differential feedback reactions on data collection and subsequent feedback delivery.

Confederates receiving feedback from participants were instructed to react in a negative, neutral, or positive manner. When confederates reacted to feedback in a negative manner, feedback accuracy decreased by 13% (although unchanged in the neutral or positive conditions). Furthermore, participants greatly reduced their frequency of feedback deliveries in the negative and neutral conditions as compared with the positive conditions. This suggests that lack of reinforcement (or even punitive) aspects of feedback for people assigned to observations and feedback delivery necessitates steps to either support the accuracy of feedback, particularly non-positive forms, through supplemental management efforts or by training recipients how to react appropriately to feedback.

In a perhaps ironic twist, despite the fact that people may avoid delivering corrective feedback, there is some evidence that recipients may prefer corrective feedback over positive feedback, at least under some circumstances. For example, Simonian and Brand (2022) allowed participants to select either corrective or positive feedback while learning a new task. Not only did all participants prefer corrective feedback over positive feedback, but their performance also improved only after receiving corrective feedback. In order to maintain the behaviors of people tasked with delivering feedback, it may be critical to shape the reactions of those receiving feedback. Both Ehrlich et al. (2020) and Walker and Sellers (2021) demonstrated that training could increase behaviors believed to be associated with better receptive skills. More research is needed to establish which feedback receptive skills have the best effects on subsequent performance of employees or influence the willingness of managers to continue delivering feedback. Furthermore, more research is needed that examines how preference for feedback and motivation to seek out feedback might be altered (Ashford & Cummings, 1983; Sleiman, Gravina et al., 2020).

Conclusion

Much research has been done investigating feedback, and given the complexity involved with this seemingly simple concept, much research is still needed. Table 1 summarizes the topics our field has investigated and the findings thus far (undoubtedly, nuances will need to be added as more research is conducted). This past information suggests several potential future research avenues. Table 1 also suggests a non-exhaustive list of feedback research questions still in need of answering. Furthermore, all of the suggested directions could be further investigated by looking at how these variable factors might combine and interact, both in controlled and applied settings, using tasks of differing levels of complexity and work types. Each of the feedback variables could also be examined in terms of effects across various demographics and cultures (Nastasi et al., 2022). Most studies on feedback performance have largely focused on productivity or

Table 1. Summary of feedback findings and future directions.

Feedback Factor	Current Findings and Understanding	Relevant Areas of Future Research
Function of feedback	There is no definitive function of feedback; rather, it is a stimulus that can acquire a number of sometimes overlapping functions	• What is the most common function of feedback in organizations? • What are the best procedures to train individuals to establish or abolish certain functions of feedback? • What commonly seen organizational procedures tend to establish or abolish certain feedback functions?
Objective and evaluative elements of feedback	Combining objective information and subjective evaluations will enhance the effects of feedback over objective or evaluative components alone.	• How do explicit and implicit evaluations compare? • What are the critical features of evaluation (e.g., content of message, tone during delivery, body language, etc.)? • What is the impact when various evaluations are in conflict with one another (e.g., self, peer, or managerial evaluations)? • What effect does the degree or severity of evaluation have (e.g., "your performance was substandard/poor/awful/atrocious/disgusting" or "I saw your data and it was improved/good/excellent/amazing/inspiring")? • Do rote statements undermine evaluations? How much variance is necessary to maintain enhancements?
Specificity of feedback	Feedback effects are enhanced as precision increases, at least for correct performance or infrequent feedback; reduced specificity might be preferable for the problem solving of mistakes; specific feedback may be unnecessary in the context of frequent feedback	• At what point, if any, does specificity become overwhelming for a performer (e.g., describing performance in terms of several dimensions of behavior or outcome measures)? • Do certain dimensions of performance (e.g., rate, accuracy, latency, creativity, duration, quality, etc.) benefit differentially from specificity? • At what point during the learning process should feedback change from general to specific? • What are guidelines for determining if feedback for errors should only indicate nonspecific results (e.g., correct or incorrect) to promote problem-solving or indicate precise corrections (e.g., steps omitted and how to fix) to foster immediate improvements?
Feedback based on comparisons	Group feedback, without an indication of an individual's placing with the group, is generally ineffective; the effects of social comparison feedback is unclear	• What are the mediating factors that determine the effectiveness of normative feedback (e.g., culture, individual position within rankings, specificity of feedback when above or below group average, are the group members familiar with each other)?
Combinations feedback of different natures	Performance is not enhanced by combining feedbacks incongruent in nature (e.g., feedback sandwich); positive feedback and negative feedback should be delivered separately	• How much time must separate positive and negative feedback sessions? • How to mitigate the emotional impact of negative feedback while maintaining the performance impact? • Do positive-negative and positive-corrective combinations of feedback have the same effect?

(Continued)

Table 1. (Continued).

Feedback Factor	Current Findings and Understanding	Relevant Areas of Future Research
Accuracy in feedback delivery	Feedback is more effective when steps are taking to ensure accuracy	• What factors will lead a performer to detect feedback inaccuracy? • Are there factors that will make a performer distrust accurate feedback? • How to correct the general distrust of feedback following a history of inaccurate feedback? • What is the effect when feedback starts out accurate but slowly becomes inaccurate and vice-versa?
Privacy of feedback	Generally, it has been cautioned to provide feedback privately when involved individual and identifiable performance	• What are the contextual factors that will differentially impact the impact of public versus private feedback?
Frequency of feedback	Feedback becomes more effective as it becomes more frequent	• When considering time, effort, and money, is there a point of diminishing returns as feedback frequency increases? • What standards should be used to determine when new performers under frequent feedback should be transitioned to less frequent feedback?
Timing of feedback	Unclear whether after-session or before-session feedback is more beneficial; slight evidence for presenting feedback about prior performance immediately before subsequent performance	• Does the complexity of the task interact with the effectiveness of feedback timing? • Is verbal mediation an important consideration to determining the effectiveness of feedback timing? • Does the size of the duration between sessions differentially impact the effectiveness of after-session or before-session feedback?
Source of feedback	Feedback from authority figure more effective than feedback from non-authority	• How do other feedback sources (e.g., self, peer, enemy, stranger, etc.) compare to one another? • Is there an interaction effect with different feedback sources and recipients (e.g., front-line employees and managers versus knowledge workers and managers)?
Feedback modality	Face-to-face feedback is most effective	• What elements make face-to-face feedback effective (and how might they be recreated through other modalities)? • What are strategies to enhance the effectiveness of remote feedback?
Feedback reception	People will distort data or avoid delivering non-positive feedback; recipients prefer corrective feedback when learning a new task	• What strategies can be used to ensure regular and accurate feedback delivery, even in the face of negative reactions from recipients? • What are the minimal elements necessary to prevent feedback reactions from being perceived as negative?

some closely related other measure, but additional dependent variables merit investigation (e.g., quality, creativity, satisfaction, well-being, cost-benefit). Much work remains to be done to understand functional properties and how to create the best systems of feedback for both the people delivering and the people receiving feedback (Balcazar et al., 1985; Johnson, 2013; Matey et al., 2021). Just as consequences may provide feedback to the organism, the findings of our research should continue to provide feedback to our practices and procedures.

Disclosure statement

We have no known conflicts of interest to disclose.

ORCID

Douglas A. Johnson http://orcid.org/0000-0002-7802-3566

References

Agnew, J. L., & Redmon, W. K. (1992). Contingency specifying stimuli: The role of "rules" in organizational behavior management. *Journal of Organizational Behavior Management*, *12* (2), 67–76. https://doi.org/10.1300/J075v12n02_04

Agnew, J. L. (1998). The establishing operation in organizational behavior management. *Journal of Organizational Behavior Management*, *18*(1), 7–19. https://doi.org/10.1300/J075v18n01_02

Aguinis, H., Gottfredson, R. K., & Joo, H. (2012). Delivering effective performance feedback: The strengths-based approach. *Business Horizons*, *55*(2), 105–111. https://doi.org/10.1016/j.bushor.2011.10.004

Aljadeff-Abergel, E., Peterson, S. M., Wiskirchen, R. R., Hagen, K. K., & Cole, M. L. (2017). Evaluating the temporal location of feedback: Providing feedback following performance vs. prior to performance. *Journal of Organizational Behavior Management*, *37*(2), 171–195. https://doi.org/10.1080/01608061.2017.1309332

Alvero, A. M., Bucklin, B. R., & Austin, J. (2001). An objective review of the effectiveness and essential characteristics of performance feedback in organizational settings (1985-1998). *Journal of Organizational Behavior Management*, *21*(1), 3–29. https://doi.org/10.1300/J075v21n01_02

Ammons, R. B. (1956). Effects of knowledge of performance: A survey and tentative theoretical formulation. *The Journal of General Psychology*, *54*(2), 279–299. https://doi.org/10.1080/00221309.1956.9920284

Ashford, S. J., & Cummings, L. L. (1983). Feedback as an individual resource: Personal strategies of creating information. *Organizational Behavior and Human Performance*, *32* (3), 370–398. https://doi.org/10.1016/0030-5073(83)90156-3

At Emery Air Freight: Positive reinforcement boosts performance. (1973). At emery air freight: Positive reinforcement boosts performance. *Organizational Dynamics*, *1*(3), 41–50. https://doi.org/10.1016/S0090-2616(73)80017-8

Bacotti, J. K., Grauerholz-Fisher, E., Morris, S. L., & Vollmer, T. R. (2021). Identifying the relation between feedback preferences and performance. *Journal of Applied Behavior Analysis*, *54*(2), 668–683. https://doi.org/10.1002/jaba.804

Baer, D. M., Wolf, M. M., & Risley, T. R. (1968). Some current dimensions of applied behavior analysis. *Journal of Applied Behavior Analysis*, *1*(1), 91–97. https://doi.org/10.1901/jaba.1968.1-91

Balcazar, F., Hopkins, B. L., & Suarez, Y. (1985). A critical, objective review of performance feedback. *Journal of Organizational Behavior Management*, *7*(3–4), 65–89. https://doi.org/10.1300/J075v07n03_05

Bechtel, N. T., McGee, H. M., Huitema, B. E., & Dickinson, A. M. (2015). The effects of the temporal placement of feedback on performance. *The Psychological Record*, *65*(3), 425–434. https://doi.org/10.1007/s40732-015-0117-4

Berger, J. (2013, June 25). *INSTANT MBA: When giving feedback, give criticism between two positives*. The Business Insider. http://www.businessinsider.com/feedbackbetween-two-positives-2013-6

Blakely, E., & Schlinger, H. (1987). Rules: Function-altering contingency-specifying stimuli. *The Behavior Analyst, 10*(2), 183–187. https://doi.org/10.1007/BF03392428

Bottini, S., & Gillis, J. (2021). A comparison of the feedback sandwich, constructive-positive feedback, and within session feedback for training preference assessment implementation. *Journal of Organizational Behavior Management, 41*(1), 83–93. https://doi.org/10.1080/01608061.2020.1862019

Brand, D., Novak, M. D., DiGennaro Reed, F. D., & Tortolero, S. A. (2020). Examining the effects of feedback accuracy and timing on skill acquisition. *Journal of Organizational Behavior Management, 40*(1–2), 3–18. https://doi.org/10.1080/01608061.2020.1715319

Brett, J. F., & Atwater, L. E. (2001). 360° feedback: Accuracy, reactions, and perceptions of usefulness. *Journal of Applied Psychology, 86*(5), 930–942. https://doi.org/10.1037/0021-9010.86.5.930

Bucklin, B. R., McGee, H. M., & Dickinson, A. M. (2003). The effects of individual monetary incentives with and without feedback. *Journal of Organizational Behavior Management, 23* (2/3), 65–94. https://doi.org/10.1300/J075v23n02_05

Chae, S., Eagle, L. M., Johnson, D. A., Moon, K., Choi, E., & Oah, S. (2020). The impact of authority relations and feedback delivery method on performance. *Journal of Organizational Behavior Management, 40*(1–2), 140–150. https://doi.org/10.1080/01608061.2020.1746476

Choi, E., Johnson, D. A., Moon, K., & Oah, S. (2018). Effects of positive and negative feedback sequence on work performance and emotional responses. *Journal of Organizational Behavior Management, 38*(2–3), 97–115. https://doi.org/10.1080/01608061.2017.1423151

Critchfield, T. S., Doepke, K. J., Epting, L. K., Becirevic, A., Reed, D. D., Fienup, D. M., Kremsreiter, J. L., & Ecott, C. L. (2017). Normative emotional responses to behavior analysis jargon or how to use words to win friends and influence people. *Behavior Analysis in Practice, 10*(2), 97–106. https://doi.org/10.1007/s40617-016-0161-9

Critchfield, T. S., & Doepke, K. J. (2018). Emotional overtones of behavior analysis terms in English and five other languages. *Behavior Analysis in Practice, 11*(2), 97–105. https://doi.org/10.1007/s40617-018-0222-3

Daniels, A. C. (2009). *Oops! 13 management practices that waste time and money (and what to do instead)*. Performance Management.

Daniels, A. C., & Bailey, J. S. (2014). *Performance management: Changing behavior that drives organizational effectiveness*. Performance Management Publication.

Daniels, A. C. (2016). *Bringing out the best in people: How to apply the astonishing power of positive reinforcement* (3rd ed.). McGraw-Hill.

DeNisi, A. S., & Pritchard, R. D. (2006). Performance appraisal, performance management and improving individual performance: A motivational framework. *Management and Organization Review, 2*(2), 253–277. https://doi.org/10.1111/j.1740-8784.2006.00042.x

Duncan, P. K., & Bruwelheide, L. R. (1985). Feedback: Use and possible behavioral functions. *Journal of Organizational Behavior Management, 7*(3–4), 91–114. https://doi.org/10.1300/J075v07n03_06

Ehrlich, R. J., Nosik, M. R., Carr, J. E., & Wine, B. (2020). Teaching employees how to receive feedback: A preliminary investigation. *Journal of Organizational Behavior Management, 40* (1–2), 19–29. https://doi.org/10.1080/01608061.2020.1746470

Emery Air Freight Corporation. (1971). *Feedback systems*. System Performance Division.

Feeney, E. J. (1972). Performance audit, feedback and positive reinforcement. *Training & Development Journal, 26*(11), 8–13.

Feeney, E. J. (1982). Performance standards, feedback, and rewards: A performance improvement system. *National Productivity Review*, *2*(1), 36–42. https://doi.org/10.1002/npr.4040020107

Ford, J. E. (1980). A classification system for feedback procedures. *Journal of Organizational Behavior Management*, *2*(3), 183–191. https://doi.org/10.1300/J075v02n03_04

Frederiksen, L. W., Richter, W. T., Jr, Johnson, R. P., & Solomon, L. J. (1982). Specificity of performance feedback in a professional service delivery setting. *Journal of Organizational Behavior Management*, *3*(4), 41–53. https://doi.org/10.1300/J075v03n04_05

Goltz, S. M., Citera, M., Jensen, M., Favero, J., &., & Komaki, J. L. (1989). Individual feedback: Does it enhance effects of group feedback. *Journal of Organizational Behavior Management*, *10*(2), 77–92. https://doi.org/10.1300/J075v10n02_06

Goodman, J. S., & Wood, R. E. (2004). Feedback specificity, learning opportunities, and learning. *Journal of Applied Psychology*, *89*(5), 809–821. https://doi.org/10.1037/0021-9010.89.5.809

Grote, D. (2002). *The performance appraisal question and answer book: A survival guide for managers*. American Management Association.

Hartwell, C. J., & Campion, M. A. (2016). Getting on the same page: The effect of normative feedback interventions on structured interview ratings. *Journal of Applied Psychology*, *101*(6), 757–778. https://doi.org/10.1037/apl0000099

Henley, A. J., & DiGennaro Reed, F. D. (2015). Should you order the feedback sandwich? Efficacy of feedback sequence and timing. *Journal of Organizational Behavior Management*, *35*(3–4), 321–335. https://doi.org/10.1080/01608061.2015.1093057

Hirst, J. M., & DiGennaro Reed, F. D. (2015). An examination of the effects of feedback accuracy on academic task acquisition in analogue settings. *The Psychological Record*, *65*(1), 49–65. https://doi.org/10.1007/s40732-014-0087-y

Jawahar, I. M. (2006). An investigation of potential consequences of satisfaction with appraisal feedback. *Journal of Leadership and Organizational Studies*, *13*(2), 14–28. https://doi.org/10.1177/10717919070130020101

Johnson, D. A., Dickinson, A. M., & Huitema, B. E. (2008). The effects of objective feedback on performance when individuals receive fixed and individual incentive pay. *Performance Improvement Quarterly*, *20*(3/4), 53–74. https://doi.org/10.1002/piq.20003

Johnson, D. A. (2013). A component analysis of the impact of evaluative and objective feedback on performance. *Journal of Organizational Behavior Management*, *33*(2), 89–103. https://doi.org/10.1080/01608061.2013.785879

Johnson, D. A., Rocheleau, J. M., & Tilka, R. E. (2015). Considerations in feedback delivery: The role of accuracy and type of evaluation. *Journal of Organizational Behavior Management*, *35*(3–4), 240–258. https://doi.org/10.1080/01608061.2015.1093055

Johnson, D. A., & Akpapuna, M. (2018). A pragmatic approach for building motivation to promote employee creativity and organizational innovation. In B. Wine & J. K. Pritchard (Eds.), *Organizational Behavior Management: The Essentials* (pp. 242-273). Hedgehog Publishers .

Johnson, D. A., & Johnson, C. M. (2022). Foundations and advances: Revisiting the past and selecting for the future. *Journal of Organizational Behavior Management*, Advance online publication.1–7. https://doi.org/10.1080/01608061.2022.2029797

Jordan, P. (Director). (1972). *Business, behaviorism and the bottom line* [Film]. CRM Productions.

Kang, K., Oah, S., & Dickinson, A. M. (2005). The relative effects of different frequencies of feedback on work performance. *Journal of Organizational Behavior Management*, *23*(4), 21–53. https://doi.org/10.1300/J075v23n04_02

Kluger, A. N., & DeNisi, A. (1996). The effects of feedback interventions on performance: A historical review, a meta-analysis, and a preliminary feedback intervention theory. *Psychological Bulletin, 119*(2), 254–284. https://doi.org/10.1037/0033-2909.119.2.254

Komaki, J. L. (1986). Toward effective supervision: An operant analysis and comparison of managers at work. *Journal of Applied Psychology, 71*(2), 270–279. https://doi.org/10.1037/0021-9010.71.2.270

Kuchinke, K. P. (2000). The role of feedback in management training settings. *Human Resource Development Quarterly, 11*(4), 381–401. https://doi.org/10.1002/1532-1096(200024)11:4<381::AID-HRDQ5>3.0.CO;2-3

Kuykendall, D., & Keating, J. P. (1990). Altering thoughts and judgements through repeated association. *British Journal of Social Psychology, 29*(1), 79–86. https://doi.org/10.1111/j.2044-8309.1990.tb00888.x

Lechermeier, J., & Fassnacht, M. (2018). How do performance feedback characteristics influence recipients 'reactions? A state-of-the-art review on feedback source, timing, and valence effects. *Management Review Quarterly, 68*(2), 145–193. https://doi.org/10.1007/s11301-018-0136-8

Lee, K., Shon, D., & Oah, S. (2014). The relative effects of global and specific feedback on safety behaviors. *Journal of Organizational Behavior Management, 34*(1), 16–28. https://doi.org/10.1080/01608061.2013.878264

Lee, J., Lim, S., & Oah, S. (2020). Effects of accurate and inaccurate feedback on work performance: The role of the awareness of inaccuracy. *Journal of Organizational Behavior Management, 40*(1–2), 46–62. https://doi.org/10.1080/01608061.2020.1746472

Malott, R. W. (1992). A theory of rule-governed behavior and organizational behavior management. *Journal of Organizational Behavior Management, 12*(2), 45–65. https://doi.org/10.1300/J075v12n02_03

Mangiapanello, K. A., & Hemmes, N. S. (2015). An analysis of feedback from a behavior analytic perspective. *The Behavior Analyst, 38*(1), 51–75. https://doi.org/10.1007/s40614-014-0026-x

Mason, M. A., & Redmon, W. K. (1993). Effects of immediate versus delayed feedback on error detection accuracy in a quality control simulation. *Journal of Organizational Behavior Management, 13*(1), 49–83. https://doi.org/10.1300/J075v13n01_05

Matey, N., Gravina, N., Rajagopal, S., & Betz, A. (2019). Effects of feedback delivery requirements on accuracy of observations. *Journal of Organizational Behavior Management, 39*(3–4), 247–256. https://doi.org/10.1080/01608061.2019.1666773

Matey, N., Sleiman, A., Nastasi, J., Richard, E., & Gravina, N. (2021). Varying reactions to feedback and their effects on observer accuracy and feedback omission. *Journal of Applied Behavior Analysis, 54*(3), 1188–1198. https://doi.org/10.1002/jaba.840

Mesch, D. J., Farh, J., & Podsakoff, P. M. (1994). Effects of feedback sign on group goal setting, strategies, and performance. *Group & Organization Management, 19*(3), 309–333. https://doi.org/10.1177/1059601194193006

Michael, J. (2004). *Concepts and principles of behavior analysis* (2nd ed.). Association for Behavior Analysis International.

Moon, K., Lee, K., Lee, K., & Oah, S. (2017). The effects of social comparison and objective feedback on work performance across different performance levels. *Journal of Organizational Behavior Management, 37*(1), 63–74. https://doi.org/10.1080/01608061.2016.1236059

Nastasi, J. A., Crowe, A., & Gravina, N. E. (2022). Reporting Demographic Variables in JOBM and JAP: A Comparison and Call to Action. *Journal of Organizational Behavior Management*, Advance online publication. 1–14. https://doi.org/10.1080/01608061.2022.2082624

Newby, T. J., & Robinson, P. W. (1983). Effects of grouped and individual feedback and reinforcement on retail employee performances. *Journal of Organizational Behavior Management*, *5*(2), 51–61. https://doi.org/10.1300/J075v05n02_03

O'Reilly, C. A., & Anderson, J. C. (1980). Trust and the communication of performance appraisal information: The effect of feedback on performance and job satisfaction. *Human Communication Research*, *6*(4), 290–298. https://doi.org/10.1111/j.1468-2958.1980.tb00150.x

Palmer, M. G., Johnson, C. M., & Johnson, D. A. (2015). Objective performance feedback: Is numerical accuracy necessary? *Journal of Organizational Behavior Management*, *35*(3–4), 206–239. https://doi.org/10.1080/01608061.2015.1093059

Palmer, M. G., Johnson, C. M., & Johnson, D. A. (2015). Objective performance feedback: Is numerical accuracy necessary? *Journal of Organizational Behavior Management*, *35*(3–4), 206–239. https://doi.org/10.1080/01608061.2015.1093059

Pampino, R. N., MacDonald, J. E., Mullin, J. E., & Wilder, D. A. (2004). Weekly feedback vs. daily feedback. *Journal of Organizational Behavior Management*, *23*(2–3), 21–43. https://doi.org/10.1300/J075v23n02_03

Park, J. A., Johnson, D. A., Moon, K., & Lee, J. (2019). The interaction effects of frequency and specificity of feedback on work performance. *Journal of Organizational Behavior Management*, *39*(3–4), 164–178. https://doi.org/10.1080/01608061.2019.1632242

Pearce, J. L., & Porter, L. W. (1986). Employee responses to formal performance appraisal feedback. *Journal of Applied Psychology*, *71*(2), 211–218. https://doi.org/10.1037/0021-9010.71.2.211

Peterson, N. (1982). Feedback is not a new principle of behavior. *The Behavior Analyst*, *5*(1), 101–102. https://doi.org/10.1007/BF03393144

Prue, D. M., & Fairbank, J. A. (1981). Performance feedback in organizational behavior management: A review. *Journal of Organizational Behavior Management*, *3*(1), 1–16. https://doi.org/10.1300/J075v03n01_01

Simonian, M. J., & Brand, D. (2022). Assessing the efficacy of and preference for positive and corrective feedback. *Journal of Applied Behavior Analysis*. Advance online publication. https://doi.org/10.1002/jaba.911

Skinner, B. F. (1953). *Science and human behavior*. Macmillan.

Sleiman, A. A., Sigurjonsdottir, S., Elnes, A., Gage, N. A., & Gravina, N. E. (2020). A quantitative review of performance feedback in organizational settings (1998-2018). *Journal of Organizational Behavior Management*, *40*(3–4), 303–332. https://doi.org/10.1080/01608061.2020.1823300

Sleiman, A. A., Gravina, N. E., Robinson, T., & Podlesnik, C. A. (2020). The role of effort in shifting preference for feedback stimuli. *Journal of Organizational Behavior Management*, *40*(1–2), 30–45. https://doi.org/10.1080/01608061.2020.1746471

So, Y., Lee, K., & Oah, S. (2013). Relative effects of daily feedback and weekly feedback on customer service behavior at a gas station. *Journal of Organizational Behavior Management*, *33*(2), 137–151. https://doi.org/10.1080/01608061.2013.785898

Staats, A. W., & Staats, C. K. (1958). Attitudes established by classical conditioning. *Journal of Abnormal and Social Psychology*, *57*(1), 37–40. https://psycnet.apa.org/doi/10.1037/h0042782

Thorndike, E. L. (1927). The law of effect. *American Journal of Psychology*, *39*(1/4), 212–222. https://doi.org/10.2307/1415413

Timberlake, W. (1977). The application of the matching law to simple ratio schedules. *Journal of the Experimental Analysis of Behavior*, *27*(1), 215–217. https://doi.org/10.1901/jeab.1977.27-215

Travers, R. M. W. (1977). *Essentials of learning* (4th ed.). Macmillan.

Trowbridge, M. H., & Cason, H. (1932). An experimental study of Thorndike's theory of learning. *The Journal of General Psychology*, *7*(2), 245–260. https://doi.org/10.1080/00221309.1932.9918465

Van Stelle, S. E., Vicars, S. M., Harr, V., Miguel, C. F., Koerber, J. L., Kazbour, R., & Austin, J. (2012). The publication history of the journal of organizational behavior management: An objective review and analysis: 1998–2009. *Journal of Organizational Behavior Management*, *32*(2), 93–123. https://doi.org/10.1080/01608061.2012.675864

Walker, S., & Sellers, T. (2021). Teaching appropriate feedback reception skills using computer-based instruction: A systematic replication. *Journal of Organizational Behavior Management*, *41*(3), 236–254. https://doi.org/10.1080/01608061.2021.1903647

Warrilow, G. D., Johnson, D. A., & Eagle, L. M. (2020). The effects of feedback modality on performance. *Journal of Organizational Behavior Management*, *40*(3–4), 233–248. https://doi.org/10.1080/01608061.2020.1784351

Weatherly, N. L., & Malott, R. W. (2008). An analysis of organizational behavior management research in terms of the three-contingency model of performance management. *Journal of Organizational Behavior Management*, *28*(4), 260–285. https://doi.org/10.1080/01608060802454643

Welsch, W. V., Ludwig, C., Radiker, J. E., & Krapfl, J. E. (1973). Effects of feedback on daily completion of behavior modification projects. *Mental Retardation*, *11*(4), 24–46.

Wine, B., Lewis, K., Newcomb, E. T., Camblin, J. G., Chen, T., Liesfeld, J. E., Matthews, K. M., Morgan, C. A., & Newcomb, B. B. (2019). The effects of temporal placement of feedback on performance with and without goals. *Journal of Organizational Behavior Management*, *39*(3–4), 308–316. https://doi.org/10.1080/01608061.2019.1632244

Pay-for-Performance: Behavior-Based Recommendations from Research and Practice

Barbara R. Bucklin, Anita Li, Manuel Manny Rodriguez, Douglas A. Johnson, and Lauren M. Eagle

ABSTRACT

The use of pay-for-performance has the potential to greatly increase the productivity of the workforce by incentivizing the act or result of performance itself rather than time spent performing. In this paper, monetary incentive approaches are examined through the lens of behavioral research and practice. Important criteria to protect both the financial health of the organization and the physical and emotional health of the workers are outlined, along with considerations for an organization to prepare for the transition to a different form of financial compensation. This paper offers best practices, as well as suggestions for future research and considerations to help overcome potential concerns from organizational and individual perspectives.

Dating back to some of their earliest works (Skinner, 1938), behavior analysts have long focused on the role of consequences in the development and maintenance of behavior. Within the context of workplace behavior, the role of financial consequences may be one of the most obvious candidates to start with if one wanted to extrapolate from laboratory findings to applied settings. Indeed, the earliest behavioral thought pieces about the workplace were quick to suggest the use of economic influence to improve productivity (Aldis, 1961; Skinner, 1953), though it was noted that financial rewards would not function as a simple instance of direct reinforcement. As Skinner (1969) explained, typical economic contingencies depend less on the delivery of the standard wage and more on a supervisor's potential threat to terminate employment and thus eliminate a needed source of income. As such, hourly wages are highly dependent on rule governance and aversive control to motivate any performance. However, by investigating alternative uses of financial compensation, such aversive control may be minimized in favor of an improved condition, one in which an employee feels as though their efforts matter because they are paid for their performance rather than just paid for their time. Thus, an early interest in pay-for-performance was born for behavioral theorists and practitioners, especially those interested in the workplace.

Although these early writings pointed toward revamping compensation systems in alignment with experimental research, the business community had long beaten the behaviorists to the punch. Probably the most renowned implementation of non-hourly wage systems comes from Lincoln Electric, frequently profiled for their unusual and highly successful compensation approach and one of the most famous business case studies (Koller, 2010; Rothe, 1947; Suri, 1970). Lincoln Electric is a manufacturer known for its welding equipment and has offered pay-for-performance to its factory workers for over 125 years. Just as a laboratory animal on a ratio schedule will receive more food or water only if it makes the target response more often, employees receive more pay if they produce more units (likewise, there is no hourly pay and poor products do not result in compensation). Although no income is guaranteed, Lincoln Electric still claims to have the highest-paid factory workers worldwide (Hartman, 1992; Henderson, 1985; Klein, 2012). Their piecework compensation system has resulted in highly productive employees and enabled Lincoln Electric to keep the largest market share within the global welding market (Klein, 2012; Perry, 1988). Lincoln Electric also guarantees lifetime employment and has one of the lowest turnover rates within U.S. manufacturing.

Another early business example of pay-for-performance could be seen through the work of Frederick Winslow Taylor, a notable contributor to the development of such systems (Dickinson, 2000). Taylor's contribution to pay-for-performance systems stems from his use of time studies to identify output standards and individualized incentive plans (Taylor, 1911). Taylor implemented differential piece-rate incentives, where those who did not meet standards were paid a lower rate than those who met or exceeded standards. The latter were rewarded beyond the base pay, which is the fixed base rate of pay for a job such as hourly or salary compensation (Peach & Wren, 1992). As a result of Taylor's contribution, many incentive plan derivatives emerged during this era. These are primarily two basic types: (1) time-wages, in which a monetary payout corresponded to a standard unit of working time, and (2) wages saved, in which incentives were based on reduced organizational costs.

Since behavioral applications in alignment with behavioral theory suggest that pay-for-performance systems can enhance employee performance, it would be instructive to provide an overview of the work done within organizational behavior management (OBM) on the topic of pay-for-performance and the use of monetary incentives. This paper will begin by surveying different compensation options (and outlined in Table 1) and the relevant research.

Table 1. Benefits and challenges of different pay-for-performance systems.

Fixed Compensation		
	For the organization, this system …	For the employee, this system …
Benefits	• Makes it easy to calculate payroll expenses • Is simple to design and administer	• Provides consistent compensation for financial certainty • Pays poor performers the same as good performers (i.e., benefits poor performers)
Challenges	• Can produce employees who only produce the minimum required to earn their fixed pay • Does not result in optimal performance results	• Is unfair to good performers • Decreases motivation to go beyond bare minimum expectations
Commissions/Individual Piece-rate Pay		
	For the organization, this system …	For the employee, this system …
Benefits	• Can produce significant improvements with as little as 3% incentive pay • Uses pay plans that are simple to develop and maintain • Can yield higher performance than more complex variable or fixed pay systems	• Usually delivers partial fixed wage for financial certainty • Provides an opportunity to earn above fixed wage, under the employee's control • Can increase motivation and individual satisfaction
Challenges	• Is not adjusted for overall performance, and is shown to only produce an increase in a single dimension • Can produce a decline in other untargeted aspects of performance • Can result in a competitive culture, leading to higher turnover rates	• Creates individual employees focused only on their own performance and decreases teamwork • Produces a competitive culture that can lead to employee dissatisfaction
Accelerated Incentive Pay		
	For the organization, this system …	For the employee, this system …
Benefits	• Produces higher performance than fixed wage systems	• Can pay significantly more as performance increases • Provides an opportunity to earn above fixed wage, under the employee's control
Challenges	• Is not more effective than linear pay • More challenging to design and administer than individual piece-rate pay systems	• May lead to fatigue or safety issues as employees accelerate their performance
Small Group Incentives When Equally Divided		
	For the organization, this system …	For the employee, this system
Benefits	• Results in sustained levels of productivity, often equal to or better than individual incentives in groups with equal performers	• Results in high productivity and satisfaction when the group members perform at equal levels
Challenges	• Can hurt productivity and morale of high performers	• May reduce performance in high performers • Can produce stress; some employees report that they do not want to let down their group
Goal Sharing, Gain Sharing, Profit Sharing		
	For the organization, these systems …	For the employee, these systems …

(*Continued*)

Table 1. (Continued).

Fixed Compensation		
	For the organization, this system ...	For the employee, this system ...
Benefits	• If arranged to do so, can align employee and department goals with organizational goals and strategies • Can increase productivity • May create employee stakeholders who are committed to the organization's success because a percentage of their pay depends on that success • (Profit sharing) Can be affordable because it is tied to organizational profit with pay outs that come directly from the profit	• May create a sense of ownership in the company because employees share in its success • Can result in significant pay outs for individual employees • Pay out higher percentages to higher paid employees (a benefit to those with higher fixed pay)
Challenges	• Do not focus on an individual's performance or contribution; they pay everyone similarly regardless of their contribution • (Goal sharing) Is not indexed to the company's profits, may payout large sums during unprofitable time periods • (Gain sharing) Requires increasing productivity year over year, which can be difficult to maintain	• Are unpredictable in their pay outs; employees cannot control the outcome • Are not under the control of the employee because they are based on organization-wide results • Payout infrequently, typically annually • May be perceived as unfair to those with lower fixed wages when payout is capped at a percentage of each individual's fixed wage • May not include all employees for eligibility (e.g., certain departments, or hourly or part time employees may be excluded)

Types of pay-for-performance systems

Commissions/individual piece-rate pay

This pay system is based only on an individual's specific behaviors or accomplishments. Typically, this model is only tied to one measure, such as sales numbers or profit earned by an individual; it is not adjusted for overall organizational performance. Commission or piece-rate can be based entirely on performance pay or combined with fixed compensation (i.e., a percentage of the wage is fixed, and a portion is based on individual performance). Research suggests that as little as 3% of total wages in variable piece-rate pay may be enough to produce significant performance improvements over fixed compensation such as hourly pay (e.g., Dickinson & Gillette, 1993; Frisch & Dickinson, 1990; LaMere et al., 1996; Matthews & Dickinson, 2000). These simple pay plans can usually yield higher performance than either complex variable pay plans or fixed pay plans (Abernathy, 2011; Bucklin & Dickinson, 2001; Slowiak et al., 2011).

Despite these advantages, piece-rate pay systems can create employee animosity, affecting emotional health (Davis, 2016). Piece-rate pay systems often generate competition between employees who are more likely to focus on their own performance and monetary gain, and less likely to focus on the department or organizational performance. This pay system can discourage teamwork, leaving employees feeling unsupported in their work. Unsupportive work climates can lead to employee dissatisfaction and high turnover rates (Komaki & Minnich, 2016). Unsupportive work cultures that embrace individualism also affect risk-taking (Deng et al., 2019). As piece-rate pay incentivizes high production, increased speed and pace of employee activity can ultimately lead to errors and negative customer outcomes (Binder, 2016). Additionally, occupational health may be compromised with increased job injury and accident risks (Davis, 2016). These systems can also be detrimental to organizations when they generate large payouts at times when the company is not profitable.

Accelerated incentive pay

In an accelerated pay-out system, the per-piece incentive increases as performance increases. Dickinson (2005) describes this as, "the more a performer completes, the more each part is worth" (p. 20). The justification for paying employees exponentially is to compensate workers at greater production levels, which becomes increasingly difficult to achieve. In theory, this would work to incentivize sustained high levels of productivity. Results from two laboratory studies (Oah & Dickinson, 1992; Smoot & Duncan, 1997) indicate that accelerated incentive pay is no more effective than linear pay, such as a piece-rate pay system with a consistent payout for each work output produced. Participants working under two conditions (accelerated and linear) performed comparably despite the fact that those participants earning accelerated payouts made significantly more money than those earning linear payouts. Although not typically measured in such studies, it would be worthwhile to also measure the levels of stress evoked by such systems when evaluating their merit.

Small group incentives, equally divided

In industries where group work is required, the above pay systems are not appropriate. Instead, organizations may utilize an incentive system based on performance tied to a group output or operational process. However, increasing group members diminishes the individual worker's control of their wages (Honeywell et al., 1997), thus the justification for a small group composition. Incentives delivered equally to members of small groups, with two to 12 employees, show relatively high-performance levels that are often comparable to, and in some cases exceed, individual monetary incentives (Honeywell et al., 1997; Honeywell-Johnson et al., 2002; McGee et al., 2006; Stolovitch et al., 2002). Research indicates this system is most effective when all employees within the group perform at equal levels. When there are differences, high performers tend to perform worse under small group incentives than they perform under individual monetary incentives, and low performers report stress caused by fear of letting down their group (McGee et al., 2006; Thurkow et al., 2000).

Goal sharing, gain sharing, and profit sharing

These organization-wide variable-pay systems are based on achieving annual organizational goals (goal sharing), organizational productivity over the previous year (gain sharing), or pre-defined annual profit levels (profit sharing). In most cases, the payout is capped at a percentage of an individual's salary or fixed wage or based on employees' levels within the organization (Department of Labor, 2020). The organization may also structure the payout to come from a bonus pool (Benson & Sajjadiani, 2017) where payouts may occur every fiscal quarter or annually. These systems appear to have mixed effectiveness. Some (Kruse, 1993; Osterman, 1994) have indicated these organization-wide incentive systems can enhance employee performance, especially when used in conjunction with other practices to improve performance. On the other hand, these systems have also been criticized for being largely ineffective (Benson & Sajjadiani, 2017). This is likely due to the variability in design and implementation by the organization. Another factor to consider is the payout's temporal remoteness to actual employee behaviors, resulting in a diluted incentive effect or even no effect on employee performance. Another disadvantage is that goal sharing is not indexed to the company's profit, unless profit is an explicit goal within the system (Abernathy, 2011). Due to the lack of laboratory research that can be conducted with this arrangement, the majority of research conducted on these pay systems are based on pre- and post-implementation and survey report, and thus limited in determining causality.

Practitioner innovations

Although behavioral consultants have long worked on compensation systems (Abernathy, 1990, 1996, 2014a), little has been done to demonstrate the effectiveness of their work in a scientific fashion (perhaps owing to an ironic lack of incentives for consultants to publish their work in peer-reviewed scholarly journals). Nonetheless, such practitioner efforts align well with OBM initiatives in general and help illustrate a behavior analytic approach to financial compensation, and therefore are worth an extended consideration. Abernathy et al. (1982) arguably solidified initial interest in pay-for-performance in OBM with their description of incentive pay systems in Virginia National Bank and Union National Bank of Little Rock, Arkansas. When the bank employees were introduced to these conditions, they increased production from just over 1,000 checks per hour to 3,500 per hour at Union National Bank (Dierks & McNally, 1987) and from 1,465 to 2,250 checks per hour at Virginia National Bank (Abernathy et al., 1982). As summarized by Duncan and Smoot (2001), four characteristics of these systems appear critical from a behavior analytic perspective: (1) a precise definition of performance, (2) frequent measures of performance, (3) specific and timely feedback based on those measures, and (4) a clear relationship between performance and pay. One example of a pay for performance system that integrates such characteristics is Abernathy (1996)'s Total Performance System (TPS). TPS integrates balanced scorecards, a profit-indexed pay structure, and performance management to mitigate the challenges of the systems described previously. The benefits and challenges of the TPS approach are summarized in Table 2.

Balanced performance scorecards

A scorecard is a performance improvement tool that aims to align employee performance goals and organizational goals and consists of multiple performance measures related to the individual, team, and department responsibilities (Abernathy, 1996; 2014a). Well-designed scorecards used across the organization, department, and individual levels are necessary and can facilitate cooperation, provide information to management about trends in performance, and foster discussions about improving performance over time (Abernathy, 1996 2014a). A balanced scorecard integrates quantitative goals from multiple perspectives of an organization. By incorporating performance goals on an individual, team, and organizational level, this can address the *one-*

Table 2. Benefits and challenges of the total performance system.

	For the organization, this system ...	For the employee, this system ...
Benefits	• Is tied to organizational strategies and balanced across more than one important variable for the individual role and organization • Does not risk one performance measurement dimension over others such as: productivity, quality, cost savings, sales/revenue • Uses a payout formula that considers both organization's profit and individual's performance (eliminates problem of paying high wages when organization experiences cash flow or profitability problems)	• Sets expectations about accomplishments (per balanced scorecard measures) and ties feedback and monetary consequences to meeting those expectations • Eliminates the 'fairness' concern with fixed wages that occurs when top performers are paid the same as low performers
Challenges	• Can be time consuming to implement • Can pose a challenge with understanding the organization as a system and balancing weights across all organizational performance measures • May result in complaints and perceptions of unfairness regarding measures and weights selected, especially early in its implementation • May produce fear in some employees about being measured and held accountable to their performance measures	• Can be described as unfair; self-monitoring of performance measures may help • May not be consistent when there is variability in an individual's job role

dimensional concern of pay for performance systems. At all three levels, scorecards typically include measures and provide performance feedback across Key Performance Indicator (KPI) dimensions to balance short-term and long-term goals. KPI dimensions could be sales and revenue, profit, expenses, cash flow, regulatory compliance, productivity, quality, customer service, and employee satisfaction.

These scorecards are balanced because weights are assigned to each measure based on its value to the organization, value to the customer, ease of improvement/control the performer has over the measure, and urgency to improve. The sum of the weights at each level equal 100%. Individuals earn a weighted score from 0% up to 100%, upon which their performance pay is based. The scorecard needs to be well understood for the tool and process to be managed properly. Providing definitions of each component of the scorecard has been viewed as helpful by the authors' clients, and illustrating the components as well, as shown in Figure 1. The following are definitions for the scorecard elements as depicted in Figure 1.

1. KPI dimension. The Key Performance Indicator (KPI) aligned across the organization.
2. Measure. A summary of what is measured.
3. Definition. A detailed description of each measure and how it is calculated or collected over the month or quarter; this makes each measure and data calculation clear to the performer and anyone viewing the scorecard.

1	2	3	4										5	6	7	8
KPI Dimension	Measure	Definition	PERFORMANCE SCALE										Raw Score	Score	Weight	Weighted Score
			1	2	3	4	5	6	7	8	9	10				
Sales	Booked revenue	Revenue booked monthly, averaged over the quarter	$583,333	$597,916	$612,500	$627,083	$641,666	$670,833	$700,000	$729,166	$758,333	$816,666	$612,500	3	10%	0.30
Expenses	Quarterly costs per case	Monthly departmental facilities allocation per case managed, reported as quarterly average	$750	$700	$600	$550	$500	$480	$475	$450	$425	$400	$450	8	10%	0.80
Productivity	Time spent per case	Hours spent by Case Managers per case, averaged across cases	25		24		22		21			20	22	5	10%	0.50
Productivity	Case load	Monthly case load (number of cases) per Case Manager, averaged over the quarter	5				6					7	7	10	10%	1.00
Quality Assurance	All mistakes identified internally	Percentage of cases returned to Case Manager for error correction over the quarter	15%	14%	13%	12%	10%	8%	6%	4%	2%	0%	12%	4	20%	0.80
Quality Assurance	Impactful mistakes identified internally	Number of dollar-costing errors identified by QA during the quarter	9	8	7	6	5	4	3	2	1	0	4	6	15%	0.90
Quality Assurance	Mistakes identified externally, by clients	Number of errors identified by clients that resulted in monetary loss	6		5		4	3	2	1		0	2	7	15%	1.05
Customer Satisfaction	Customers satisfied with service	External quarterly customer satisfaction survey results, averaged over the quarter	80%	85%	90%	92%	95%	96%	97%	98%	99%	100%	98%	8	7%	0.56
Regulatory Compliance	Internal Survey	Internal quarterly survey as percent marked "Consistently" across all three metrics, subtracting the N/A answers	55%	58%	60%	65%	70%	75%	80%	85%	90%	100%	58%	2	3%	0.06
			THRESHOLD				TARGET					STRETCH			100%	5.97

Figure 1. Total performance system balanced scorecard example.

4. Performance scale. A range from 1 to 10, with: 1 = the minimal threshold of acceptable performance; 5 = the target or goal that an average performer should achieve; 10 = the stretch goal or maximum performance.
5. Raw score. For each measure, this is the actual performance achieved during a month or quarter.
6. Score. For each measure, this is the performance scale number corresponding to the raw score. The number is multiplied by the weight to determine the weighted score.
7. Weight. This number is assigned to the measure based on its value to the organization, value to the customer, ease of improvement/control the performer has over the measure, and urgency to improve. The sum of the weights = 100%.
8. Weighted score. For each measure, the score (corresponding to the performance scale) is multiplied by the weight. The sum of the weighted score for each measure = the overall score for that individual or department. The overall weighted score ranges from 0 to 10.

Balanced scorecards encompass several elements shown in OBM research to improve performance. For example, under antecedent control, they provide explicit metrics to employees to set expectations of performance, as well as provide feedback after performance, which can function as behavioral consequences (Aljadeff-Abergel et al., 2017; Daniels & Bailey, 2014; Johnson, 2013). Moreover, the monetary incentives linked to scorecard feedback may further strengthen balanced scorecards as useful tools for improving performance. Research has suggested that evaluative feedback combined with incentives may be more effective than either alone (Bucklin et al., 2003; Goomas & Ludwig, 2007; Johnson et al., 2008).

Profit indexed performance pay

One concern of performance pay is that the employee payouts are not tied to the profitability of an organization. Abernathy (2011) proposes using an organizational multiplier, a complex formula that indicates an organization's profitability to guide pay for performance systems. In order to determine what value to use for the organizational multiplier, the organization must first determine its threshold amount to ensure the profitability of the organization. Then the organization must determine a percentage of the profit to share with employees and the exposure amount. In order to determine the organizational multiplier, the exposure is divided by the percentage of the profit and then added to the threshold amount. This value is set at 1. Typically, organizational multipliers range in value from 0 to 3. To create the organizational multiplier scale, divide the exposure by the percentage of profit times the desired multiplier scale value (e.g., 2 or 3) before adding the threshold amount. If the company is not profitable, then there are no payouts beyond an employee's base pay regardless of individual performance scores. If the company achieves its maximum profitability, employees can potentially earn up to three times the organization's established percent of base pay. By incorporating the organizational multiplier in a formula called Profit-Indexed Pay (Abernathy, 1996, 2011, 2014a), the financial health of the organization is reflected in the payout. The complete Profit-Indexed Pay formula comprises the multiplier of an employee's quarterly salary or base pay, a basis percentage set by the organization, the organizational multiplier, and the individual scorecard performance, all multiplied together which equals performance pay. Although the Profit-Indexed Pay formula is straightforward and only involves four metrics multiplied together, determining the organizational multiplier scale is complex and time-consuming. Unfortunately, the complexity of this formula can leave some organizations hesitant to use it. A simpler adaptation to the original formula may be multiplying the quarterly salary or base pay, times a percentage of profit, times the individual scorecard performance, which equals performance pay. This adapted profit-indexed performance pay is a simple *profit-sharing* approach to establish a static budget available for individual payouts each year, quarter, or month. For example, if payouts happen quarterly and the organizational profit is $25,000 in a quarter, that is the amount available for pay-for-performance across the organization in the following quarter. This solution is transparent to employees with the ability for the organization's leaders to define what will be available as pay-for-performance based on the individual employee's balanced scorecard result.

Performance management

The performance management element of the Total Performance System provides a focus on data to evaluate performance, troubleshoot problem areas, and implement solutions toward maximizing performance. OBM practitioners engage clients to use performance management techniques such as the ABC analysis (Braksick, 2007; Daniels & Bailey, 2014), diagnostic tools such as Austin's (2000) Performance Diagnostic Checklist (Gravina et al., 2021), and Mager and Pipe's (1970) problem solving questions. These techniques, coupled with direct observations, data gathering and analysis, and collaboration with organizational management on identifying solutions, become a foundational element of performance management. During implementation, there is a heavy focus on individual, group, and organization-wide performance feedback. Abernathy (1996; 2011, p. 2014) emphasizes a rich feedback loop to ensure the success of other elements of the Total Performance System.

Little empirical research has validated the Total Performance System in its entirety as a result of the multilevel components and complexity. However, components such as scorecards and performance management have had successful empirical demonstrations. In a controlled field study, LaMere et al. (1996) implemented a pay system that closely resembled the Total Performance System. The organization was a waste disposal firm that employed 22 roll-off truck drivers. When given the opportunity to earn 3%, 6%, or 9% of their total wages in incentive pay, drivers' performance across several measures immediately increased. The increase averaged approximately 20% over baseline, for 28 weeks for the group with the longest intervention in the study. While the researchers referred to this as a piece-rate pay system, it had many of the characteristics of a multidimensional pay system, such as: (1) several performance measures that were assigned point values, and taken together comprised the primary performance measure – percentage of jobs completed in less time than baseline; (2) performance management used in the form of feedback based on measures, and incentive pay delivered weekly; and (3) incentive payout values derived from projected labor-cost savings, which made the program affordable to the organization.

In recent applied studies in health and human service settings, researchers implemented balanced scorecards across multiple performance dimensions, either alone (Griffin et al., 2019), or as part of a treatment package along with training, coaching, and publicly posted feedback (Szabo et al., 2012). Both studies used multiple baseline designs and showed increased staff performance for the intervention period of up to nine weeks and 16 weeks, respectively, at a low cost to the organizations. Additional empirical research would be beneficial as organizations, such as healthcare settings, are increasingly interested in seeing evidence-based approaches for improving performance (Rosenthal & Dudley, 2007).

Parallels with research outside of organizational behavior management

Although the current paper is focused on behavior analytic innovations with monetary incentive systems, it would be remiss if non-behavioral research was not at least briefly considered. Even if explanations about data are steeped in mentalistic terms, if performance data exists it should not be ignored simply because it was generated by someone from a different theoretical paradigm (after all, data are data). Overall, this research aligns well with behavioral research. Two meta-analyses found positive overall effect sizes for individual monetary incentives when analyzing 146 (Garbers & Konradt, 2014) and 7,987 (Kim et al., 2021) studies. Kim et al. (2021) conducted a meta-analysis to examine the relationship between incentives and overall performance, for which they found a positive effect size (δ = .52). Further, to follow up and extend previous meta-analyses with conflicting results regarding the impact of monetary incentives on performance in interesting tasks (Jenkins et al., 1998; Weibel et al., 2010), they found a positive incentive–performance relationship in both interesting (δ = +.58) and non-interesting tasks (δ = +.52). These findings were consistent across moderators such as task intensity, different types of performance, and work autonomy. Furthermore, these findings were contrary to often-stated claims that incentives have a negative effective on interesting tasks and thus undermine intrinsic motivation (Deci, 1972; Deci et al., 2017; Pink, 2009). In fact, research suggests monetary rewards improve overall motivation regardless of intrinsic motivation and that pay-for-performance can sustain improvement even after removal (Benzer et al., 2013; Hendijani et al., 2016).

Garbers and Konradt (2014) examined effects of individual and team-based incentives on performance and found a positive overall effect size ($\delta = +.32$). In their analysis of moderators, they found larger effect sizes for field studies ($\delta = +.34$) than for laboratory studies ($\delta = +.29$) and smaller effect sizes for less-complex tasks ($\delta = +.19$) than other types of tasks. Similar to our description earlier in this paper of small group incentives, this meta-analysis found consistently positive incentive-performance relationships for team-based incentives, which were comparable to the results of individual incentives, and further found that effect size decreased as the number of team members increased.

Even though the explanatory mechanisms vary, the basic conclusion reached across disciplines is the same: namely that monetary incentives can be successful, when implemented carefully with thoughtful design. Of course, that last added qualification is quite vital and highlights the importance of reviewing the literature for caveats in implementation (to be discussed shortly). For anyone interested in a particular topic within monetary incentive approaches (e.g., gainsharing), they would be well advised to consult the vast research literature available.

Incentive systems and "the greater promise"

OBM has long been concerned with using our interventions (including those with monetary incentive components) for the good of the worker first and foremost. In what is likely the first full OBM article ever published, Aldis (1961) considered how basic experimental research might inform our incentive systems (e.g., greater immediacy, piece-rate, etc.) to increase productivity. Nonetheless, he concluded his article by noting that the "greater promise is that such experiments may lead to happier workers as well." (p. 63). Throughout his writings, Abernathy saw that the true potential of pay-for-performance was to ensure fairness for the workers and to improve the human condition in general (Abernathy, 2014b). Our discipline should not simply be a tool to help corporations make more money, but rather an approach to improve the lives of people while at work.

Without careful thought and attention, application of our science could be to the detriment of workers. In laboratory research, we can arrange conditions such that the animal will behave in suboptimal ways, especially as deprivation levels for the animal increases, even to the point that the energy expended to get a food reinforcer exceeds the energy that the food provides

(Christopher, 1988; Zentall, 2014). Skinner (1953) once pointed out that we can get a pigeon to respond as fast as five times per second and to maintain that rate for hours. It is not difficult to imagine how such arrangements could be used for the exploitation and ill health of workers, especially among the most vulnerable or deprived members of society. In laboratory settings, any potential dangers to the health of the experimental animal are mitigated, for example, by careful maintenance of the animal body weight so that any losses are offset with additional feed away from the experimental chamber (Ferster & Skinner, 1957). No such provision is inherently provided for the care of people when they are overworked by their employers. Therefore, any OBM professional must be mindful of ethical considerations when advocating for the redesign of monetary systems.

Returning to our earlier example of Lincoln Electric's pure incentive pay system, even though the company may boast of low turnover rates, that outcome may obscure some negative aspects of their approach. With the exception of job-related illnesses or injuries, Lincoln Electric offers no paid holidays or sick leave (Klein, 2012), which induces many employees to work while struggling with illnesses (Hartman, 1992). If aging employees are unable to work as fast, then they simply earn less. In short, there is no safety net at a company like Lincoln Electric, for both good and bad. It is a high-pressure work environment that sees 20–50% of new hires quitting within 3 months (Hodgetts, 1997). The overall turnover rate remains positive because employees who make it past the first 90 days tend to become lifelong productive employees and hiring is done infrequently. Such outcomes work well for a single company but could be problematic for the overall employment culture if implemented at a larger scale.

Although our work needs to be financially feasible for the organization, it is important to not become preoccupied with the measure of money alone (or any measure that indirectly stands in for money, such as productivity). This is true of any work within OBM, even if the issue is more salient when the topic involves monetary incentives. Within the context of incentive pay, Davis and Hoyt (2020) found that piece rate pay was associated with negative effects on worker health, with greater risks found among women, minorities, and low-income workers. Johansson et al. (2010) reported that piece rate pay was correlated with risk taking and mistakes. However, they noted that they could not conclusively determine that such monetary incentives will always produce negative side effects. Instead, they suggested that the appropriate answer about the impact of pay-for-performance is, "it depends on." In other words, the details of the implementation are critically important to the success or failure of any incentive system.

For example, Oxenbridge and Moensted (2011) studied room attendants who were paid by piece-rate and found that the payment method increased the speed at which employees worked. Unfortunately, it also led to an observed increase in employees working unsafely and routinely exposing themselves to greater injuries. The work setting in this study only measured and rewarded the completion of clean rooms, with little training or emphasis on safety. From a behavioral perspective, these risky and undesirable outcomes should not be surprising. As the old adage goes, you get what you pay for. If you only pay for increased productivity, then you will get all forms of increased productivity, including the unsafe forms (or perhaps exclusively the unsafe forms, if unsafe performance is easier or less time consuming). If one wants to improve both productivity and safety, then measures and consequences need to exist for both productivity and safety. If other measures matter, such as quality, timeliness, teamwork, or creativity, then those measures need to be reflected as well. Evaluating performance via a single metric creates the risk of unmeasured performance worsening for other criteria. The net effect of an intervention may depend upon a consideration of all these systemic factors.

A balanced approach with pay-for-performance

We must design our incentive systems holistically to ensure fair working conditions that are optimal from the perspective of both the employer and employee. Failing to address this leaves us open to criticisms of being anti-labor or misunderstanding what really motivates employees. One of the advantages of a performance scorecard is that several measures can be used to balance different needs, making sure that employees are rewarded not just for working harder, but also working in alignment with safety, quality, or other standards. Incentives can be integrated in coordination with other safety and total health initiatives to ensure the well-being of employees (Ludwig & Laske, 2021; Olson et al., in press). Incentive systems can have criteria in place for quality. Finally, we can involve employees in the selection of measures and design of incentive systems to promote satisfaction and allow transparency about the structure and reasoning for incentive measures. Research has suggested that workers will perform better when they help design an incentive system, as compared with an identical incentive systems designed without employee input (Caza et al., 2015; Cooper et al., 1992). When unions or employees in general are involved in the design of reward systems, workers show improved satisfaction, greater trust in management, and a greater tendency to remain with the organization (Jenkins & Lawler, 1981; Schwarz, 1989).

Therefore, a balanced approach suggests that monetary incentives should be implemented as part of broader supportive system, and not as a cure-all single component. Compensation metrics must take into account issues such as quality, safety, health, and satisfaction through a cooperative framework. Part of Lincoln Electric's success with incentive pay comes from the supportive elements such as profit sharing, job security, and employee input on managerial decision making. During a tour of Lincoln Electric, union executives from other companies had difficulty finding a need for a union at the manufacturer (which has never had a union) and noted that most of the Lincoln employees were already getting what they had been fighting for at their respective unions. However, it is rare that corporations will put forward such a comprehensive approach, or as one of the union leaders put it, "I'm not worried that unions are going to become irrelevant because most of you are too dumb to run your companies this way!" (Solman, 2011).

Although the focus of this paper has been on economic influences, it would be negligent if the possibility of non-monetary incentives was not acknowledged, especially when monetary incentives are not feasible. For example, feedback, praise, recognition, and celebrations have also been used successfully to drive performance (Daniels & Bailey, 2014; Johnson, 2013). The key variable is to not be wholly dependent on hourly wages as the only source of motivation and acknowledgment for workers. Mixed models are also possible, such as including an hourly base pay that could ensure financial security for employees, but with additional monetary incentives to promote discretionary effort and recognition to those who do more than the minimum. Regardless of whether incentives are to be implemented as supplemental reward or as part of a complete pay-for-performance system, implementation should be done with a careful consideration of the necessary supporting factors.

Making sure that the organization is prepared for a change in compensation practices

Taking into consideration everything discussed in this paper, as well as recommendations by pay-for-performance experts (Abernathy, 2014a; Daniels & Bailey, 2014; Garbers & Konradt, 2014), effective performance-based pay at the individual and organizational level should:

- Be structured on company values and strategic objectives
- Be agile to adapt to changing business needs
- Consider both the organization's profit as well as the individual's performance
- Be focused on employee contributions and used to maintain or increase performance
- Be transparent: scorecards, measures, and results are shared to set expectations and are aligned with feedback and incentives
- Be contingent on an employee's own performance
- Measure performance within the performers' control, and/or obstacles to performance be within managers' control to remove in support of the performers
- Be based on clearly specified behaviors or accomplishments

- Be certain, ethical, and fair (i.e., if the performance occurs, the individual will always receive the pay)
- Be paid as soon after the performance as possible, or at least linked with frequent feedback
- Be based on measures agreed upon by both the employee and supervisor
- Be designed to avoid ethical concerns or potential discomfort expressed by employees about working under a pay-for-performance system

Pay-for-performance readiness factors

Based on our experience, if an organization is not ready, the system will be ineffective at best and detrimental at worst. Prior to implementing a pay-for-performance system, we recommend the conditions outlined next to avoid potential organizational and individual challenges or ethical dilemmas that can result from pay-for-performance systems.

Executive and management readiness

Executive and senior leaders need to spend time identifying organizational-level results aligned with their business strategies. This will take time, energy, and oversight from the start. It is not only important for management to use scorecards as tools to discuss and provide consequences for department and individual performance; they must *own* the scorecards, meaning the scorecards are used by the employee to self-manage their own performance, raise issues, and hold themselves accountable to their performance. The process of managing performance and pay for performance will not be successful unless management is committed to this system as a new way to manage performance across all levels of their organization. Sharing return-on-investment data helps executive leaders *buy in* to pay-for-performance systems.

Manager and supervisor buy-in is also crucial. For many organizations, this type of system changes the behaviors required by managers and supervisors, which may be time-consuming and discouraging at first. It is up to executive leaders to create and deliver positive consequences for their managers and supervisors, contingent on engaging in those new behaviors. This is especially true at the beginning when requirements change, more work is involved, and pay is not yet attached to the scorecard results (i.e., design, development, and baseline phases). As with any change initiative, over time managers and supervisors will experience the benefits (i.e., natural positive consequences) of their scorecard-related management activities.

Participant readiness

Employees may resist working under a pay-for-performance system for a number of reasons, and therefore, it is important to design a fair and ethical system, obtain participant collaboration and buy-in, and clearly communicate all features of the system prior to implementation. These considerations are described next, along with techniques to ensure participants are prepared to work under such a system.

Fair and ethical system design

To ensure fairness and compliance, compensation systems must adhere to local and federal Human Resource (HR) regulations. As an OBM consultant or practitioner, it is important to understand compensation laws for the organization's location (e.g., see https://www.dol.gov/general/aboutdol/majorlaws for a summary of the major laws of the U.S. Department of Labor). For new employees hired under an existing pay-for-performance system, clearly communicate the performance measures and pay contingencies to avoid surprises and adhere to HR regulations.

In addition to fearing the unknown, participants may worry that these systems are management's efforts to get more work for less pay. O'Brien (1990) suggested data-driven collaboration between labor and management to help management be less punitive and more reinforcing with OBM solutions such as pay-for-performance. Systems designed to benefit both the organization as well as the employee, with input from all stakeholders including participants or their representatives (e.g., unions), can result in a positive, ethical work environment (O'Brien, 1990).

Communication

Once the system is designed and ready to be implemented, it is important to communicate to participants how the variable pay system follows HR regulations, benefits the employees as well as the organization, and is fair and attainable for all participants. As mentioned above, participants may fear punitive consequences associated with clear behavioral measures. To assuage these concerns, Warman et al. (2020) conducted multiple informational sessions and private meetings with participants in a health and human service setting just prior to pay-for-performance system implementation. OBM consultants must partner with participants, including management, to identify and agree upon measures, clarify what those measures will and will not be used for, and to ensure ethical practices are followed (Abernathy, 1996). As noted by Warman et al. (2020), due to the limited prevalence of pay-for-performance systems, OBM consultants must work with the organization's management to communicate expectations, explain new pay contingencies and formulas, and verify participants' understanding. This communication is often delivered during training sessions or performance appraisals.

Performance measures/data collection systems

For scorecards to function most effectively, the organization must have IT systems in place to collect data and populate scorecards. When scorecards rely on too much manual data collection and analysis, they become cumbersome and are therefore abandoned. The IT system is typically purchased or created during the pay-for-performance system design.

The organization should have a system for sharing scorecard results "at a glance." This can be integrated within the IT data collection system. The more frequently and easily employees and their managers or supervisors can view current scorecard data, the more effective the program will be. The system will not work if delays are long between the behavior and when employees see their scores and/or earn payouts. With scorecards being visible and shared such as using an online database, employees should immediately see scores that bridge the gap between behavior and payout.

Even with the most robust data collection systems, managers need time allocated to complete or review (in the case of automated scorecards) their department and employees' weekly, monthly, and/or quarterly scorecards, and provide feedback to their employees based on results. When adequate time is not allocated, competing work tasks may take precedence, resulting in an improperly implemented or abandoned system.

Program design and implementation resources

The following personnel, time, and financial resources are crucial for designing and implementing successful pay-for-performance systems.

Program champion

With the most successful pay-for-performance scorecard systems, the organization identifies a program champion to serve as a single point of contact. This person should be able to answer questions and provide support. He or she must have access to the IT system(s) and scorecard data. The program champion is often someone in a quality control, training and development, or human resource role.

Scheduled time to design, implement, and test

Time needs to be set aside to fully design, implement, and test the scorecard system and measures (i.e., collect baseline data) prior to attaching it to performance-based pay. As described earlier, if employees do not have control over the measures, there are likely to be problems, such as fear of punitive consequences. During pilot testing/baseline, the organization should gather frequent feedback from employees in every department and revise the measures as appropriate.

Organizational financial stability

The organization should be financially stable. Ultimately, pay-for-performance scorecards produce impressive returns on investment in quality, productivity, customer service, employee retention, that all contribute to financial health. However, if the organization cannot afford the initial payouts, employees and their managers will not receive contingent performance pay and the return on investment will be much lower.

Clear expectations

In successful pay-for-performance scorecard systems, organizations initially, and on an ongoing basis, set clear expectations with managers and employees about what is required of them and how the system aligns with and contributes to the organization's goals.

Any added time and work commitments related to collecting, reviewing, and reporting scorecard data should be set before baseline data are collected. If managers and supervisors will be collaborating with a program champion and/or data analyst, those relationships should be made explicit. Everyone should be given instructions about who answers any questions.

Managers, supervisors, and employees also need a clear description about how individual scorecard measures and the overall system align with the organization's goals and strategies. This transparency helps to overcome potential concerns or confusion participants may have when the system is introduced.

Per the Executive and Management Readiness sections above, it is important for executive leaders to deliver ongoing feedback to managers and supervisors about their participation in the program. This includes reviewing scorecards with managers/supervisors and following up on how they share data with employees. These executive, management, and supervisory behaviors should be included on their individual scorecards as well to encourage leadership behaviors as part of the whole process (Abernathy, 2011).

Frequent, contingent consequences and incentives

This condition may seem out of place, given that pay-for-performance scorecard systems *are* monetary incentives. However, other consequences and incentives should be considered as well.

It is important for executive leaders to provide relief from activities occurring in participants' jobs that could compete with successful work on scorecards. This is particularly true in the beginning.

As mentioned earlier, in successful scorecard systems, executive leaders provide social recognition and praise to managers and supervisors when they successfully use scorecards to manage their teams. This is also important during the program baseline before monetary payouts are available.

Readiness checklist

Organizations considering pay-for-performance should check all the following boxes in Figure 2 before they embark on a pay-for-performance scorecard system.

READINESS CHECKLIST

- ☐ Our **executive leaders** report that they see value in pay-for-performance scorecards, and they expect a return on their scorecard investment.
- ☐ Our **executive leaders** have time to focus on identifying organizational strategies with which the scorecards will be tied.
- ☐ **Positive consequences** will be available **for managers and supervisors** who engage in scorecard design, development, and baseline data collection for their departments and employees.
- ☐ Our organization has **IT systems and a portal** in place to collect, report, analyze, and share scorecard data, OR we have a plan/budget to purchase or create IT system(s).
- ☐ We've identified an **internal program champion** to serve as a single point of contact to answer questions and provide support related to pay-for-performance scorecards.
- ☐ We plan to take the **time necessary to fully design, test, and analyze** the scorecard system prior to delivering pay based on scorecard results.
- ☐ Our organization is **financially stable.**
- ☐ We have, or plan to, set **clear expectations about the time and work commitments,** across the organization, necessary to make the program a success.
- ☐ We will communicate regularly about how the scorecard system **aligns with the organization's goals and strategies.**
- ☐ Executive leaders are prepared to deliver **ongoing social recognition to managers and supervisors based on their successful participation** in the program.
- ☐ Our organization is prepared to re-structure managerial and supervisory job duties, as necessary, to **remove contingencies that compete with scorecard-related activities.**

Figure 2. Total performance system, pay-for-performance, readiness checklist.

Conclusion

Although the concept of pay-for-performance rather than pay-for-time-at-work is a simple idea, the actual implementation can be complicated, especially when it disrupts standard practices and implementers are mindful about ensuring fairness and equity. Research will continue to be needed as society and businesses evolve. As reflected in our summary of pay-for-performance research, very few applied studies examine pay-for-performance systems in real work settings. There are concerns cited by most of the researchers whose work is summarized here that their laboratory research may not generalize to work settings (e.g., Bucklin et al., 2003; Johnson et al., 2008; McGee et al., 2006; Slowiak et al., 2011). Extending any of the individual monetary incentive research to real-world work settings would be of tremendous value to the business world.

Conceptually, we know a lot about the potential benefits for both the organization and the individual employee under pay-for performance systems, yet very few organizations have reported their results. We are aware of dozens of applications of pay-for-performance using scorecard systems, mostly consistent with our descriptions. We believe this is partly because of propriety concerns, however, we encourage these organizations when possible to publish their approaches and results as case studies for others to learn from and extend to other industries.

As outlined in this paper, extensive pay-for-performance research and practice over time has led to several recommended behavior-based practices. Any system needs to be balanced and weighted across variables important to both the individual and the organization. To ensure that it is likely to succeed and that it is administered fairly and ethically, we implore readers to adhere to the factors described and summarized in the readiness checklist. We encourage OBM researchers and practitioners to continue implementing, analyzing, and researching pay-for-performance systems while exercising caution against potential drawbacks. Pay-for-performance can have a positive economic and cultural impact for both organizations and individuals when implemented appropriately. The contrary is also true, inadequate compensation systems could lead to unintended and potentially disastrous outcomes, such as unfair pay distribution to certain performers, punitive intentions by management, competitive cultures, or issues related to employee fatigue, safety, or stress. To avoid or mitigate unintended drawbacks, effective and ethical pay-for-performance systems, as outlined in this paper, should involve all stakeholders including participants in the design, payout equitably contingent incentives across multiple performance dimensions, clearly define conditions under which incentives are earned, and follow through on performance expectations. When used carefully and with broad consideration, monetary incentives can be a powerful tool to potentially improve the social condition, aligning the good of the business with the good of the employee.

Disclosure statement

No potential conflict of interest was reported by the author(s).

ORCID

Douglas A. Johnson http://orcid.org/0000-0002-7802-3566

References

Abernathy, W. B. (1990). *Designing and managing an organization-wide incentive pay system.*

Abernathy, W. B. (1996). *The sin of wages: Where the conventional pay system has led us and how to find a way out.* PerfSys Press.

Abernathy, W. B. (2011). *Pay for profit: Designing an organization-wide performance-based compensation system.* Performance Management Publications.

Abernathy, W. B. (2014a). Beyond the Skinner box: The design and management of organization-wide performance systems. *Journal of Organizational Behavior Management, 34*(4), 235–254. https://doi.org/10.1080/01608061.2014.973631

Abernathy, W. B. (2014b). *The liberated workplace: Transitioning to Walden Three.* Performance Management Publications.

Abernathy, W. B., Duffy, E. M., & O'Brien, R. M. (1982). Multi-branch, multi-systems programs in banking: An organization-wide intervention. In R. M. O'Brien, A. M. Dickinson, & M. P. Rosow (Eds.), *Industrial behavior modification: A management handbook* (pp. 370–382). Pergamon Press.

Aldis, O. (1961). Of pigeons and men. *Harvard Business Review, 39*(4), 59–63.

Aljadeff-Abergel, E., Peterson, S. M., Wiskirchen, R. R., Hagen, K. K., & Cole, M. L. (2017). Evaluating the temporal location of feedback: Providing feedback following performance vs. prior to performance. *Journal of Organizational Behavior Management, 37*(2), 171–195. https://doi.org/10.1080/01608061.2017.1309332

Austin, J. (2000). Performance analysis and performance diagnostics. In J. Austin & J. E. Carr (Eds.), *Handbook of applied behavior analysis* (pp. 321–350). Context Press.

Benson, A. M., & Sajjadiani, S. (2017). Are bonus pools driven by their incentive effects? Evidence from fluctuations in gainsharing incentives. *ILR Review, 71*(3), 567–599. https://doi.org/10.1177/0019793917726066

Benzer, J. K., Young, G. J., Burgess, J. F., Baker, E., Mohr, D. C., Charns, M. P., & Kaboli, P. J. (2013). Sustainability of quality improvement following removal of pay-for-performance incentives. *Journal of General Internal Medicine, 29*(1), 127–132. https://doi.org/10.1007/s11606-013-2572-4

Binder, C. (2016). Integrating organizational-cultural values with performance management. *Journal of Organizational Behavior Management, 36*(2–3), 1–17. https://doi.org/10.1080/01608061.2016.1200512

Braksick, L. W. (2007). *Unlock behavior, unleash profits: Developing leadership behavior that drives profitability in your organization* (2nd ed.). The McGraw-Hill Company.

Bucklin, B. R., & Dickinson, A. M. (2001). Individual monetary incentives: A review of different types of arrangements between performance and pay. *Journal of Organizational Behavior Management, 21*(3), 45–137. https://doi.org/10.1300/J075v21n03_03

Bucklin, B. R., McGee, H. M., & Dickinson, A. M. (2003). The effects of individual monetary incentives with and without feedback. *Journal of Organizational Behavior Management, 23* (2–3), 65–94. https://doi.org/10.1300/J075v23n02_05

Caza, A., McCarter, M. W., & Northcraft, G. B. (2015). Performance benefits of reward choice: A procedural justice perspective. *Human Resource Management Journal, 25*(2), 184–199. https://doi.org/10.1111/1748-8583.12073

Christopher, A. B. (1988). *Predisposition versus experiential models of compulsive gambling: An experimental analysis using pigeons* [Unpublished Ph.D. dissertation]. West Virginia University.

Cooper, C. L., Dyck, B., & Frohlich, N. (1992). Improving the effectiveness of gainsharing: The role of fairness and participation. *Administrative Science Quarterly, 37*(3), 471–490. https://doi.org/10.2307/2393453

Daniels, A. C., & Bailey, J. (2014). *Performance management: Changing behavior that drives organizational effectiveness* (5th ed.). Performance Management Publications.

Davis, M. E. (2016). Pay matters: The piece rate and health in the developing world. *Annals of Global Health, 82*(5), 858–865. https://doi.org/10.1016/j.aogh.2016.05.005

Davis, M. E., & Hoyt, E. (2020). A longitudinal study of piece rate and health: Evidence and implications for workers in the US gig economy. *Public Health, 180*(1), 1–9. https://doi.org/10.1016/j.puhe.2019.10.021

Deci, E. L. (1972). The effects of contingent and noncontingent rewards and controls on intrinsic motivation. *Organizational Behavior & Human Performance, 8*(2), 217–229. https://doi.org/10.1016/0030-5073(72)90047-5

Deci, E. L., Olafsen, A. H., & Ryan, R. M. (2017). Self-determination theory in work organizations: The state of a science. *Annual Review of Organizational Psychology and Organizational Behavior, 4*(1), 19–43. https://doi.org/10.1146/annurev-orgpsych-032516-113108

Deng, H., Leung, K., Lam, C. K., & Huang, X. (2019). Slacking off in comfort: A dual-pathway model for psychological safety climate. *Journal of Management, 45*(3), 1114–1144. https://doi.org/10.1177/0149206317693083

Department of Labor. (2020, November). *Profit sharing plans for small businesses*. https://www.dol.gov/sites/dolgov/files/EBSA/about-ebsa/our-activities/resource-center/publications/profit-sharing-plans-for-small-businesses.pdf

Dickinson, A. M. (2000). The historical roots of organizational behavior management in the private sector: The 1950s-1980s. *Journal of Organizational Behavior Management, 20*(3–4), 9–58. https://doi.org/10.1300/J075v20n03_02

Dickinson, A. M. (2005). Are we motivated by money? Some results from the laboratory. *Performance Improvement, 44*(2), 18–24. https://doi.org/10.1002/pfi.4140440306

Dickinson, A. M., & Gillette, K. L. (1993). A comparison of the effects of two individual monetary incentive systems on productivity: Piece rate pay versus base pay plus monetary incentives. *Journal of Organizational Behavior Management, 14*(1), 3–82. https://doi.org/10.1300/J075v14n01_02

Dierks, W., & McNally, K. A. (1987, March). Incentives you can bank on. *Personnel Administrator, 32*, 61–65.

Duncan, P. K., & Smoot, D. T. (2001). Pay for performance. In C. M. Johnson, W. K. Redmon, & T. C. Mawhinney (Eds.), *Handbook of organizational performance: Behavior analysis and management* (pp. 255–276). The Haworth Press.

Ferster, C. B., & Skinner, B. F. (1957). *Schedules of reinforcement*. Appleton-Century-Crofts.

Frisch, C. J., & Dickinson, A. M. (1990). Work productivity as a function of the percentage of monetary incentives to base pay. *Journal of Organizational Behavior Management, 11*(1), 13–33. https://doi.org/10.1300/J075v11n01_03

Garbers, Y., & Konradt, U. (2014). The effect of financial incentives on performance: A quantitative review of individual and team-based financial incentives. *Journal of Occupational and Organizational Psychology, 87*(1), 102–137. https://doi.org/10.1111/joop.12039

Goomas, D. T., & Ludwig, T. D. (2007). Enhancing incentive programs with proximal goals and immediate feedback: Engineered labor standards and technology enhancements in stocker replenishment. *Journal of Organizational Behavior Management, 27*(1), 33–68. https://doi.org/10.1300/J075v27n01_02

Gravina, N., Nastasi, J., & Austin, J. (2021). Assessment of employee performance. *Journal of Organizational Behavior Management, 41*(2), 124–149. https://doi.org/10.1080/01608061.2020.1869136

Griffin, M., Gravina, N. E., Matey, N., Pritchard, J., & Wine, B. (2019). Using scorecards and a lottery to improve the performance of behavior technicians in two autism treatment clinics. *Journal of Organizational Behavior Management, 39*(3–4), 280–292. https://doi.org/10.1080/01608061.2019.1632241

Hartman, R. (Producer). (1992, November 8). *60 Minutes.* [Television broadcast]. CBS News.

Henderson, R. I., Jr. (1985). *Compensation management: Rewarding performance* (4th ed.). Reston Publishing Company.

Hendijani, R., Bischak, D. P., Arvai, J., & Dugar, S. (2016). Intrinsic motivation, external reward, and their effect on overall motivation and performance. *Human Performance, 29* (4), 251–274. https://doi.org/10.1080/08959285.2016.1157595

Hodgetts, R. M. (1997). A conversation with Donald F. Hastings on the Lincoln Electric Company. *Organizational Dynamics, 25*(3), 68–74. https://doi.org/10.1016/S0090-2616(97)90048-6

Honeywell-Johnson, J. A., McGee, H. M., Culig, K. M., & Dickinson, A. M. (2002). Different effects of individual and group monetary incentives on high performance. *The Behavior Analyst Today, 3*(1), 88–103. https://doi.org/10.1037/h0099964

Honeywell, J. A., Dickinson, A. M., & Poling, A. (1997). Individual performance as a function of individual and group pay contingencies. *The Psychological Record, 47*(2), 261–274. https://doi.org/10.1007/BF03395224

Jenkins, G. D., & Lawler, E. E. (1981). Impact of employee participation in pay plan development. *Organizational Behavior and Human Performance, 28*(1), 111–128. https://doi.org/10.1016/0030-5073(81)90018-0

Jenkins, G. D., Mitra, A., Gupta, N., & Shaw, J. D. (1998). Are financial incentives related to performance? A meta-analytic review of empirical research. *Journal of Applied Psychology, 83*(5), 777–787. https://doi.org/10.1037/0021-9010.83.5.777

Johansson, B., Rask, K., & Stenberg, M. (2010). Piece rates and their effects on health and safety: A literature review. *Applied Ergonomics, 41*(4), 607–614. https://doi.org/10.1016/j.apergo.2009.12.020

Johnson, D. A. (2013). A component analysis of the impact of evaluative and objective feedback on performance. *Journal of Organizational Behavior Management, 33*(2), 89–103. https://doi.org/10.1080/01608061.2013.785879

Johnson, D. A., Dickinson, A. M., & Huitema, B. E. (2008). The effects of objective feedback on performance when individuals receive fixed and individual incentive pay. *Performance Improvement Quarterly, 20*(3–4), 53–74. https://doi.org/10.1002/piq.20003

Kim, J. H., Gerhart, B., & Fang, M. (2021). Do financial incentives help or harm performance in interesting tasks? *Journal of Applied Psychology, 107*(1), 153–167. http://dx.doi.org/10.1037/apl0000851

Klein, G. D. (2012). Creating cultures that lead to success: Lincoln Electric, Southwest Airlines, and SAS Institute. *Organizational Dynamics, 41*(1), 32–43. https://doi.org/10.1016/j.orgdyn.2011.12.005

Koller, F. (2010). *Spark: Lessons from Lincoln Electric's unique guaranteed employment program.* PublicAffairs.

Komaki, J. L., & Minnich, M. L. (2016). A behavioral approach to organizational change: Reinforcing those responsible for facilitating the climate and hence promoting diversity. *Journal of Organizational Behavior Management, 36*(2–3), 154–184. https://doi.org/10.1080/01608061.2016.1200514

Kruse, D. (1993). *Does profit sharing affect productivity?* (NBER Working Paper Series, 4542). National Bureau of Economic Research.

LaMere, J. M., Dickinson, A. M., Henry, M., Henry, G., & Poling, A. (1996). Effects of a multi-component monetary incentive program on the performance of truck drivers: A longitudinal study. *Behavior Modification, 20*(4), 385–406. https://doi.org/10.1177/01454455960204002

Ludwig, T. D., & Laske, M. M. (2021). *Behavioral safety: An efficacious application of applied behavior analysis to reduce human suffering.* [Manuscript submitted for publication]. Department of Psychology, Appalachian State University.

Mager, R. F., & Pipe, P. (1970). *Analyzing performance problems.* Fearon.

Matthews, G. A., & Dickinson, A. M. (2000). Effects of alternative activities on productivity under different percentages of incentive pay. *Journal of Organizational Behavior Management, 20*(1), 3–27. https://doi.org/10.1037/h0099964

McGee, H. M., Dickinson, A. M., Huitema, B. E., & Culig, K. M. (2006). The effects of individual and group monetary incentives on high performance. *Performance Improvement Quarterly, 19*(4), 107–130. https://doi.org/10.1111/j.1937-8327.2006.tb00387.x

O'Brien, R. M. (1990). Working the other side of the street. *Journal of Organizational Behavior Management, 11*(1), 193–205. https://doi.org/10.1300/J075v11n01_12

Oah, S., & Dickinson, A. M. (1992). A comparison of the effects of linear and exponential performance pay function on work productivity. *Journal of Organizational Behavior Management, 12*(1), 85–115. https://doi.org/10.1300/J075v12n01_05

Olson, R., Cunningham, T., Nigam, J., & Anger, W. K. (in press). Total worker health and organizational behavior management: Emerging opportunities for improving worker well-being. *Journal of Organizational Behavior Management.*

Osterman, P. (1994). How common is workplace transformation and who adopts it? *Industrial and Labor Relations Review, 47*(2), 173–188. https://doi.org/10.1177/001979399404700202

Oxenbridge, S., & Moensted, M. L. (2011). The relationship between payment systems, work intensification and health and safety outcomes: A study of hotel room attendants. *Policy and Practice in Health and Safety, 9*(2), 7–26. https://doi.org/10.1080/14774003.2011.11667759

Peach, E. B., & Wren, D. A. (1992). Pay for performance from antiquity to the 1950s. *Journal of Organizational Behavior Management, 12*(1), 5–26. https://doi.org/10.1300/J075v12n01_02

Perry, N. J. (1988, December 19). Here come richer, riskier pay plans. *Fortune*, 51–58.

Pink, D. (2009). *Drive: The surprising truth about what motivates us.* Penguin.

Rosenthal, M., & Dudley, R. (2007). Pay-for-performance: Will the latest payment trend improve care? *Journal of American Medical Association, 297*(7), 740–744. https://doi.org/10.1001/jama.297.7.740

Rothe, H. F. (1947). Review of Lincoln's incentive system [Review of the book Lincoln's incentive system, by J. F. Lincoln]. *Journal of Applied Psychology, 31*(3), 344–345. https://doi.org/10.1037/h0050780

Schwarz, R. M. (1989). Participative decision making; Comparing union-management and management-designed incentive pay programs. *Group & Organizational Studies, 14*(1), 104–122. https://doi.org/10.1177/105960118901400109

Skinner, B. F. (1938). *The behavior of organisms: An experimental analysis.* Appleton-Century-Crofts.

Skinner, B. F. (1953). *Science and human behavior.* Macmillan.

Skinner, B. F. (1969). *Contingencies of reinforcement: A theoretical analysis.* Appleton-Century-Crofts.

Slowiak, J. M., Dickinson, A. M., & Huitema, B. (2011). Self-solicited feedback: Effects of hourly pay and individual monetary incentive pay. *Journal of Organizational Behavior Management, 31*(1), 3–20. https://doi.org/10.1080/01608061.2011.541816

Smoot, D. A., & Duncan, P. K. (1997). The search for optimum individual monetary incentive pay system: A comparison of the effects of flat pay and linear and non-linear incentive pay systems on worker productivity. *Journal of Organizational Behavior Management, 17*(2), 5–75. https://doi.org/10.1300/J075v17n02_02

Solman, P. (2011, July 18). *Were we too easy on Lincoln Electric?* PBS Newshour. https://www.pbs.org/newshour/rundown/2011/07/were-we-too-easy-on-lincoln-electric.html

Stolovitch, H. D., Clark, R. E., & Condly, S. J. (2002). Incentives, motivation and workplace performance: Research & best practices. *International Society for Performance Improvement and the SITE Foundation.*

Suri, G. K. (1970). The Lincoln Incentive System: Its relevancy to Indian Industry. *Indian Journal of Industrial Relations, 6*(3), 297–302.

Szabo, T. G., Williams, W. L., Rafacz, S. D., Newsome, W., & Lydon, C. A. (2012). Evaluation of the service review model with performance scorecards. *Journal of Organizational Behavior Management, 32*(4), 274–296. https://doi.org/10.1080/01608061.2012.729408

Taylor, F. W. (1911). *The principles of scientific management.* Harper & Brothers.

Thurkow, N. M., Bailey, J. S., & Stamper, M. R. (2000). The effects of group and individual monetary incentives on productivity of telephone interviewers. *Journal of Organizational Behavior Management, 20*(2), 3–25. https://doi.org/10.1300/J075v20n02_02

Warman, A. S., Wine, B., & Ernest, R. (2020). An application of pay-for-performance in a human services setting. *Journal of Organizational Behavior Management, 40*(3–4), 273–283. https://doi.org/10.1080/01608061.2020.1819514

Weibel, A., Rost, K., & Osterloh, M. (2010). Pay for performance in the public sector—Benefits and (hidden) costs. *Journal of Public Administration: Research and Theory, 20*(2), 387–412. https://doi.org/10.1093/jopart/mup009

Zentall, T. R. (2014). Suboptimal choice by pigeons: An analog of human gambling behavior. *Behavioral Processes, 103*, 156–164. https://doi.org/10.1016/j.beproc.2013.11.004

Assessment of Employee Performance

Nicole Gravina, Jessica Nastasi, and John Austin

ABSTRACT

Assessments are commonly used in organizational behavior management (OBM) to identify performance targets, determine environmental variables contributing to poor performance, and devise appropriate interventions. This paper describes the role of assessment at the individual performer level in OBM and the assessment process. It also reviews four common types of OBM assessments: historical assessments, functional assessments, preference assessments, and procedural acceptability and discusses the research support, weaknesses, and opportunities for future research for each. Finally, we conclude with recommendations for the future of assessment in OBM, including incorporating technology, using ongoing question-asking to informally assess performance and the environment, developing and validating survey instruments and other assessment tools, and attending to cultural variables in assessments.

In organizations, most results are directly or indirectly a function of what people say and do or their *behavior*. The body of research in behavior analysis tells us that behavior is driven by its environment, and most notably, the consequences in the environment. The environments which drive employee behavior are mostly created by the nature of the work and the people who work in the organization, especially the leaders. Arguably, the ultimate goal of organizational behavior management (OBM) is to scientifically study and understand the role of various work environments in influencing leader and employee behavior and the results they produce.

Organizations can be evaluated at three levels: the organization level, the process level, and the performer level (McGee & Crowley-Koch, 2020; Rummler & Brache, 1995). While assessing and intervening at the organization and process level can lead to large-scale organizational changes, they still require an understanding of the performer level because performers drive process and organizational change. Without environments that support performers in upholding process improvements and organizational changes, those improvements will fail. Thus, it is critically important to understand how the environment influences employee behavior and how it can be changed to encourage different behaviors. This paper will focus exclusively on performer-level assessments that can help us understand the factors influencing people's behavior in organizations.

Researchers and practitioners have developed several different performance assessments to help understand and influence organizational behaviors. In this paper, we will review the role of performance assessment, discuss the assessment process, and focus on four broad classes of assessments related to individual and employee performance:

1) Historical assessments, which analyze past data to derive optimal performance targets that deliver organizational results.
2) Functional assessments, which analyze the environment to discover the causes of poor performance or barriers to improved performance.
3) Preference assessments, which measure a person's relative preference for various items as potential reinforcers for their own behavior.
4) Procedural acceptability assessments, which measure the extent to which the treatments developed and implemented by researchers or practitioners are preferred by consumers or end-users.

We will describe the role and process of performer level assessments, review each of these types of assessments, including recent developments, suggest future research in each area, and then look forward to the next 20 years of research and practice in OBM performance assessment.

The role of assessment in OBM

Performance assessments in OBM serve a variety of functions. Practitioners use assessments to identify performance issues in need of intervention (Sulzer-Azaroff & Fellner, 1984), determine environmental factors causing performance issues (Austin, 2000), and select functionally appropriate interventions (Carr, Wilder, Majdalany, Mathisen, & Strain, 2013). Also, as part of the intervention process, the practitioner may engage employees from the outset, build rapport, and learn more about an organization's processes and jargon, improving subsequent intervention implementation (Sigurdsson & Austin, 2006). This initial investment of time pays dividends when an intervention is implemented later. A deep understanding of the work environment can help identify the most critical performance targets.

Furthermore, a functional intervention based on an understanding of the current work environment is likely to be more effective than using a generic "off-the-shelf" solution or blindly using a solution that worked in a different environment. In addition, function-based solutions are potentially less effortful and less costly. Further, employees may be more likely to buy into the solution when they know a manager or consultant spent time learning about their organization and gathering input (McSween, Myers, & Kuchler,

1990). Moreover, an assessment produces a valuable permanent product for the organization, which can provide initial evidence of the practitioner's potential contributions to the organization and result in continued engagement. Therefore, assessments of various types should be standard practice in OBM.

In 2018, Wilder and colleagues reviewed research published in the *Journal of Organizational Behavior Management (JOBM)* from 2000 to 2015 and found that assessments were included in 28% of all OBM field studies and 48% of a subset of safety-related studies. Ninety percent of the behavioral safety studies that included assessments used a historical assessment, which often involved examining the incident and first aid data from the site to select intervention targets. Taken together, these data suggest that OBM researchers use assessments, but there is an opportunity to expand their use in OBM field research and practice. Furthermore, in some cases, it makes sense to combine assessment procedures, and limited scholarly work guides the selection of intervention tools as part of the assessment process.

Assessment process

The assessment process usually includes three stages: pre-assessment, assessment, and intervention planning, aptly described by Cunningham and Geller (2012). Assessments aimed at one, well-defined and easily observed performance target (e.g., cleaning at the end of shift) will quickly move through this process, but larger-scale assessments (e.g., identifying safety behaviors that will lead to a reduction in injuries) will require more time in each stage. Following this process will help researchers and practitioners select the best assessments, identify the appropriate stakeholders, and reap the most value from the assessment.

Pre-assessment

During the pre-assessment stage, the practitioner and organizational stakeholders must agree on the assessment's goal and scope (Cunningham & Geller, 2012). This is particularly important in large-scale assessments and those aimed at identifying performance issues because a myriad of other problems can surface, and the assessment can grow in scope. For example, a practitioner conducting an assessment to improve safety behaviors performed by workers may learn that the maintenance staff is not performing necessary safety-related repairs in a timely fashion, and this could require a separate analysis. An agreed-upon plan can limit scope creep and keep the team focused. Identifying the scope can also help identify who should be involved in the assessment process. For example, an interview-based assessment could be conducted with both the employees whose performance is being assessed and their supervisor.

There are several other choices for practitioners and stakeholders to make during pre-assessment planning. For example, the practitioner must select the appropriate assessments, decide how they will be administered, and identify resources needed. We will describe some of the assessments available in the next section. An assessment can be administered by record review, individual or group interviews, observation, survey, or a combination of these methods. The administration will be, in part, dependent on who will contribute to the assessment and what fits best with the chosen assessment and the employees' jobs. For example, some people may not have a dedicated work computer, and therefore, they may be more likely to respond to a survey administered using paper during a meeting. Some employees may also prefer anonymity. Resources required might include documents or data already available, access to the work areas for observation, employee time, access to employee e-mail addresses, access to scheduled meetings, and a space to work. The goal of the planning stage is to use forethought to design an assessment plan to gather useful information as efficiently as possible. An inefficient assessment process will waste valuable time and resources and delay the start of an intervention. However, proceeding without an assessment could be more costly if an intervention does not produce the desired results.

Assessment

During the assessment phase, the practitioner uses the assessments to gather information. Consider planning the assessment in a way that leads to optimal information gathering. For example, administering a survey before an interview means that the results can help guide interview questions. Anonymous surveys may also yield different information than group or individual interviews because they gather honest input with less fear of repercussions. Practitioners may also want to create a plan to keep the information collected organized so that it is easy to locate relevant information later.

Although the scope should be identified prior to the assessment, it is wise to allow some flexibility in the process so that the practitioner can gather as much relevant information as possible. For example, when using a structured interview like the Performance Diagnostic Checklist (PDC, Austin, 2000), which will be described later, practitioners can ask follow-up questions to clarify responses and gather more nuanced information. Suppose that during the PDC interview, the client responds that the supervisor is not present during task completion (question 5). In that case, the practitioner can directly observe task completion to confirm the response and ask follow-up questions to determine if this would improve the performance. A survey could include open-ended questions so that employees can provide information not stated in the survey, allowing practitioners to learn more about the performance issue and organization.

At the end of the assessment, practitioners often create a report to discuss with the site. For a small-scale assessment that employs one assessment tool, a graphical display and summary are likely sufficient to communicate the results. Larger-scale assessments might include a report with an executive summary that describes the assessment process followed and results, followed by more details and then recommendations. Reports should consist of both strengths identified by the intervention (e.g., employees have been sufficiently trained and materials are readily available) and opportunities for improvement (e.g., performance feedback is lacking) to improve leader buy-in.

Intervention planning

After the assessment is complete, the findings can be used to select appropriate interventions. Although describing examples of sample interventions is beyond this paper's scope, we would like to offer a few suggestions to consider during intervention planning. First, interventions that are most likely to be implemented effectively and consistently should be selected. A well-selected intervention is not useful if it is not implemented. During the assessment process, practitioners have learned about the organization, the intervention targets that might work best for them, and barriers to implementation. Therefore, they can design an intervention that fits the client's needs and environment. In many OBM studies that employed assessments, researchers started with one intervention component and then added components as needed (e.g., Cruz et al., 2019). This approach allows the practitioner to use the least intrusive intervention necessary to produce the desired results and shape the organizational behaviors required to maintain the solution. It also provides evidence for the organization that all intervention components included must be maintained to sustain the improvements.

Now that we have described the assessment process, we will discuss assessments that researchers and practitioners can use to learn more about the performance issues. Each of these assessments has advantages and disadvantages and is suitable in different contexts, determined during the pre-assessment phase.

Historical assessment

Many organizations already measure relevant behaviors or correlative outcomes (e.g., sales, absenteeism, turnover, product rejects, reported injuries) before the consultation. In some cases, those data may be used to identify performance targets or inform the development of intervention procedures (Bumstead & Boyce, 2005). This method is sometimes referred to as a historical assessment and is similar to a records review, typical in clinical behavior analysis. Historical assessments are one of the most common assessment methods utilized in OBM, perhaps due to the low effort and cost required compared to other methods (Wilder, Lipschultz, King, Driscoll, & Sigurdsson, 2018). Historical assessments have been used in a variety of settings, including manufacturing, retail, human services, sales, public transportation, food services, and construction (Fante, Gravina, & Austin, 2007; Hermann, Ibarra, & Hopkins, 2010; Lebbon, Austin, Rost, & Stanley, 2011; Lee, Shon, & Oah, 2014; Olson & Austin, 2001).

Historical assessments can provide vital information to help select intervention targets and conditions under which behaviors might be more or less likely to occur and are used most often in behavioral safety (Wilder et al., 2018). Historical assessments may be particularly amenable to behavioral safety because industrial organizations must collect data to comply with the Occupational Safety and Health Administration (OSHA) requirements. Therefore, measures such as recordable injuries, compensation claims, and lost time injuries may be available across several years. Furthermore, historical assessments are considered a best-practice assessment method for instituting behavior-based safety processes (McSween, 2003). In human service settings, researchers and practitioners can use historical data to identify which procedures or programs are consistently followed, billing trends, trends in absences and turnover, arrangements that lead to the best client outcomes, and potential monetary savings in addressing the performance. The utility of historical assessments may hinge on the accuracy and reliability of data collected before intervention procedures; thus, researchers and practitioners should inquire further to evaluate the quality of data to be used for historical assessments.

Although historical assessments can be a useful starting point to narrow the focus onto the most critical performance targets, they are typically combined with other assessment procedures (e.g., direct observation, interviews) to inform intervention selection. For example, a historical assessment might find that injuries to the hand comprise most of the injuries over the past five years at a company. Still, the most appropriate solution might involve supervisors requiring employees to wear gloves, monitoring the behavior, and praising it when it happened. In this case and many cases, the intervention targets are different from the controlling variables, and different types of assessment may be required to understand each of these. Thus, a functional assessment may be needed to devise an effective solution.

Performance analysis

In 1999, Austin et al. lamented that OBM had not kept pace with other areas of behavior analysis in developing functional assessments to improve the selection of effective interventions. They identified three reasons for the glaring omission. First, OBM interventions appear to be effective without assessment procedures. However, previous research in clinical behavior analysis indicates that functional assessment procedures can enhance interventions and subsequent outcomes compared to default intervention procedures (Wacker, Berg, & Harding, 2014). Second, employees typically possess well-developed language skills and the ability to accurately describe contingencies and other aspects of their work environment, and therefore much of their work behavior will include rule-governed components. Finally, OBM is concerned with increasing behavior, and in clinical behavior analysis, most of the assessments were designed to understand harmful behaviors that should be decreased or replaced. These differences do not negate the relevance of assessment procedures, but the assessments employed in OBM are necessarily distinct from assessments used in other behavior analysis areas. In fact, some argue that the term performance analysis is a better fit for assessments used in organizations, because the procedures and outcomes do not directly map onto clinical functional assessments.

Austin and colleagues went on to describe performance analysis tools developed by behavior analysts that guided examining variables that could contribute to performance issues, including Gilbert's (1978) vantage analysis and troubleshooting guide, Mager and Pipe (1997) simple flowchart, and Rummler and Brache (1995) systems tools. The authors also discussed the ABC Analysis described by Daniels and others for analyzing performance (Daniels & Bailey, 2014). Each of these assessments help trained professionals analyze performance, but they did not directly suggest interventions. Austin and colleagues suggested that performance analyses should consider four areas: Antecedents, equipment and processes, knowledge and skills, and consequences. They also argued that although interviews may not be as effective as more direct assessment procedures such as descriptive or experimental analysis in clinical behavior analysis, they may be sufficient and the most practical for business settings.

In 2000, Austin published a book chapter that included an assessment tool, the Performance Diagnostic Checklist (PDC), that spanned the four areas mentioned above. The PDC could be used to interview employees, conduct observations or collect data, and aid in selecting an effective intervention, all of which will be described in more detail later in the chapter. A flurry of studies followed that employed and extended the tool. Following the PDC, other assessment procedures were incorporated into OBM research, including a pre-intervention analysis involving antecedent manipulations (Therrien, Wilder, Rodriguez, & Wine, 2005), a structural analysis (Fante, Gravina, Betz, & Austin, 2010), and a fluency-based skill assessment to identify skill deficits (Pampino, Wilder, & Binder, 2005). Austin's papers were published at a time that, along with many others' work, helped propel OBM into a more contemporary behavioral approach for addressing performance issues in organizations while simultaneously revealing more research questions. Twenty years have passed since the PDC was published, and since then, researchers have examined and expanded upon the assessment and incorporated other functional assessment methods into research and practice. OBM practitioners and researchers have leaned on the behavior analysis knowledge to further develop assessment methods for organizations. Behavior analysis typically utilizes three types of assessments: indirect assessment, direct assessment, and experimental analysis (Kelley, LaRue, & Roane, 2014), and many OBM assessments use more than one of these methods in concert (Wilder et al., 2018).

Indirect assessments

An indirect assessment involves gathering information to understand variables impacting a performance issue without directly observing those behaviors. Practitioners often use indirect assessments such as surveys, rating scales, and interviews because they are easy and quick to administer, require minimal training, and enable input from various sources. Below, we describe two common indirect assessment methods in OBM: the PDC and its variations and the ABC Analysis.

Performance diagnostic checklist

As opposed to identifying targets of interventions, the PDC is a quick, low-effort tool for forming a hypothesis about the function of target behaviors and informing the selection of intervention procedures and may be used in a variety of settings. It is one of the most common assessments utilized in OBM, and its usage appears to be on an increasing trend (Wilder et al., 2018). The PDC was created to be a more specific version of the Behavior Engineering Model created by Gilbert (1978); the categories and some of the exact questions were based on a protocol analysis of expert OBM consultants' problem solving (Austin, 1996). An early version of the PDC appeared in other publications such as Mattaini and Thyer (1996). The intent was to create a tool that novices could use to identify effective solutions to organizational problems. While the PDC is a list of questions, researchers and practitioners can collect descriptive data to inform some of the answers.

Research has demonstrated that interventions informed by PDC results yield desirable intervention outcomes (e.g., Amigo, Smith, & Ludwig, 2008; Doll, Livesey, McHaffie, & Ludwig, 2007; Eikenhout & Austin, 2005; Gravina, VanWagner, & Austin, 2008; Pampino, Heering, Wilder, Barton, & Burson, 2004; Rodriguez et al., 2006). For example, Pampino et al. (2004) increased the completion of maintenance tasks in a coffee shop with intervention procedures informed by PDC results. Specifically, PDC results suggested that low task completion may occur because of a lack of adequate antecedent and consequence manipulation instead of training deficits or issues with equipment and processes.

Whereas the four domains of the PDC (i.e., antecedents and information, equipment and processes, knowledge and skills, and consequences) apply to performance in various settings, the original 20-item checklist is not always specific enough to identify contingencies operating in certain domains. Therefore, more precise iterations of the PDC have been developed and applied, including the PDC for human services (PDC-HS; Carr et al., 2013), the PDC for occupational safety (PDC-S; Martinez-Onstott, Wilder, & Sigurdsson, 2016), and the PDC for parents (PDC-P; Hodges, Villacorta, Wilder, Ertel, & Luong, 2020).

The PDC-HS was developed to assess the performance of employees responsible for providing direct care to other individuals (Carr et al., 2013). Carr et al. (2013) posed a few unique considerations for the performance of employees in human service settings, including inadequate treatment integrity, inaccurate data collection, deficits in program development, issues with attendance or tardiness, insufficient reporting, and poor graph construction. The authors administered the PDC in an autism treatment center providing early intervention services, then made revisions according to the conditions specific to human service organizations, and the inclusion of sections for scoring and corresponding intervention recommendations. Modifications included updated domain titles to a) training, b) task clarification and prompting, c) resources, materials, and processes, and d) performance consequences, effort, and competition. Next, 11 behavior analysts were asked to pilot and assess the PDC-HS, and revisions were made accordingly. Finally, the predictive validity and utility of the last version of the PDC-HS were assessed by comparing the use of indicated and non-indicated interventions as identified by the PDC-HS. Results showed that performance improvements were greater after implementing the PDC-HS indicated intervention compared to a non-indicated intervention, suggesting that the PDC-HS may be a valuable tool for identifying performance deficits and subsequent intervention recommendations in a human service setting (Carr et al., 2013).

Since its publication, the PDC-HS has been utilized in a variety of settings, including schools (Bowe & Sellers, 2018; Merritt, DiGennaro Reed, & Martinez, 2019), retail stores (e.g., Loughrey, Marshall, Bellizzi, & Wilder, 2013; Smith & Wilder, 2018), and further evaluation in autism treatment clinics (Ditzian, Wilder, King, & Tanz, 2015; Wilder et al., 2018). A review conducted by Wilder, Cymbal, and Villacorta (2020) indicated that the performance consequences, effort, and competition domains were endorsed most often across settings. Future research may bolster support for using the PDC-HS by evaluating the tool compared to other assessment methodologies and assessing its utility in additional human service settings (e.g., residential facilities, clinics for the treatment of substance use, crisis intervention services, geriatric facilities).

Two additional iterations of the PDC include the PDC-Safety (PDC-S; Martinez-Onstott et al., 2016) and the PDC-Parent (PDC-P; Hodges et al., 2020). Martinez-Onstott et al. (2016) made modifications to the PDC to include safety-specific language with the addition of a Likert scale response measure and formal scoring instructions. The authors used the adapted tool to identify deficits contributing to noncompliance with personal protective equipment (PPE) requirements among three landscaping professionals. Assessment results indicated deficits in a performance consequence, and an intervention employing the use of graphic feedback increased proper PPE usage across participants, but there was no comparison between indicated and non-indicated interventions. A study conducted by Cruz et al. (2019) used the PDC-Safety to evaluate variables influencing noncompliance with hand hygiene protocols at a center-based treatment facility for individuals with developmental and intellectual disabilities. Results suggest that the intervention indicated by PDC-Safety was effective at increasing hand hygiene compliance compared to the non-indicated intervention. Hodges et al. (2020) adapted the PDC to assess barriers to treatment implementation by parents for children with problem behavior and evaluated the effectiveness of indicated versus non-indicated interventions. In experiment one, assessment results indicated a task clarification and prompting intervention, which increased parents' treatment integrity. In experiment two, the authors demonstrated that the indicated intervention was more effective than the non-indicated intervention at improving parent performance (Hodges et al., 2020). Further research is needed to evaluate the effectiveness of indicated versus non-indicated interventions for all PDC iterations.

Some additional recommendations for future research on the efficacy, feasibility, and validity of the PDC and PDC iterations may be considered. First, although preliminary research suggests acceptable validity and test-retest reliability for the PDC-HS (Cymbal, Wilder, Thomas, & Ertel, 2020; Wilder, Lipschultz, Gehrman, Ertel, & Hodges, 2019), additional research assessing the reliability and validity of the PDC and its iterations with a larger sample size is warranted. Replications of previous findings may be extended to novel settings and compare the use of the PDC to specialized iterations of the PDC like the PDC-HS, PDC-Safety, and PDC-Parent as well as other formal assessment tools. Comparisons could examine the quality of recommendations yielded from the assessment and the time, cost, and resources required. In addition, future research should systematically evaluate the relationship between PDC domain scores and intervention efficacy. Although some early projects using the PDC were carried out by undergraduate students and coached by graduate or doctoral-level behavior analysts (e.g., Austin, Weatherly, & Gravina, 2005; Rohn, Austin, & Lutrey, 2002; Shier, Rae, & Austin, 2003) suggesting that the tool does not require extensive experience to use it, the level of skill necessary to use the PDC could be further examiined. Cymbal et al. (2020) evaluated whether Master's, Bachelor's, and Associate's degree (or high school diploma) level practitioners trained in behavior analysis could use the PDC-HS to accurately identify domains responsible for a performance problem described in three vignettes. The results indicated that Master's and Bachelor's level practitioners were slightly better at accurately identifying the correct domains for the performance problem than Associate's level practitioners, but the difference was small (~5–6%). Researchers should also compare the PDC against a more informal interview across novice practitioners and OBM experts.

Future studies should evaluate whether the type of individual interviewed (e.g., manager or performer, high-performer or low-performer) differentially impacts the information gathered and selecting appropriate intervention procedures. For example, low performers may find it more difficult to describe the barriers to performance, while high performers may have identified barriers and employed workarounds to produce good results. Researchers could also further refine the PDC by including a rating of importance for each item. Finally, future iterations of the PDC could incorporate culturally responsive questions into the tool to guide users to be culturally sensitive when asking the questions and selecting interventions (See Appendix A for an updated PDC with many of these considerations embedded).

ABC analysis

An ABC Analysis is an assessment in which practitioners identify antecedents and consequences that support and discourage desired and undesired performances (Connellan, 1978; Daniels & Bailey, 2014) ABC Analyses are typically constructed based on information known about the performance concerns, but interviews could provide additional information. ABC analyses appear to be common in business because they are easy to teach, help leaders understand variables that may contribute to poor performance and can be applied to many situations. However, the ABC Analysis findings may make intervention development less intuitive than the PDC since the ABC analysis is framed in terms of antecedents and consequences rather than specific solutions such as feedback, training, equipment, or praise. Despite the seemingly common application of ABC Analysis in organizations, limited research demonstrates their utility for selecting interventions. Researchers could examine whether insight gleaned from ABC Analyses improves intervention selection by practitioners with various experience levels.

Despite being easy and quick to administer, previous clinical research on indirect assessments indicates that this use alone may be insufficient because they can yield inaccurate or incorrect information compared to direct assessments (Fisher, Piazza, Bowman, & Amari, 1996; Lennox & Miltenberger, 1989; Umbreit, 1996). Although there are concerns about indirect assessments within behavior analysis, OBM research has repeatedly demonstrated the utility of indirect assessments for identifying performance issues and selecting interventions in organizational settings. Indirect assessments may be more informative in OBM because they are typically conducted with adults who have the language skills to describe their current environment. However, OBM researchers have never directly compared indirect assessments with descriptive or experimental assessments. A comparison of assessment methods could help researchers identify boundary conditions for when indirect assessments are suitable and when more rigorous assessment methods are required. Finally, none of the current indirect assessments used in OBM ask questions about culture (within and beyond the organization) or learning history, which could be important factors in intervention design and make indirect methods more valuable.

Direct assessments

Direct assessments involve the direct observation and recording of behavior without manipulating the environment. Direct assessments yield descriptive data on behavior and the conditions when it is most and least likely to occur and are more rigorous than indirect assessments. Direct assessments are usually informed by indirect assessments conducted prior to the direct assessment (Thompson & Borrero, 2014). In OBM, direct assessments may involve observing high and low performers to compare differences in how they work and monitoring work performance under naturally occurring conditions (e.g., in the presence and absence of customers or the supervisor). Data can be collected using data sheets or A-B-C or narrative recording (i.e., recording the antecedents, behaviors, and consequences). Sometimes, data are analyzed visually (e.g., scatterplot), statistically (e.g., correlations), or using a probability analysis or lag sequential analysis (e.g., calculating the probability that a specific consequence is more likely to follow a specific behavior).

Narrative recording

Narrative recording entails observing and recording antecedents, behaviors, and consequences as they occur in the natural environment. A book chapter published in 1982 described a descriptive assessment procedure designed to identify effective sales behaviors (Crawley, Adler, O'Brien, & Duffy, 1982). The researchers followed top-performing salespeople and low-performing salespeople and took detailed data on their behaviors and subsequent sales engagements. When they interviewed top salespeople and asked why they were effective at selling (indirect assessment), they did not gather much useful information. However, the direct observations yielded information about behaviors top sellers engaged in, and they created a checklist. Later, the researchers taught low-performing salespeople to follow the checklist, and their sales increased dramatically. When the checklist and training were implemented organization-wide, they saw a dramatic increase in sales.

Direct observation

OBM researchers collect data under various conditions during baseline to help identify an intervention. For example, Fienup, Luiselli, Joy, Smyth, and Stein (2013) collected data on the start and end times of consecutive meetings and the transition time required between meetings. They found that meetings that started and ended late affected punctuality at the next meeting. Fante et al. (2010) noticed that the high variability of pharmacist safe performance appeared to be due to the presence and absence of a makeshift wrist support. After a variable baseline phase, the researchers collected descriptive data on the improvised wrist support presence and found a strong correlation; the use of wrist supports resulted in safer wrist positioning. These simple observations led to powerful interventions that may not have been obvious without direct observation.

Scatterplot

A scatterplot presents collected data visually so that patterns can be detected. For example, Anbro et al. (2020) used a scatterplot in a study that evaluated virtual reality (VR) to assess a training procedure to improve communication and situational awareness among medical and nursing students. The VR technology recorded eye gaze, and observers recorded correct communication steps. A scatterplot revealed that the training improved communication but not looking at the patient. Scatterplots are useful for identifying temporal patterns or relationships between two variables. However, sometimes it can be difficult to detect patterns in responding using a scatterplot, specifically if the measures plotted are not presented in the appropriate analysis unit. If no patterns emerge, another assessment procedure may be required.

Although direct assessments are more rigorous than indirect assessments, there are some disadvantages worth mentioning. Because direct assessments require direct observation, data collection, and analysis, they necessitate more time and training to complete. A culturally competent assessment will require even more training. Also, while direct assessments involve direct observations of behavior and conditions, they do not demonstrate a functional relationship because no environmental variables are manipulated. Therefore, they may require a similar amount of time as an experimental analysis but yield less informative results. Finally, it may be problematic to observe and take data on all the behaviors and conditions of organizations' concern. For example, collecting descriptive data on unsafe work behaviors could be problematic if they occur infrequently and unethical if they are not intervened upon immediately.

Experimental analysis

Experimental analyses are more rigorous than indirect and direct assessments, and they can also yield more definitive information about causal variables and lead to optimal interventions. In an experimental analysis, researchers or practitioners systematically manipulate environmental variables and observe responses in each condition (Wacker et al., 2014). The variables manipulated are usually chosen based on the results of an indirect or direct assessment. For example, if an observer notices that employees behave differently in the presence and absence of the supervisor, they could manipulate their presence to see if a functional relationship emerges. By showing that the behavior changes when the experimenter changes the environmental condition, we become more confident that the environmental variable is responsible for behavior changes. The more demonstrations of this relationship, the more confident we can be in our conclusions. This process is similar to the elements of prediction, verification, and replication, as seen in design methodology (Cooper, Heron, & Heward, 2020; Erath et al., 2020). For practical reasons, when conducted as part of an assessment, these manipulations usually occur in short segments (e.g., 5 to 30 min), which enables the experimenter to identify functional relationships quickly.

Safety performance may be amenable to an experimental analysis if the conditions tested do not put employees at prolonged or unnecessary risk. For example, following the direct assessment conducted with pharmacy employees conducted by Fante et al. (2010) mentioned above, the researchers conducted an experimental manipulation. Because they observed that pharmacy employee posture appeared to be safer when the makeshift wrist support was in place, they manipulated the presence of the wrist support. They concluded that it was functionally related to safety performance. Low-risk, low-effort experimental analyses like those conducted by Fante et al. (2010) may be modified and applied in other contexts to assess the variables impacting performance and inform the selection of intervention procedures.

Experimental analyses may also involve manipulation of aspects of the physical environment like sounds, light, and the presence of others. Therrien et al. (2005) also manipulated a series of variables in an alternating fashion to determine which increased the likelihood of employees greeting customers at a sandwich shop. Although they found that having the radio did not appear to influence performance, the door chime was most likely to encourage customer greetings, followed by the presence of a manager. The researchers then combined the door chime and manager presence and demonstrated substantial improvement in greetings over baseline conditions. Finally, the experimenters added feedback, which increased performance to 100% for the last two sessions. The experimental analysis employed by Therrien and colleagues demonstrates how stimuli presumed to serve a discriminative function can be verified via experimental analysis.

Finally, Pampino et al. (2005) included a performance analysis in their study to increase correct entering of job codes by construction supervisors. Job codes were used for billing, and entering incorrect codes could result in over or under billing the client. The researchers broke the task into component skills (remembering codes, locating codes, and typing codes) and evaluated the supervisor's performance for each skill. Once they identified deficits, they used fluency training to improve their accuracy and their speed of performance. Thus, the assessment resulted in more precise and efficient training procedures.

Despite many successful examples of experimental analyses in clinical behavior analysis, limited research using this assessment approach exists in OBM. In some cases, it may be too challenging to manipulate variables while people work, especially if it may interfere with job performance or safety. Improving virtual reality and other simulation technology could enhance our ability to conduct experimental analyses without risking harm or lost productivity in the future. However, employees may behave differently under contrived conditions than during their everyday work. Still, an experimental analysis may be more efficient than testing interventions over a more extended period using an experimental design. Furthermore, it may provide more accurate information than traditional surveys employed in Industrial-Organizational Psychology. OBM researchers should continue to develop experimental analysis methods to help identify effective interventions.

Reinforcer and preference assessments

The identification of reinforcers is integral to developing and implementing any effective consequence-based intervention component (Simonian, Brand, Mason, Heinicke, & Luoma, 2020). Presumed reinforcers may not function as such, wasting time and money. Therefore, stimulus preference assessments (identification of putative reinforcers) and reinforcer assessments (identification of stimuli demonstrated to increase behavior) are a cornerstone of behavior analytic interventions (Fisher et al., 1992; Roscoe, Iwata, & Kahng, 1999). Common preference assessment formats in clinical behavior analysis include forced-choice procedures (i.e., selection between stimuli such that a hierarchy may be established) such as the paired-stimulus preference assessment (Fisher et al., 1992), ranking procedures, and multiple stimulus preference assessments with (MSW; Windsor, Piché, & Locke, 1994) or without replacement (MSWO; DeLeon & Iwata, 1996).

Preference and reinforcer assessments are ubiquitous in applied behavior analytic research conducted with individuals with developmental disabilities yet are seldom utilized with typically developing adults or employees (Wine,

Kelley, & Wilder, 2014). Previous research indicates managers are poor at predicting employee preferences, and in practice, they often request help in identifying the reinforcers of their employees, thus the use of more formal preference and reinforcer assessment methodology with employees may be warranted (Wilder, Harris, Casella, Wine, & Postma, 2011; Wilder, Rost, & McMahon, 2007). Also, employee preferences may change over time; thus, preference should be reassessed over extended periods of employment (Wine, Gilroy, & Hantula, 2012; Wine et al., 2014).

Waldvogel and Dixon (2008) compared the use of a ranked survey and multiple stimulus preference assessment without replacement with four direct-care staff. They found that assessment ranks correlated across formats for three out of four employees, but no reinforcer assessment was conducted to determine whether or not preferred stimuli functioned as reinforcers. Wilder et al. (2007) compared the use of stimuli identified by a ranked survey to stimuli identified with a verbal choice format. Then a reinforcer assessment was used to determine whether stimuli identified functioned as a reinforcer. Results indicated that the survey format was more accurate in identifying reinforcers compared to the verbal choice format. Wine, Reis, and Hantula (2014) compared using a ranking procedure, survey, and MSWO and conducted a subsequent reinforcer assessment with three direct-care staff members. All preference assessment formats identified reinforcers, but the results of social validity measures indicated that the MSWO was rated as more cumbersome, less preferred, and took more time than ranking and survey formats.

Practitioners can also identify preferred job tasks and working arrangements to improve job assignments and identify strategies to make aversive tasks more palatable. For example, Green, Reid, Passante, and Canipe (2008) created an assessment tool they termed the Task Enjoyment Motivation Protocol (TEMP), which involved supervisors interviewing staff to identify which job tasks were least preferred and the aspects of those tasks that made them less preferred. Supervisors then attempted to remove undesirable properties of tasks reported as less preferred (e.g., eliminate interruptions while reviewing timesheets). One participant disliked conducting staff observations because staff appeared to dislike being observed. The researchers added a performance lottery so that the participant could deliver lottery tickets based on observations, resulting in staff rating being observed as more favorable on a rating scale. The researchers also attempted to increase desirable stimuli associated with the task (e.g., providing snacks during paperwork). Results indicated that the tasks were rated and ranked higher after making changes based on the TEMP assessment.

OBM researchers have also evaluated feedback preferences. For example, Reid and Parsons (1996) demonstrated that staff in a clinical, residential setting preferred immediate versus delayed feedback. Sigurdsson and Ring

(2013) found that undergraduate students preferred feedback on correct quiz performance compared to incorrect quiz performance, even though both resulted in similar quiz performance scores. Researchers have also demonstrated that employees prefer different delivery modes of feedback. For example, Hardesty, Orchowitz, and Bowman (2018) found that therapists in a clinical setting preferred to view data in a line graph, while direct care employees preferred bar graphs.

Research indicates that the most practical and accurate preference assessments in OBM differ from clinical behavior analysis, which is to be expected. While research on directly assessing preferences exists in OBM, it is mostly related to tangible reinforcers, which may not be practical in all organizations. Some practitioners would argue (the 3rd author, for example) they are less effective than social reinforcers. Green et al. (2008) demonstrated that changing aspects of the work task could improve the task rating and ranking, which warrants more research. Other researchers have shown that participants prefer different aspects of feedback delivery (e.g., Sigurdsson & Ring, 2013). OBM researchers have a tremendous opportunity to evaluate practical strategies that allow leaders to identify employee preferences for reinforcers and other work-related factors and improve work productivity and enjoyment. More focus on assessments related to work and preferences could result in designing interventions that employees find acceptable and enjoyable.

Procedural acceptability assessments

The term social validity encompasses the social significance of goals selected, the acceptability of intervention procedures, and the importance of intervention outcomes (Wolf, 1978). Assessments of social validity generally solicit information from consumers of an intervention to inform the initial development and long-term viability of intervention procedures (Schwartz & Baer, 1991). Specifically, these assessments may indicate the need for further education or training, detect undesirable intervention effects, and allow us to protect the rights of consumers (Hawkins, 1991; Kazdin, 1977). Although the term social validity has been subject to debate, there is immense value in assessing the acceptability of intervention goals, procedures, and outcomes for consumers. Assessments of procedural acceptability may be particularly useful in OBM to predict undesirable intervention outcomes and increase the probability that institutionalization will occur (Nastasi, Simmons, & Gravina, 2020; Sigurdsson & Austin, 2006). Unacceptable management procedures may increase absenteeism, turnover, disputes, and arbitrations between labor and management (Parsons, 1998). Therefore, this section will specifically focus on measures of procedural acceptability (see pre-assessment section for the selection of targets).

Interviews, questionnaires, rating scales, and choice procedures are the most common methods used to assess procedural acceptability in OBM (Nastasi et al., 2020). It would be valuable if researchers or practitioners developed a valid protocol to evaluate consumer use or nonuse of behavioral interventions as the dependent variable to predict acceptability, and that can be used in practice to increase adoption of behavioral technology. Due to the subjective nature of these measures, the utility of procedural acceptability assessments may hinge on the conditions under which those assessments were employed (Schwartz & Baer, 1991). Therefore, researchers and practitioners should consider a few variables when conducting procedural acceptability assessments. First, procedural acceptability must be assessed using a representative sample of relevant consumers across an organization. Researchers and consultants should also consider how other variables such as the anonymity or the availability of results to an immediate supervisor may alter consumer responding. Procedural acceptability should also be assessed at multiple time points across an intervention. The assessment results can then be used to alter the intervention or supplement intervention procedures as needed to maximize outcomes and maintenance. Researchers could use this information to examine how the acceptability changes based on how the intervention is produced and the changes in performance it creates over time. Finally, procedural acceptability could be used as a tool for improving cultural awareness during intervention development and adjusting interventions to be more culturally sensitive.

Although the benefits of assessing procedural acceptability are numerous, limited research exists on the use of procedural acceptability assessments in OBM. This observation is ironic since virtually every OBM practitioner encounters challenges when encouraging clients to change their behavior and adopt behavioral recommendations and/or systems. Future research should evaluate the accuracy and reliability of results across different types of procedural acceptability measures. Procedural acceptability by customers or clients may also differ across components of an intervention; thus, further research is needed to determine which aspects of an intervention may be more or less acceptable to those who interact with employees exposed to interventions. Furthermore, researchers should assess the variables impacting the accuracy of subjective measures across organizational settings. Finally, researchers and practitioners should recognize that acceptability should be the bare minimum. Organizational leaders should ultimately strive to maximize intervention outcomes and improve job satisfaction among all members of an organization (Hantula, 2015).

Reflections on the current state of assessment in OBM

OBM currently utilizes several performer level assessments that help identify intervention targets, select interventions likely to improve performance and help learn employee preferences. Each of these assessments improves our understanding of the behaviors of employees and the environment where they work. That understanding can lead to more sophisticated, tailored, and effective interventions, which researchers have demonstrated.

Despite the increase in assessments employed in OBM research, there is still tremendous opportunity for growing and refining the research and application of assessments. Although researchers have studied assessments, there have been only modest attempts to evaluate the validity and reliability of the assessments (e.g., Carr et al., 2013; Cymbal et al., 2020; Johnson, Casella, McGee, & Lee, 2014; Wilder et al., 2019). In other words, we do not know whether the assessment procedures are leading to the best possible behavior targets and interventions or if practitioners would choose the same targets and interventions without the aid of an assessment. Furthermore, we do not know if selecting these target behaviors, and interventions leads to optimal organization outcomes (Daniels & Bailey, 2014). This question could be, at least partially, answered by conducting a meta-analysis to compare effect sizes of applied intervention studies that employed an assessment with those that did not. It might also be useful to compare intervention selection among experts and novices for a variety of performance issues with and without the aid of an assessment tool.

Although practitioners acknowledge that assessments offer additional benefits such as building rapport and learning more about the client, the work, and the organizational jargon, these benefits have not been documented in the research literature. Pre-post surveys could evaluate practitioner-client relationships, and pre-posts tests could evaluate the knowledge acquired about the work and organization. Practitioners could also be surveyed to learn more about their experiences with employing assessments in organizations.

Although researchers have assessed preferences for reinforcers and tasks, there is an opportunity to expand this area by developing tools to determine preferences for other aspects of work like meeting arrangements, feedback discussions, task preferences, and other aspects of the work experience. Furthermore, researchers could evaluate whether accommodating employee preferences for various task arrangements leads to improved work performance or job satisfaction.

Finally, researchers have used assessments to identify interventions that are likely to be useful, but they have rarely assessed the social validity of interventions before implementation. Doing so could allow researchers to determine if expected acceptability predicts effectiveness. It could also increase our understanding of intervention "buy-in" if acceptability were assessed periodically through the intervention process.

Looking forward, the next 20 years

Given the assumed focus on behavior driving results and environment driving behavior, one possible direction for research and practice is to help leaders and managers understand critical environmental factors to more easily improve performance and the workplace. For example, it's not hard to imagine digital tools requiring no behavioral training for leaders to conduct assessment (historical, functional, reinforcer preference, or procedural acceptability-focused) and derive behaviorally-sound solutions. Of course, the problem of proper deployment would remain, and OBM has always had the challenge of teaching people to effectively implement behavioral interventions, so that should also be a focus in the next 20 years.

A low-tech and informal method that has promise for assessing the function of various environmental influences on target behaviors is question asking. In recent years, a growing number of articles in large publications such as the *Harvard Business Review* has featured question asking. Simple observation in virtually any organizational setting reveals that we often reinforce the behavior of people who get the right answer, but rarely the person who asks a question. Researchers have found that leaders do not ask enough questions; when people ask more questions, it improves learning and interpersonal bonds (i.e., in some situations, people like the questioner more); and that certain types of questions are more effective than others (Brooks & John, 2018). OBM researchers could teach leaders to ask questions that are more effective at uncovering the causes of poor performance to derive more effective and more acceptable solutions. Regular question-asking about performance could lead to more agile and preventative solutions.

Over the next 20 years, OBM has a tremendous opportunity to develop new assessments, including behavior-based surveys, that could help identify performance targets and effective interventions and then validate them. For example, OBM researchers could create an assessment to evaluate the overall level of reinforcement in the work environment and examine whether that predicts good performance. Validated and useful assessments may serve to disseminate OBM by helping leaders readily understand the work environment and drivers of behavior.

Finally, as behavior analysts become more culturally informed, OBM has an opportunity to embed culturally sensitive questions and procedures into assessments. For example, feedback assessments should consider the broader culture where the organization operates and how feedback typically works in that culture. Cultural humility is a process of learning about the culture of others and understanding your own beliefs and cultural identities and how these might impact your behavior, expectations, and decisions. This approach is important and relevant for the field of OBM, as well as consultants and leaders in the context of improving performance because it can be culturally insensitive, not to mention behaviorally less effective, to assume you know all of the required elements for performance improvement. We argue that a more effective and culturally humble approach is to collect data, to ask questions, to conduct a variety of assessments as described in this chapter, and to learn about the people in the work environment and engage them in deciding on solutions before taking the most appropriate course of action. The last 20 years of OBM research and practice has seen an increase in the use of assessments. The next 20 years should focus on expanding and refining them to improve our impact on employees and organizations.

Disclosure statement

No potential conflict of interest was reported by the authors.

ORCID

Nicole Gravina http://orcid.org/0000-0001-8210-7159

References

Amigo, S., Smith, A., & Ludwig, T. (2008). Using task clarification, goal setting, and feedback to decrease table busing times in a franchise pizza restaurant. *Journal of Organizational Behavior Management*, *28*(3), 176–187. doi:10.1080/01608060802251106

Anbro, S. J., Szarko, A. J., Houmanfar, R. A., Maraccini, A. M., Crosswell, L. H., Harris, F. C., . . . Starmer, L. (2020). Using virtual simulations to assess situational awareness and communication in medical and nursing education: A technical feasibility study. *Journal of Organizational Behavior Management*, *40*(1–2), 1–11. doi:10.1080/01608061.2020.1746474

Austin, J. (1996). *Organizational troubleshooting in expert management consultants and experienced managers* [Unpublished doctoral dissertation]. Florida, USA: Florida State University, Tallahassee.

Austin, J. (2000). Performance analysis and performance diagnostics. In J. Austin & J. E. Carr (Eds.), *Handbook of Applied Behavior Analysis* (pp. 321–350). Oakland, CA: Context Press.

Austin, J., Weatherly, N., & Gravina, N. (2005). Using task clarification, graphic feedback, and verbal feedback to increase closing task completion in a privately owned restaurant. *Journal of Applied Behavior Analysis*, *38*(1), 117–121. doi:10.1901/jaba.2005.159-03

Bowe, M., & Sellers, T. P. (2018). Evaluating the performance diagnostic checklist-human services to assess incorrect error-correction procedures by preschool paraprofessionals. *Journal of Applied Behavior Analysis*, *51*(1), 166–176. doi:10.1002/jaba.428

Brooks, A. W., & John, L. K. (2018 May-June). The surprising power of questions. *Harvard Business Review*, 60–67. https://hbr.org/2018/05/the-surprising-power-of-questions

Bumstead, A., & Boyce, T. E. (2005). Exploring the effects of cultural variables in the implementation of behavior-based safety in two organizations. *Journal of Organizational Behavior Management*, *24*(4), 43–63. doi:10.1300/J075v24n04_03

Carr, J. E., Wilder, D. A., Majdalany, L., Mathisen, D., & Strain, L. A. (2013). An assessment-based solution to a human-service employee performance problem. *Behavior Analysis in Practice*, *6*(1), 16–32. doi:10.1007/bf03391789

Connellan, T. K. (1978). *How to improve human performance*. New York, NY: Harper and Row.

Cooper, J. O., Heron, T. E., & Heward, W. L. (2020). *Applied behavior analysis* (3rd ed.). Upper Saddle River, NJ: Pearson.

Crawley, W. J., Adler, B. S., O'Brien, R. M., & Duffy, E. M. (1982). Making salesmen: Behavioral assessment and intervention. In *Industrial behavior modification: A management handbook* (pp. 184–199). Oxford, United Kingdom: Pergamon Press.

Cruz, N. J., Wilder, D. A., Phillabaum, C., Thomas, R., Cusick, M., & Gravina, N. (2019). Further evaluation of the performance diagnostic checklist-safety (PDC-Safety). *Journal of Organizational Behavior Management, 39*(3–4), 266–279. doi:10.1080/01608061.2019.1666777

Cunningham, T. R., & Geller, E. S. (2012). A comprehensive approach to identifying intervention targets for patient-safety improvement in a hospital setting. *Journal of Organizational Behavior Management, 32*(3), 194–220. doi:10.1080/01608061.2012.698114

Cymbal, D., Wilder, D. A., Thomas, R., & Ertel, H. (2020). Further evaluation of the validity and reliability of the performance diagnostic checklist-human services. *Journal of Organizational Behavior Management*, 1–9. doi:10.1080/01608061.2020.1792027

Daniels, A. C., & Bailey, J. S. (2014). *Performance management: Changing behavior that drives organizational effectiveness* (5th ed.). Atlanta, Georgia, USA: Aubrey Daniels International, Inc.

DeLeon, I. G., & Iwata, B. A. (1996). Evaluation of a multiple-stimulus presentation format for assessing reinforcer preferences. *Journal of Applied Behavior Analysis, 29*(4), 519–533. doi:10.1901/jaba.1996.29-519

Ditzian, K., Wilder, D. A., King, A., & Tanz, J. (2015). An evaluation of the performance diagnostic checklist–human services to assess an employee performance problem in a center-based autism treatment facility. *Journal of Applied Behavior Analysis, 48*(1), 199–203. doi:10.1002/jaba.171

Doll, J., Livesey, J., McHaffie, E., & Ludwig, T. D. (2007). Keeping an uphill edge: Managing cleaning behaviors at a ski shop. *Journal of Organizational Behavior Management, 27*(3), 41–60. doi:10.1300/j075v27n03_04

Eikenhout, N., & Austin, J. (2005). Using goals, feedback, reinforcement, and a performance matrix to improve customer service in a large department store. *Journal of Organizational Behavior Management, 24*(3), 27–62. doi:10.1300/J075v24n03_02

Erath, T. G., Pellegrino, A. J., DiGennaro Reed, F. D., Ruby, S. A., Blackman, A. L., & Novak, M. D. (2020). *Experimental research methodologies in organizational behavior management. [Manuscript submitted for publication]*. JOBM: Department of Applied Behavior Science, University of Kansas.

Fante, R., Gravina, N., & Austin, J. (2007). A brief pre-intervention analysis and demonstration of the effects of a behavioral safety package on postural behaviors of pharmacy employees. *Journal of Organizational Behavior Management, 27*(2), 15–25. doi:10.1300/J075v27n02_02

Fante, R., Gravina, N., Betz, A., & Austin, J. (2010). Structural and treatment analyses of safe and at-risk behaviors and postures performed by pharmacy employees. *Journal of Organizational Behavior Management, 30*(4), 325–338. doi:10.1080/01608061.2010.520143

Fienup, D. M., Luiselli, J. K., Joy, M., Smyth, D., & Stein, R. (2013). Functional assessment and intervention for organizational behavior change: Improving the timeliness of staff meetings at a human services organization. *Journal of Organizational Behavior Management, 33*(4), 252–264. doi:10.1080/01608061.2013.843435

Fisher, W. W., Piazza, C. C., Bowman, L. G., & Amari, A. (1996). Integrating caregiver report with a systematic choice assessment to enhance reinforcer identification. *American Journal on Mental Retardation*. https://psycnet.apa.org/record/1996-01619-002

Fisher, W. W., Piazza, C. C., Bowman, L. G., Hagopian, L. P., Owens, J. C., & Slevin, I. (1992). A comparison of two approaches for identifying reinforcers for persons with severe and profound disabilities. *Journal of Applied Behavior Analysis, 25*(2), 491–498. doi:10.1901/jaba.1992.25-491

Gilbert, T. F. (1978). *Human competence*. New York, NY: McGraw-Hill.

Gravina, N., VanWagner, M., & Austin, J. (2008). Increasing physical therapy equipment preparation behaviors using task clarification, graphic feedback and modification of work environment. *Journal of Organizational Behavior Management*, *28*(2), 110–122. doi:10.1080/01608060802100931

Green, C. W., Reid, D. H., Passante, S., & Canipe, V. (2008). Changing less-preferred duties to more-preferred: A potential strategy for improving supervisor work enjoyment. *Journal of Organizational Behavior Management*, *28*(2), 90–109. doi:10.1080/01608060802100899

Hantula, D. A. (2015). Job satisfaction: The management tool and leadership responsibility. *Journal of Organizational Behavior Management*, *35*(1–2), 81–94. doi:10.1080/01608061.2015.1031430

Hardesty, S. L., Orchowitz, P. M., & Bowman, L. G. (2018). An evaluation of staff preference for graphic characteristics. *Journal of Organizational Behavior Management*, *38*(4), 345–353. doi:10.1080/01608061.2018.1524338

Hawkins, R. P. (1991). Is social validity what we are interested in? Argument for a functional approach. *Journal of Applied Behavior Analysis*, *24*(2), 205. doi:10.1901/jaba.1991.24-205

Hermann, J. A., Ibarra, G. V., & Hopkins, B. L. (2010). A safety program that integrated behavior-based safety and traditional safety methods and its effects on injury rates of manufacturing workers. *Journal of Organizational Behavior Management*, *30*(1), 6–25. doi:10.1080/01608060903472445

Hodges, A. C., Villacorta, J., Wilder, D. A., Ertel, H., & Luong, N. (2020). Assessment and improvement of parent training: An evaluation of the performance diagnostic checklist–parent. *Behavioral Development*, *25*(1), 1–16. doi:10.1037/bdb0000092

Johnson, D. A., Casella, S. E., McGee, H., & Lee, S. C. (2014). The use and validation of pre-intervention diagnostic tools in Organizational Behavior Management. *Journal of Organizational Behavior Management*, *34*(2), 104–121. doi:10.1080/01608061.2014.914009

Kazdin, A. E. (1977). Assessing the clinical or applied importance of behavior change through social validation. *Behavior Modification*, *1*(4), 427–452. doi:10.1177/014544557714001

Kelley, M. E., LaRue, R. H., & Roane, H. S. (2014). Indirect behavioral assessments: Interviews and rating scales. In W. W. Fisher, C. C. Piazza, & H. S. Roane (Eds.), *Handbook of applied behavior analysis* (pp. 472–488). New York, NY: Guilford Press.

Lebbon, A., Austin, J., Rost, K., & Stanley, L. (2011). Improving safe consumer transfers in a day treatment setting using training and feedback. *Behavior Analysis in Practice*, *4*(2), 35–43. doi:10.1007/BF03391782

Lee, K., Shon, D., & Oah, S. (2014). The relative effects of global and specific feedback on safety behaviors. *Journal of Organizational Behavior Management*, *34*(1), 16–28. doi:10.1080/01608061.2013.878264

Lennox, D. B., & Miltenberger, R. G. (1989). Conducting a functional assessment of problem behavior in applied settings. *Research and Practice for Persons with Severe Disabilities*, *14*(4), 304–311. doi:10.1177/154079698901400409

Loughrey, T. O., Marshall, G. K., Bellizzi, A., & Wilder, D. A. (2013). The use of video modeling, prompting, and feedback to increase credit card promotion in a retail setting. *Journal of Organizational Behavior Management*, *33*(3), 200–208. doi:10.1080/01608061.2013.815097

Mager, R. F., & Pipe, P. (1997). *Analyzing performance problems*. Atlanta, GA: Center for Effective Performance Inc.

Martinez-Onstott, B., Wilder, D., & Sigurdsson, S. (2016). Identifying the variables contributing to at-risk performance: Initial evaluation of the Performance Diagnostic Checklist–Safety (PDC-Safety). *Journal of Organizational Behavior Management*, *36*(1), 80–93. doi:10.1080/01608061.2016.1152209

Mattaini, M. A., & Thyer, B. A. (Eds.). (1996). Finding Solutions to Social Problems: Behavioral Strategies for Change. Washington, DC: American Psychological Association Press

McGee, H. M., & Crowley-Koch, B. J. (2020). *Types of organizational assessments and their applications [Manuscript submitted for publication]*. Department of Psychology, Western Michigan University.

McSween, T. E. (2003). *Values-based safety process: Improving your safety culture with behavior-based safety*. Hoboken, NJ: John Wiley & Sons.

McSween, T. E., Myers, W., & Kuchler, T. C. (1990). Getting buy-in at the executive level. *Journal of Organizational Behavior Management, 11*(1), 207–221. doi:10.1300/J075v11n01_13

Merritt, T. A., DiGennaro Reed, F. D., & Martinez, C. E. (2019). Using the Performance Diagnostic Checklist–Human Services to identify an indicated intervention to decrease employee tardiness. *Journal of Applied Behavior Analysis, 52*(4), 1034–1048. doi:10.1002/jaba.643

Nastasi, J., Simmons, D., & Gravina, N. (2020). Has OBM found its heart? An assessment of procedural acceptability trends in the journal of organizational behavior management. *Manuscript submitted for publication.*

Olson, R., & Austin, J. (2001). Behavior-based safety and working alone: The effects of a self-monitoring package on the safe performance of bus operators. *Journal of Organizational Behavior Management, 21*(3), 5–43. doi:10.1300/J075v21n03_02

Pampino, R. N., Jr, Heering, ,. P. W., Wilder, D. A., Barton, C. G., & Burson, L. M. (2004). The use of the performance diagnostic checklist to guide intervention selection in an independently owned coffee shop. *Journal of Organizational Behavior Management, 23*(2–3), 5–19. doi:10.1300/J075v23n02_02

Pampino, R. N., Wilder, D. A., & Binder, C. (2005). The use of functional assessment and frequency building procedures to increase product knowledge and data entry skills among foremen in a construction organization. *Journal of Organizational Behavior Management, 25* (2), 1–36. doi:10.1300/J075v25n02_01

Parsons, M. B. (1998). A review of procedural acceptability in organizational behavior management. *Journal of Organizational Behavior Management, 18*(2–3), 173–190. doi:10.1300/J075v18n02_09

Reid, D. H., & Parsons, M. B. (1996). A comparison of staff acceptability of immediate versus delayed verbal feedback in staff training. *Journal of Organizational Behavior Management, 16*(2), 35–47. doi:10.1300/j075v16n02_03

Rodriguez, M., Wilder, D. A., Therrien, K., Wine, B., Miranti, R., Daratany, K., ... Rodriguez, M. (2006). Use of the performance diagnostic checklist to select an intervention designed to increase the offering of promotional stamps at two sites of a restaurant franchise. *Journal of Organizational Behavior Management, 25*(3), 17–35. doi:10.1300/J075v25n03_02

Rohn, D., Austin, J., & Lutrey, S. (2002). Decreasing cash shortages using verbal and graphic feedback. *Journal of Organizational Behavior Management, 22*(1), 33–46. doi:10.1300/J075v22n01_03

Roscoe, E. M., Iwata, B. A., & Kahng, S. (1999). Relative versus absolute reinforcement effects: Implications for preference assessments. *Journal of Applied Behavior Analysis, 32*(4), 479–493. doi:10.1901/jaba.1999.32-479

Rummler, G., & Brache, A. (1995). Improving performance: How to manage the white space on the organizational chart San Francisco: Jossey-Bass.

Schwartz, I. S., & Baer, D. M. (1991). Social validity assessments: Is current practice state of the art? *Journal of Applied Behavior Analysis, 24*(2), 189–204. doi:10.1901/jaba.1991.24-189

Shier, L., Rae, C., & Austin, J. (2003). Using task clarification, checklists and performance feedback to increase tasks contributing to the appearance of a grocery store. *Performance Improvement Quarterly*, *16*(2), 26–40. doi:10.1111/j.1937-8327.2003.tb00277.x

Sigurdsson, S. O., & Austin, J. (2006). Institutionalization and response maintenance in organizational behavior management. *Journal of Organizational Behavior Management*, *26* (4), 41–77. doi:10.1300/J075v26n04_03

Sigurdsson, S. O., & Ring, B. M. (2013). Evaluating preference for graphic feedback on correct versus incorrect performance. *Journal of Organizational Behavior Management*, *33*(2), 128–136. doi:10.1080/01608061.2013.785889

Simonian, M. J., Brand, D., Mason, M. A., Heinicke, M., & Luoma, S. M. (2020). A systematic review of research evaluating the use of preference assessment methodology inn the workplace. *Journal of Organizational Behavior Management*, 1–19. doi:10.1080/01608061.2020.1819933

Smith, M., & Wilder, D. A. (2018). The use of the performance diagnostic checklist-human services to assess and improve the job performance of individuals with intellectual sisabilities. *Behavior Analysis in Practice*, *11*(2), 148–153. doi:10.1007/s40617-018-0213-4

Sulzer-Azaroff, B., & Fellner, D. (1984). Searching for performance targets in the behavior analysis of occupational safety: An assessment strategy. *Journal of Organizational Behavior Management*, *6*(2), 53–65. doi:10.1300/J075v06n02_09

Therrien, K., Wilder, D. A., Rodriguez, M., & Wine, B. (2005). Preintervention analysis and improvement of customer greeting in a restaurant. *Journal of Applied Behavior Analysis*, *38* (3), 411–415. doi:10.1901/jaba.2005.89-04

Thompson, R. H., & Borrero, J. C. (2014). Direct observation. In W. W. Fisher, C. C. Piazza, & H. S. Roane (Eds.), *Handbook of applied behavior analysis* (pp. 472–488). New York, NY: Guilford Press.

Umbreit, J. (1996). Functional analysis of disruptive behavior in an inclusive classroom. *Journal of Early Intervention*, *20*(10), 18–29. doi:10.1177/105381519602000104

Wacker, D. P., Berg, W. K., & Harding, J. W. (2014). Functional and structural approaches to behavioral assessment of problem behavior. In W. W. Fisher, C. C. Piazza, & H. S. Roane (Eds.), *Handbook of applied behavior analysis* (pp. 472–488). New York, NY: Guilford Press.

Waldvogel, J. M., & Dixon, M. R. (2008). Exploring the utility of preference assessments in organizational behavior management. *Journal of Organizational Behavior Management*, *28* (1), 76–87. doi:10.1080/01608060802006831

Wilder, D. A., Cymbal, D., & Villacorta, J. (2020). The performance diagnostic checklist-human services: A brief review. *Journal of Applied Behavior Analysis*, *53*(2), 1170–1176. doi:10.1002/jaba.676

Wilder, D. A., Harris, C., Casella, S., Wine, B., & Postma, N. (2011). Further evaluation of the accuracy of managerial prediction of employee preference. *Journal of Organizational Behavior Management*, *31*(2), 130–139. doi:10.1080/01608061.2011.569202

Wilder, D. A., Lipschultz, J., Gehrman, C., Ertel, H., & Hodges, A. (2019). A preliminary assessment of the reliability and validity of the performance diagnostic checklist-human services. *Journal of Organizational Behavior Management*, *39*(3–4), 194–212. doi:10.1080/01608061.2019.1666772

Wilder, D. A., Lipschultz, J. L., King, A., Driscoll, S., & Sigurdsson, S. (2018). An analysis of the commonality and type of preintervention assessment procedures in the *journal of organizational behavior management* (2000–2015). *Journal of Organizational Behavior Management*, *38*(1), 5–17. doi:10.1080/01608061.2017.1325822

Wilder, D. A., Rost, K., & McMahon, M. (2007). The accuracy of managerial prediction of employee preference: A brief report. *Journal of Organizational Behavior Management*, *27*(2), 1–14. doi:10.1300/J075v27n02_01

Windsor, J., Piché, L. M., & Locke, P. A. (1994). Preference testing: A comparison of two presentation methods. *Research in Developmental Disabilities, 15*(6), 439–455. doi:10.1016/0891-4222(94)90028-0

Wine, B., Gilroy, S., & Hantula, D. A. (2012). Temporal (in)stability of employee preferences for rewards. *Journal of Organizational Behavior Management, 32*(1), 58–64. doi:10.1080/01608061.2012.646854

Wine, B., Kelley, D. P., III, & Wilder, D. A. (2014). An initial assessment of effective preference assessment intervals among employees. *Journal of Organizational Behavior Management, 34*(3), 188–195. doi:10.1080/01608061.2014.944747

Wine, B., Reis, M., & Hantula, D. A. (2014). An evaluation of stimulus preference assessment methodology in organizational behavior management. *Journal of Organizational Behavior Management, 34*(1), 7–15. doi:10.1080/01608061.2013.873379

Wolf, M. M. (1978). Social validity: The case for subjective measurement or how applied behavior analysis is finding its heart. *Journal of Applied Behavior Analysis, 11*(2), 203–214. doi:10.1901/jaba.1978.11-203

Performance Assessment of Organizations

Heather M. McGee and Brian J. Crowley-Koch

ABSTRACT

As Organizational Behavior Management was borne out of Applied Behavior Analysis, so too is its approach to assessing environmental variables before implementing solutions for behavior change. This article discusses several types of organizational assessments used by researchers and practitioners. Behavior Systems Analysis (BSA) and Performance Management (PM) are the two most common assessment and intervention approaches used in OBM. These two methods are compared and contrasted and the levels and analyses within BSA are discussed. Also included in this article are common organizational assessments that are used by consultants and human resources professionals that are not typically used by OBM practitioners (change readiness, culture/engagement, and pulse surveys). These traditional assessments are approached through a behavior analytic lens and ways in which OBM practitioners can use them to assess and influence behavior is provided. A sustainability (otherwise known as maintenance or generalization) assessment is also included that builds upon previous research (e.g.) and experience through private practice.

Organizational assessment refers to "a systematic process for obtaining valid information about the performance of an organization and the factors that affect performance" (Jones, Lusthaus, Adrien, & Stanley, 2006, p. 4). Generally, organizational assessment can occur at any level of performance within and across the organization, from individual performer to macro-system, provided it (a) assesses the overall performance of the organization or factors that affect that performance, and (b) follows a systematic process. Additionally, we stipulate that to be considered an organizational behavior management (OBM)-based organizational assessment, the process and tools must use a behavior analytic or behavioral systems framework. Previous work shows the behavioral and behavioral systems perspective follows a systematic analysis process (Austin, 2000; Diener, McGee, & Miguel, 2009; Gilbert, 1978; Johnson, Casella, McGee, & Lee, 2014; McGee, 2017, 2018a; McGee & Crowley-Koch, 2019; Rummler, 2004; Rummler & Brache,

2013). Our focus will be on describing a selection of organizational assessments used in OBM-based management consulting, as well as traditional assessments that can be useful to the OBM practitioner. Finally, throughout this paper we use assessment and analysis interchangeably. When we use the term "analysis," we are not referring to experimental analysis, such as functional analysis.

Assessment and improvement efforts in OBM are often categorized into two categories: Behavioral Systems Analysis (BSA) and Performance Management (PM) (Wine & Pritchard, 2018). Behavioral Systems Analysis is an OBM methodology for improving performance that blends applied behavior analysis (ABA) and general systems theory by providing a framework for the analysis of both the organizational system and the behaviors of the individuals who work within that system (McGee & Crowley-Koch, 2019). More specifically, BSA involves understanding the organization as an adaptive and interconnected system. An adaptive system is one in which performers at all levels track and quickly and effectively respond to changes in the internal and external environments. An interconnected system means that a change in one part will affect other parts of the system. Additionally, BSA involves viewing an organization as cross-functional with various levels of performance to be analyzed. Again, changes in one part of the system affect other parts across levels as well as within levels of performance.

Organizational systems are complex; therefore, most BSA practitioners analyze anywhere from three to six different levels of performance along with the behaviors of individuals within each level (Addison & Haig, 2013; Gilbert, 1978; Malott, 2003; Rummler, 2004; Rummler & Brache, 2013). This means that BSA is not a single assessment, but rather a collection of interrelated assessments designed to produce a picture of how the organization currently operates and how it should operate to be successful. Perhaps the most common multi-level framework in BSA is Rummler and Brache's (2013) three levels approach. This involves analyzing the performance of the organization as a whole, critical processes within, and critical jobs and behaviors of organizational performers. Several assessment tools are available and relevant to each of these levels; a full systems analysis likely requires multiple tools/analyses at each level of performance.

Performance Management is the application of behavior analysis to the performance of individuals or groups within the workplace. While PM is a necessary component of BSA, it can be used on its own. That is, you cannot do BSA without PM, but you can do PM without BSA. This is because, regardless of the level of performance (organization, process, performer), there will always be people whose behavior shapes and is shaped by the system. You can redesign a process, but both the old and new process are performed by people engaging in behaviors. You can reallocate resources across organizational functions, but reallocation requires the behavior of individuals to decide, carry out, and support performance in affected functions. If you use BSA tools and ignore behavior, you are not doing BSA; you simply are using general systems theory.

The interrelatedness of PM and BSA makes classifying organizational assessments as strictly one or the other difficult. It is possible to do PM at any level and all BSA involves PM to some extent. Therefore, we present all of our traditional OBM (PM and BSA) assessments as OBM assessments and organize them by the level of performance at which the assessments are typically conducted. We also explain, when relevant, the conditions under which an assessment could be used at other levels. In addition to the typical OBM assessments, we introduce assessments that are more commonly found in traditional management consulting, but which could prove valuable to an OBM professional. These assessments are especially helpful for project scoping purposes, so we will begin with those. Finally, the goal of any organization assessment is that it results in lasting, meaningful change. Therefore, we will end our assessment descriptions with a sustainability assessment.

Types of assessments

Traditional management consulting assessments

The assessments presented here (change readiness, culture/engagement, and pulse surveys) are often designed, implemented, and evaluated using cognitive constructs or "fuzzy" terms to both assess and explain performance drivers (e.g., personality, leadership style, drive, self-efficacy, autonomy, engagement, etc.). Unfortunately, this might lead OBMers to pass up these assessments without a second thought, especially given that research in management/ Organizational Behavior/Organizational Development/etc. (and therefore the research on such assessments) often involves verbal report measures only, and includes more model testing than direct assessment of the impact of the tools on intervention selection and implementation. However, we argue that there is value in using these assessments and that it actually does not take much to convert these construct-based driver descriptions into more useful and behavioral terminology. What makes these assessments valuable is their emphasis on the distal factors that influence behavior and results, which are typically missing from OBM assessments (even the behavioral systems analysis assessments).

Change readiness

The roots of change management are found in an early publication by Coch and French (1948), who explored employees' resistance to changing work processes and tools in a manufacturing plant. The authors ask two questions at the end of their introduction: 1) Why do people resist change so strongly, and 2) What can be done to overcome this resistance? The answer to the second question is understood through an assessment of the organization through a change management lens.

Change readiness assessments provide an opportunity for an organization to determine if they are ready for a significant change. Holt, Helfrich, Hall, and Weiner (2010) described readiness as "the degree to which those involved are individually and collectively primed, motivated, and technically capable of executing the change" (p.50). While much has been written about change readiness in other psychological and research paradigms (e.g., Rafferty, Jimmieson, & Armenakis, 2013) little has been written from a behavior analytic perspective. We provide a brief change readiness assessment that focuses on systemic variables.

Organizational changes can include implementing a new process to replace existing ones, technological advancements, changes to the external business environment, mergers and acquisitions, and organizational restructuring, including physical change (e.g., moving organizations to new geographical locations or buildings). The change readiness assessment breaks down into four categories, (1) Clarity and Alignment, (2) Skills and Abilities, (3) Time, Tools, and Resources, and (4) Feedback and Accountability.

The Clarity and Alignment category seeks to understand how well the organization's employees and leaders understand the change effort. Practitioners should assess how well employees grasp the what, why, and how of the change. Additionally, employees should be aware of what is expected of them in their roles to contribute to the initiative's success. Practitioners, working with organization leadership, should link the change to organizational strategy and goals, and communicate the purpose of the change. Typically, organizations will draft and communicate a "case for change" that details the rationale behind the change as well as details around what is changing (processes, peoples, job description) and what is staying the same. Practitioners should reconcile the change with other initiatives and organizational or functional strategies to ensure that there are no competing priorities or initiatives and that the employees are receiving consistent messaging regarding the change initiative. Leaders in the organization should also be clear on what their leader stewardship behaviors are to communicate, set expectations, and reinforce the desired behaviors of the initiative.

The Skills and Abilities category is focused on the employees' competency to ensure that they have the necessary knowledge, skills, and abilities to perform the new or different behaviors required of the organizational or functional change. A knowledge or skill gap assessment (either formal or informal) should be conducted to assess how fluent the performers are and ascertain what existing gaps might be rectified by training or upskilling. Similarly, leader skills should be assessed to identify how well the organization's leaders can deal with resistance to change and provide feedback and reinforcement to the new behaviors and results.

The third category, Time, Tools, and Resources, assesses whether the performers and organization functions have the required resources to support new behaviors associated with the change initiative. The theme of this assessment category is to ensure that the workforce is set up for success, especially if they are engaging in new and different behaviors. This category also assesses whether there are competing resources (e.g., time) for other organizational or functional priorities. In addition to the necessary resources (time, materials, autonomy, money, tools, processes), there should be an issue resolution process to identify resource issues and work to resolve them expediently.

The final change readiness assessment category covers Feedback and Accountability. Feedback and reinforcement systems should be in place to ensure that performers come into contact with performance feedback and reinforce the new behaviors required by the change. An assessment of the natural and contrived consequences should help identify areas needing additional support in terms of feedback and reinforcement. Additionally, site leadership should be engaging with performers early on in the change as performance coaches to listen to feedback, address problems, and provide positive and constructive feedback. This category also covers the accountability of new behaviors and processes, which should all have identified owners and responsibilities for the new or changed processes.

OBM practitioners have a competitive advantage during change management and readiness initiatives in that skilled practitioners are well suited to link business results of the change to pinpointed behaviors necessary to create the desired results. Once the link between results and behaviors have been established practitioners can then use performer level tools (see below) to understand the change through the perspective of employees enduring the change. In other words, by understanding the necessary or missing antecedents and consequences to the change behaviors OBM practitioners can then seek solutions to influence the correct or desired behaviors. At a higher level, OBM practitioners can also use relationship mapping and process mapping to understand how processes and procedures either support or hinder behaviors, and how the change will affect other business functions.

Culture/engagement assessment

If a Google search is evidence of popularity, we find 8.65 million results for "organizational culture" and 15.7 million results for "employee engagement." Additionally, 9 out of 10 executives surveyed reported that Organizational Culture (OC) and employee engagement are "important or very important" to their organization (Deloitte Culture Perspectives, 2016). Although not typically discussed in behavior analytic terms, organizational culture and employee engagement, as they relate to organizational behavior, can become useful tools for assessment. There are several definitions of both concepts; OC describes employees' point of view and whether their perspective aligns with the organizations' or functions' mission, vision, and values. Employee engagement measures employees' "commitment, motivation, sense of purpose, and passion for their work and organization" (Managing Employee Surveys, n.d.). This section combines these assessments because they collect data on employees' opinions and are used similarly in practice. This section covers behavioral literature on both topics, discusses the use of surveys in organizations, and suggests how both OC and employee engagement can be useful as assessment tools to OBM practitioners.

Researchers in Organizational Behavior and Industrial/Organizational psychology have provided several definitions for OC: the languages, values, attitudes, beliefs, and customs of an organization (Muchinsky, 2003), a set of characteristics that the organization values (Robbins, 2003), and a set of shared assumptions that guide behaviors (Ravasi & Schultz, 2006). Behavioral consultancies also address OC. Aubrey Daniels International defined culture as "shaped by what people say and do, and the practices that are encouraged and discouraged over time, whether intentional or otherwise" (Build a positive, sustainable culture, n.d.). ALULA defined culture as "A pattern of behavior that is encouraged or discouraged by people and by systems over time" (Jacobs, 2013, p. 153). Varying degrees of definitions aside, OC is indirectly implicated in how work gets done, and how the organization and its people react to changing environments. Olson (2002) summarizes traditional OC concepts and endorses a behavioral systems analysis model to address traditional OC variables through a behavioral lens.

Employee engagement also has many definitions. Kahn (1990) first defined engagement as "the harnessing of organization members' selves to their work roles; in engagement people employ and express themselves physically, cognitively, and emotionally during role performances" (page 694). Towers Perrin (2003) state that engagement is "a strong sense of personal accomplishment from one's job," and "the extent to which employees understand their role, and their unit's role, relative to company objectives." (p. 5). The fact remains, similarly to organizational culture, there is no agreed upon definition of "employee engagement" and the above definitions aren't necessarily helpful for defining what a practitioner should assess when attempting to alter "engagement." Summarizing this sentiment nicely, Daniels (2009) said that engagement is a "non-specific non-scientific term used to describe the amount of positive reinforcement available in the workplace for value-added behavior" (p. 7). A recent behavior analytic interpretation of employee engagement by Ludwig and Frazier (2012) explains the limitations of traditional approaches and definitions, namely covert states and correlational data. They provide a behavior analytic perspective on what the actual drivers of employee engagement are: reinforcement, adequate resources, management behaviors, autonomy, and experimental causality.

Practitioners build OC and engagement surveys around themes of inquiry and importance to the organization. Questions around the organization's mission/vision, innovation, teamwork, business results, perception of compensation, and perceptions of leadership are found on OC surveys. Themes like job fit, resource allocation, recognition, accountability, cross-functional collaboration, and professional development exist in engagement surveys. There are no set established categories or industry standards; the questions and themes are included based on whether the organization believes it is a "culture" issue, or an "engagement" issue.

Although detailed descriptions of survey design and implementation can be found elsewhere, the authors suggest following a few basic steps for conducting an engagement or OC survey. Setting a survey strategy will help ensure you are asking the right questions and the purpose for the survey is bound to an overarching organizational strategy. The strategy should also identify how results will be communicated, how often the survey will occur, and who will be held accountable for identifying and implementing changes based on survey results. First, identify what it is you are trying to measure and why. Aligning on survey goals (what and why) will help determine themes and categories of interest, and therefore will assist in question development. Second, identify the resources for designing and conducting the survey. If there are no resources within the organization with survey design skills and capabilities it may be necessary to hire outside help. Timing for surveys can vary. However, organizations typically use an annual cycle and should be careful not to schedule analyses around cyclical events that might skew the results (e.g., performance reviews, bonuses). Survey questions should be simple and straightforward taking care to avoid double-barreled items (questions that include two topics couched into one question). Answers to questions should be standardized (scales of 1–5 are common) to ensure that survey analysis is consistent and uncomplicated. It is also important to ask the same questions every time you survey so that changes in responses over time can be assessed. Anonymity of survey respondents is paramount to receiving honest opinions. Careful design of internet surveys goes a long way to ensuring high response rates including compatibility with older browsers and slow connections, keeping questionnaires short for voluntary surveys, minimizing response effort where possible, and careful placement of instruction/directions to avoid unnecessary scrolling. For additional guidance on survey design, readers are encouraged to read Dillman, Smyth, and Christian (2014). Once a survey has been completed the results should be communicated to the group surveyed. Communication should identify common positive, neutral and negative themes and what themes require action or mitigation from the organization. Based on the results of the survey and the objectives of the organization, Human Resources and related teams focus on efforts to improve on low scoring themes. The next survey measures attempts for improvement from the past year. Consistent successful surveys and subsequent Human Resource efforts to improve low scoring categories have the positive benefit of establishing those surveys as effective antecedents for change. As the organization works to use the survey information to improve the company and communicate to its employees the steps they are taking, the more likely the employees are to participate honestly in such surveys. The opposite is also true. If there is little to no change in the organization when surveys are completed, respondents may be less likely to take surveys seriously in the future.

The results of OC and Engagement surveys identify areas that need additional focus. For example, an OC assessment might find a mismatch between how employees feel about the organization's stated goals and how things actually operate in the business. If the gap is large, practitioners or leadership may find it necessary to rethink the mission/vision/goal statement by completing further analyses. Understanding employee perceptions of the organization can lead to additional OBM assessments like PM and BSA. Other catalysts can prompt OC assessments besides the passage of time. An upcoming merger or acquisition is an excellent example of when an OC assessment can help understand how big a gap exists between the two merging organizations. Practitioners use this information to determine how many resources and efforts are required to close critical gaps. In addition to understanding organization or performance gaps, practitioners and organizational leadership can share survey results with the employees so staff has a better grasp of current events and the possibility for upcoming organizational changes or potential layoffs.

While behavior analysts do not typically rely on survey data, skilled behavior analysts can infer the environmental causes that likely produce the verbal behavior measured by such surveys. Behavioral relations can then be verified via observations of pinpointed behaviors, antecedents, and consequences to determine root causes and ultimately develop solutions. For example, an engagement survey might find a low score for perceptions of leadership. As an initial step, a behavior analyst could initiate follow-up interviews and assessments to pinpoint which behaviors leaders are engaging in too little or lacking entirely. Once pinpointed and vetted by leadership, the OBM practitioner can then implement interventions to increase the desired leadership behavior and systemic analyses and changes to support the interventions.

Pulse survey

Pulse surveys are another assessment tool that has become popular in the last decade. Contrasted with more extensive organizational surveys completed annually (e.g., OC or engagement surveys), pulse surveys are short, can be completed at any time, and can be about any subject that is important to an organization or function. Welbourne (2016) links the popularity of pulse surveys with the availability of survey technology and the disillusionment with traditional annual surveys.

Because of the newness of pulse surveys and the lack of rigor in definition, pulse surveys can assess anything that is deemed important. The approach to pulse surveys should follow the above recommendations for survey design and implementation with a few differences. Because pulse surveys are meant to be quick and easy, they could require less resources and are more prone to be conducted internally. Timing is an obvious difference from traditional annual surveys. The name "pulse" implies that these types of surveys are quick checks over time. Repeated questions are encouraged as the measurement over time will help track progress, but consideration should be given to allow enough time between surveys for performance to change. The following are a few examples of ways that OBM practitioners can use pulse surveys as assessment tools. Note that most of the following examples use pulse surveys as addendums to the surveys discussed above.

One application of a pulse survey could be to assess the communications and preparation work leading up to change implementation. Practitioners may be interested in determining whether the communications they have created and disseminated for the change have achieved their objective. By creating a focused pulse survey and asking questions about the change's critical components, consultants can determine whether more work needs to be done or if what has been completed already is sufficient. Consultants may be concerned with understanding if their employees know when the change will take place, the reasons for the change, and how the change will affect their function and role. Additionally, practitioners will want to understand if the organization is ready for the transition to occur and if messaging and communications for the change have been useful. Asking these types of questions before implementation can provide insight into how well the change work permeates the organization and can potentially address critical issues before an implementation goes live.

Consultants and practitioners also use pulse surveys after a change implementation as a "postmortem" to assess the different facets of the change and how they affected the organization, different functions, and individual employees. Asking questions around elements such as resource allocation, communication, leadership behaviors, reinforcement, changes in role, and metrics help practitioners understand what went well and what may need additional effort for upcoming engagements.

Practitioners also use pulse surveys as a secondary measure of leader or employee behavior. For example, the second author used pulse surveys with a client going through a merger via acquisition. With the consulting team's help, the executive sponsors had identified four leadership behaviors that were critical to stewarding the change, especially during the initial transition period. The sponsors were interested in gauging how well their functional leaders were displaying those behaviors. The pulse survey was deployed organization-wide three times, each time asking questions about leader behavior expected during the transition. After the consulting team analyzed the data and developed themes, the executive sponsors then used the pulse survey reports to provide feedback to their functional leaders on their progress and barriers.

In addition to the leader behavior questions, the team used the survey to provide feedback on how well those behaviors were permeating the organization. This is also an example of another use for pulse surveys – data dissemination. The consultant team provided the client with summarized key messages from each iteration of the survey. Client leadership then distributed the results to the organization so the employees could see the results of their efforts and items that still needed work. Data dissemination through pulse survey tools could bolster the content of all surveys mentioned above, depending on the organization's communication needs and strategy.

Pulse surveys can uncover issues that may not be addressed in other surveys or by exploring themes that were outcomes of different assessments. For example, an engagement survey may reveal low scores on compensation and benefits. A pulse survey consisting of open-ended questions about perceptions and issues regarding compensation and benefits may uncover the underlying issues that a generic survey cannot. As the answers to the open-ended questions are analyzed, follow up pulses can then pinpoint the problem so a solution can be determined.

Pulse surveys also address issues that require attention but fall outside the scope of extensive assessments of cyclical nature. For example, the authors drafted this article during the COVID-19 global pandemic. A large organization housing thousands of people would be interested in using a pulse survey to identify the needs of their employees during a crisis. A Human Resources team may be interested in understanding the safety needs of their employees while also communicating work from home protocols and collecting feedback on whether or not the organization is providing enough communication and support. As new information comes in, the organization can update its employees on employee health information, resources, and other relevant data.

OBM assessments

Within OBM, assessment of organizations can and does occur at multiple levels and from various vantage points. However, assessments may be most easily organized according to a three levels approach: Organization, process, and performer (Rummler & Brache, 2013). Assessments occurring at the organization level typically comprise the system as a whole, while assessments at the process level look at specific workflows within the organization. Finally, performer level assessments focus on individual jobs, performances, and tasks/behaviors of interest.

As with the traditional management consulting assessments, some OBM assessments have more empirical support than others. Following our three levels organization, performer level assessments generally have the most empirical support while organization level assessments generally have the least. For a more detailed treatment of the empirical support of OBM assessments, readers are encouraged to read Dickinson (2000), Johnson et al. (2014), McGee (2017, 2018a), McGee and Crowley-Koch (in press), Rummler (2007), and Sigurdsson and McGee (2015).

The organization level

Strategy assessment. Many organizations find it helpful to have strategic goals – goals that are long range in nature (often 3–5 years out). Strategic goals are usually much bigger/broader than operational goals (which are typically written 0–2 years out), and serve to link the operational goals more clearly to the organization's mission, or major purpose for existing. Strategic goals are typically created during strategy assessment, also referred to as strategic planning. Rummler and Brache (2013) described the strategic planning and implementation process in their book, *Improving Performance: How to Manage the White Space on the Organizational Chart*. Additionally, Gilbert's (1978) Vantage Level analysis has been used for strategic purposes, such as reducing conflict within organizations and creating interventions consistent with organizational values (Shevchik, 1982; Smith & Chase, 1990). However, we only know of two specific OBM assessment tools directly targeting strategic planning. Ludwig and McGee's (2016) Strategy Tool guides the user through creating and/or analyzing an organizational vision and mission, completing a competitive analysis, and developing strategy statements.

McGee (2018b) expanded on Ludwig and McGee's (2016) Strategy Tool by creating the Strategic Planning and Implementation Tool. This more recent tool comprises two sections: strategic planning and strategy implementation. In the strategic planning section, the traditional S.W.O.T. (strengths, weaknesses, opportunities, and threats) analysis, which is common in traditional strategic planning (Helms & Nixon, 2010), is reconceptualized using the BSA framework to provide more context for the analysis of each S.W.O.T. factor. Specifically, competitive advantages and disadvantages are analyzed through the lens of the functioning of specific departments/functions across the organization that contribute to the design, development, and delivery of the products and services (see **Functional Relationships Assessment** section). Their strengths and weaknesses determine the overall strengths and weaknesses around each product/service, and our organization as a whole.

Opportunities and threats are analyzed through the lens of specific environmental variables (e.g., regulatory/legal, economy, culture, geopolitical, natural environment) – the industry and community factors that, while not under the control of the organization, impact how it makes strategic and operational decisions (see **External Environment Assessment** section). Armed with the results of these analyses, users begin to generate broad strategies using a T.O. W.S. (threats, opportunities, weaknesses, and strengths) analysis (Weihrich, 1982). T.O.W.S. analysis uses the results of the S.W.O.T. analysis to guide brainstorming of ways in which the organization might (a) use its strengths to take advantage of opportunities and (b) use its strengths to minimize threats, (c) improve weaknesses by taking advantage of opportunities, and (d) eliminate weaknesses to avoid threats. The aim is not to create a list of specific goals, but rather to generate ideas from which goals could be created. The final step of the strategic planning section is the creation of S.M.A.R.T. strategic goals. S.M.A.R.T. refers to specific, measurable, accountable (typically, this is "achievable" in the S.M.A.R.T. acronym), realistic, and time-bound. These goals are created by indicating (a) the direction of the change, (b) the accomplishment itself, (c) the amount of the change, (d) when the accomplishment will be achieved, and (e) the individual (owner) responsible for tracking the goal over time and ensuring progress. For example, a S.M.A.R.T. strategic goal might be that the organization will increase the number of clients served by 25% within five years, and Heather owns this goal.

The second section of the tool is the strategy implementation. Strategic planning is only valuable insofar as it produces behavior and systems change. In order to achieve different results, we must engage in different behaviors. In order to identify the necessary behavior changes, we first need to break the long-term, broad goals down into more close-in, objective sub goals. For example, if the strategic goal were a 5-year goal, begin by breaking down the overall into smaller goals for the end of years four, three, and two. Next, break down year-one goal into 4th, 3rd, 2nd, and 1st quarter goals. This process makes it more apparent what milestones need to be reached to achieve the overall goal. Next, analyze how the organization's customers, resources, products/services, and functions will impact and be impacted by the goal and determine what changes need to be made to each to achieve both milestones and the overall goal. Armed with this information, we can create an action plan for our 1st quarter goals, and make new action plans each quarter until the goal is achieved. These action plans focus on the behavior changes that must occur to create the system changes that will result in the achievement of our goals.

External environment assessment. There are two main types of behavioral systems analyses that are conducted on the organization as a whole: an analysis of the external factors impacting the organization, and an analysis of the relationships between the internal functions of the organization. In smaller organizations, the analyst might be able to combine these into a single analysis, but this becomes very messy and confusing in larger organizations, rendering the value of the visuals associated with such analyses as communication devices useless. Therefore, we will discuss each of these assessments individually.

Several tools exist for assessing the external environment in which an organization (or any system) operates. Examples are Brethower's (1972, 1982, 2000) Total Performance System (TPS), Rummler and Brache (2013) Super System Map, and Ludwig and McGee's (2016) Organization Analysis Tool. While this assessment is typically conducted on the entire organization (organization level of performance), these could assess only a function, process, job, performance, or even task.

Brethower's (1972, 1982, 2000) TPS is a system diagram that shows seven critical organizational components: mission/goal, products/services, customers/stakeholders, external feedback (customer measures), processing system, inputs, and internal feedback (processing system measures). The user completes the diagram by identifying the components, as they currently exist within the organization, and then analyzing them to determine opportunities for system improvement. In such an assessment, you might have data to suggest that one or more components are not operating at optimal levels or you are missing components altogether (e.g., missing feedback loops). It is important to remember that any changes you make will have system-wide impacts, even if the change is made within a single component. For example, an organization's leaders might decide to add a new product/service to its offerings. It will require resources (inputs) to make the new product (people, equipment, money, technology), and those resources, or at least some of them, might have to come from another product offering's resources, affecting the ability of the organization to effectively produce that original product, and affecting the workload of individuals involved in the production of both products. Table 1 shows the components of the TPS and the information when building the diagram. Rummler and Brache (2013) expanded the original TPS by two additional elements: environmental variables (e.g., government regulations, economy) and competition (for inputs and customers), and called their expanded diagram the Super System Map (See Figure 1). Even though the organization does not directly control these external components, it is impacted by them and therefore should be responding quickly and effectively to changes in each.

Both the TPS and the Super System are diagram/map-based tools. They are visual representations of the organizational system. These diagrams serve both as prompts for the analyst to gather the relevant systems information (a blank map prompts the gathering of information regarding each system component in order to create a completed map, as well as to identify any problems within the system) and as devices for communicating their findings to the

Table 1. The total performance system.

Tps components	Description
1. Mission/Goal	Why does this system exist?
2. Products/Services	What products & services are produced by the processing system?
3. Customers/Stakeholders	Who receives the product or service? The financial outputs of the organization?
4. External Feedback (Customer Measures)	What information does the organization get from its customers and stakeholders about the impact or value the product/service/financial output has on them?
5. Processing System	How does the organization convert inputs into products/services?
6. Inputs	What resources are used by the system?
7. Internal Feedback (Processing System Measures)	How does the organization measure performance internally to determine whether it is meeting its goals?
8. Environment*	What environmental factors impact the system (economy, government, culture, natural environment, and marketplace)?
9. Competition*	Who are the system's competitors for inputs or customers?

*system components added in Rummler and Brache (2013) Super System Diagram.

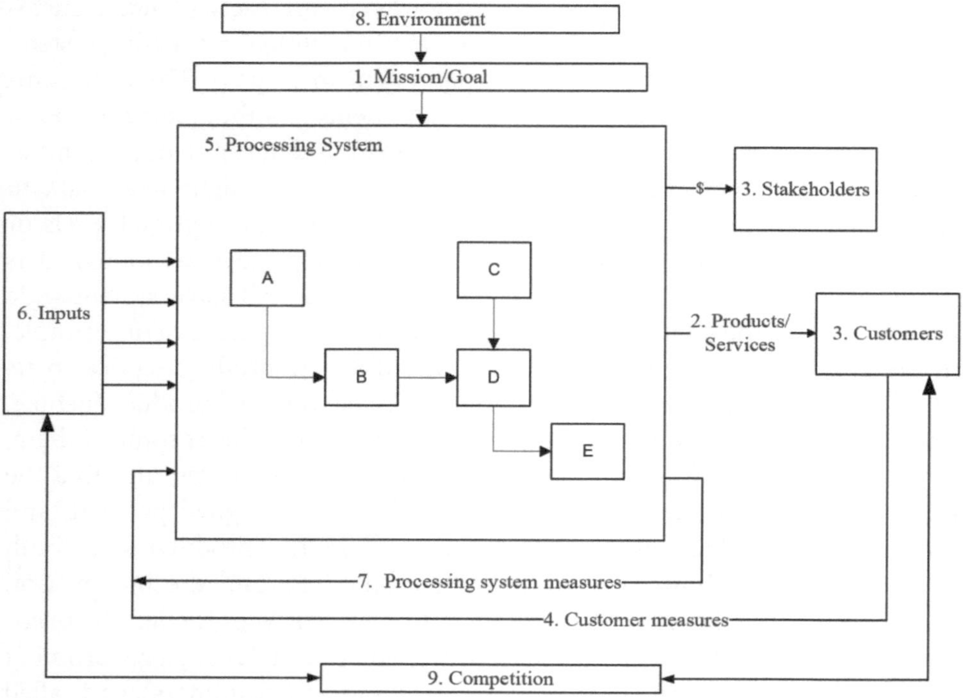

Figure 1. Organizational system map.

organizational client. This requires that the tool user already know exactly what information to gather to complete the map, including the best questions to ask and the most important data to gather. Ludwig and McGee (2016) created their Organization Analysis Tool based on their experiences with students and clients who struggled to identify those questions and data and, therefore, struggled to produce compelling and informative systems diagrams.

Their tool does not introduce a new diagram/map, but rather provides the user with a set of questions to ask and data to gather to complete a TPS/Super System diagram/map. The tool provides guided questions to help the practitioner (1) collect organizational information on the nine system components previously described; (2) identify measures and goals around components; (3) collect baseline data (gather data if it already exists or observe and collect data if it does not); (4) analyze the current state of each of the components and identify any disconnects between the current state and the ideal state of those components; (5) create an organizational system map that provides a visual depiction of the system and disconnects; (6) analyze the overall functioning of the system by asking questions around the interactions between and among the functions as well as general preparedness for changes in the external environment; (7) organize the opportunities for improvement based on root cause analysis of each of the identified disconnects; (8) analyze both the potential positive and potential negative impacts of taking action on those opportunities in terms of their short- and long-term effects on workflow efficiency, customer and employee satisfaction, resource allocation and consumption, revenues, etc.; and (9) make initial recommendations for solutions, determine the individuals who must be involved in design and implementation of changes, and set deadlines for action items.

Functional relationships assessment. Rummler and Brache (2013) Relationship Map (see Figure 2) illustrates the various departments or functions of the organization, what each department/function produces, and which function(s) or customer(s) receives those outputs. While this assessment is typically done

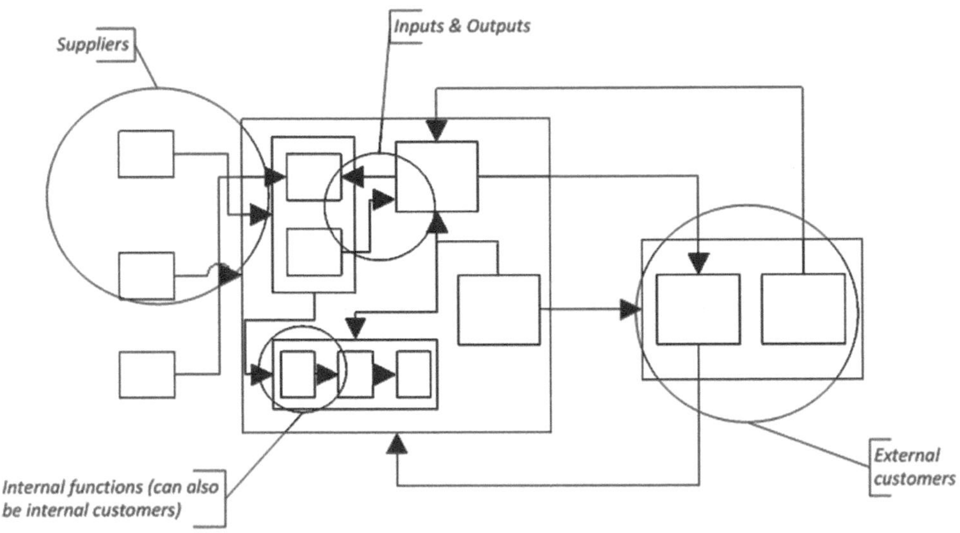

Figure 2. Functional relationships map.

at the organization level, it can be used to analyze job relationships as well, and in small organizations or organizations without traditional functional structures, this is how the assessment is more likely to be used. The functional relationships assessment is used to identify who produces what for whom, as well as where goals, standards, and feedback loops exist (or should exist) between the functions. These input/output relationships are then analyzed to determine whether any are missing, unnecessary, confusing, or misdirected. Goals, standards, and feedback loops for both functions in the relationship are assessed to determine whether they are designed in a way that supports success of both the supplier function and the customer function. Additionally, the overall picture can show how specific relationships can even affect other functions of the organization, by tracing the flow of a process through the various functions and eventually to the external customer. As with their Organization Analysis Tool, Ludwig and McGee's (2016) Functional Relationships Tool does not present a new or different map/diagram. Instead, it provides guided questions to help the practitioner (1) collect cross-functional information (see Relationship Map description); (2) identify measures and goals around those inputs and outputs; (3) collect baseline data (gather data if it already exists or observe and collect data if it does not); (4) analyze the components and identify any disconnects between the current state and the ideal state of those components; (5) create a functional relationships map that provides a visual depiction of the relationships and current disconnects between the organization's suppliers, departments/functions, and customers; (6) analyze the overall functioning of the organization's departments or functions; (7) organize the opportunities for improvement based on root cause analysis of each of the identified disconnects; (8) analyze both the potential positive and potential negative impacts of taking action on those opportunities; and (9) make initial recommendations for solutions, determine the individuals who must be involved in the design and implementation of changes, and set deadlines for action items.

The process level

Process assessment. Process assessment involves analyzing how work gets done. A process is a series of steps designed to produce a product or service (Rummler & Brache, 2013). Though process assessment is common outside of OBM and typically associated with Six Sigma or Lean, within OBM Rummler and Brache (2013) cross-functional process map is the most well-known tool. As with the Super System and Relationship Maps, Rummler and Brache's process assessment is a map-based tool. Process assessment involves first identifying the steps of the process, as they currently occur in the organization, and creating a cross-functional process map to provide a visual depiction of the process from beginning to end (see Figure 3). A cross-functional process map is organized into "swim lanes" or horizontal bands, each of which

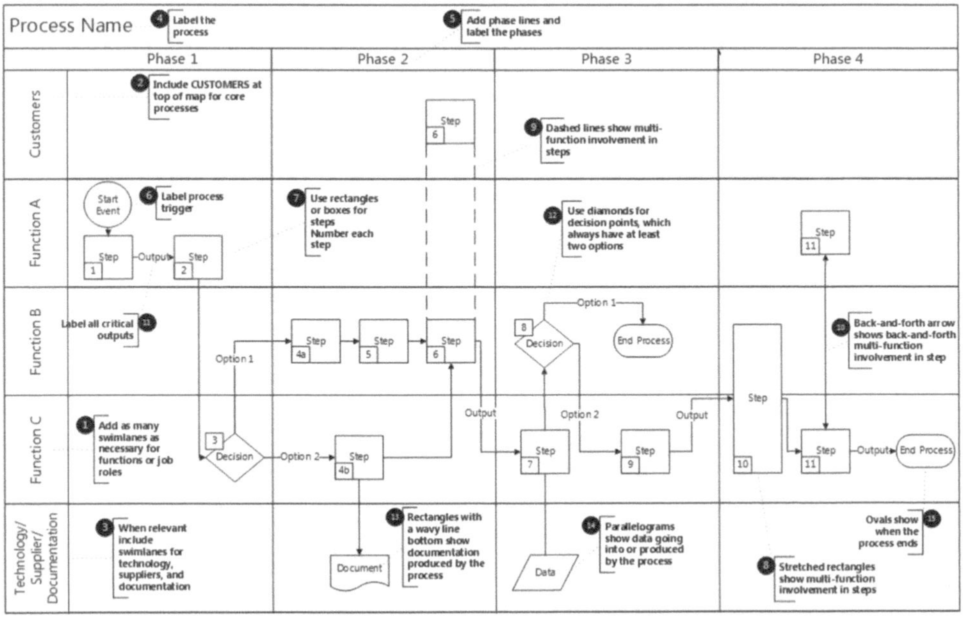

Figure 3. Cross-functional process map.

represents a function of the organization involved in the process to some extent. Each step (represented by a labeled box) and decision (represented by a labeled diamond) in the process is displayed in the swim lane of the function responsible for that step. The steps/decisions are connected by arrows and are organized linearly (as much as possible), moving from left to right in the map to show the progress of the process over time. In situations where multiple functions are engaging in different steps at the same time, those steps would appear at the same point in the map moving from left to right, but would still appear in the swim lane belonging to the function responsible for that step. If no steps occur concurrently, each step would appear after the previous step in the process, and in the appropriate swim lane.

Creating a process map allows you to identify (a) the scope of process being analyzed (where it starts and stops); (b) the functions involved in the process (or performers if it is either a single function process analysis or if you are working with an organization that does not have traditional functional structures); (c) the steps or tasks involved, including any decisions and all decision options; and (d) the inputs, outputs, and standards of each step. Once you have mapped the process, you can analyze it to identify any issues with respect to missing, redundant, or convoluted steps, standards, time, and resources involved. From there, you can redesign the process to improve performance, and a new map can be created to illustrate the future-state process.

As with their Organization Analysis and Functional Relationships Tools, Ludwig and McGee's (2016) Process Mapping Tool does not present a new or different map/diagram. Instead, it provides guided questions to help the practitioner (1) define the process; (2) identify process phases (typically 3–5 critical milestones of the process) and steps; (3) identify measures and goals around those phases and steps; (4) collect baseline data; (5) analyze the components and identify disconnects; (6) create a cross-functional process map that provides a visual depiction of the phases and steps, along with any identified disconnects within or between steps; (7) analyze the overall functioning of the process; (8) organize opportunities for improvement based on root cause analysis; (9) analyze the impact of performance improvement opportunities; and (10) make initial recommendations for solutions, determine the individuals who must be involved in design and implementation of changes, and set deadlines for action items.

Though not an actual assessment tool, Ramias (2013) article *Seeing a Process: The Power of Visual Analysis* is an excellent resource for process analysis and improvement. In the article, Ramias describes eight common process issues, along with how to identify and improve them. These issues are (a) serial versus parallel process steps; (b) excess reviews, approvals, and inspections; (c) unnecessary, non-value-adding steps; (d) redundant activities; (e) batch processing; (f) multiple process variations; (g) bottlenecks; and (h) rework loops. It is beyond the scope of this paper to describe each of these issues in detail, so readers are encouraged to review the original article.

The job/performer level

Job analysis. Job analysis involves examining and improving the design of a job as a whole by identifying and analyzing all of the accomplishments associated with a particular job. Job analysis, as with process assessment, is common outside of OBM and is typically associated with industrial-organizational psychology and human resource management. Within OBM, some tools available for analyzing and improving job design are job models (Garza, McGee, Schenk, & Wiskirchen, 2018; Rummler & Brache, 2013), Ludwig and McGee's (2016) Job Management Tool, and Rummler and Brache's (2013) Role and Responsibility Matrix. Job models are typically table-based tools that can include any or all of the following information: (a) accomplishments; (b) sub-accomplishments; (c) tasks; (d) measures and critical dimensions of performance; (e) performance standards; (f) feedback and consequences; and (g) knowledge, skills, and abilities (KSAs) required. Once the components currently in place for the job are identified, they are analyzed to determine where performance or performance support could be improved. See Figure 4 for a sample Job Model design.

Ludwig and McGee's (2016) Job Management Tool provides guided questions to help the practitioner (1) define the job's outputs; (2) determine the critical tasks that produce those outputs; (3) determine the resources required to complete the tasks (i.e., time, tools/equipment/materials, foundational skills

Job: Enter Job Title Here Job Purpose: Enter Job Purpose Here Supervisor: Enter Job Role This Job Directly Reports to Here

Responsibilities	Accomplishments	Measures	Goals/Standards	Tasks	KSAs
What is a primary responsibility of the job?	What is a primary accomplishment associated with this responsibility?	What are the measure associated with the accomplishment? In other words, what are the critical aspects of the accomplishment that should be assessed to determine whether it has been achieved?	What is the goal/standard for each measure of this accomplishment? In other words, what does performance excellence along each measure look like for this accomplishment?	What is a primary task associated with this accomplishment?	What KSAs, if any, are required to perform this task?
				What is a primary task associated with this accomplishment?	What KSAs, if any, are required to perform this task?
				What is a primary task associated with this accomplishment?	What KSAs, if any, are required to perform this task?
	What is a primary accomplishment associated with this responsibility?	What are the measure associated with the accomplishment? In other words, what are the critical aspects of the accomplishment that should be assessed to determine whether it has been achieved?	What is the goal/standard for each measure of this accomplishment? In other words, what does performance excellence along each measure look like for this accomplishment?	What is a primary task associated with this accomplishment?	What KSAs, if any, are required to perform this task?
				What is a primary task associated with this accomplishment?	What KSAs, if any, are required to perform this task?
				What is a primary task associated with this accomplishment?	What KSAs, if any, are required to perform this task?
	What is a primary accomplishment associated with this responsibility?	What are the measure associated with the accomplishment? In other words, what are the critical aspects of the accomplishment that should be assessed to determine whether it has been achieved?	What is the goal/standard for each measure of this accomplishment? In other words, what does performance excellence along each measure look like for this accomplishment?	What is a primary task associated with this accomplishment?	What KSAs, if any, are required to perform this task?
				What is a primary task associated with this accomplishment?	What KSAs, if any, are required to perform this task?
				What is a primary task associated with this accomplishment?	What KSAs, if any, are required to perform this task?

Figure 4. Job model.

and knowledge, training, and information); (4) identify measures and goals around outputs and tasks, along with how performers receive feedback on their performance; (5) collect baseline data; (6) analyze the outputs, tasks, and resources and identify disconnects related to these components; (7) analyze the overall functioning of the job; (8) organize opportunities for improvement based on root cause analysis; (9) analyze the impact of performance improvement opportunities; and (10) make initial recommendations for solutions, determine the individuals who must be involved in design and implementation of changes, and set deadlines for action items.

Rummler and Brache's (2013) Role and Responsibility Matrix clarifies responsibilities across multiple jobs within a function, based on each job's contributions to an overall process. The matrix design allows a supervisor or manager to determine how each job within their function contributes to overall process goals by first identifying the functional accomplishments associated with the process, and then identifying the individual job accomplishments and goals associated with each major functional accomplishment and process step.

Performance assessment. Sometimes it is important to analyze a particular job performance in detail. This calls for performance assessment and most OBM performance assessments can be seen as variants of Rummler's (1972) Human Performance System. The Human Performance System assesses six specific job performance variables: performance specifications, task support, consequences, feedback, knowledge/skill, and individual capacity . Gilbert's (1978) Behavior Engineering Model (BEM) and Binder's (1998) Six Boxes^{TM} models also assess these variables, though they use different language to describe the six components. The BEM describes the six variables as data, instruments, incentives, knowledge, capacity, and motives and organizes the HPS into a matrix format, with each of the six variables falling under one of two main categories: environmental supports (data, instruments, incentives) and person's repertoire of behavior (knowledge, capacity and motives). The Six Boxes^{TM} model translated the BEM into a more user-friendly diagnostic tool using nontechnical language. Austin's (2000) Performance Diagnostic Checklist (PDC) provides a more condensed analysis, with four categories (antecedents and information, equipment and processes, knowledge and skills, and consequences). The PDC also uses a checklist format, making it a relatively easy to use tool on the job (Gravina, Nastasi, & Austin, in press). Abernathy's (2009, 2010) Performance Analysis/Performance Constraint Analysis comprises three general categories (opportunity, capability, context) with two to three subcategories under each category (work input and time under opportunity; competence, resources, and processes under capability; and prompts, feedback, and consequences under context). Abernathy further breaks down each subcategory into two to three sources of performance variation under each subcategory. Work input is broken down into work availability, work input quality, and work distribution. Time is broken down into employee utilization, employee scheduling, and employee attendance. Abernathy breaks competence down into employee selection and employee training, resources into work supplies and work tools, and processes into work methods and work flow. Finally, he breaks each of prompts, feedback, and consequences down into manager/employee and organization/employee.

Task analysis. Task analysis involves breaking a specific job performance down into its component tasks to determine whether those tasks are necessary and efficiently arranged, as well as for training purposes. In many ways, task analysis is similar to process assessment. For example, each of Ramias (2013) process issues can also occur within a single performance of a particular job. Task analysis differs from process assessment in that (a) you are analyzing the performance of a single individual or job role as opposed to performance across multiple job roles or functions, and (b) task analyses typically present information in flowchart or numbered outline form as opposed to a map.

Mager's (1997) approach to task analysis involves starting with a specific job and breaking it down into its component tasks. Though similar to job modeling, it is not likely that the tasks in a job model would have been broken down in enough detail as to be helpful for the purposes of task analysis. Once the job tasks have been identified, each task is broken down into component task steps, along with the knowledge, skills, and abilities (KSAs) required to complete those task steps. It should be noted that Mager described the task analysis process as identifying and breaking down all tasks associated with a particular job; however it is not typically carried out that way. It is much more common, for either analysis or training purposes, to identify a single job performance, task, or responsibility and break it down into a detailed task step and KSA listing, including breaking down decision points within the performance. In fact, the decision breakdown is one of the most useful aspects of task analysis, as these are often the points in the performance where new learners and poor performers struggle the most (McGee, 2016). For example, the performance of a manager giving feedback to an employee might include the task "determine whether follow up is necessary and, if so, schedule the follow up." The inclusion of "determine" tells us that this is a decision point that should be broken down. For example, we must identify what the various decision outputs are (e.g., follow up necessary or follow up unnecessary) and under what specific conditions each of those outputs would be appropriate (e.g., follow up is unnecessary if there was no constructive feedback or if there was only minor constructive feedback provided on non-critical task/accomplishment and performer identified issue and solution immediately, whereas follow-up would be required under any other circumstance).

Task analysis is perhaps most common outside of OBM (in I-O Psychology), where it is typically used for training and selection purposes. When used for training purposes, the task analysis will likely take the form that we have described. When used for selection purposes, however, the task analysis will look more like a job model in that it will comprise a series of task statements, along with the KSAs required to complete those tasks. In this application, it is typical to write the task statements at the level of a whole job responsibility, rather than specific steps associated with a given responsibility.

Contingency analysis. Any performance can be broken down into component tasks or behaviors and each of those tasks/behaviors can be analyzed individually. The most basic approach for this is the ABC Analysis. In an ABC Analysis, you identify the behavior of interest and then observe the behavior over time to determine the antecedents and consequences operating on the behavior. Daniels and Bailey's (2014) PIC/NIC Analysis and Braksick's (2007) E-TIP Analysis are two tools that expand on the basic ABC Analysis by building consequence diagnostics into the analysis.

To conduct a PIC/NIC Analysis, first identify both the desired behavior as well as the undesired (or currently occurring) behavior (Daniels & Bailey, 2014). Next, identify the antecedents and consequences associated with each behavior, as you would do in a basic ABC Analysis. Finally, categorize the consequences as either positive or negative (from the performer's perspective), immediate or future, and certain or uncertain. Once completed, identify which consequences – whether programmed or naturally occurring – suppress desired behavior and/or support undesired behavior. The advice from these analyses is to provide immediate and certain consequences to influence behavior, using positive versions of these consequences to support behavior and negative versions of these consequences to discourage behavior (as well as eliminating antecedent and consequences that run counter to the intended performance whenever possible). The E-TIP Analysis (Braksick, 2007) follows a similar process: (a) identify the desired and undesired behavior; (b) observe behavior to determine antecedents and consequences; and (c) analyze each of the consequences to determine its Effect (encouraging or discouraging), Timing (immediate or delayed), and Probability (likely or unlikely). Where the E-TIP differs from the PIC/NIC is in the addition of an analysis of the Importance (high or low) of the consequence, from the performer's perspective.

A final contingency analysis tool is Ludwig and McGee's (2016) Behavior Change Tool. This tool provides guided questions to help the practitioner (a) define an essential task to be analyzed; (b) determine the essential behaviors that must be performed to consider the task complete, as well as the competing behaviors that are currently occurring; and (c) analyze the antecedents, behaviors, and consequences to determine root causes of behavior issues and identify potential solutions. Begin by determining a task, critical to the success of a job performance or responsibility that is not occurring as it should. Next, break the task down into its component task steps or behaviors, much as you would in a task analysis. Then, determine whether each of those behaviors occurs (a) at the right time, (b) every time it is supposed to occur, (c) accurately, and (d) completely. For any behaviors not occurring at the right time, every time, accurately, and completely, continue with an analysis of the antecedents and consequences. First, identify what the performer does instead of the essential (desired) behavior (i.e., the competing behavior). Next, observe performance to determine the antecedents associated with the both the essential behavior and the competing behavior. Conduct an analysis on the antecedents by determining the probability of them occurring. Then, identify the positive, negative, immediate, and delayed consequences (for both the performer and the organization) for the essential behaviors, along with the competing behaviors, and determine the probability of those consequences occurring. Use this information to develop solutions, determine individuals who must be involved in design and implementation of changes, and set deadlines for action items.

Sustainability assessment

Ostensibly, the goal of performance and systems improvement efforts are to create lasting behavior change. After the project or initiative is complete, the effects should not disappear along with exiting consultants. Redmon and Agnew (1991) provided anecdotal evidence that OBM practitioners tend to focus their efforts on the "middle" phases of the consultation process (implementation, evaluation) rather than beginning phases (pre-entry, entry) or the end phases (maintenance, withdrawal, follow-up). Sigurdsson and Austin

(2006) provided an extensive review of the history of "institutionalization," "adoption," and response maintenance of OBM interventions followed by an analysis of four elements that increase chances of institutionalization of OBM interventions (involvement in design, training of internal staff, formal data collection system, and a formal system of dispensing consequences). Results of their review of JOBM articles found varying degrees of implementation of those four variables. The authors recommend incorporating institutionalization variables into OBM work that seeks to foster lasting change and sustainability of programs and interventions. Conard, Johnson, Morrison, and Ditzian (2016) also discuss the sustainability of interventions in their comprehensive review. After discussing different definitions of what we are referring to as "sustainability", namely "institutionalization" (i.e., generalization of behavior change over time) and "maintenance" (i.e., partial or full continuation of an intervention by the organization after the consultant or researcher has departed the setting), the authors suggest using "temporal generality" as an encompassing term and then discuss 12 of those tactics (intervene and hope, sequential modification, introduce to natural maintaining contingencies, use of indiscriminable contingencies, mediate generalization, behavior systems analysis, promotion of social validity, use of instructional design, involvement in intervention design, training internal staff, formal data collection system, and formal system of dispensing consequences). Given the importance of sustaining useful OBM interventions, there is a need for a more systemic approach to assessing OBM applications' sustainability.

At the end of their review, Conard et al. (2016) discussed one limitation of their review was that it was limited to publicly known data, thus excluding potential trade secrets that might be withheld for the purposes of a competitive edge in consultation or simply a lack of incentives for consultants to publish. We provide recommendations for a sustainability assessment, based on previous research above and experience through private practice, which will assist practitioners in thinking through items that will affect intervention adoption and sustainability. The sustainability assessment comprises five categories: *Sponsorship & Alignment, Measures, Antecedents, Behavior, and Consequences*. Assessing whether an intervention or project will sustain should start early in the consultation process. If the consultant(s) waits until the end of the project to assess the adoption of the initiative, it is more than likely that they will have undervalued or underestimated elements that are crucial for success for long-term maintenance.

The first category, *sponsorship & alignment*, assesses how well the planned initiative aligns with organizational values and whether there is adequate senior level sponsorship for the project. For example, the project should have an executive sponsor – a project owner that will approve budget(s), act as a final decision maker, help to communicate and socialize the initiative with other executives and business units and assist in identifying and removing barriers to project success. In addition to an executive sponsor, and based on the initiative's size and scope, project champions may be helpful. Project champions are typically senior leaders who have a stake in the initiative and can help steward the project in different areas or functions. In initiatives where the implementation is enterprise or organization-wide, a project champion is someone who acts as a subject matter expert (SME) for that initiative and how it interacts with their function. That project champion then acts as an SME for both the initiative and how it relates to their function. Project champions are usually members of the project team, which is where they develop their credentials as SMEs. The alignment category also includes "involvement in design" from Sigurdsson and Austin (2006) as members of the project team should be involved in the assessment and design of interventions.

Organizational alignment is also assessed in this category. The initiative should be viewed through a systemic lens to understand if it aligns with the organizations mission, vision, values, and patterns of behavior (culture). The short- and long-term goals should also be assessed to ensure that they mesh with overachieving organization or functional goals. Horizontal alignment is also critical. In other words, the goals of the initiative should reconcile and complement the other functions of the organization. Finally, the project or initiative should be assessed to determine if it is creating new stand-alone systems or if the systems can be incorporated into existing processes or programs, the former being more complicated and resource intensive.

The second category, measures, addresses the important issue of project metrics. Many OBM interventions involve ongoing data collection of behavior, results or both (while Human Resources does collect data in the form of surveys it is typically not pinpointed behavior tied to business results). Ideally, a measurement system should be in place to capture behaviors, results, or both that are correlated with success of the initiative. The measurement system should be accurate – measuring what it says it measures and thereby increasing trust in the metrics as well as the program overall. If behaviors are primarily measured by the system, they should be sufficiently pinpointed. If the system measures results only, there should be little guesswork from employees to understand what behaviors produce those results. Additionally, management should determine and clearly communicate whether observations and measurement should occur in the open (in full view and with full knowledge of those being observed) or more unobtrusively (potentially without the knowledge of those being observed). In general, transparency in performance analysis, improvement, and ongoing maintenance is encouraged. However, there may be situations in which overt observation could produce artificial or exaggerated responses. In these situations, covert observation might be preferred. However, covert observation does have its drawbacks – mainly mistrust and paranoia. Ownership and maintenance of the measurement system should also be addressed to ensure that the system is valid and that changes and updates to the measurement system are made as priorities or behaviors/results change.

The third category, antecedents, has five subcategories, all of which can be classified as environmental stimuli that come before behavior and prompt behavior. The first subcategory of antecedents is roles and responsibilities. The roles and responsibilities should be clear for all employees that are affected by the change. The boundaries of their roles should also be delineated to prevent role crossover and confusion. Roles and responsibilities should include who is responsible and accountable for results and ensuring that those are communicated and understood throughout the organization. Lastly, changes in roles, responsibilities, and job descriptions should be formally captured in Human Resources systems to reflect the changes implemented.

Competency is the next subcategory. Simply put, employees should be able to perform the tasks that are expected of them to reach the desired results. Training should be effective and delivered at the right time (preferably, close to when the behaviors occur or start). Additionally, the hiring and selection processes should incorporate the new skills and abilities into job posting and hiring processes.

Processes and procedures is the next subcategory. Most significant changes occur at this level and it is crucial that the procedures and processes in which the employees work support their new behavior. Changes to systems and processes should be documented and should incorporate critical behaviors and any necessary significant changes to processes and procedures. Practitioners should also document and approve the roles and responsibilities of process owners. Process owners should also be trained on the changes to existing processes or the implementation of new processes. Resources required for processes should also be analyzed to ensure that performers have what they need to be able to work fluently and efficiently within the new or changed system. Processes should focus on reducing response effort for performers where possible and building reinforcement into the system.

Goals and objectives is the next subcategory for antecedents. Short, medium, and long-term goals for the initiative should be identified that reconcile with the overall strategy of the organization. These goals should be communicated to all performers and the link between their performance and desired results are clear. Goals should be challenging and attainable. From a systemic lens, the organizations performance management system should incorporate these goals and objectives into cyclical review cycles.

Communication is the last subcategory of antecedents. Employees should be aware of important changes and the status of critical organizational systems and any changes that effect their work or the work of others. Communication methods should reach intended audiences in their preferred format, so the message is received and not dismissed (e.g., e-mail blasts). A communication forum should be established so that front-line employees and leaders can provide feedback on the health of the initiative, taking care not to show preference to the type of employee providing feedback.

The next category is behavior. Ideally, behaviors should be pinpointed (Daniels & Bailey, 2014) so that performers know exactly what to do and when to do it. The performers should also cease to engage in competing behaviors if they exist. There should be direct connection between the pinpointed behaviors and the results to be achieved as well as the connection being continually assessed. Leaders should also continue to clarify performance expectations and show connections between performer behavior and results. Leaders also have an additional responsibility of modeling pinpointed or desired behaviors and usage of tools, processes, or systems.

The last category is consequences. Formal (e.g., pay for performance) and informal (e.g., manager feedback) consequence systems should be in place and operating as intended. Feedback should be based on the metrics that are captured in the measurement system. Results metrics should be incorporated into standard meetings so that progress and barrier removal can be discussed. Consequence systems should provide the quality and quantity of reinforcement to overcome the reduced emphasis when practitioners leave and the initiative is "business as usual." Leaders should continue to coach, provide feedback, and reinforce behaviors often. Reinforcement of behaviors should itself be reinforced through senior leadership. Milestones and goal achievement should receive special attention and reinforcement. Table 2 provides an overview of the sustainability assessment elements and suggested questions for each element.

Summary

Organizational assessments presented in this article could help OBM and other ABA professionals within a wide range of jobs (supervisor, academic, consultant, trainer, etc.) employ a systematic and systemic approach to workplace performance analysis and improvement. Practitioners should not assume it involves a one-time effort. In fact, a continuous improvement element could be added to the end of each assessment described above.

Rarely are the results of initial projects or assessments flawless, which is why a process of continuous improvement is essential to making incremental changes that improve the quality of the assessment or implementation. Practitioners should establish a forum or process where issues are identified, tracked, escalated (if required), and resolved. Once issues arise, they should be given the proper time and attention and addressed in a timely matter. Leaders should also encourage an open forum where issues are brought to the table and resolved rather than punishing the behavior of bringing new issues to light. Best practices and lessons learned should also be captured in an organized process to inform future initiatives and changes. As organizations and the

Table 2. Sustainability assessment.

Categories	Questions
Sponsorship & Alignment	(1) Sponsorship Are the right people involved in the initiative from the beginning and does it have strong executive sponsors and champions? (2) Are the right stakeholders involved in the design of the initiative? (3) AlignmentDoes the initiative align with the organization's cultural values? (4) Does the initiative align with the organization mission, vision, and strategy? (5) Are the organization's short- and medium-term goals aligned to support the initiative? (6) Do the objectives or goals of the initiative reconcile with other functions of the organization? (7) Is the initiative creating brand new systems or processes? Can these be integrated into existing systems?
Measures	(1) Is an effective measurement system in place that captures behaviors, results or both? (2) Are behavior measures sufficiently pinpointed? (3) If only results are being measured do the performers know what behaviors produce those results? (4) Has an owner and process been identified for maintaining the measurement system and report-generating processes? (5) Do leaders help maintain the measurement system and provide feedback on its effectiveness?
Antecedents	(1) Roles and ResponsibilitiesAre roles and responsibilities clear for all employees affected by the change? (2) Are the boundaries within which employees should operate clearly defined? (3) Has the appropriate level of responsibility and accountability for actions and results been established, communicated, and understood? (4) Have job descriptions for changed roles been revised to reflect the required changes to behaviors, results, and responsibilities? (5) CompetencyHave all affected employees acquired the skills they need to execute their roles? (6) Is training effective and delivered at the right time to build skills or prompt behavior? (7) Do hiring and selection processes provide sufficient emphasis on knowledge, skill, ability, and experience needed to perform the key job responsibilities? (8) Processes & Procedures Are changes to the impacted processes updated to incorporate the changes and new behaviors? (9) Have long-term process owners been identified? (10) Have process owners been oriented and trained? (11) Are key resources (time, technology, tools, etc.) to the process in place and functioning? (12) Are processes working as intended to support desired behaviors and outcomes? (13) Are processes designed to reduce response effort where possible? (14) Goals & Objectives Are short, medium, and long-term goals identified and communicated? (15) Are goals challenging yet attainable? (16) Are goals tied to behaviors as well as consequences that are delivered? (17) Have leaders and performers revised their performance objectives and performance management plans to reflect new behaviors and results? (18) Communication Are employees given communication to update them on the health and status of the initiative? (19) Do the communication methods reach the intended audience by means in which the audience prefers? (20) Is there two-way communication from front-line employees and management on the health of the initiative? (21) Are employees given the correct prompts at the right time, so they know exactly what to do and when to do it?
Behavior	(1) Are the desired behaviors pinpointed and communicated in a way that leaves no room for ambiguity? (2) Are most performers actually performing the desired behaviors and not performing competing behaviors? (3) Are the desired behaviors linked to the desired results? (4) Are leaders continuing to clarify performance expectations and to foster the connection between behaviors and results? (5) Is the impact of behaviors on targeted results continually assessed? (6) Are leaders' role-modeling behaviors, and usage of tools, procedures, and processes?

(*Continued*)

Table 2. (Continued).

Categories	Questions
Consequences	(1) Are formal and informal consequences delivery systems in place? (2) Are leaders providing feedback based on data from the measurement system? (3) Are all stakeholders receiving the feedback they need about results through the measurement system? (4) Do planned consequence systems provide the quality and quantity of reinforcement needed to sustain behaviors after the initiative becomes "business as usual"? (5) Are results metrics being incorporated into standing meetings? (6) Is reinforcement delivered to those who provide consequences? (7) Is success and goal achievement consistently reinforced? (8) Do leaders continue to coach, give feedback, and reinforce behaviors often (daily or weekly)?

environments they operate within change, the systems that make up the organization must also change. Organizations must revisit their goals and strategies, structures, processes, and jobs. Organizational assessment is an ongoing requirement for sustainable organizational improvement and overall health.

Disclosure statement

No potential conflict of interest was reported by the authors.

References

Abernathy, W. B. (2009). Walden two revisited: Optimizing behavioral systems. *Journal of Organizational Behavior Management*, *29*(2), 175–192. doi:10.1080/01608060902874567

Abernathy, W. B. (2010, May/June). A comprehensive performance analysis and improvement method. *Performance Improvement*, *49*(5), 5–17. doi:10.1002/pfi.20146

Addison, R. M., & Haig, C. (2013, January). A walk on the human performance side—Part 4. *Performance Improvement*, *52*(1), 38–42. doi:10.1002/pfi.21320

Aubrey Daniels International. (n.d.). *Build a positive, sustainable culture*. Retrieved from https://www.aubreydaniels.com/organizational-culture

Austin, J. (2000). Performance analysis and performance diagnostics. In J. Austin & J. E. Carr (Eds.), *Handbook of applied behavior analysis* (pp. 321–349). Philadelphia, PA: Context Press.

Binder, C. (1998). The six boxes™: A descendent of Gilbert's behavior engineering model. *Performance Improvement*, *37*(6), 48–52. doi:10.1002/pfi.4140370612

Braksick, L. W. (2007). *Unlock behavior, unleash profits: Developing leadership behavior that drives profitability in your organization*. New York, NY: McGraw Hill Professional.

Brethower, D. M. (1972). *Behavioral analysis in business and industry: A total performance system*. Kalamazoo, MI: Behaviordelia, Inc.

Brethower, D. M. (1982). The total performance system. In R. M. O'Brien, A. M. Dickinson, & M. P. Rosow (Eds.), *Industrial behavior modification: A management handbook* (pp. 350–369). New York, NY: Pergamon Press.

Brethower, D. M. (2000). A systematic view of enterprise: Adding value to performance. *Journal of Organizational Behavior Management, 20*(3/4), 165–190. doi:10.1300/J075v20n03_06

Coch, L., & French, J. R. P. (1948). Overcoming resistance to change. *Human Relations, 1*(4), 512–532. doi:10.1177/001872674800100408

Conard, A. L., Johnson, D. A., Morrison, J. D., & Ditzian, K. (2016). Tactics to ensure durability of behavior change following the removal of an intervention specialist: A review of temporal generality within organizational behavior management. *Journal of Organizational Behavior Management, 36*(2–3), 210–253. doi:10.1080/01608061.2016.1201036

Daniels, A. C. (2009). *Oops! 13 management practices that waste time and money (and what to do instead)*. Atlanta, GA: Performance Management.

Daniels, A. C., & Bailey, J. S. (2014). *Performance management: Changing behavior that drives organizational effectiveness*. Atlanta, GA: Performance Management Publications.

Deloitte Culture Perspectives. (2016). *Culture vs. engagement*. Deloitte. Retrieved from https://www2.deloitte.com/us/en/pages/human-capital/articles/culture-versus-employee-engagement-strategy.html

Dickinson, A. M. (2000). The historical roots of organizational behavior management in the private sector: The 1950s-1980s. *Journal of Organizational Behavior Management, 20*(3–4), 9–58. doi:10.1300/J075v20n03_02

Diener, L. H., McGee, H. M., & Miguel, C. F. (2009). An integrated approach for conducting a behavioral systems analysis. *Journal of Organizational Behavior Management, 29*(2), 108–135. doi:10.1080/01608060902874534

Dillman, D. A., Smyth, J. D., & Christian, L. M. (2014). *Internet, phone, mail, and mixed-mode surveys: The tailored design method*. Indianapolis, IN: John Wiley & Sons.

Garza, K. L., McGee, H. M., Schenk, Y. A., & Wiskirchen, R. R. (2018). Some tools for carrying out a proposed process for supervising experience hours for aspiring board certified behavior analysts®. *Behavior Analysis in Practice, 11*(1), 62–70. doi:10.1007/s40617-017-0186-8

Gilbert, T. F. (1978). *Human competence: Engineering worthy performance*. New York, NY: McGraw-Hill.

Gravina, N., Nastasi, J., & Austin, J. (in press). Assessment of employee performance. *Journal of Organizational Behavior Management*.

Helms, M. M., & Nixon, J. (2010). Exploring SWOT analysis—where are we now? A review of academic research from the last decade. *Journal of Strategy and Management, 3*(3), 215–251. doi:10.1108/17554251011064837

Holt, D. T., Helfrich, C. D., Hall, C. G., & Weiner, B. J. (2010). Are you ready? How health professionals can comprehensively conceptualize readiness for change. *Journal of General Internal Medicine, 25*(1), 50–55. doi:10.1007/s11606-009-1112-8

Jacobs, S. (2013). *The behavior breakthrough: Leading your organization to a new competitive advantage*. Austin, TX: Greenleaf Book Group LLC.

Johnson, D. A., Casella, S. E., McGee, H. M., & Lee, S. C. (2014). The use and validation of pre-intervention diagnostic tools in organizational behavior management. *Journal of Organizational Behavior Management, 34*(2), 104–121. doi:10.1080/01608061.2014.914009

Jones, R., Lusthaus, C., Adrien, M.-H., & Stanley, C. (2006). *Organization assessment guide: Prepared by the evaluation division performance and knowledge management branch*. Canadian International Development Agency. Gatineaux, Quebec.

Kahn, W. A. (1990). Psychological conditions of personal engagement and disengagement at work. *The Academy of Management Journal, 33*(4), 692–724. doi:10.2307/256287

Ludwig, L. H., & McGee, H. M. (2016). *Performance analysis toolkit [electronic toolkit]*. Performance Blueprints. Retrieved from https://www.performanceblueprints.com/tools/

Ludwig, T. D., & Frazier, C. B. (2012). Employee engagement and organizational behavior management. *Journal of Organizational Behavior Management, 32*(1), 75–82. doi:10.1080/01608061.2011.619439

Mager, R. F. (1997). *Making instruction work: A step-by-step guide to designing and developing instruction that works.*Atlanta, GA: CEP Press.

Malott, M. E. (2003). *Paradox of organizational change.* Reno, NV: Context Press.

McGee, H. M. (2016, October). *Task analyzing complex staff performances.* Invited presentation at the annual Michigan Autism Conference, Kalamazoo, MI.

McGee, H. M. (2017). Consultation practices: Organizations. In J. K. Luiselli (Ed.), *Applied behavior analysis advanced guidebook* (pp. 259–283). Cambridge, MA: Elsevier. doi:10.1016/B978-0-12-811122-2.00011-5

McGee, H. M. (2018b, September). *A behavioral systems analysis approach to strategic planning.* Invited presentation at the annual Minnesota Northland Association for Behavior Analysis Conference, Minneapolis, MN.

McGee, H. M. (2018a). Process assessments and redesign. In B. Wine & J. Pritchard (Eds.), *Organizational behavior management: The essentials*(pp. 274-318). Hedgehog Publishers.

McGee, H. M., & Crowley-Koch, B. J. (2019). Using behavioral systems analysis to improve large scale change initiatives in autism service organizations. *Perspectives on Behavior Science, 42*(4), 931–954. doi:10.1007/s40614-019-00231-0

McGee, H. M., & Crowley-Koch, B. J. (in press). Behavioral systems analysis in organizations. In R. A. Houmanfar, M. Fryling, & M. Alavosius (Eds.), *Applied behavior science in organizations: Consilience of historical and emerging trends in organizational behavior management.* Kalamazoo, MI: Association for Behavior Analysis International.

Muchinsky, P. M. (2003). *Psychology: Applied to work.* Belmont, CA: Wadsworth/Thomson Learning.

Olson, R. (2002). Organizational culture: Putting the organizational culture concept to work. *The Behavior Analyst Today, 3*(4), 471–481. doi:10.1037/h0100001

Rafferty, A. E., Jimmieson, N. L., & Armenakis, A. A. (2013). Change readiness: A multilevel review. *Journal of Management, 39*(1), 110–135. doi:10.1177/0149206312457417

Ramias, C. (2013, March). Seeing a process: The power of visual analysis. *BPTrends.* Retrieved from http://www.bptrends.com/bpt/wp-content/publicationfiles/03-05-2013-COL-Perf%20Improvement-Seeing%20the%20Process-Ramias-Wilkins-v1.pdf

Ravasi, D., & Schultz, M. (2006). Responding to organizational identity threats: Exploring the role of organizational culture. *Academy of Management Journal, 49*(3), 433–458. doi:10.5465/amj.2006.21794663

Redmon, W. K., & Agnew, J. L. (1991). Organizational behavioral analysis in the United States: A view from the private sector. In P. A. Lamal (Ed.), *Behavioral analysis of societies and cultural practices* (pp. 125–139). Washington, DC: Hemisphere Publishing Corp.

Robbins, S. P. (2003). *Essentials of organizational behavior.* Upper Saddle River, NJ: Prentice Hall.

Rummler, G. A. (1972). Human performance problems and their solutions. *Human Resource Management, 11*(4), 1–10. doi:10.1002/hrm.3930110402

Rummler, G. A. (2004). *Serious performance consulting according to Rummler.* International Society for Performance Improvement. Silver Spring, MD.

Rummler, G. A. (2007). The past is prologue: An eyewitness account of HPT. *Performance Improvement, 46*(10), 5–9. doi:10.1002/pfi.166

Rummler, G. A., & Brache, A. P. (2013). *Improving performance: How to manage the white space on the organization chart* (3rd ed.). San Francisco, CA: Jossey-Bass.

Shevchik, P. S. F. (1982). *Vantage level analysis: A potential tool for reducing conflict in a labor union* (Master's thesis), Western Michigan University. ProQuest Dissertations Publishing.

Sigurdsson, S. O., & Austin, J. (2006). Institutionalization and response maintenance in organizational behavior management. *Journal of Organizational Behavior Management, 26* (4), 41–77. doi:10.1300/J075v26n04_03

Sigurdsson, S. O., & McGee, H. M. (2015). Organizational behavior management: Systems analysis. In H. Roane, J. E. Ringdahl, & T. Falcomata (Eds.), *Clinical and organizational applications of applied behavior analysis* (pp. 627–647). Cambridge, MA: Academic Press.

Smith, J. M., & Chase, P. N. (1990). Using the vantage analysis chart to solve organization-wide problems. *Journal of Organizational Behavior Management, 11*(1), 127–148. doi:10.1300/J075v11n01_09

Society for Human Resource Management. (n.d.). *Managing employee surveys.* Retrieved from https://www.shrm.org/resourcesandtools/tools-and-samples/toolkits/pages/managingemployeesurveys.aspx

Towers Perrin. (2003). Working today: Understanding what drives employee engagement. *Towers Perrin Talent Report.* Retrieved from http://www.keepem.com/doc_files/Towers_Perrin_Talent_2003%28TheFinal%29.pdf

Weihrich, H. (1982). The TOWS matrix—A tool for situational analysis. *Long Range Planning, 15*(2), 54–66. doi:10.1016/0024-6301(82)90120-0

Welbourne, T. M. (2016). The potential of pulse surveys: Transforming surveys into leadership tools. *Employment Relations Today, 43*(1), 33–39. doi:10.1002/ert.21548

Wilder, D., Lipschultz, J., King, A., Driscoll, S., & Sigurdsson, S. (2018). An analysis of the commonality and type of preintervention assessment procedures in the journal of organizational behavior management (2000–2015). *Journal of Organizational Behavior Management, 38*(1), 5–17. doi:10.1080/01608061.2017.1325822

Wine, B., & Pritchard, J. K. (2018). Behavior analysis in organizations. In B. Wine & J. Pritchard (Eds.), *Organizational behavior management: The essentials*(pp. 8-12). Orlando, FL: Hedgehog Publishers.

Epilogue[1]

Douglas A. Johnson and C. Merle Johnson

When the *Handbook of Organizational Performance: Behavior Analysis and Management* was published two decades ago we observed the remarkable development of organizational behavior management (OBM) during our field's first quarter century (Johnson et al., 2001). Now a new generation of OBM researchers and practitioners allow us to envision an even brighter future than existed at the beginning of the 21st century. The collection of articles in this volume of the *Handbook of Organizational Performance: Foundations and Advances* illustrates the excellent foundation shown in the field of OBM.

First, as co-editors we described how the foundations in this volume, as well as the advances in Volume 2, evolve from several levels of variation and selection (Johnson & Johnson, 2022). Next, Brethower et al. (2022) provided a nice summary of how the field progressed from applications in higher education to assorted workplace settings that continue to expand today. The subsequent articles provide great summaries and reviews of OBM terms (Johnson & Ferguson, 2023), research designs (Erath et al., 2021), antecedent strategies (Choi & Johnson, 2022), and measurement and maintenance approaches (Wilder & Cymbal, 2023). Behavioral assessment of employees (Gravina et al., 2021) as well as organizational operating systems (McGee & Crowley-Koch, 2021) enable supervisors and stakeholders to make pragmatic and legal decisions for managing individuals, teams, divisions, or entire organizations. Providing effective performance feedback, rather than just global ratings of efficacy, allows employees and managers to improve efforts and supervision (Johnson et al., 2023). Finally, pay-for-performance has been a major contribution by OBM researchers for managing employees for decades (Abernathy, 1996; 2014). Bucklin et al. (2022) provide an outstanding synopsis of this critical area while carefully suggesting prudent ways to implement such systems with minimal resistance and maximal efficacy.

As a field OBM continues to show major contributions in these historically important areas. We should be proud of our accomplishments since Ed Feeney's major milestone half a century ago showing how performance feedback improved both employee and organizational productivity (Feeney, 1972). These foundational areas of study are well-grounded empirically and have withstood scientific scrutiny for the past 50 years. In Volume 2 the contributors will expand the foundational applications of OBM as the field continues to evolve. We hope you enjoy all these contributions; may they inspire you to join this developing field.

Finally, similar to what the co-editors agreed to carry out in the original *Handbook of Organizational Performance: Behavior Analysis and Management* (Johnson et al., 2001), we are donating all royalties for both volumes of the current *Handbook of Organizational Performance: Foundations and Advances* to help fund the D. Chris Anderson Student Research Grant for the OBM Network. We want to support quality research carried out by students as they foster the development of OBM for another 50 years.

Note

1. We have no known conflicts of interest to disclose.

References

Abernathy, W. B. (1996). *The sin of wages: Where the conventional pay system has led us and how to find a way out.* PerfSys Press. www.aubreydaniels.com/store/books/the-sin-of-wages

Abernathy, W. B. (2014). *The liberated workplace: Transitioning to Walden Three.* Performance Management Publications. www.aubreydaniels.com/store/books/the-liberated-workplace

Brethower, D. M., Dickinson, A. M., Johnson, D. A., & Johnson, C. M. (2022). A history of organizational behavior management. *Journal of Organizational Behavior Management, 42*(1), 3–35. https://doi.org/10.1080/01608061.2021.1924340

Bucklin, B. R., Li, A., Rodriguez, M., Johnson, D. A., & Eagle, L. M. (2022). Pay-for-performance: Behavior-based recommendations from research and practice. *Journal of Organizational Behavior Management, 42*(4), 309–335. https://doi.org/10.1080/01608061.2022.2047868

Choi, E., & Johnson, D. A. (2022). Common antecedent strategies within organizational behavior management: The use of goal setting, task clarification, and job aids. *Journal of Organizational Behavior Management, 42*(1), 75–95. https://doi.org/10.1080/01608061.2021.1967834

Erath, T. G., Pellegrino, A. J., DiGennaro Reed, F. D., Ruby, S. A., Blackman, A. L., & Novak, M. D. (2021). Experimental research methodologies in organizational behavior management. *Journal of Organizational Behavior Management, 41*(2), 150–181. https://doi.org/10.1080/01608061.2020.1869137

Feeney, E. J. (1972). Performance audit, feedback and positive reinforcement. *Training & Development Journal, 26*(11), 8–13.

Gravina, N., Nastasi, J., & Austin, J. (2021). Assessment of employee performance. *Journal of Organizational Behavior Management, 41*(2), 124–149. https://doi.org/10.1080/01608061.2020.1869136

Johnson, C. M., Mawhinney, T. C., & Redmon, W. K. (2001). Epilogue. In C. M. Johnson, W. K. Redmon, & T. C. Mawhinney (Eds.). *Handbook of organizational performance: Behavior analysis and management* (pp. 457–459). Routledge. https://doi.org/10.4324/9780203048184

Johnson, D. A., & Ferguson, R. (2023). On terms within organizational behavior management. *Journal of Organizational Behavior Management, 43*(2), 162–188. https://doi.org/10.1080/01608061.2022.2099504

Johnson, D. A., & Johnson, C. M. (2022). Revisiting the past and selecting for the future: An introduction to *Handbook of Organizational Performance: Foundations and Advances*. *Journal of Organizational Behavior Management, 42*(3), 203–209. https://doi.org/10.1080/01608061.2022.2029797

Johnson, D. A., Johnson, C. M., & Dave, P. (2023). Performance feedback in organizations: Understanding the functions, forms, and important features. *Journal of Organizational Behavior Management, 43*(1), 64–89. https://doi.org/10.1080/01608061.2022.2089436

McGee, H. M., & Crowley-Koch, B. J. (2021). Performance assessment of organizations. *Journal of Organizational Behavior Management, 41*(3), 255–285. https://doi.org/10.1080/01608061.2021.1909687

Wilder, D., & Cymbal, D. (2023). Pinpointing, measurement, procedural integrity, and maintenance in organizational behavior management. *Journal of Organizational Behavior Management, 43*(3), 221–245. https://doi.org/10.1080/01608061.2022.2108537

Review Questions

Chapter 1

a) State and describe the three levels of variation and selection contingencies Skinner noted (1981; 1987; 1990) and compare them with the corresponding three levels for OBM noted by Johnson, Redmon, & Mawhinney (2001).
b) How will artificial intelligence (AI) and automation influence jobs in OBM in the future? How should employees trained for occupations in OBM respond to changes in work settings?
c) Explain the statistical concept of "regression to the mean." How did Tversky and Kahneman apply regression to the mean when flight instructors disagreed with their recommendation to praise students' appropriate rather than criticize poor performance? Do you agree with the flight instructors' conclusion that praise is detrimental to learning and verbal punishment is beneficial? Why or why not?

Chapter 2

a) Why does Lincoln Electric in Cleveland utilize piece rate rather than hourly wages to pay their workers? Do you agree with their *incentive management* system that does not pay employees for days in which they are absent, but guarantees no worker is laid off during economic downturns? Also, explain and critique Lincoln Electric's profit-sharing bonus system.
b) What is *programmed learning* and why is it different than traditional training or educational approaches? What are the advantages of this approach and why do you think it is not utilized more today, despite empirical evidence of its efficacy?
c) Explain one of the International Society for Performance Improvement (ISPI) standards, "Partner with Clients," by detailing their mnemonic, "RSVP" (Results, System, Value-added, Partner).
d) Explain von Békésy's quote, "First, make the analysis; second, make the synthesis; the synthesis tells you if your analysis is correct." Justify how his expression concerning analysis/synthesis/evaluation-confirmation sets the foundation for the experimental analysis of behavior, applied behavior analysis, behavioral systems analysis, OBM, and scientific analysis in general.
e) Historically, people working in OBM were academics, consultants, or salaried personnel (trainers, safety experts, organizational development, or quality improvement specialists). Recently, Board Certified Behavior Analysts (BCBAs) have started to join these three professional specializations.

How might this impact OBM as a profession as well as organizations such as the OBM Network?

f) Explain the relevance of two quotes from Brethower and his colleagues: "Let the data be the guide" and "If you can't maintain it, don't train it!" Then elaborate on the second quote, leading pioneers in OBM to admonish trainers to emphasize consequences over simply training employees. In your explanation include these characteristics of consequences: frequency-altering effect (reinforcing or punishing), magnitude (large or small), impact (personal or organizational & other), timeliness (immediate or delayed), and probability (certain or uncertain).
g) Describe the Total Performance System and apply this tool to a problem in an organization in which you are currently employed or have worked in previously.
h) Explain how survey, interview, or other self-report data used as the sole or primary measure of employee performance is subject to errors in memory or outright distortion. Thus, OBM eschews these verbal reports alone even though traditional management, industrial-organizational (I-O) Psychology, and International Society for Performance Improvement (ISPI) often rely on these methods of data collection. However, applied behavior analysis and OBM employ these types of measures for social validity data. Why do these forms of perception data have utility?
i) Select two authors from this list of 21st century writers who have made important contributions to organizational performance and justify why you believe their work made a lasting impact on the field of OBM: Aubrey Daniels, Bill Abernathy, Leslie Wilk Braksick, Roger Kaufman, Dick Grote, Danny Langdon, Geary Rummler, Tom Gilbert, and Maria Malott.
j) Will an OBM-oriented approach emphasizing a Skinnerian philosophy of reinforcement contingencies change the world for the better compared to authoritarian/dictatorship methods of aversive control? Why or why not?

Chapter 3

a) How does applied behavior analysis in general and OBM specifically differ from social sciences such as economics, social psychology, political science, and industrial-organizational Psychology? As an applied behavioral science, does OBM offer more promise for humane intervention and improvement of work conditions and employee performance, thus improving organizational efficacy?
b) Why do researchers and practitioners in OBM focus on both behavior and outcomes (results) when carrying out contingency analyses in organizational settings? Also, why do we focus on stimulus and response classes rather than discrete stimuli or behaviors? Although we focus on worthy results, what is the problem with only measuring results without considering the work behavior that led to the outcome?
c) What are covert events? How should OBM researchers and practitioners respond to criticisms that behavior analysis does not include thinking and cognition in their narrow field?

d) Advertisers sign celebrities to contracts to associate these individuals with specific products, services, or companies. Customers who like the celebrity then develop positive feelings toward the product, service, or company. This, in turn, helps to drive sales in a respondent conditioning paradigm. Explain why advertising companies put clauses in these agreements that allow them to negate the contract "for cause."
e) Are humans free of their genetics? If so, why do critics of behavior analysis get a "free pass" when they claim to have "free will?" Explain the OBM perspective that behavior in organizations is a function of the history of consequences for work behavior, current workplace conditions, and prevailing physical and social contingencies in that environment.
f) Explain how performance feedback may function as reinforcement, punishment, or extinction when it no longer increases behavior.
g) During training, such as in a college classroom, trainees and students seldom check their social media because they want to avoid admonishment from trainers, instructors, or professors. Once out of class or training sessions they often check these sources; thus, the behavior is persistent. What happens during subsequent classes or training sessions if the instructor is late to class? That is, if not talking to other students around them, what behaviors do most students engage in while waiting for a tardy professor?
h) From the previous example, what happens when the instructor finally arrives? That is, note the antecedents (S^D and S^Δ) and subsequent behaviors.
i) What are conditioned motivating operations (CMOs)? Give original examples in a workplace of both a CMO-R and a CMO-T.
j) Why do OBM researchers and practitioners study delayed consequences and indirect acting contingencies in addition to direct contingencies with immediate consequences?
k) Contrast rule-governed behavior to contingency-shaped behavior for an entrepreneur creating a start-up company on her own. That is, describe how she allocates her time and effort on her first day and note whether most of her behavior is likely to be rule-governed or contingency-shaped.
l) Why do we conceptualize rules as contingency-specifying stimuli? Explain how direct-acting contingencies often maintain rule-governed behavior through overt and covert self-supplied verbal consequences. Provide an original example of your own behavior.
m) What is the problem with labeling most responding at work as just rule-governed behavior and not engaging in a thorough analysis? For example, criticize the following statement. "My co-worker is a real 'go-getter', and I just don't have any self-control for this job." Provide a remedy for this employee from an OBM perspective.
n) How does OBM differ from other perspectives in the analysis of organizational change? Does the future for OBM appear fruitful despite this variant theoretical approach?

Chapter 4

a) Science involves systematic observations of natural phenomena as well as studying functional relations between variables. To determine possible causality, controlled experiments are carried out between independent variables and dependent variables. What is meant by internal validity when carrying out such experiments? State at least four types of threats to internal validity for such experiments.
b) What is external validity? What is ecological validity? What is translational research and does research in OBM appear to span this basic laboratory to applied continuum?
c) Briefly describe single-case experimental designs and note two advantages as well as one limitation to this type of research design.
d) Describe the AB design and explain the weakness in this type of research. Why would an OBM researcher employ an AB design despite this weakness?
e) Explain why an ABAB design is methodologically superior to an AB design. What is at least one limitation of an ABAB design? Give an example of an ABCBC design studying employee behavior in a human service setting.
f) Explain how multiple baseline designs are a series of staggered AB designs across (a) participants' or groups' behavior, (b) behaviors of the same participant or group, or (c) conditions. What is a nonconcurrent multiple baseline, a variation of the standard type of design? Finally, how do multiple probe designs differ?
g) Describe multi-element (alternating treatment) designs. Now describe how a musician performing a concert one night might ascertain which type of song to play (independent variable) based on how enthusiastic the crowd applauds (dependent variable) in a multielement design.
h) Describe changing-criterion designs. Now describe how an organization could use this type of design to gradually change a group of sedentary employees who volunteer to begin walking during lunch breaks based on feedback to the group.
i) Briefly describe a parametric analysis for a single-case design. Explain how this type of research design could investigate different levels of individual feedback on the amount of time employees spend on social media while at work.
j) What is meant by a component analysis for single-case designs? Describe how a feedback package could be dismantled in a component analysis for training employees learning a new software program.
k) Describe group design research. Note an advantage and a disadvantage of group designs compared to single-case designs.
l) Explain between-subjects designs, noting potential threats to internal validity. Although group designs are often advantageous to control threats to external validity, how do single-case design researchers reduce these threats and improve generality?
m) Compared to random assignment of participants in between-subjects design, matched-pairs designs have advantages and disadvantages. Indicate at least one advantage as well as one limitation.

n) Give an example of a factorial design for studying how frequently to test airline pilots for illicit drug usage to comply with U.S. government Federal Aviation Administration (FAA) regulations.
o) Explain how within-subject group designs are similar to and differ from single-case designs. Do these designs have similar threats to internal validity?
p) What are mixed methods designs? Give an example for student drivers learning how to safely drive cars.
q) Critics of single-case designs complain that these lack power and external validity. Respond to these critiques by advocating for the benefits of single-case research designs.

Chapter 5

a) Antecedent control of employee behavior appears to be a common strategy for managers and supervisors, but consequences usually receive more credit in OBM literature. Explain why this supposition may not be valid considering multiple control of operant behavior. Include rule-governed behavior in your explanation.
b) Research on goal setting shows goal difficulty and performance typically increase together until goals seem unachievable, then performance deteriorates. Explain why these findings appear consistent across many disciplines. Does the use of subgoals mitigate these outcomes?
c) "Do your best" to answer this question: Does specificity of goal achievement matter?
d) Should goals be assigned by supervisors or participatively set with management? Why? Are individual, group, or combined goals the best for improving performance? Again, why?
e) Explain how goal setting has potential for both discriminative and motivational control when responding at work. In addition, note how goal setting controls immediate and delayed behavior via self-generated rules.
f) Should organizations combine goal setting with explicit contingencies? Why or why not?
g) How is task clarification similar to goal setting as antecedents? How do they differ? How does task clarification relate to training?
h) Could task clarification function as a CMO? Why or why not?
i) Although classified as antecedents like goal setting and task clarification, how do checklists and job aids differ?
j) How can managers ensure that checklists and job aids initiate as well as maintain behavior change?
k) Goal setting, task clarification, checklists, and job aids prompt responding when managing employee behavior. Should we caution supervisors to be sure to neither ignore nor minimize contingencies of reinforcement when implementing antecedent control? What types of contingencies would you recommend?

Chapter 6

a) Although similar in many respects, how does OBM differ from applied behavior analysis (ABA)? Do you consider OBM a subdiscipline of ABA? Why or why not?

b) Both OBM and industrial-organizational (I-O) psychology focus on outcomes in organizational settings; note two similar measures from each discipline and another measure in which the disciplines differ.

c) Although considered a behavior science, how do OBM measures differ from other disciplines?

d) Describe each of these characteristics for pinpointing target performance: precise, reliable, measurable, and observable.

e) Should behaviors or outcomes (results) be measured? Justify your answer. Provide an example of each. What is a PIP? Provide an original example.

f) How does measurement of performance in OBM differ from a typical performance appraisal in traditional management and I-O psychology?

g) Provide a rebuttal to the criticism that OBM is only concerned with measuring individual performance, thus limited in application to group and/organizational performance.

h) In *Human Competence* (2007) Gilbert suggested three dimensions for measuring performance: quality, quantity/productivity, and cost. Briefly describe each of these three dependent variables and give an original example of each.

i) Explain the two primary methods of measuring performance advocated by Daniels and Bailey (2014): counting and judgment. Indicate one strength and one limitation of each approach. Also describe Abernathy's performance matrix for judging pinpoints.

j) OBM research and practice measure performance (work behavior and results), secondary measures of social validity such as procedural acceptability are inconsistently collected. Explain why these may be necessary in organizational settings—both for employees and for customers or consumers.

k) Should organizations encourage employees to measure their own behavior? Does self-monitoring obfuscate "real" performance? How could reliability be carried out for self-monitoring?

l) What is procedural integrity in OBM and how should this be carried out? Argue for or against this and provide rationale for the necessity of measuring fidelity if intervention is implemented automatically (e.g., computer-generated feedback of an outcome measure).

m) Note the similarities between response maintenance and institutionalization in OBM. Then indicate differences between these concepts noting the issue of single compared to interlocking behavioral contingencies. Does OBM research and evaluate these very well? Why or why not?

Chapter 7

a) Define performance feedback in OBM and note how it generally is not as automatic as most forms of feedback (with or without corresponding consequences).
b) Explain what is missing in the immortal maxim: *Practice makes perfect.*
c) Feeney's classic use of feedback at Emery Air Freight initiated OBM studies of this intervention; it is the most common independent variable in OBM research. Does performance feedback function as an antecedent, consequence, or both? Justify your answer.
d) Explain how respondent conditioning can make feedback emotionally positive or negative. Then describe how feedback could function as a conditioned punisher or a conditioned reinforcer, based on an employee's personal history.
e) Similarly, explain how performance feedback may serve discriminative functions based on the employee's history at work.
f) Provide an original example of how performance feedback from a supervisor could function as a conditioned motivating operation (CMO).
g) Similarly, present another original example of a supervisor providing feedback that does not immediately evoke a response, but generates rule-governed behavior by a worker.
h) Presenting feedback alone does not guarantee improvement, but pairing feedback with goal setting and/or consequences enhances performance. Why do you believe that when managers and supervisors provide erratic feedback they are puzzled by inconsistent outcomes?
i) Which is better, objective or evaluative feedback? Does combining the two enhance performance? Compare these three types of feedback to no feedback and make a recommendation based on this comparative research.
j) Summarize the controlled research on feedback specificity and performance outcomes. What seems to be the general conclusion of these findings?
k) Is group feedback effective? Why or why not? Would combining individual and group feedback enhance performance? Again, why or why not?
l) Is it beneficial to mitigate negative critiques by mixing them with positive comments when providing corrective feedback? Explain why.
m) Why should performance feedback be accurate?
n) Why should individual performance feedback be presented in a confidential manner?
o) How frequently should performance feedback be presented? Compare seasoned employees to trainees or new employees.
p) Describe the research on feedback timing and possible rule-generated self-statements. That is, why does performance feedback before a work session seem to be as effective as post-session feedback?
q) Explain the findings concerning feedback source (supervisor, peer, self, family member, stranger, or automatically presented from a computer). Why do you believe these outcomes have been found in the literature?
r) Is face-to-face better than computer generated, text, or remotely presented feedback? What caveats exist based on published controlled research?

s) When supervisors deliver corrective feedback, does it matter how the employees respond to the delivery? That is, how important is feedback reception? Explain your answer regarding performance feedback preferences for both supervisors and employees.

Chapter 8

a) Like James Lincoln's *incentive management* system at Lincoln Electric, Frederick Taylor's *scientific management* involved pay-for-performance at the genesis of the 20th century. Explain his differential piece-rate incentive system and compare it to hourly pay or salary compensation.
b) Describe advantages and problems with individual piece-rate incentive systems (including commission only for sales agents) for both the employee and the organization. Combined fixed and performance-based pay systems improve productivity compared to fixed systems alone. How small can the performance-based pay yield productivity increases for combined systems?
c) Compare accelerated incentive pay to linear payout systems such as straight piece rate. Which appears better, including how to administer such pay-for-performance systems? Explain the rationale for your preference.
d) Explain benefits, as well as limitations, for small-group incentive pay systems that have equal payouts for all group members.
e) Describe goal sharing, gain sharing, and profit sharing pay systems. Explain why these lose their ability to improve productivity due to delayed and typically equal payouts such as end-of-year bonuses.
f) Briefly describe Abernathy's Total Performance System and why it seemed to improve performance at the banks that utilized his incentive pay. Note at least two benefits for both the employees and the organization as well as one challenge for both parties.
g) Describe Abernathy's balanced performance scorecard. Evaluate performance scorecards designed to manage and compensate employees.
h) What is profit-indexed performance pay? Do you believe this variant is an improvement to the Total Performance System? Why or why not?
i) Performance management is the crux of OBM. Briefly explain how performance scorecards dovetail into a system of direct observation of behavior, outcome measures, goal setting, incentives, and evaluation at the individual, group, and organization-wide level of analysis.
j) Does pay-for-performance put intrinsic motivation at risk? Why or why not, based on controlled empirical research?
k) Why do OBM theoreticians, researchers, and practitioners not use these empirical controlled-research findings to their advantage when interacting with Wall Street financial operatives, corporate executives, and entrepreneurs since so many organizational psychologists and managers claim external incentives are harmful and ruin intrinsic motivation? (Hint: This is one reason why these financial experts think "psychology" is touchy feely and somewhat weird).

l) Explain the authors' warning of potential problems by only having a productivity measure with incentive management. That is, is the axiom, "You get what you pay for"—a concern that we should consider when implementing monetary incentives? Elaborate on this issue.
m) What considerations should executive and management personnel be ready to address before implementing a pay-for-performance system such as performance scorecards?
n) Similarly, what should employees consider before accepting one of these systems?
o) What kinds of legal and regulatory considerations need to be addressed, in addition to ethical issues?
p) How should the new pay-for-performance incentive system be communicated internally to the organization as well as externally to consumers/customers and interested third-party persons (e.g., local press, relatives of employees)?
q) Similarly, what incentives and other considerations should be addressed for human resources (HR) and information technology (IT) departments/personnel for their additional time and effort implementing these performance scorecards and pay systems?
r) Critique the readiness checklist before implementing a pay-for-performance scorecard system. Do you agree with these 11 points? Which do you support, and which do you question?
s) Why are there so few pay-for-performance programs in organizations? Do you agree with the authors' conclusions? Why or why not? Why do so many organizations pay their employees by the hour only rather than utilize pay-for-performance systems? How effective is straight salary compensation?

Chapter 9

a) The authors categorize the assessment of individual employees of an organization based on four broad classes. List and briefly explain each of these four classes.
b) Note at least four possible reasons to assess individual employee performance in organizations.
c) What should happen during the pre-assessment phase between the OBM practitioner and management or other stakeholders?
d) What processes and outcomes result from the assessment phase? Why do the authors suggest practitioners consider anonymous or confidential interviews and surveys?
e) When designing interventions post-assessment, why should recommended interventions be expected to be successful and consistently applied? Why should practitioners recommend one initially and then build additional interventions later?
f) What are historical assessments? Why are these combined with other sources such as direct observation and interviews?

g) How is performance analysis in OBM similar to a functional analysis in ABA? Why might these analyses be missing in the literature during the first two decades of OBM studies? Describe the four areas that Austin and colleagues developed for performance analysis in the Performance Diagnostic Checklist (PDC).
h) Briefly describe the PDC and note three variations: PDC-HS, PDC-Safety, and PDC-Parent. Do these variations seem to be reliable and valid instruments of indirect assessment?
i) Describe an ABC analysis in OBM. State at least one advantage of this type of indirect assessment as well as one possible limitation. Why is this possible limitation generally not deemed a concern by most practitioners?
j) Explain direct assessment in OBM and briefly note three variations: narrative recording, direct observation, and scatterplots.
k) Describe an experimental analysis of assessing employee behavior at work. Do these hold promise compared to traditional survey information typically collected by I-O psychologists? Why should we be cautious recommending an experimental analysis for safety behavior?
l) Briefly describe possible reinforcer and preference assessments in OBM. Why might these be less pervasive than in ABA? Is this a valid issue for performance feedback preferences?
m) What are procedural acceptability assessments? What are some of the methods of carrying out these assessments and what precautions should be taken? Why do you think these are not more prevalent in OBM?
n) Summarize the reliability and validity of measures and preferences concerning individual assessment in OBM. Furthermore, how should OBM address cultural issues of employees in the workplace?

Chapter 10

a) Describe and contrast the two categories of organizational assessment: Behavioral Systems Analysis (BSA) and Performance Management (PM). Explain how these two categories are related.
b) What rationale do the authors provide for OBM researchers and practitioners to consider when reviewing traditional management measures? That is, what possible value are cognitive constructs such as autonomy, leadership style, or engagement?
c) Describe the construct of change readiness and the categories: clarity and alignment; skills and abilities; time, tools, and resources; and feedback and accountability. Why should leadership communicate timely rationale for change readiness to their employees?
d) How can findings from employee surveys measuring organizational culture (OC) and employee engagement be valuable to OBM practitioners? Reinterpret these two traditional constructs from a behavior analytic perspective so an OBM practitioner can understand and find them beneficial for organizational change.

e) How do pulse surveys differ from typical annual surveys? Are they administered as repeated measures across time and situations, like behavior analysis measures? Why should data from pulse surveys be disseminated as truthful feedback to all personnel within the organization?
f) Standards for return rates (e.g., minimum of 50 to 65%), reliability, and validity exist for survey administration, as do standards for interobserver reliability and other ABA measures. Why are these important for conclusions from survey data, like a minimum of 80% interobserver reliability is for ABA results? What types of erroneous conclusions could be made if an insufficient number of employees respond to a survey? (See the Dillman et al. (2014) gold standard for more information).
g) Explain and differentiate the three levels of organizational assessment in OBM: organizational, process, and performer.
h) At the organizational level, what are strategic goals or strategic planning and how do these differ from operational goals? Explain both parts of McGee's Strategic Planning and Implementation Tool.
i) Describe how to carry out an external environment assessment using Brethower's Total Performance System (TPS). Include the seven components of TPS.
j) Explain how Rummler and Brache's Super System Map expanded TPS to include two additional external components. Note how and why Ludwig and McGee changed the TPS and Super System Map in their Organization Analysis Tool.
k) What is a functional relationship assessment? Why are goals, standards, and feedback loops identified as well as who in the organization produces what to whom?
l) What is a process assessment? Describe steps, decisions, and swim lanes for Rummler and Brache's cross-functional process map at this assessment level. After mapping is complete, what processes are identified and analyzed during redesign? Use Ludwig and McGee's process mapping tool or Ramia's power of visual analysis in this redesign.
m) What is the performer level of an organizational assessment? Include a job analysis in your answer. Describe a job model, either Ludwig and McGee's Job Management Tool or Rummler and Brache's Role and Responsibility Matrix.
n) What is a performance assessment? When might this be needed? Why do many practitioners prefer Austin's PDC when conducting a performance assessment?
o) What is a task analysis and how is it similar to process assessment? Describe Mager's task analysis and provide a rationale as to why identifying decision points is critical. How might a task analysis be used for training new employees? How might it be used for selection of which employee to hire or to promote?
p) Describe utilizing a contingency analysis for component tasks or behaviors from a task analysis. Explain how consequences in an ABC contingency can be examined through Daniels and Bailey's PIC/NIC analysis. Similarly, explain Braksick's E-TIP approach noting her addition to a PIC/NIC contingency analysis.

q) As another variant, Ludwig and McGee's Behavior Change Tool adds what features to the previous contingency analyses?
r) What is meant by incorporating institutionalization variables into an OBM project to increase sustainability? How well do consultants and practitioners in the field do this and what activities and contingencies can be employed to ensure sustainability?
s) What five categories do the authors recommend to consultants and practitioners to include in a sustainability assessment? Explain each of these categories.
t) Rarely are organizational projects, including those in OBM, perfect the first time in design and execution. *Kaizen*, the Japanese manufacturing approach of continuous improvement, shook the American auto industry in the late 20th century when they borrowed W. Edward Deming's statistical process control (SPC) (Redmon & Dickinson, 1988). McGee & Crowley-Koch (2021) emphasize the need for organizational assessment throughout sustainable improvement. How and why?

Index

Note: Figures are indicated by *italics*. Tables are indicated by **bold**.